CONTEMPORARY PERSPECTIVES IN COMPARATIVE EDUCATION

REFERENCE BOOKS IN
INTERNATIONAL EDUCATION
(VOL. 16)

GARLAND REFERENCE LIBRARY
OF SOCIAL SCIENCE
(VOL. 703)

Reference Books in International Education

Edward R. Beauchamp
General Editor

1. *Education in East and West Germany: A Bibliography*, by Val D. Rust
2. *Education in the People's Republic of China, Past and Present: An Annotated Bibliography*, by Franklin Parker and Betty June Parker
3. *Education in South Asia: A Select Annotated Bibliography*, by Philip G. Altbach, Denzil Saldanha, and Jeanne Weiler
4. *Textbooks in the Third World: Policy, Content and Context*, by Philip G. Altbach and Gail P. Kelly
5. *Education in Japan: A Source Book*, by Edward R. Beauchamp and Richard Rubinger
6. *Women's Education in the Third World*, by David H. Kelly and Gail P. Kelly
7. *Minority Status and Schooling*, by Margaret A. Gibson and John V. Ogbu
8. *Teachers and Teaching in the Developing World*, by Val D. Rust and Per Dalin
9. *Russian and Soviet Education, 1731–1989: A Multilingual Annotated Bibliography*, by William W. Brickman and John T. Zepper
10. *Early Childhood Education in the Arab World: A Source Book*, by Byron G. Massialas and Layla Jarrar
11. *Education in Sub-Saharan Africa: A Source Book*, by George E.F. Urch
12. *Youth in the Soviet Union*, by Anthony Jones
13. *Education in Israel: A Source Book*, by Yaacov Iram
14. *Arab Education in Transition: A Source Book*, by Byron G. Massialas and Samir A. Jarrar
15. *Education and Cultural Differences: New Perspectives*, by Douglas Ray and Deo H. Poonwassie
16. *Contemporary Perspectives in Comparative Education*, edited by Robin J. Burns and Anthony R. Welch
17. *Education in the Arab Gulf States and the Arab World: An Annotated Bibliographic Guide*, by Nagat El-Sanabary
18. *International and Historical Roots of American Higher Education*, by W.H. Cowley and Don Williams
19. *Education in England and Wales: An Annotated Bibliography*, by Franklin Parker and Betty June Parker
20. *Chinese Education: Problems, Policies, and Prospects*, edited, with an introduction, by Irving Epstein
21. *Early Childhood Education in Asia and the Pacific: A Source Book*, edited by Stephanie Feeney
22. *Understanding Educational Reform in Global Context: Economy, Ideology, and the State*, edited by Mark B. Ginsburg

CONTEMPORARY PERSPECTIVES IN COMPARATIVE EDUCATION

edited by

Robin J. Burns
Anthony R. Welch

GARLAND PUBLISHING, INC. • NEW YORK & LONDON
1992

Library of Congress Cataloging-in-Publication Data

Burns, Robin J., 1943–
Contemporary perspectives in comparative education / Robin J. Burns, Anthony R. Welch.
p. cm. — (Garland reference library of social science ; vol. 703. Reference books in international education ; vol. 16)
Includes bibliographical references (p.) and index.
ISBN 0-8240-9603-7 (alk. paper)
1. Comparative education—Australia. 2. Comparative education—New Zealand. 3. International education—Australia. 4. International education—New Zealand. I. Welch, Anthony R. II. Title. III. Series: Garland reference library of social science ; v. 703. IV. Series: Garland reference library of social science. Reference books in international education ; vol. 16.
LB43.B87 1992
370.19'5—dc20 91-21631
CIP

Printed on acid-free, 250-year-life paper
Manufactured in the United States of America

Contents

Series Editor's Foreword

This series of scholarly works in comparative and international education has grown well beyond the initial conception of a collection of reference books. Although retaining its original purpose of providing a resource to scholars, students, and a variety of other professionals who need to understand the role played by education in various societies or regions of the world, it also strives to provide up-to-date information on a wide variety of selected educational issues, problems and experiments within an international context.

Contributors to this series are well-known scholars who have devoted their professional lives to the study of their specialization. Without exception these men and women possess an intimate understanding of the subject of their research and writing. Without exception they have not only studied their subject in dusty archives, but they have also lived and travelled widely in their quest for knowledge. In short, they are "experts" in the best sense of that often overused word.

In our increasingly interdependent world, it is now widely understood that it is a matter of survival that we not only understand better what makes other societies tick, but that we also make a serious effort to understand how others, be they Japanese, German or Chilean, attempt to solve the same kinds of educational problems that we face in North America. As the late George Z.F. Bereday wrote: "[E]ducation is a mirror held against the face of a people. Nations may put on blustering shows of strength to conceal public weakness, erect grand facades to conceal shabby backyards, and profess peace while secretly arming for conquest, but how they take care of their children tells unerringly who they are" (*Comparative Method in Education*, New York: Holt, Rinehart & Winston, 1964, p. 5).

Perhaps equally important, however, is the valuable perspective that studying another education system (or its problems) provides us in understanding our own system (or its problems). To step outside of our own limited experience and our commonly held assumptions about schools and learning in order to look back at our system in contrast to another places it in a very different light. To learn, for example, how the Soviet Union or Belgium handle the education of a multilingual society; how the French provide for the funding of public education; or how the Japanese control admissions into their universities enables us to understand that there are alternatives to our own familiar way of doing things. Not that we can often "borrow" directly from other societies; indeed, educational arrangements are inevitably a reflection of deeply rooted political, economic and cultural factors that are unique to a society. But a conscious recognition that there are other ways of doing things can serve to open our minds and provoke our imaginations in ways that can result in new approaches that we would not have otherwise considered.

Since this series is intended to be a useful research tool, the editor and contributors welcome suggestions for future volumes as well as ways in which this series can be improved.

Edward R. Beauchamp
University of Hawaii

Preface

This volume provides a window onto current work in comparative and international education in Australia and New Zealand. The vigour of much research and writing is clearly evident, at a time when institutional factors are constraining the expansion of related teaching programmes. The volume highlights the capacity of many researchers here to contribute actively to the worldwide development of comparative and international education.

It may be too early to point definitively to a distinctively Australian or New Zealand approach to the field. Nonetheless, a local style may well be forming, the product of several forces. One is the fundamental economic and cultural shift currently underway that is forging a new definition of relationships with Europe (notably the United Kingdom), in favour of the immediacy and intimacy of ties with Asia, the Pacific, and Pacific Rim, to an extent and depth barely conceivable a generation ago. Much work here in comparative and international education has this aspect of international relations in education clearly in view and is designed to help forge the character of these relations. Secondly, the rapid diversification of local culture, which is itself the product of complex and changing patterns of immigration, as well as other forces. Multiculturalism is having a strong impact on comparative and international education, as is the growing sensitivity within the research community to its relationships with indigenous Australians and New Zealanders. Third may be detected the tendency for researchers here to take careful account of those various traditions of scholarship originating in North America, the United Kingdom, continental Europe, and many parts of the 'South'. This increasing eclecticism, in my view at least, is unmatched by researchers in other parts of the world.

It is not possible to claim the present volume to be a perfect illustration of these trends and characteristics. Yet its contents provide substantial evidence for them, and is on this basis commended to a wide readership as a particular contribution of the Australian and New Zealand Comparative and International Education Society.

Phillip W. Jones
ANZCIES President (1989–1990)

Introduction: Reflections upon the Field

ANTHONY WELCH AND ROBIN BURNS

School of Social and Policy Studies in Education,
Faculty of Education, University of Sydney
New South Wales

•

Centre for Comparative and Policy Studies,
School of Education
La Trobe University, Victoria

Like many other subjects, comparative and international education is a heterogeneous field, and even the association of comparative with international in the title is more grounded in convenience than in epistemological necessity. It is therefore little wonder that every few years another 'state of the art' volume, or symposia occurs. It is also little wonder that comments on diversity, lack of agreement on methodology, or lack of clarity of definition, abound in reflective essays and meta-analyses. Paulston (1990) claims that this reflects the increased diversity in those sciences, mainly social and behavioural, which underlie research in general. And since comparative education can be regarded as interdisciplinary, it is no surprise that a number of methodologies exist in the field. This is true amongst comparativist and international educators within a nation or region, as well as in the field as a whole (Halls 1990).

RECENT CONSIDERATIONS OF THEORY

This volume in the current series of Garland Reference Books in International Education goes to press at a particular historical point. This observation is nonetheless important as an explanation of developments in comparative educational theorizing. As examples, Nicholas Hans' classic work (*Comparative Education*, 1949) was published at a time of postwar reconstruction, while that of Brian Holmes' (*Problems in Education*, 1965), as that of George Bereday (*Comparative Method in Education*, 1966) and Harold Noah and Max Eckstein (*Towards a Science of Comparative Education*, 1969) were published in a decade characterized by an ebullient postwar optimism, and faith that science and technology could solve social problems, and perhaps transcend political differences, perhaps issuing in the 'end of ideology' (Bell, 1960).

What is distinctive about the time at which the current volume appears, particularly for scholars of comparative education? There are a number of elements, which together form a very different climate of opinion, or ideological matrix, to that which surrounded the works of some of our famous forebears. Firstly the Enlightenment faith in science and technology as a basis of social reform, including in education, has largely corroded. No longer do we believe so readily, with Condorcet and other Philosophes, that science forms the basis for progress in all fields, in the human or moral sciences (as J.S. Mill called them) as much as in the physical. On the contrary, the view is now argued that, too often, the domination of nature has presaged the domination of individuals: that science often attempts, in practice, to bring nature, philosophy and society under control. The recognition of this relationship is at least as old as Francis Bacon (Bacon 1856) but is a feature of an emerging critical orientation within the contemporary social sciences.

The Enlightenment faith in what Passmore has called the perfectibility of man through science (Passmore 1972) is a defining feature of what we now understand as positivism (Von Wright in Adorno et al. 1976). Most evident in postwar comparative education in the work of Brian Holmes, and Noah and Eckstein, the belief that the future of the subject lay within the bounds of debates in philosophy of natural science, characterized the scholarship of the 1960s. (See Price, and Welch in this volume.) It also informed in broadly similar terms the belief in modernization theory (see Hindson in this volume), and licensed attendant ideas such as the Green Revolution.

The more recent withdrawal of faith in scientific methodology, however, is not just explicable in terms of having witnessed the breakdown of both the inductive and deductive nomological scientific paradigms (Feyerabend 1975, 1976, 1978, 1987, Salmon 1989), or even the repeated demonstration that scientific predictions and solutions have failed in both the natural and social sciences. (See Toh and Farrelly, this volume.) Added to these phenomena, is the growing belief that solutions based upon natural scientific methodologies are often predicated upon technical values of efficiency and economy (Habermas 1971, 1976, 1978; Marcuse 1968; Feyerabend 1975, 1978). These values, which celebrate systemic efficiency at the cost of older values of human freedom and development, devalue the ethical realm and legitimate a view of the world whereby the rationality of decisions in any field is ultimately perceived in terms of their conformance with the canons of scientific orthodoxy. Such procedures, while underpinning much of the research in the social sciences, including comparative education, of the 1960s are no longer so readily thought to be appropriate as a basis for social and educational reform of the *fin de siecle*. Indeed episodes in which scientific notions of management, or efficiency, have been used to reform education, have been shown to be biassed in particular ways (Callahan 1962; Altbach et al. 1985; Aronowitz and Giroux 1986), and the incursion of such a techno-logic into education continues to provoke critical scrutiny by comparative scholars, among others (Weiler 1990, Welch 1990).

Another element of the different ideological climate is revealed in contemporary historical events, including the brief, bloody war in the Arabian gulf in early 1990, and the social and economic transformation of many Eastern European and allied states beginning in the late 1980s. It is not possible to predict with confidence the major outcomes of each of these cataclysmic events, although the latter has thus far shown to have had a greater and more direct impact on comparative research.

Nonetheless, the educational impact of the former in terms of the renascence of a vital and, at times, fundamentalist Islam, the perception of the war as a form of foreign intervention by some in both Arab states and the West, and the potential challenge to more multiculturalist forms of comparative education (see Simkin and Gauci, this volume) are not to be overlooked.

But it is the transformation of Central and Eastern Europe which is already having a substantial impact upon comparative education. Not only are conferences devoting chapters to the study of this transformation (CESE 1990), but in the face of such profound problems, scholars are even more reluctant to maintain the traditional theory-practice split, which is another hallmark of positivist research (Bottomore 1975; Giddens 1979). As we approach the end of the twentieth century, it is no longer so commonly held that, as educationists, we should attempt to emulate our more prestigious cousins in the sciences, and simply collect (or establish) the facts, or relevant theories, and leave questions of value for others to determine. Problematic issues of political and economic transformation, including national sovereignty, migration, ethnic schism, and racism, all demand urgent practical responses, and in the face of such pressing problems in countries such as the USSR, Poland and Yugoslavia, any continuation of scholarly explanations solely in terms of theory and methodology is increasingly being seen as the equivalent of a theological debate about how many angels can dance on the head of a pin.

This observation is not in any sense a denial of the role of theory; rather it is a restatement of the relationship between theory and practice. Theory is, from this point of view, a kind of practice (Wittgenstein 1968; Feyerabend 1975, 1978), and can only gain meaning from its employment in practical situations. Practical employment brings dead rules to life, and it is this insight, together with the ethical implication which it implies, which is informing a newer generation of more critically oriented scholars. (See *inter alia* Price, Scrase, Burns, and Welch, this volume.)

It is not, however, the case that the positivist paradigm has vanished from comparative education altogether. Indeed there are still powerful currents of this form of methodology (Psacharopoulos 1990) in our field, just as in other social sciences, while at the same time more theoretical, and more critical studies (Masemann 1982, 1990; Carnoy 1974, 1982; Weiler 1983), continue to be underrepresented in the literature. Nor is it the case that the melioristic impulse which has always been present in some form in comparative education, and formed part of its rationale, has vanished. Rather, a new literature is developing which, although still advancing an interest in the betterment of the human condition, is less likely to base such desires or related methodologies upon the monolithic claims of methodology in the natural sciences. (See Price, Burns, Welch, in this volume.)

While the above describes general trends in comparative educational research over the last two decades or more, it would be wrong to characterise the current scene as monolithic. For example, in his recent review essay, Paulston contrasts a predominantly North American overview with a European one. Both point to diversity. The former, represented in Altbach's and Kelly's analysis, considers diversity as an obstacle, and calls for more concern with challenges to the field of comparative which are coming from critiques of nation-state studies, of quantification and system models, of structural-functionalism and from new approaches based on conflict perspectives on international capitalism (Paulston 1990: 249). The latter, through Schriewer's analysis, welcomes diversity, and suggests an approach to dealing with it through reflective sociohistorical description. Comparison is a mental operation which seeks relationships between observable facts; it is also a social scientific method for establishing relationships between relationships. Through reflection theory, the two aspects of comparison can be bridged with the concept of self-reference, which can be placed on an equal level with scientific truth. These two are different ways of dealing with and understanding experience; through this common task, diverse social phenomena can be brought together for reflective understanding and for bringing practice and theorising in education together under an internal system of reflection.

CONSIDERATIONS OF CONTENT

It is perhaps through the experiential, or the field of practice, that the work of comparative and international educators is known to other educationists, theorists, pedagogues, policy makers and planners. A question that is asked of us as well as by us, is: what does comparative and international education have to offer? (See e.g. Simkin 1983.) Postlethwaite listed the research agenda for comparativists in the early 1980s as follows:

> economics of education, educational planning and policy, pre-school education, teaching and teacher education, curriculum, educational statistics, higher education, non-formal education, adult education, human development. (Halls 1990: 44)

Reviewing regional studies from around the world, Halls reported at the end of the decade that the following had been research themes:

> pre-school, primary and basic education; post-compulsory and vocational education, higher education, educational reform, educational planning and administration, reforms and innovation, issues related to education and modernisation, the application of technology to education and working life, educational thought and culture, moral and religious education, adult especially non-formal education, and educational processes and content. (ibid.: 50–54)

CONSIDERATIONS OF METHOD

From one point of view, the agendas of comparativists have included most of the major themes in educational practice. There has been little study of the ways in which these themes are developed, although comparativists are in a good position to do so. The fact that comparativists now look at intra-national differences and apply some of their tools, especially the analysis of educational context, in such studies, does not necessarily mean that any accumulation of theory or understanding of these news studies takes place. Rather, lack of opportunities to do comparative research abroad, or the political agendas of governments or agencies for whom comparativists may happen to be working abroad, are as likely determinants. Any specific impact of comparative methods and theories on the policy and the practice of education has yet to be evaluated. Individual comparativists may contribute, and it may be splitting hairs to ask if they do so as comparativists or simply because they have the opportunity to do a particular job and revert to another discipline or selectively borrow theories and methods to do so.

An evaluation of how this manner of working affects comparative and international education, however, is timely, for two main reasons. One is a possible direct threat to comparative as a cross-national collegial activity. Comparativists are potentially important in the new drive to commodify and sell education internationally. Part of the commodification process depends on defining knowledge and its producers as the property of those who pay for its development or 'consumption'. The use of comparativists to target, package and market one nation's educational services abroad may be a way of finding legitimacy and funding. However, it threatens not just academic freedom but collegiality and the short-term concern with any chance to 'do' comparative must be weighed against even medium-term serious consequences. A critical and comparative perspective is possible, but unwelcome among policy makers at least (Burns 1986; Welch 1986a, 1988). Other ways of doing comparative research may become increasingly limited, which would be another type of threat to the activity. The second reason for looking at the impact of comparative research is to provide a better understanding of the relationships between opportunities to undertake comparative work, and the generation of issues for research, which in turn affects theorising. Insofar as opportunities arc limited by the availability of funds, and researchers have little say in the setting of funding agendas, the ability to do alternative work not only threatens our collegiality and integrity, but also the ongoing development of comparative itself. Some of the heat surrounding this relationship between research and funding, the setting of agendas and the supposed relationships between being 'useful' and fitting in with other people's agendas have been illustrated in recent debates in the *Comparative Education Review* (see especially 34(3), 1990 and 35(3), 1991) and in national Comparative and

International Education Society conferences (see e.g. Gillespie and Collins 1986; Welch 1986b; Burns 1988).

INTERACTIONS SHAPING COMPARATIVE EDUCATION TODAY

One of the more direct external effects to the infrastructure of comparative education has been the changes in Eastern Europe referred to above. Although the fluid nature of historical change in many of these societies at the current time does not allow a general assessment to be made, it is true to say that already, the changes in Eastern Europe have wrought substantial changes to the infrastructure of comparative education. As only one example, the unification of Germany has already brought about the demise of the premier educational research establishment in the former German Democratic Republic, the Akademie der Pädagogischen Wissenschaften, together with its several hundred staff. It is expected that the well established comparative journal *Vergleichende Pädagogik* will shortly cease publication as a result (despite the efforts of some comparative scholars in both of the former Germanies, and elsewhere), and is unlikely to be replaced. To what extent this event will be mirrored in other states undergoing radical political and educational transformations will only be known over time.

There are also, however, factors internal to comparative and international education, which are related to methodological and sociological factors surrounding the practice of the field. These have also played an important role in determining subject matter. So long as the focus is on educational systems, there tends to be a parallel concern with the nation-state as the unit of analysis. Insofar as there are consistent methodological bases for comparative, this level has become the way in which educational phenomena are approached. Educational inequality, the education of women and girls, ethnicity and education, the transfer of educational resources and ideas and the role of international agencies in educational development have been studied by comparativists in recent years. However, this has been largely undertaken from within nation-state frameworks, by looking at issues about the education and society links in national systems. This focus in turn has led to criticism of the extent to which the state has been the major unit of analysis, and assessment of inputs and outcomes has been a major tool in the study of education and development (Kelly and Altbach 1986). Added to the challenges Altbach and Kelly discerned, cited above, are the challenges from other disciplines studying, for example, the education of women and girls (see in particular Yates in the present volume), from other methodologies, especially critical ethnography with its focus on the micro level (e.g. Masemann 1982, 1990; and Crossley in the present volume), from studies of literacy (Lankshear and Lawler 1987) and text (see Scrase in the current volume), and from macro theories such as world systems theory as a way of conceptualising actors and institutions at the supra-nation level (see e.g. Carnoy, Zachariah, and Apple, in Altbach and Kelly 1986).

Further issues arise when we consider the nature of large-scale comparative undertakings. The International Association for the Evaluation of Educational Achievement (IEA) studies are the obvious example, and Holmes' description is apt:

> The research was not policy oriented. Flawed though the approach is, the amount of data collected is impressive. . . . These studies rely heavily on psychometric techniques and undoubtedly set a new trend in empirical comparative education research. (1985: 333)

The positivistic assumptions on which the research has been based have been criticised (see Heymann 1979) as have the lack of policy direction, and the lack of problem conception (Purves and Levine 1975), or 'educational or societal problem' (Holmes 338) underlying its instigation and implementation. And very few comparativists were actually involved in either its conception or implementation (Sheehan 1983: 166). Other educational data bases have been collected by such institutions as the International Bureau of Education (IBE) and increasingly by funding agencies, most notable of which is the World Bank (Jones 1991).

The role of empirical data in furthering the field of comparative education depends on one's orientation as well as on the ways in which the data have been gathered. Holmes, for example, emphasises a problem-posing approach which starts with the identification and analysis of problems to which at least some of the assumed solutions are educational, and ends with prediction of the outcomes of or possible outcomes of policy. Despite criticism of his tendency to uncritically accept the parameters of the research situation, and for the non-applied nature of much of his work, Holmes argues that, by carefully collecting and classifying as well as critically reflecting on data which the problems suggest need gathering, 'comparative education research can contribute to the planned reform of education' (Holmes 1981: 14–15). Ethnographers such as Masemann and Heymann, by contrast, are more concerned with the significance of different sorts of data in the process of educational delivery and change, although elements of this tradition have been criticised too by comparativists (Welch 1985b) while the positivistic tradition is evident in the managerial and efficiency studies of inputs and outcomes typified by the work of Psacharopoulos (1990). It seems that large cross-national empirical studies may be seen by agencies and governments seeking international funds or external legitimation for their policies, as the contribution which comparative education can make to educational development and change.

Envisaging alternatives is harder than criticising what has been done, however. The belief that education could pave the way to economic growth, and that this was a 'good thing,' dominated much of the work of comparativists (alongside economists, agriculturalists, and a galaxy of agencies) from the 1960s till disillusion began to set in by the mid-1970s. Their way of posing problems clearly lay in projecting from the experience of the capitalist industrial nations, and while education was seen as a key in bringing about the desired changes, in supporting 'modernisation' and indeed, in bringing 'modernisation of consciousness' about, it took several decades, school push-outs, and un- and under-employment of school graduates to draw attention to questions about the type of education and its relationship to the particular society in question.

There was something of a reversal during the 1980s in particular, with education being blamed for a number of economic and social ills (Aronowitz and Giroux, 1986, Altbach et al., 1985; Apple 1987; Welch 1990). Comparativists have tended to look at the similarities in educational and related problems in different parts of the world, and in some instances have been party to the framing of general strategies to deal with them. What has happened less frequently is the turning of their skills to problems either within their own nation, or at a more micro level. That this is beginning to happen more frequently reflects the 'paradigm' shift that Kelly and Altbach, Holmes, Paulston and others suggest. That opportunity and perhaps even necessity, or response to concerns about 'relevance' has preceded new methodological developments may have been significant in enabling changes to take place. 'Pollution' from theoretical developments in related disciplines, together with a sense in many circles that a moratorium on too much concern with methodological issues have, arguably, contributed to the possibility of the new breakthrough in the way the field is studied and theorised.

RATIONALE FOR THE PRESENT VOLUME

The preceding sections have argued that comparative education is at a new stage in defining its missions, its methodologies and by implication, its identity. If Cowen (1981) saw a breakthrough from a dominant historical paradigm in the 1970s, Schriewer (1988) anticipated an amalgam and possible transformation of the structural-functional and positivistic approaches which continue to inform much educational research. With the exception of the recent IBE volume (Halls 1990), debate at least in the English literature, has gone on as if comparativists lived only in North America or Europe, with case material being contributed from elsewhere. And despite the recent plethora of retrospective pieces and *Festschrifte* as a particularly significant generation of post-war comparativists have retired—together with yet more analytic books on the field—little has been written that is prospective in intent, and based on the view from a different geographical region.

This volume had its origins in both a critical conference of the Australian (now Australian and New Zealand) Comparative and International Education Society, and the subsequent sense that the Society, while not quite ready to establish a journal, nevertheless had an important contribution to make. As the epilogue shows, many of the comparativists here have been trained in comparative abroad. Yet the practice here, as elsewhere, both of teaching and research, is limited by situation-specific opportunity and framed by the issues which we confront first in our educational institutions, then in interaction with society, and also in our possibilities for international research and collegial contact. What has that enabled comparative and international educators here to do? In seeking to look at this through a publication, an issues paper was circulated which posed the following challenges:

1. What do comparativists offer to the task, depicted in Nicholas' pithy way, of providing 'profiles' of education and schooling as 'temporary but locally satisfying solutions to what is otherwise an insoluble puzzle, namely how to square a triangle made up of the conflicting needs, wants, desires, interests, etc. of (1) individuals (2) society—and all this in relation to (3) varying definitions of worthwhile, useful knowledge'? (1983: 206)

2. What do we contribute to what Holmes defines as a 'paradigm of theories dealing with: knowledge, and how it can be acquired (epistemology); causation (aetiology); mental and physical difference between individuals (ethnology); learning (psychology); and the nature of society (sociological and political science theories)'? (1982: 12)

3. How may education be 'phased and programmed and experienced in a life of rapidly shifting relationships at home at work, in communications of every kind'? (King 1985: 218)

4. How can we address questions of the content of education within groups, as well as the interrelationships between groups 'in a way that can assist those who conduct schooling in particular societies'? (White 1981: 317)

5. How do we acknowledge, in the light of the foregoing, that reform has been 'one of the chief purposes of comparative studies in education'(Watson and Wilson 1985: 7) but on the one hand, comparative education perspectives on this have tended to be limited to one particular conservative theoretical orientation

> (Welch 1987: 220) and on the other, too divorced from the needs of the practitioners? (Simkin 1983: 111)

The aim of the project which resulted in the present volume and which began in 1988, was to provide some light on these issues from the perspective of a particular set of scholars, drawn largely from a particular geographical region, and often responding to its problems. The participation in the early stages by Dr Ibrahim Alladin issued in invitations to other comparativists whose work highlights the issues with which we are dealing here, and whose experience often includes the same area, loosely described as the Pacific Rim, which is the main focus of Australian and New Zealand comparativists. We also sought to show how particular issues which arise out of local concerns are contributing to the growth and change of comparative theory and methodology. The issues include the legitimation of educational knowledge; critical reflections on comparative education, race, ethnicity and gender; youth, the new vocationalism and post-compulsory education; international agencies; education and development; and reconceptualising the role of education. Contributors were asked to address substantive issues, with case material from the Pacific Rim area as far as possible, and with attention to the significance of the work for the theory and practice of comparative education. We thus tried to go beyond the agenda described by Arnove, Kelly and Altbach for the 1980s: 'educational expansion and reform and equality of educational opportunities and outcomes' (1981: 1) and at the same time to show that comparative education has a distinctive agenda and contribution since the one described above could apply to most educational fields of inquiry.

In this present volume, in addition, individual contributors raise pointedly the consistent themes summarized below, in different contexts and in different ways:

1. The ethics of research: Here, there is a common thread of a denial of the ethics of the older positivist models of research, such as those used variously by the major comparativists of the 1960s. What is evident instead is the elaboration of newer forms of theory, based on the ethics of feminist research, critical theory,

and varieties of Marxism/neo Marxism. All of the above reject the technicist underpinnings of scientistic forms of theorizing in comparative education, whether practised by the older generation of Holmes, Bereday, or Noah and Eckstein, or members of the current generation such as Psacharopoulos. In this volume Price raises these concerns most explicitly.

2. Reconceptualising the education-planning-development links: Here again, the work around this theme in the present volume reflects substantial changes since the postwar 'modernization' era (Welch 1985a). Contributors dealing with development no longer accept that the social and economic development of Third World nations will necessarily be served by a slavish adoption of Western technology, institutions and values. Instead, a concern with the impact of Westernization, especially upon the broad mass of people in Third World nations, is evident, and thus aid, planning and development are all given more critical scrutiny. The chapters by Toh and Farrelly, and Collins and Gillespie address these issues in different ways.

3. The role of international agencies and agents in social and educational change: This area too is gaining increasing attention, including from Australian scholars (Jones 1987, 1991; Welch 1988; and Toh and Farrelly, Hindson, Collins and Gillespie, and Burns in this volume). No longer is it assumed that international agencies and exchanges are always motivated by simple considerations of the good of the host nation(s). At least since Carnoy (1974, Arnove 1980) and similar studies, comparativists have been concerned with inequities in international economic and political power, which often act to the detriment of the mass of Third World people that are the supposed beneficiaries of 'aid'. Alliances between small, Westernised elites in Third World countries, and major international aid agencies or large capitalist interests (see Collins and Gillespie in this volume) have become an increasing focus of critical interest, as is the political and cultural context of the 'host' nation.

4. The educational challenge of inequality: While older work in comparative education often spoke of access, or assumed that educational expansion was either inevitable or desirable, or both, contemporary thought focuses on ways in which particular groups are disadvantaged. Class analysis in national or international contexts has undergone something of a renascence, while comparative studies of gender and race/ethnicity have gained increasing sophistication. Perhaps the increasing recognition of the complex interrelationships in culture between marginalised and mainstream groups, by figures such as Scrase and others, may allow comparativists to further prove their worth in this area.

5. Comparative education and educational practice: The increasingly wide range of interests which comparativists demonstrate is now often oriented towards questions of practical reform. Comparativists in Australia have interested themselves keenly in the development of policies and practices in the area of international students, and have often been critical of the wholesale change in rationale from 'aid' to 'trade'. (See Burns, and Toh and Farrelly n this volume.) Comparisons with practices elsewhere have shown some of the pitfalls in this area (Welch 1988). Equally, comparativists from this region have shown critical interest in Australia's role in the South Pacific, or what has been called Australia's international relations in education. This interest in educational practice is shared by many other educational researchers in Australasia and has led comparativists into some fruitful work with colleagues from other disciplines. This is all the more likely given the relatively limited pool of comparativists in the region.

6. Legitimacy: The development of legitimacy as a theme in comparative education has occurred over the last twenty years or so. To a fair extent, research has centred upon the question: How does the taken-for-granted become legitimate, or naturalised? Initially the question, itself provoked by reorientations within British sociology of education around the 1970s, dealt with the relational qualities of knowledge in particular settings. This

yielded a number of case studies examining how certain knowledge came to be structured in particular ways at specified times and places. Later, the relationship of knowledge and legitimation was systematically broadened to analyse the ways in which the legitimation of knowledge connected with the ongoing need for legitimacy by the political system. In this process, Australians such as Burns and Welch have played a role, while the chapter by Scrase in the current volume deals with relevant concerns.

THE INDIVIDUAL CONTRIBUTIONS

These range broadly across groups and themes, often challenging accepted wisdom, developing innovative theoretical strains in comparative educational research, or employing different units of analysis. BRANSON AND MILLER explore the prospects of post-structuralist feminism for an understanding of girls' education in Bali, Indonesia. In an era of multiculturalism, culture is being recognised as an increasingly powerful determinant of knowledge transmission, yet the scientific and rational western model of education still tends to dominate, including among academics who write and act in the Third World. This dependence upon a unitary and technical logic, whose history is also intimately linked with the rise of Western capitalism, can license the construction of abstract categories such as 'the Balinese'. The spread of this scientific ideology by its missionaries is part of the spread of Western capitalism into post-colonial regimes, which often becomes part of the fabric of the host nation, and in particular becomes associated with those in power in those societies, forming a bridge to elites in metropolitan countries. Pre-colonial modes of knowing are systematically eroded, devalued and supplanted with scientific models derived from the West.

In Bali, education is important for girls studied in this investigation, because education can be a means toward a prestigious, non-manual job, and may be important in her future marriage. Literacy has traditionally been associated with power in Balinese society, and was reserved for the few. Literacy has often been imbued with the sacred, or divine. The Dutch influence accentuated class and status divisions in Indonesian society, while at the same time raising general aspiration levels. It was not until 1959 that Bali had its first senior secondary schools. Since then there has been an educational explosion.

'Modern' education, however, has increasingly marginalized Balinese women, who traditionally had an important and powerful role in Balinese society. Modern female roles in Indonesian society, including textbooks, emphasise the roles of homemaker, or as teachers, nurses etc. Traditional female dominance of trading has largely been supplanted by models of Western femininity: beautiful, privatized and passive. Now, in the face of this modern education, Balinese girls are dropping out at rates much higher than their male peers, and express less confidence in their ability levels.

SCRASE picks up some of these themes in a study of a different Third World context: West Bengal, India. Scrase reviews the potential of reproduction and resistance theory, including Bowles and Gintis, Giroux, Willis, Bourdieu, Gramsci, and others for explaining the way in which textbooks distort the reality of Indian life, in particular the life of the mass of working class Indians. Textbooks show neat, urban settings, replete with Western style houses, cars and gadgetry. Slums do not rate a mention, and poor people are often portrayed in less than flattering terms.

This process of the distortion of everyday reality is all the more insidious, in that it is this group (i.e. the poor) who have least power to control the schooling they experience, but who are also served least well by it. The realities of life for the majority of people in contemporary India are systematically distorted. It is middle class Western experience which is most conventionally portrayed in the textbooks which Scrase investigates, while the actual lives of working class Indians are distorted and, at times, disdained. The ideology which Scrase discerns in the texts under study is largely consonant with that of the Westernized middle class in West Bengal, and operates structurally in similarly discriminatory fashion to the old caste system of ancient India, but supplanting those older notions of caste with more contemporary concepts of class. Both serve to maintain a form of cultural hegemony.

PRICE, too, attacks distortion, but from a different perspective. He argues that, along with Epstein and others, research, and methodology, in comparative education has been distorted by its predominant refusal to accept its ideological role. In part, this is a legacy of an outmoded, value-free model of the natural sciences, which focuses on what is, and thus falls victim to a form of mechanistic understanding, a technical orientation which Price argues is not only outmoded in the natural sciences, but has also distorted discussion about methodology in the social sciences, including comparative education, at the same time. Certainly, much debate in comparative education turned on the question of scientific methodology, and its appropriateness as a metaphor and model for research. This was particularly so in the 1960s when figures such as Bereday, Holmes, and Noah and Eckstein each claimed to have discovered the model of the natural sciences most appropriate. With hindsight, such efforts can be seen as another example of positivistic social science, and Price argues that such models are inadequate to the task of a reformulated, and reformist, comparative education. Price, like several of the newer and more critically oriented scholars, holds to a vision of a better world, less infected by extremities of wealth and poverty, war and pollution. Can comparative education make any difference to these profound and pressing, global problems? For Price, part of the problem is seeing all these problems in isolation, and it is here that the synthesizing study of comparative education can make a modest contribution.

More than this however, and as Price argued in his latest book, we need to give due acknowledgement to the many forms of teaching and learning which go on outside the formal institutions of education, and often for individuals well outside the age range of conventional schooling. On this account, the women's movement, the peace movement, trade unions and, presumably, ecological movements merit our attention as educative in function. And Price raises once again the question of the role of work in relation to education, as also the theme of moral-political education.

WELCH also considers critically theoretical silences in comparative education. In tracing, and contributing to, the development of legitimation as a theme in comparative research, he argues that work by some of our leading comparativitists in the area of curriculum change often embraced substantially different conceptions of knowledge, culture and power. In reviewing some of the precursors—Kandel, Hans and Holmes—to studies of changes to the social constructions of knowledge, however, he finds that functionalist underpinnings were only really present in the latter.

Later, as comparativists were increasingly moved to consider the implications of the 'new' sociology of education of the 1970s, the notion of hierarchies of educational knowledge and changes in the knowledge stock were examined and theorized in comparative perspective. The most recent, current stage of the debate owes more to developments in critical theory, particularly the work of Offe and Habermas, with their emphases on system legitimacy, and the theory of the state in modern society. With this stage, the connections between the legitimacy of knowledge and that of the political system is finally made explicit, and offers new definitions of knowledge, culture and power.

YATES also casts a critical eye over comparative education, and its methods, drawing upon recent developments in feminist theory and methodology, which she argues is also concerned with the act of comparison. For example, consciousness raising, which Yates defines as the sharing of experience without a formal leader, is in fact a comparing of like with like: that is, using the common experience of wife, mother, woman to gradually come to see a new reality, perhaps with an eye to the transformation of prevailing reality. The analogy with the work of Freire here is palpable, and acknowledged, although Yates argues that with women's consciousness raising groups, there is an even lesser influence upon 'outside' knowledge. The second form of comparison Yates examines is that which pits the experience of girls with that of boys. Here again the distinctiveness of the female experience raises similarities with Freire: the notion of 'knowing a situation and knowing it differently'. Activist practitioners and practically oriented social scientists need to use 'imagined alternatives' against which to test current situations. A good deal of what Yates calls 'mapping research' has been inspired over the last decade or so by this perspective. The third form of comparison is that of cross-cultural research, which has given rise to increasing numbers of studies of similarities and differences among the achievements of girls from different cultures and which, according to Yates, has, in turn, stimulated further theorizing about gender.

Positivism, liberalism, and relativities of power are also raised as significant problems for the development of a feminist ethic in education. Positivism, Yates asserts, fails to acknowledge that 'terms' and 'facts' may be susceptible to different interpretations, while liberalism pervades the taken-for-granted understanding behind key terms such as 'equality,' 'fairness,' and 'individual'. The failure to take into account differences in power, particularly differences in the ability to define the legitimate, vitiates the utility of techniques such as values clarification in areas such as human relations courses for girls.

SIMKIN AND GAUCI also focus on the failure to recognize difference, in particular ethnic difference in the Australian educational context. The paper, in line with many other analyses of multiculturalism, separates out the analysis of indigenous and non-indigenous minorities and concentrates on the latter, in particular the translation of multiculturalism into educational rhetoric and reality. The predominant framework within which multiculturalism is defined in Australia, according to Simkin and Gauci, is that of social cohesion: multiculturalism must not be allowed to threaten that fundamental value, a concern which has become even more manifest since Asian immigration to Australia has become a larger proportion of the overall intake. Part of the question rests on the definition of culture, which although recognized, at times, as dynamic, nonetheless operates within an overall taken-for-granted of a core Australian 'common culture'. It is perhaps for this reason that most policy documents persist in attributing educational disadvantage to the lack of English language skills, failing to recognize the structural parameters of minority affiliation.

There are also significant differences within the states, as to the extent to which those with different 'cultural capital' may contribute to curriculum development, policy development etc. Some states operate according to a common curriculum, others work via an emphasis on the learning of other languages, still others insist that while all schools must offer multicultural perspectives, that only some will also offer, for example, community languages, or bilingual education. Following a wide ranging review of comparative approaches to ethnic diversity, including allusions to examples outside Australia, Simkin and Gauci argue that comparative researchers will have a role to play for some considerable time, by developing case studies of different (state) practices and programmes, and possibly in evaluating the relevance of overseas models for use in the Australian context. The overall assessment of Simkin and Gauci is that in Australia, comparative theory building has been weak, and academic research in comparative education has not played much of a role in the development of policies or practices in multicultural education. In the face of an ongoing diversity of cultural input, perhaps aspects of Australia's traditional xenophobia will continue to inform Australian responses.

COLLINS AND GILLESPIE also examine the South Asian context, and focus on the vexed relationship between education and employment, which in turn raises the issue of clashes between values of equity and efficiency. The Philippines is used as a case study of a Third World state: rich in people, but poor in technological development. Moreover, it is crippled with overseas debt problems, the repayment of which now consumes more than half of the annual budgetary allocation, while the country also still reveals the legacy of colonial domination, mainly from America. In this context, it is not surprising that pragmatic concerns with building the economy through education overwhelm the frequently cited concerns with equity and democracy.

Ultimately, argue Collins and Gillespie, such logic depends upon the adoption of Human Capital economic theories which, as advanced by spokesmen such as Theodor Schultz, see individuals as a form of economic input and investment, to be compared with other forms of investment, like machinery. Equally, the assumption goes, individuals only seek education to further their economic advantage. In the developing countries context, the economy is often seen to be divided into modern and traditional sectors, the latter of which is often seen as a cause of slower growth. In fact, the link between education and economic growth is not that simple, as the work of Ronald Dore, John Oxenham and others has shown. Employers may well increase the level of qualification demanded for a paricular job, independently of any demonstrated need for that level of skill, a process which reflects the glut of well qualified, perhaps over qualified, applicants. This in turn, is parasitic upon rising demand for education, especially in the developing world. Credentialism, then, and the associated unemployment and underemployment, is a feature of education in the Philippines, too. Retention rates, too, are low, as with other developing countries, and there are wide disparities of esteem associated with different educational institutions. The private sector, however, is very substantial, more than in many other Third World states, and these institutions are often patronized by students from wealthier and better educated backgrounds. Schools reflect a conventional academic bias, as in other Third World contexts, which yields a surfeit of well schooled young people who compete fiercely for the limited number of white collar jobs.

What does this pattern mean for employment and education in the Philippines? Studies quoted by Collins and Gillespie show substantial, and tragic, wastage of human ability and resources. As many as six out of ten three year college graduates fail to find work. This under-utilization rate has more than doubled in the last three decades; when seen in either economic or in educational terms, it represents an enormous loss, resulting, in part, in an export industry of educated Filipinos. Collins and Gillespie show how difficult it is for the Aquino government to resist the mass democratic aspirations of the Filipino people for more education, especially of the kind which carries the prospect of white collar employment, although the resulting economic imbalance, and personal loss, is enormous. The vocationalizing of education, while reasonable from one point of view, may well be resisted by the populace, interested in having their children enter white collar employment.

In the end, the answers to this development dilemma lie not only within education, but include economic and social strategies of import substitution, public investment in infrastructure, and making the quality of rural life richer, and hence more attractive.The latter might well involve direct redistribution of land to farmers, in a country where the best land is owned by a few, and where cronyism is rampant. Are these remedies, then, likely to be entertained and adopted in the Philippines?

Collins and Gillespie are pessimistic, and current evidence suggests their assessment may well be accurate.

CROSSLEY raises political and ethical issues as the context within which education in the South Pacific needs to be considered. His major concern is with the development and application of comparative and international education in the Australia-Pacific region. To some extent, current work by 'outsiders' can be seen as a 'betrayal' of former Australian efforts to develop formal western education within the Pacific, as the trend is to provide training and research contracts whose major aim is to benefit the Australian tertiary institution. While this is a pronounced and explicit trend in Australian and other industrialised country aid since the early 1980s, it has in fact built on practices already in place, and on the competitive awarding of 'development' contracts by agencies such as the World Bank. The importance of both the trend, and indigenous criticism of it, is that it is comparative educators whose training and experience places them in a strong position to successfully compete for contracts, especially at a time when other sources for their research have dried up. This in turn highlights ethical and methodological issues for comparativists, including concern about the relationships between theory and practice.

The issues which Crossley points to in his examples of 'outsider' applied research include the power and prestige of recommendations especially for external funding agencies, and the irony of specific recommendations which reduce the role of indigenous institutions and enhance that of industrial country ones. The fact that such research has been done 'on' rather than 'with' local people only enhances the gap between perspectives and the potential damage to the autonomy of local researchers and policy makers who are dependent on outside funds. This mirrors in some ways the dilemmas of researchers in Australia and elsewhere who are also increasingly dependent on tied funds. It also raises questions, especially in an applied field such as education, about the sources of legitimacy of knowledge and the process of its selection and application in educational systems.

Two pointers to ways out of the situation of researchers becoming more tightly bound to the processes of dependency are suggested by Crossley. He demonstrates how critical research and theorising by comparativists from around the world, and in some instances crystallised in the themes of their annual conferences, is available both for understanding what is going on and as material and ideas for indigenous educators, researchers and policy makers to use in the process of developing their own alternatives. While this does not get out of the bind of a one-way traffic in educational ideas, his second proposal does: diversified research paradigms emphasising ethnographic approaches, both for their concern with multiple perspectives, respect for values and context as an important aspect of understanding a situation, and for establishing collaborative research partnerships including in the critical area of evaluation.

If Crossley's chapter is an analysis of the strengths of comparative education and critical ethnography to resist enhancing dependency in the South Pacific, that by BURNS focuses on the 'other side' of the processes, the push towards privatisation of education and other services within industrialised countries, and the effects on debates with respect to both general education and development.

TOH AND FARRELLY take up the issues of educational development and the role of foreign training in accelerating the production of indigenous middle and high level personnel. Looking at the rise of study abroad programs, they acknowledge that they have provided advanced technological knowledge and skills, and generated 'international understanding' through their presence abroad. However, there has never been a consideration that this is an important two-way process, and the fostering of goodwill towards the former host rather than enhanced understanding is seen as a desirable outcome for the visiting students. In fact, it has been stated ever more clearly by politicians that the taking of overseas students is as much to benefit the host country, both through goodwill which should lead to continuing economic and political contacts with the former hosts and through the actual work which they do, especially those undertaking research. Do they also make a significant contribution to the economic and social development of the source countries, especially the poor majorities in those countries?

While there has been research on overseas students for decades, there has been little inquiry about their actual orientation to development issues and the explicit and implicit orientations, if any, of their overseas courses. Toh and Farrelly review this extensive international literature, critically examine development theories and models, and then look at the assumptions of students and their courses. Their study was of a sample of students undertaking postgraduate courses in Australia related to rural development (agricultural science, extension and economics) at four universities. The students came from 13 different Third World countries. Open-ended interview schedules were used to elicit both student and academic information about students' knowlege of and attitudes to Third World development issues, perceptions of the relevance of the academic programs, their motivations for study abroad, students' future career plans in development, and background details. In addition to finding that the overwhelming percentage of students were middle class and oriented to the modernisation view of development if they held any articulated view at all, it was found that the topics of research and the methodologies were largely narrowly technical and positivistic, very much like those of their lecturers and supervisors. The outcomes are viewed from different development, methodological and ethical perspectives, but especially through questioning the value to Third World development, particularly of the poor, of such training.

It is for that group that non-formal education (NFE) is seen as a 'critical resource' for acquiring the skills and knowledge to become more effective members of society. For women in particular, it is also a more attainable resource than, for example, capital or land, enabling them to become 'integrated' in the development process. STROMQUIST begins her chapter with a critique of that depiction of women, arguing that they are integrated but under conditions of subordination which restrict their attainment of collective benefits and oppress them through the unfair social division of labour. Seen from this perspective, NFE has a critical role for women, too, but for emancipation. How have the NFE programs supported by international agencies affected the conditions of women?

Stromquist encountered a major problem in investigating this question, which affects most assessments of the role of education in development, namely, there is frequently an education or training component of development projects, but it is rarely explicit, and the actual amounts specifically put into NFE are small in aid budget terms. Further, the World Bank, one of the major educational funders, concentrates on formal education. At the home government level, programs tend to be segmented along the lines of ministries and different public sectors leading to fragmented, highly specific courses which do little to address issues related to women's current, especially reproductive roles, or future possibilities. Yet reproduction, production and emancipation are considered key issues for change for women, difficult as they are to incorporate in NFE programs or in development as it is generally conceived by governmental and international agencies.

A different picture emerges from the NFE programs of non-governmental organisations (NGOs): these tend to be more diverse, creative and comprehensive, and include childcare arrangements to assist women's participation. They 'combine skills with gender awareness'. Looking for the bases for the different potentials of NFE programs for women, Stromquist is critical of the development model of most states and large international agencies. They tend to be neither oriented to the neediest people, nor to women, not least because women are rarely represented on the teams that assess and develop projects. Women tend to be better represented at all stages of NGO projects, and provide thereby a training ground for confidence and skill building. Minimal training and financial resources are crucial for women to become successful project managers and implementers. This is being recognised by some governments which are increasing their funding of NGOs, with a considerable amount being for NFE and for women.

Three key issues emerge from the review of NGO strengths and potential, and the over-riding need of poor women for access to money: micro verus macro strategies for social and economic change; women-only versus integrated development projects; and the role of the state in national development, especially since it can constrain or facilitate the work of NGOs.

BACCHUS asserts, following Carnoy and Levin, that a concept of the State must underlie any serious analysis of the educational system. His focus is on formal education and the ways in which the State carries out its functions of accumulation and legitimation. His particular concern is to examine these processes in the less developed countries.

The chapter provides a major review of the phases in the emergence of colonial education as the background to the post-colonial dilemmas. The newly enfranchised masses were prepared to grant legitimacy to the State, or at least to a particular government, insofar as it was able to provide for them. In educational terms, this led to demands for an education which would increase the opportunities for the social and economic mobility of their children; in turn, the State had to ensure continued economic growth to meet such demands, including the demand for jobs as well as for the training for them. This they have been increasingly unable to do, largely due to continued economic dependency as a result of the social and economic infrastructure established during the colonial period.

As in industrialised countries, one solution to the dilemma of service provision has been privatisation, often following a period of heavy borrowing in an attempt to provide a public solution. Both a fiscal and a legitimacy crisis has followed, the one from debt and the other from both its consequences and from the general inability of the State to fulfil its promises. An alternative solution to the private one has been less expensive public services, which has further decreased the mass legitimacy of regimes but, since elites have become less dependent on the masses for their sources of legitimacy, they can afford to ignore the needs of the masses.

Bacchus echoes Crossley's concern that educational 'experts' may have a crucial role, especially as outside advisors, policy makers and trainers of indigenous educational elites. They cannot stand aside from a concern with the base of their operation (mass versus elite), with the implications of their findings and recommendations, and the models and processes which they use. Based on Habermas' concept of three major knowledge-guiding interests, Bacchus shows the implications of each for the practice of education and development. An unacknowledged or inadequate knowledge should no longer inform educational research and practice, and he advocates serious exploration of the emancipatory potential of education by researchers, teachers, policy makers and administrators.

Yet another chapter echoes concern with economic and educational development, the ways their inter-relationships are conceived, and the models on which further developments are premised. HINDSON applies his analysis to the small island states of the South Pacific, partly in recognition of interest both in small island states in general, and in the South Pacific as a geographical and strategic region. His particular concern is with the inadequacies of the formal western educational planning process for these island states.

In reviewing the emergence of formal educational planning, Hindson teases out some of the major elements of the economics-education nexus. High levels of economic growth were supposed to 'trickle down' to the masses who, with an injection of literacy and numeracy as well as the 'right' modern values, would be able to participate in the new economic opportunities. The economists had their own version, which focused on human productive capacities and became known as human capital theory. Both modernisation and human capital theory influenced educational planners, in the drive to expand education for economic purposes, and state and foreign agency financing of education enhanced the role of the planners. They brought with them international comparison as a tool for national planning. In the late 1960s, social scientists and educators began to question the way the education-economy link was framed, not least because it was not delivering the goods to the masses, or to a sustained economic growth. And the use of international comparison became discredited because it ignored crucial local conditions and imposed a universalising set of expectations and approaches. Comparativists have been at the forefront of criticising universal educational and developmental panaceas. A decade ensued of searching both for new educational and new theoretical approaches.

An alternative approach to educational development which fits certain cultural frames within the South Pacific uses a responsive rather than a proactive process oriented to specific local tensions and needs. It is depicted as an ongoing search for educational direction and Hindson applies it to the understanding of two decades of educational planning in the South Pacific. Educational quality, relevance, conflict between academic and vocational education and between economic and social objectives were found to be the main conflicts determining educational change. The tensions often led to positive action and to context-relevant solutions and readjustment of educational aims and goals.

BURNS is concerned with the ways in which the state depicts education and how questions of quantity and quality in education are manipulated in educational discourses as different economic conditions prevail. As with other contributors, notably Bacchus, she considers the issue of different interests in education and looks at them in relationship to quantity-quality considerations, especially as they are used in decisions about education's role in development. The tensions between educational professionals, students and parents, on the one hand, and other 'clients' for educational outcomes on the other, are explored through the concept of 'crisis' and the ways in which professionals use it in relationship to educational provision itself, and other interest groups use the more general socio-economic situation as the basis for educational decision-making.

Her example which is worked through in depth is the re-definition of education as a commodity or service, the sale of which can both assist with financing the expansion of education at home and which is still somehow considered to benefit foreign nationals whose own educational services are inadequate. There is a general trend towards privatisation of education, as Stromquist, and Collins and Gillespie have raised in relationship to the problems of educational provision in developing countries. The linking of privatisation to expanded opportunities both for fee-paying nationals and for recruiting overseas students sets a major apparent concern in education, equality, at variance with other considerations. Further issues about thc effects of privatisation on knowledge itself, especially through the commodification of research, are being offset in the debate against the benefit to the common good of more applied research.

Thus, the whole discourse has shifted, and national interest has been posed as an over-riding good to which services such as education should be subsidiary. How one defines a national interest is left unproblematic. That it cannot remain so is shown in the effects on higher education of the whole commercialisation and privatisation push. The effects, however, have not been to de-legitimate the discourse, but the notions of education and knowledge, and of state responsibility for service provision more generally, which are at present out of step with the state-industry alliance.

Details regarding the relationship between education and employment are taken up by KING. He shows how a number of different worldviews nevertheless are based on the assumption that the future is foreseeable, plannable and contrivable by means of formal education under the control of the state. At present young people subject to formal education are no longer just 'manpower': they are nearly young adults and as such, and for technological, political and educational reasons they have become a source of anxiety to the adult world. Employment is one key aspect of this anxiety. In turn, the relationship of education to employment has become a pivotal issue in educational decision-making, including decisions about quality and quantity.

King reports an extended comparative study of youth, employment and education, focussing on post-compulsory education for young adults who, he points out, constitute a group in their own right in society today and are outside the ambit of formal academic education. The research itself has had to come to grips with new realities of educational and training needs, technology, the labour market and the whole educational policy-making process. New research partners have had to be recruited in order to understand the situation and the different perspectives within which decisions are being made and institutions shaped and re-shaped. While he maintains that 'realistic' studies must be country and culture specific, and hence beyond the grand studies and attempted theory-making of traditional comparative education, nevertheless the commonality of the problem suggests a cross-national research effort. The situation is thus a challenge to comparative education and an opportunity to show its relevance to local educators and bureaucrats.

In a sense, King's chapter brings considerations full circle, from a critique of Western educational imperialism to a plea for understanding of the local context in industrialised countries in order to bridge some theory-practice gaps in comparative educational research and in the processes of educational change. In so doing, his chapter also points to some persistent issues which have occurred throughout these chapters. The major ones are the relationship between education as a human right and as a tool for greater human equality and liberation and the society within which it is taking place; the role of interest groups in determining educational inputs and outcomes including local, national, regional and global ones; the need for new understanding of the local and national context and of changing requirements from the various clients for education; the need for researchers to reflect critically on their relevance, their methodologies, their role in change and the ethical implications of the type of research they undertake and for whom, and the challenge to comparative education as a field of intellectual endeavour. There is in fact very little concern with issues which were once of major concern, namely the nature of comparative research and theorising. Concern with theory is rather expressed through various pleas for relevance in practice, and implicitly through concern with the way data are gathered both in relationship to those researched, and those who pay for the research.

It is tempting to suggest that comparative and international education has moved out of the missionary phase, when grand theory and universal practice were its desired outcomes. Rather, it has emerged from some serious concern that it has no relevance either to students of education or to educators and educational policy makers, to engage with major educational issues and in the struggle, new approaches and new questions are emerging. The chapters in this volume are part of that struggle, written mostly by the middle generation of recent doctoral graduates and mid-career educators who have been trained in comparative education yet who do not teach or apply it in their major work. In their efforts to relate that day-to-day educational work and their research interests, critical reflection on the field and new concepts, problems and approaches are emerging.

REFERENCES

Adorno, T., et al. (1976) *The Positivist Dispute in German Sociology*. London, Heinemann.

Altbach, P., Kelly, G., and Weiss, L., (1985) *Excellence in Education*. Buffalo, Prometheus Press.

Altbach, P.G. and Kelly, G.P. (eds.) (1986) *New Approaches to Comparative Education*. Chicago, University of Chicago Press.

Apple, M. (1987) 'Foreword'. Lankshear and Lawler, *Literacy*.

Arnove, R. (1980) *Philanthropy as Cultural Imperialism. The Foundations at Home and Abroad*. Boston, G.K. Hall.

Arnove, R.F., Kelly, G.P. and Altbach, P.G. (1981) 'Approaches and Perspectives'. In P.G. Altbach, R.F. Arnove and G.P. Kelly (eds.), *Comparative Education*. New York, Macmillan, 1981: 3–11.

Aronowitz, S., and Giroux, H. (1986) *Education Under Siege. The Conservative, Liberal and Radical Debate over Schooling*. London, Routledge.

Bacon, F. (1856) 'Novum Organum and The Advancement of Learning'. In J. Spedding (ed.), *Collected Works*, London, Longman & Co.

Bell, D. (1960) *The End of Ideology*. London, Free Press of Glencoe.

Bereday, G. (1966) *Comparative Method in Education*. New York, Holt, Rinehart and Winston.

Bottomore, T. (1975) *Marxist Sociology*. London, Macmillan.

Burns, R. (1986) 'Implications of the Accelerated Commercialisation of Higher Education and Research'. In R.R. Gillespie and C.B. Collins (eds.), *Education as an International Commodity*. Brisbane, ANZCIES, 145–162.

Burns, R. (1988). 'The Scientific Is Political: Educational Research in Comparative Perspective'. Paper presented at the annual meeting of the Comparative and International Education Society, Atlanta, Georgia, March.

Callahan, R. (1962) *Education and the Cult of Efficiency*. Chicago, University of Chicago Press.

Carnoy, M. (1982) 'Education, Economy, and the State'. In M. Apple (ed.), *Cultural and Economic Reproduction in Education*. London, Routledge.

Carnoy, M. (1974) *Education as Cultural Imperialism*. New York, McKay.

Comparative Education Society of Europe (CESE) Conference (1990). Madrid, July.

Cowen, R. (1981) 'The Place of Comparative Education in the Educational Sciences'. Paper presented at the Comparative Education Society of Europe conference, Geneva.

Cowen, R. (1981) 'Sociological Analysis and Comparative Education'. *International Review of Education*, 27 (4).

Feyerabend, P. (1975) *Against Method.* London, New Left Books.

Feyerabend, P. (1976) 'On the Critique of Scientific Reason'. In C. Howson, *Method and Appraisal in the Physical Sciences.* London, Cambridge University Press.

Feyerabend, P. (1987) *Farewell to Reason.* London, Verso.

Feyerabend, P. (1978) *Science in a Free Society.* London, New Left Books.

Giddens, A. (1979) 'Positivism'. In T. Bottomore and R. Nisbet (eds.), *A History of Sociological Analysis.* London, Heinemann.

Giddens, A. (1974) *Positivism and Sociology.* London, Heinemann.

Gillespie, R.R. and Collins, C.B. (eds.) (1986) *Education as an International Commodity.* Brisbane, ANZCIES.

Habermas, J. (1971) 'Technology and Science as Ideology'. *Toward a New Society,* London, Heinemann.

Habermas, J. (1978) *Knowledge and Human Interests.* London, Heinemann.

Habermas, J. (1976) *Legitimation Crisis.* Boston, Beacon Press.

Halls, W.D. (1990) *Comparative Education: Contemporary issues and trends.* London, Jessica Kingsley Publishers/Paris, UNESCO.

Halls, W.D. (1990) 'Trends and Issues in Comparative Education'. In W.D. Halls (ed.), *Comparative Education,* op. cit.

Hans, N. (1949) *Comparative Education.* London, Routledge.

Heymann, R. (1979) 'Comparative Education from an Ethnomethodological Perspective'. *Comparative Education* 15(3).

Holmes, B. (1982) 'Muddles and Confusion in Comparative Education'. In R. Cowen and P. Stokes (eds.). *Methodological Issues in Comparative Education.* London, The London Association of Comparative Educationalists, 6–14.

Holmes, B. (1985) 'Trends in Comparative Education'. *Prospects* 15(3): 25–346.

Holmes, B. (1981) *Comparative Education: Some considerations of method.* London, George Allen and Unwin.

Holmes, B. (1965) *Problems in Education. A Comparative Approach.* London, Routledge.

Jones, P. (1987) *International Policies for Third World Development: UNESCO, Literacy and Development.* London, Routledge.

Jones, P. (1991) *World Bank Financing of Education. Lending, Learning and Development.* London, Routledge.

Kelly, G.P. and Altbach, P.G. (1986) 'Comparative Education: Challenge and Response'. *Comparative Education Review* 30(1): 89–107.

King, E. (1985) 'Comparative Studies and Educational Reform'. In K. Watson and R. Wilson (eds.) *Contemporary Issues in Comparative Education.* London, Croom Helm, 208–219.

Lankshear, C., and Lawler, M. (1987) *Literacy, Schooling and Revolution.* Brighton, Falmer.

Marcuse, H. (1968) *One Dimensional Man.* London, Sphere.

Masemann, V.L. (1982) 'Critical Ethnography in the Study of Comparative Education'. *Comparative Education Review* 26(1): 1–14.

Masemann, V.L. (1990) 'Ways of Knowing'. *Comparative Education Review* 34(4): 465–473.

Nicholas, E.J. (1983) *Issues in Education: A Comparative Analysis*. London, Harper and Row.

Noah, H., and Eckstein, M. (1969) *Towards a Science of Comparative Education.* New York, Macmillan.

Passmore, J. (1972) *The Perfectibility of Man.* London, Duckworth.

Paulston, R.G. (1990) 'Toward a Reflective Comparative Education?' *Comparative Education Review* 34(2): 248–255.

Psacharopoulos, G. (1990) 'Comparative Education: From theory to practice, or are you a: \neo.* or b: *.ist?' *Comparative Education Review* 34(3): 369–380.

Purves, A., and Levine, D. (1975) *Educational Policy and International Assessment*. Berkeley, McCutchan, 1975.

Salmon, W. (1989). *Four Decades of Scientific Explanation*. Minneapolis, University of Minnesota Press.

Schriewer, J. and Holmes, B. (eds.) (1988) *Theories and Methods in Comparative Education.* Frankfurt am Main, Peter Lang.

Sheehan, B. (1983) 'Comparative Education: Phoenix or Dodo?' In B.A. Sheehan (ed.), *Comparative and International Studies and the Theory and Practice of Education.* Melbourne, ANZCIES, 161–178.

Simkin, K. (1983). 'Educational Comparisons and the Educator'. In Sheehan (ed.), op. cit.: 108–124.

Watson, K., and Wilson, R. (1985). *Contemporary Perspectives in Cooperative Education.* London, Croom Helm.

Watson, K. and Wilson, R. 'Introduction'. In Watson and Wilson, op. cit.: 1–8.

Weiler, H. (1983) 'Legalization, Expertise and Participation: Strategies of Compensatory Legitimation in Educational Policy'. *Comparative Education Review* 27(2).

Weiler, H. (1990). 'Comparative Perspectives on Educational Decentralization: An Exercise in Contradiction?' *Educational Evaluation and Policy Analysis:* 12 (4): 433–448.

Welch, A. R. (1986a) 'Education and the Cult of Efficiency: the Reality and the Rhetoric'. Presidential address, ANZCIES conference, Brisbane, December.

Welch, A. R. (1986b) 'For Sale, by Degrees: the Commodification of Higher Education in Australia and the United Kingdom'. Paper presented at the ANZCIES conference, Brisbane, December.

Welch, A. (1985a) 'The Functionalist Tradition in Comparative Education.' *Comparative Education* 19 (2): 5–19.

Welch, A.R. (1985b). 'A Critique of Quotidian Reason in Comparative Education.' *Journal of International and Comparative Education* 1 (1) 1986: 37–62.

Welch, A. (1991) 'La Ciencia Sedante: El Funcionalismo como Base para la Investigación en Educación Comparada.' In J. Schreiwer and F. Pedro, *Educación Comparada: Teorías, Perspectivas, Investigaciones.* Barcelona, Herder: 1–27.

Welch, A. (1990) 'Education and the Cult of Efficiency. Comparative Reflections on the Reality and the Rhetoric." Auckland University, ANZCIES.

Welch, A.R. (1987) 'Prolegomenon to a Critical Comparative Education'. In A. Williamson (ed.). *Educational Exchanges and their Implications. Challenge and Response.* Sydney, ANZCIES, 220–232. See a revised version of the same article in *Journal of International and Comparative Education* 9 (1) 1991: 506–520.

Welch, A.R. (1988) 'For Sale, by Degrees: International Students and the Commodification of Higher Education in Australia and the U.K.'. *International Review of Education* 34 (3): 387–395.

White, D. (1983) 'The Methodology of Comparative Education and Its Clarification as a Basis for Its Contribution to the Theory and Practice of Education'. In Sheehan (ed.), op. cit.: 101–107.

White, D.C. (1981) 'The Foundations and Standpoint of Comparative Education'. Unpublished PhD dissertation, La Trobe University.

Wittgenstein, L. (1968) *Philosophical Investigations.* Oxford, Blackwell.

CONTEMPORARY PERSPECTIVES IN COMPARATIVE EDUCATION

Privatisation and Educational Crisis in Comparative Perspective

ROBIN J. BURNS

Centre for Comparative and Policy Studies,
School of Education,
La Trobe University, Victoria

Crisis is often used to describe the state of education, and other social institutions, in recent years. Rarely used in the medical sense of a turning point, implying a short term state, it has become, rather, a way of describing an ongoing situation. The sense of suspense is maintained, at one level of discourse, to urge haste in adopting new solutions. The first part of this chapter explores some of the ways in which the crisis, at this level, is depicted in education, especially looking at issues of quantity, quality and their inter-relationships.

Crisis is also seen to exist in other social institutions as well, suggesting that solving the educational aspects will contribute to wider change, especially in the economy. The next section of this chapter argues that through the almost exclusive linkage of education and the economy, mediated through limited notions of development, the economically useful aspects of education have been reified as the only legitimate social function which it serves. It is only a short step, therefore, to the third level of discourse which considers education as a commodity, subject to the same forces as other commodities even though a subset, 'services', is recognised. If education is so redefined, then privatisation of the service is an obvious step in a capitalist, free market economy, the only decision that the state has to make being how much support to give it.

Allocation of educational resources has been a responsibility for the state since its acceptance of a role in the formal process. The difference, it is argued, is that when education becomes a service which is exchanged like other commodities, the change from a normative to an instrumental basis for considering the various elements of education delegitimates or at least places a lower value on other discourses, including the pedagogical, ethical and cultural. It is here, rather than in the debates about quantity and quality, that the true educational, political and socio-cultural crisis lies, posing problems for the very concept of the state especially where there is still a surface allegiance to a social-democratic ideology (Camilleri 1986). These issues will be illustrated through an examination of the privatisation of higher education.

EDUCATIONAL CRISIS IN THE 1980S

Consideration of the educational crisis has focussed on issues of quantity, quality and their inter-relationships.

1. Educational quantity

In the history of the development of educational provision, periods of expansion and non-expansion can be discerned. What triggers the change from one period to another? If we take the beginning of the modern industrial revolution as a starting point, the whole pressure for mass education can be seen as intervention on the part of the state in '"managing" the transition from child to worker' (Clarke and Willis 1984: 8). It is the future worker who is central, and the needs of the employers and their concerns which are uppermost not only in the extension of schooling to new categories of children but in the nature of that schooling. Other justifications may be used, for example "doing something" for the children's moral and even individual development, especially with the introduction of laws prohibiting child labour, and with the general welfare concerns that enabled such laws to be enacted. But practice comes to be based on anticipated pragmatic outcomes.

Extension of the franchise has been another rationale for basic schooling and, depending on political and ideological concerns, the concept of the "good citizen" has also been used as a basis for formal public schooling. Thus, the State's role in mass schooling can be interpreted as both economic and ideological: to pay for basic worker and citizen formation.

Similar dynamics can be discerned in the lengthening of the period of mass schooling. The relationship between the type of educational provision and the needs of the economy at the time is evidence of this. It is argued that it is only during a period of economic buoyancy that more "liberal" and comprehensive mass education flourishes. At other times, the state sponsors education, or rather training, more narrowly defined in terms of the needs of the economy. Clarke and Willis argue that British capitalism in particular has always 'taken an interest in "surplus labour"' (1984: 8), an interest in which the state colludes to a greater or lesser extent. But a point is reached where the costs of providing for that surplus both in school provisions and in welfare payments for unemployed labour exceed the willingness or capacity to pay even for maintenance of the same amount and type of mass education. A new phase is then entered where the quality, often expressed as concern for the content of education, rather than the quantity, becomes a central issue.

2. *Educational quality and content*

There is some consideration of quality and content in expansionary educational phases, for example through a change in the rationale for formal education, including the need for its expansion. This is seen in the previous example of industrialisation and mass schooling, or the basic literacy and numeracy work in post-revolutionary developing countries. However, the issue is highlighted by the state in non-expansionary phases. Even when the issues are more or less left in the hands of the professional educators, state intervention becomes a way of showing that it is still responsive to lobby groups, or of using resources which have been freed once quantitative aspects have stabilised. A balance is achieved between professional and other interests through the use of selective funding of curriculum innovation, special programmes for example for so-called disadvantaged groups, and community or teacher (especially teacher union) demands for extra resources. The nature of innovations are the outcome of conflict between professionals and providers, but the innovation rather than its contribution to the training of the labour force, and political-ideological rather than predominantly economic considerations are uppermost.

This point can be illustrated in the debate from the 1960s onwards over comprehensive education. In Scandinavia for example, especially Sweden, the 1960–80 period has seen a systematic introduction of comprehensive compulsory education, with research on the curriculum centrally directed and results implemented nationwide. The state's desire to provide equality of opportunity through equality of educational provision stems from the social democratic ideology and its particular form in practice there (see e.g. Burns 1981; Marklund, S. 1981), tempered with comparative study of the role of comprehensive education in the US in particular. At the same time, while a similar push for comprehensive institutions took place in the UK, Australia and West Germany, for example, curriculum innovation took a different form. In the UK and Australia in particular the focus was on school based curriculum development partly accompanied by national curriculum projects (Crossley 1983). Towards the end of the 1970s the processes began to be reversed: the introduction of more space for local initiatives in Sweden, in response in part at least to a realisation that equality of input didn't produce equal outcomes (Husen 1974) and to growing "disciplinary" and "motivational" problems in schools. On the other hand, in Australia and to some extent the UK, the move was towards at least a "core curriculum". This can be seen as a response to concerns voiced but not adequately evidenced by employers about "declining standards" of school leavers and often ill-defined concern about the management of diversity and the provision of a common informational and value base for the nation's young (e.g. Curriculum Development Centre 1980).

3. *Quantity versus quality*

Taking both a long-range and a global view of public education, quantity and quality can be seen to be competing criteria for the provision of publicly funded educational institutions. So long as the focus is on "bodies in the classroom"—whether to meet economic, political or other socio-cultural demands—the question of quantity will provide the major focus for the allocation of resources. When demand has caught up with supply at one level, either improving quality at the saturated level or increasing quantity at the next level becomes possible, so long as there is no overall drop in finance. As with other educational supply decisions, there are four major interest groups vying to decide this issue: government, educational professionals, educational planners and managers, and the clients of education (students, their parents, and potential employers). If interests can be divided into the instrumental and normative, and recognising that each interest group may not be unitary and also differs in how it defines what appears on the surface to be a shared interest, the expectations of education might look something like this:

FIGURE 1

INTERESTS		
Interest Group	*Instrumental*	*Normative*
Government	Satisfied voters (personally and economically)	"Good citizens"
Ed. professionals	"Successful" learners (defined by theory)	"Socialised" youth (defined ideologically)
Ed. managers	Efficient delivery	—
Students	Skills and "knowledge"	Personal satisfaction
Parents	"Successful" offspring (defined by economic and class/gender/ethnic values)	Socialised, "happy" youth
Employers	Choice from among skilled workers	"Good workers" (defined by behaviour and productivity)

How can these conflicting interests be channelled into either/or decisions on quantity and quality? To satisfy both would quickly require either more expenditure to meet rising expectations as places expand at each level and as quality improvements at lower levels increase the eligible pool for higher ones, or more diversified goals for education. The latter implies a greater de-linking of the education-work relationship and greater emphasis on personal satisfaction and cultural rather than socio-economic variables as desired educational outcomes. However, as the reproduction theorists and radical educational sociologists of the 1970s have indicated, there are limits to enhancing personal satisfaction in a society which still rewards people overwhelmingly in unequal monetary and status terms. Even cultures of resistance can only go so far in supporting the individual's need for identity and self-esteem in an overtly unequal social system backed up by punitive legal sanctions when economic incentives fail (Willis 1977).

Are educational outcomes determined solely on the basis of the power struggle between different interest groups? It is suggested that one struggle is to de-legitimate normative interests, and to refine instrumental ones so that different parties can attempt to maximise their satisfactions. Seen in another light, the conflict is between education as an instrument of the economy, and education as a cultural phenomenon, or the relative weights given to instrumental or normative bases and their perceived inter-relationships.

When crisis considered centrally as economic is used as a framework for decision-making, economic development is one way of problematising the role of the state in framing and resourcing services. The outcomes for the ways in which education is defined, the role of the state and the relationship of education to non-economic, especially socio-cultural considerations, of different approaches to education and development are explored next.

EDUCATION AND DEVELOPMENT

Arguments favouring education for *economic development* have rested on the relationship between the quantity of people with given levels of qualifications and national and comparative indicators of economic growth. Education is considered instrumental for the achievement of growth, albeit only one such instrument. However, the crudity of the quantity-growth equation is seen in the diverse instrumental interests in expansion. Surplus labour, for example, is only valuable to employers if the potential workers have the skills required. Or diversity of teacher and parental expectations defies a simple assumption that X number of pupils reaching Y educational level is sufficient or subject to consensual definition and evaluation. Further, government and students might both admit that getting a job given particular qualifications is not the full story on educational satisfaction. Those whose interests seem best served by confining the debate to the instrumental are the managers and planners. They have focussed increasingly on issues of efficiency and effectiveness, predominantly using cost-benefit terms for evaluation, with an emphasis on systems rather than on details of inputs and outputs in more than numerical terms.

However, once questions of quality are admitted to the debate, the room for diversity is increased. If normative interests are related to issues of quality, or at least to the relationship between quantity and quality, then each interested party has a distinctive perspective on the nature of desired outcomes, and of course on the means to achieve them. The debate has tended to revolve around complaints about educational achievement, with attempts to use diachronic national data such as age-related literacy and numeracy scores or synchronic comparative data such as the IEA studies, to determine the validity of claims, ignoring problems with the validity and interpretation of such data. Non-school variables such as employer expectations or student motivation, or the changing role of teachers especially in western countries, have received insufficient attention in attempts to assess their efficiency and effectiveness of education. In the absence of clear and widely accepted alternatives, and under pressure especially from industry, to "improve" various aspects of the youth workforce, efficiency in financial management has become the way in which quality debates are largely contained. The location of training and its workforce relevance tend to dominate discussion.

A major way of looking at *social development* and education is as a normative debate about the proper goals of education. That is, however, a subset of the philosophical concern about goals. Individual development is being left further and further behind or subsumed within the overall issues of social development: since the individual has to exist in a society, the individual has to "fit in" or be socialised to live satisfactorily in society. Thus the individual/social contradiction is denied through emphasis on the individual's social destiny. A different way in which the individual's needs could have been re-asserted, through an emphasis on equality, has been framed in group terms: class, sex, ethnicity and so on. A new contradiction is thereby exposed, between individual and group, for in a hierarchical society there will always be an underclass. The reward of individual merit, emphasising that class, for example, should not be a barrier to personal mobility, can only be at the expense of others. And even if the "working class" becomes progressively more bourgeois, a new category of welfare recipients has been created below it (see e.g. Stretton 1987 ch. 15).

Thus equality of opportunity is an example of a normative educational and social goal to be programmatised. In so doing, not only are sectional interests to be taken into account, but the means sought to implement effective measures. An overview of the different directions taken by social democratic governments with central control of education and others, of various political tones and de-centralised educational decision-making, leads to the observation that political will appears to be central to the pursuit of equality. A central role for education, and its consonance with other institutional goals, are necessary but not sufficient conditions for either enhanced educational equality or social development. Resources are also needed, and a programme to identify obstacles and opportunities and to implement changes to reduce inequality.

Beyond such social issues, broader cultural ones receive even less attention except perhaps among educational professionals, even in richer nations. And it is around resource questions, and their inter-relationships with providers serving interests which may be contrary to those of more than small sections of the national population, that critical educational debates tend to be framed in developing countries.

There is one more source of conflict in these countries, which has the capacity to affect far broader areas of the economy than the supply of various workforce cohorts (e.g. Carnoy 1986): outside agents of "development assistance".

THE PRESENT CRISIS: EDUCATIONAL SERVICES AS A COMMODITY

It is argued here that the financial and fiscal difficulties presently facing most nations, and particularly those facing the industrialised market economies, have overtaken the educational crisis in such a way that the economic crisis has subsumed the educational one (e.g. Price 1984/5).

The overall effect is to place not only financial brakes on the measures being taken to address questions of social development and educational aspects of this, but to substitute economic criteria for social and educational ones in the resourcing and evaluation of social programmes. This can be seen as an underlying political project in recent reviews of efficiency and effectiveness of education (e.g. CTEC 1986; Karmel 1985; the British White Paper, Department of Education and Science 1987; Committee of Vice-Chancellors and Principles 1985; US National Commission on Excellence in Education, 1983).

Two major strands are emerging. One focuses on the need for general national austerity, and education is a consistent target for reduced percentages of government spending. "We all have to make do with less", but in the initial stages at least, there is no overt departure from goals such as equality. The other focuses on challenging the value of particular types of public expenditure through questioning the underlying values on which they are based. Selective targets for reduced expenditure are chosen, and both the normative base for expenditure as well as the effectiveness of previous expenditure are questioned. Social goals, even under government regulation, are dismissed or downplayed. The language and logic of the free market is invoked as the appropriate means to distribute social as well as economic rewards, the "proof" of the superior mechanisms of the market being demonstrated in the "poor returns" to various programmes, for example for the disadvantaged (implicit at least in McLean's 1988 analysis of recent British educational reform, and in the fate of policies such as the US Head Start and Australian Participation and Equity programmes). Particular areas of study, such as peace, or even politics, are questioned.

The two strands share some features in common. Better management of resources is called for by both, as is change in the allocation of resources. But the criteria for "better" and the bases for change differ so long as the normative bases for the two approaches are at variance. And what is becoming increasingly apparent is a contradictory discourse of convenience which requires a higher social rate of return from education whether it is considered directly economic (higher productivity) or mixed (higher productivity and higher participation rates). But on the basis of individual rates of return an attempt is made to shift the costs back to the participants (individuals/families at least on a means-tested basis, and/or future employers).

The most dramatic effect of this change in discourse is that education is becoming specifically designated as a commodity. So far, the lower levels of education have been left alone, but at the post-compulsory stages, especially tertiary education, questions of inputs and outputs are discussed in terms of productivity, efficiency is equated with "better resource management" and access defined in terms of the needs of the economy. Given the better-than-average employment and income of the more highly educated, however, education is seen as an income-producing service for which the user should pay.

The "services" which educational institutions are expected to provide are also increasingly related to the economy. The "new vocationalism" in school programmes, especially in the marriage between careers education and life-skill learning pressured 'towards an emphasis on adjustment and industrial requirements' (Bates 1984: 212), is expected to produce the right attitudes to work and alternative activities for the young unemployed. This is affecting the traditional distinction between education and vocational preparation. Even when more progressive, humanistic, pedagogical practices are employed in careers and life skills classes, the nature of their content tends to offload 'the necessity to pursue what are perhaps the more difficult educational aims in relation to "less able" children in favour of a "skills" emphasis with its utilitarian flavour' (Bates 1984: 213). Individual adjustment is also stressed as teachers are expected to be social workers, counsellors, parental liaison officers, curriculum specialists and behavioural managers despite a continued fall behind in wages (Orivel 1987: 202).

At post-compulsory levels, a combination of devalued qualifications, poor employment prospects and attempts to reduce youth unemployment benefits keeps more in the classroom, where vocational programmes and preparation for further study sit uneasily side-by-side. And in tertiary institutions, with decreased finance, poorer staff-student ratios, and other changing conditions which tend to reduce the morale of employees, better pass rates are expected ("efficiency"), with students better prepared for industry ("effectiveness"). Research is also expected to be attuned to the needs of industry. These are presented as the most desirable (and by definition by the critics, most ignored) services institutions should provide.

In Australia, as elsewhere, the relationship between educational crisis and economic crisis has become so ideologically aligned that the former is reduced to victim of or a subsidiary partner with the latter. It is not surprising therefore, that once educational services are re-defined as a commodity, questions of access and "ownership" take on a new direction. Since government has to raise the money to pay for public education, and since it has to appease the voters especially the powerful lobby groups, it has to decide how to raise its funds and distribute them, a problem which is both fiscal and ideological. The world economic crisis is most frequently cited as the major cause of domestic problems, though answers are primarily sought not internationally but by re-arrangement at the domestic level. Yet, as Camilleri notes: 'Advanced industrial societies in both East and West are beset by a cultural malaise which their centralized structures can neither conceal nor resolve' (1986: 48). This results from deep-seated and interacting imbalances: (i) systematic—unequal exchange, stratification and fragmentation on a global scale; (ii) ecological—a disturbance of the equilibrium between the human species and its biophysical environment; (iii) psycho-social—the decline of normative discourse and the heightened vulnerability of the individual to political and psychological manipulation (Camilleri 1986: 48–9).

What results at the national level, as one politician notes, is a 'game of push and shove' (Staples 1986: 9), with often minimal attempt to acknowledge the transnational dimension in the ways the traditional ingredients are pushed and shoved around. Thus, the balance between private and public ownership, and private and public payment is defined in domestic terms, ignoring the extent to which private ownership in most peripheral nations is transnational rather than national. The extent to which the public/private debate is ideological rather than fiscal can be seen in the conflict for dominance of a free market approach. Any attempt at government regulation except in private interests is denounced, as is public ownership of assets (despite the fact that publicly owned enterprises need not be less profitable or less efficient than private ones, especially if the debts and profits from the latter are incurred or transmitted overseas: Stretton 1987: 25–9). This masks a concern not so much with ownership per se but with the ways in which profits are distributed.

What we are seeing now is not private initiative in the face of state neglect, but an attempt to limit the rescue operations and initiatives of the state in all spheres of life to the interests of the private sector, regulated not by an interaction between the two but the so-called logic of the free market. That this attempt applies to ever-increasing fields of human social life is seen in the commodification of services, scarcely a large step if we accept Marginson's argument (1987) that even the construction of the individual in free market discourse is as an atomised consumer. Private suppliers should be allowed to compete with public ones, client choice should thereby be increased, and the believed greater efficiency of the market used to regulate supply and demand. Once clients are designated the sole determiners, there is no room for overtly normative bases for supply. At lower levels of education, government is still expected to pay for but not necessarily supply the service, but users should be compensated for paying more for their preferred supplier. And, at higher levels, while government should continue a financial contribution, this should be limited and suppliers freed or coerced into finding alternative sources of income, helped by government incentives to others to provide this. Thus, accelerated privatisation of education is seen as a desirable means to bring it under the rules of the market. It appears that precisely this logic is used in the contemporary British situation (McLean 1988; Walford 1988; Welch 1986, 1988). What is perhaps more interesting is that the US, traditionally suspicious of state intervention, nevertheless has a far more extensive public school system than the UK or Australia, choice and responsibility giving rise to different policy outcomes.

THE PRIVATISATION OF HIGHER EDUCATION

Nations differ in the extent to which provision of services, and the types, levels and funding of services, are an accepted government responsibility, even without a crisis mentality to highlight such issues. The account of education with which this chapter began deliberately omitted consideration of the nature and role of private education, which has preceded and continued to exist in different ways side-by-side with mass public education. In the industrialised world, patterns differ from the emphasis on primary and secondary private schools in the UK and Australia, to the tertiary focus in both the US and in Japan. Private schools in particular tend to be for the preservation and selective transmission of social and cultural capital (see e.g. Connell et al. 1982; Mangan 1981). In developing countries, they are more mixed in quality and purpose, including attempts by some to by-pass state provision or inadequacy of provision, even purported gains from a particular type of private education. In most instances they receive some form of state recognition for the relief they provide to the state educational system. In analytical terms, they provide an alternative to the state system for those able to pay, and a range of real and perceived advantages to clients. They have been condoned, tolerated or assisted to varying degrees depending on the effectiveness of their lobbying power, as much as on the ideology of the government of the day.

Rather than continuing in generalities, moves to privatisation of higher education in Australia will be examined in order to see the extent to which the discourse of crisis has provided the framework for fundamental changes in thinking about higher education and the implications of this, both for the state and for the practice of higher education, especially as it has been undertaken by a social-democratic government.

1. Privatisation in Australian higher education and research

The privatisation of education debate in Australia exemplifies the deliberate shifting of responsibility to a subset of the users of educational services: the students and their families. Industry has been invited, even financially rewarded, for contributing, but very little progress in this has been achieved. Where training is involved, companies have tended to open up their own courses rather than pay for employees to attend existing institutions. The instigation of the first private university, by one of the then most successful businessmen, Alan Bond, and its offer to provide industry-specific sponsored programmes, is an example of the way industry sees existing institutions but also of higher education generally since Bond University has not been much more successful in capturing industrial support for training than the state universities. It is only in the field of research services that the users are exhorted to pay, and the debate here is taking on extraordinary dimensions since it incorrectly assumes a prior vacuum, and fixes the blame for poor Research and Development (R & D) onto lack of appropriately qualified graduates and lack of university "industrial conscience" and entrepreneurship rather than the reluctance of industry to engage in R & D (e.g. ASTEC 1987). Yet the evidence is mounting in Australia to show that most significant discoveries by scientists in Australia have to be sold overseas for development into commercial products, fewer post-graduate scientists and engineers are qualifying because of lack of employment opportunities both inside universities (with no-growth periods succeeded by lack of suitable or interested applicants even when places are increased) and outside, and most industries, especially local branches of transnational corporations, find it more convenient to buy patents from overseas and simply undertake the manufacturing side here.

As the debate proceeds domestically, two opposing views are proposed: the one from within and the one from without. The *view from within* acknowledges spiralling costs, but points to the multiple functions of education. While individual development is mentioned almost apologetically, cultural development and the contribution to the social, international as well as national, stock of knowledge is asserted. From this follow conditions for maintenance of such a function, from selection of well qualified students to standards of staffing and the conditions required to guarantee this and to protect the institution from undue outside interference (e.g. Bessant 1986; Smart 1986 and the consistent pronouncements of the Australian-Vice Chancellors' Committee). The concerns include regulation of staff conditions, the need for pay rates high enough and flexible enough to attract "good" people when market rates outside are much higher than university pay and the implications of increasing external as well as internal-managerial interference with the academic tasks. It is further asserted that there is a necessary link between teaching and research to ensure quality especially in the former (see e.g. Ben David 1977 for historical treatment of this), even if various pressures have transformed a great deal of education 'into course-work, making it a kind of technical learning. The introduction of learning-machines simply completes this process of the rationalization of education' (Redner 1987: 55). The social role of education and research is at least ideally international, and not just there for the highest bidder. Responsibility consists not in gratuitous cost-cutting and money-grabbing or serving any client, but ensuring the quality of teaching and research according to academic rather than economic standards, and making this as accessible as possible.

The *outsiders' views* are diverse. An underlying theme stresses the responsibility to the community, especially the paying public and industry. Universities have no special rights to privileges, such as different conditions of employment or the pursuit of interests just for their own sake. It is a demand-driven approach, with education little different from other commodities, and whether the demands are politically-ideologically or purely profit motivated, the right to decide is largely an external not an internal affair.

There is illogic and entrenched stubbornness and unresponsiveness on both sides. Universities and colleges have become more diverse in aims and activities, as well as sources of funding. Their funding requirements have been increasingly under-supplied which is often masked in public announcements, e.g. the Australian Research Grants Scheme increased, in constant dollars, by $6 million since 1966, but so did the size of university staffs and the number of annual applications (250 percent increase p.a.). The 1987 additional allocation of $1 million was specifically for equipment, with a new cut of $1 million mid-year (Topsom 1987). Subsequent increases through the newly-created Australian Research Council have been at the expense of institutions' individual capacity to fund research activities using their own criteria, a deliberate attempt to capture research in the national interest (Dawkins 1988; Department of Employment, Education and Training 1988; Harman and Meek 1988). This is at best ironic at a time when performance indicators are under consideration and research productivity is a major element of these.

Institutions have been responsive to new demands for courses and services such that the promise of funds seems almost sufficient rationale for change in some areas, giving rise to new concerns about responsibilities to students especially in "disadvantaged" categories, and there is increasing diversification of funding sources. Industry has proved so unwilling to take up the challenge that incentives such as Science Parks (with increased access to university facilities) and hefty tax concessions for research have still not led to a rush to capture academic researchers. The worst illogicality is the accusation of university unresponsiveness coupled with the superior right of industry to decide what should be done, and the right not to make those results available to others. I will not engage here in detailed debate about the nature of research, the university's social responsibility or more than a ritualistic invocation of academic freedom. One must note, however, that the frequent outside accusation that all university research is "pure", and the ignorance of the relationships between pure, mission-oriented and applied research, is cause for concern. In a new public research strategy in Sweden, a country with one of the highest R & D expenditures in the world (and also a higher per capita expenditure per soldier than per citizen: Sivard 1985: 40), the conflict between "scientifically"-initiated and "socially"-initiated research is considered both a healthy and a necessary one. This is especially so when both types of research are undertaken in the same institution (the university) and preferably by the same individuals (Marklund, I. 1981).

The Swedish example stresses again the role of ideology in determining both public/private roles in R & D, and combinations of desirable types of research activity. It also illustrates a planned approach with at least a medium term planning horizon, rather than the political manipulation of stop/go approaches of countries like the UK and Australia, and the planning difficulties to which these give rise. It is not the purpose here to look in detail at the pros and cons of different types of research or locations for research. However, the problems of public educational institutions using contract money as the basis for planning cannot be over-emphasised, with examples coming interestingly from the US, a country well-used to contract as a basis for research (see e.g. Cheit 1971; Dalyell 1983; Finn 1978; Noble 1977). Such contract money includes government contracts, and the implications of the huge proportions of the world's scientists engaged in military-related work cannot be overlooked in consideration of the financing and philosophy of higher education. Other aspects needing consideration include the implications for scholarly exchange at all levels of privately funded and potentially confidential research, and also the issue of access for the public at large if a user-pays principle, even without confidentiality, is uppermost.

2. *The export of educational services*

A new and complex dimension of the new rhetoric of higher educational crisis is the seeking of new markets for educational services overseas. This illustrates further the new normative base on which education is being planned, and has implications both for the "exporting" (predominantly North) and "importing" (predominantly South) countries (see Barber, Altbach and Myers 1984). It also illustrates further the location of educational issues in the economic sphere.

Australia's recent initiatives in this field are a case in point, especially when the major target for educational export is Malaysia. Malaysia has approximately 30,000 students enrolled in its seven national universities, and twice that many, predominantly of Chinese origin, overseas (Palmer 1986). Of the Malaysian students in Australia in 1987 (approximately 11,000). Ninety percent were private students, paying 45 percent of a notional $10,000 per capita per annum "full cost recovery" in the form of an Overseas Service Charge which went directly into consolidated revenue. This cost was increased over the next two years so that the notional cost-recovery point was reached and the subsidy was abolished. All overseas students are to be charged; agencies such as the Australian International Development Assistance Bureau pay for selected persons from 1990 onwards. The rhetoric surrounding this bears elaboration: under the guise of "allowing institutions" to offer over-quota places to overseas students at full-cost recovery (interestingly, set at $7,000 p.a., also the average level of funding for Australian students, but lower than the nominal level on which the Overseas Student Charge was levied), and to develop special full-cost courses both on-shore and off-shore, 'while protecting Australian students' rights of access to higher education' (Ryan 1985), education has been designated a significant area for export success. It was anticipated that by allowing full fee paying students and new course development, an "entrepreneurial spirit" would be encouraged "amongst institutions, with the possibility of generating earnings" (Commonwealth Ministry of Education 1985).

> It is important because successful marketing of education services represents one of the few areas of untapped growth potential at a time of serious national balance of payments difficulties; it is also important as a means by which involved institutions might break the straitjacket of limited public funding and evolve in more relevant directions than might otherwise be possible. (Buckingham 1986: 1)

There has been widespread debate on the issues arising from this new language and conception of education (see e.g. Gillespie and Collins 1986; McCulloch and Nicholls 1986; Welch 1986; Ong 1986), though it has been overshadowed by the rush to set up courses, and confused, competitive attempts to recruit students for the programmes.

What has been frequently overlooked is the fact that the initial stimulus for this has come from two reports on Australia's overseas *aid* programme (Goldring 1984; Jackson 1984), the former more cautious on the diplomatic and normative implications than the latter, and an investigatory Education Trade Mission in 1985, on which neither the Education nor Foreign Affairs Ministries were represented.

Leaving aside financial details, there are serious implications which must be faced and openly discussed which arise out of the impetus to export Australian tertiary educational services. These fall into ten areas:

(i) Educational: the question of standards becomes crucial for special courses in Australia and off-shore tailored to overseas "needs". Levels of entry and exit will be difficult to set and maintain, especially if there is pressure to 'concertina' course lengths because of costs, to lengthen the teaching year, take short-cuts in access to laboratory facilities, begin to make equitable library access arrangements and so on. Questions of bridging courses, language and study skills assistance, have not been addressed in detail. Inter-institutional and even intra-institutional conflict is built in to such a system.

(ii) Research: although this is not even mentioned in the documents relating to the sale of education, questions to be raised include:

- Will research training be a component of courses?
- What provisions will be made, especially at the post-graduate level, for research facilities?
- What are the effects on the research capacity and even practice in overseas students' home countries if they mainly work on research of direct benefit to the Australian economy while in Australia?
- Will the contract staff who will be used for much of the teaching be employed with the same research expectations as other university staff? Do we have staff with relevant overseas country research experience?

(iii) Student welfare: there are pressures on existing student welfare and advisory services from new funding formulae and targetting of 'disadvantaged' students. Overseas students have already been

excluded from some new welfare provisions. When budgetting is tight, welfare is often easiest to omit, especially in order to maintain 'competitive' fees. In order to avoid discrimination and two-tiered service systems, there is likely to be increased pressures on the services for *all* students.

(iv) Industrial issues: at least in the UK, one rationale for full fee-paying students has been to take up aspects of assumed under-utilisation of resources including staff. Either institutions are pulling the wool over everyone's eyes such that the rising staff-student ratios being reported are false, or we are headed for a more generalised confrontation, hinted at in the CTEC Review of the Efficiency and Effectiveness in Higher Education, over appropriate teaching commitments and use of facilities in institutions. Further, student choice may be changing, but those undersubscribed areas are even less likely to interest overseas students.

Given difficulties which have occurred in the maintenance of adequate funding levels and employment levels for researchers (e.g. ASTEC 1987), and declining employment conditions in universities (e.g. Barlow 1989), there is some talk of a staffing crisis in universities within five years (Maslen 1990). The use of contract staff is increasing, and is particularly evident in special courses for overseas students. Recruitment of staff is particularly difficult in areas paying highly in commerce and even the public service, leading to suggestions of de-regulating academic salary awards. While the university may be such a complex institution that a single system of employment is no longer appropriate, efforts to re-conceptualise it are fragmented and conflictual so far, representing neither a clearly meritocratic nor a market approach.

Maintaining conditions for Australian staff on secondment to off-shore courses is also problematic, as is the possibility that overseas staff will be hired under different conditions to teach Australian award courses off-shore, which has already taken place in one contract scheme. And what of levels of support staff?

(v) The status of women: firstly, privatisation of the overseas sector is likely to affect the newly-achieved approach to sexual parity in initial undergraduate enrolments, since women constituted only 25 percent of

subsidised overseas students. It is further likely adversely to affect proportions of local females, especially mature-age ones (Marginson 1989).

Secondly, the areas highlighted for special development (science, including medicine and veterinary science, engineering, technology, agriculture, economics and business) are the most male-dominated, both in staff and students. Further imbalances are likely to be created through accelerated development and expansion in these fields.

Thirdly, even were more women eligible for employment, privatisation of either the overseas student sector or the whole system is likely to increase the pool of female untenured staff if more get employment, but under less favourable conditions than in the past. This may well be happening merely on the basis of change without privatisation as an add-on feature.

(vi) Administration: even the optimists are concerned at the uneven marketing strategies (Buckingham 1988). Universities in Australia have not been organised or staffed for entrepreneurial activities, and while some especially newer institutions are proving adept at it, the push to keep fees competitive is leading to inefficiencies and stresses both at central management and faculty levels. No central funding has been available for such new activities, nor government services to assist in organisation beyond some mission-based Department of Foreign Affairs and Trade assistance. And new managerial structures are being created, often using outdated or inappropriate business models (Bessant 1988).

(vii) Distortion in the system: a dual tertiary education system is envisaged, to replace the old binary one with separate types of institutions. The new system has a number of facets, including two types of staff, students and courses, dual facilities and 'privileges', dual standards and dual funding.

A further aspect of distortion is the replacement of a reasonably balanced planning system combining social needs with some educational and epistemological principles, with a market-driven, constantly-changing set of 'relevant' courses. There is a difference between responsiveness as a facility, and as a major organising principle, especially given the potential for flaws in a market-driven basis for organisation of courses which may be responding to a different market by the time graduates are ready for employment. Laissez-faire may allocate students more effectively; for whom is this efficient, and on what time scale?

(viii) Equity: the introduction of a Higher Education Contribution Scheme (HECS) in 1989 is supposedly a system which, since repayments (with interest: there are rebates for up-to-date payment in full) are not required until post-graduation income reaches certain levels, does not keep poorer students out. Are poorer students prepared to incur future debt in order to study? No scheme has been in operation long enough to be assessed for its impact on equity issues. The principle of fees, and the vision of a privatised system, including private universities, are problematic at a time when social inequalities, especially among the young, are being highlighted. Existing inequalities in the dual schooling system raise further concerns about costs and equity. There is no indication that profits from overseas students will benefit local ones, though the 'costs' of a subsidised scheme was one argument used to abolish it. Can two discourses, the market and the welfare state, co-exist for two different groups of students?

(ix) International relations, aid and trade: since the Education Trade Mission which set the scene for the sale of education overseas, and which excluded the Department of Foreign Affairs, Trade and Foreign Affairs have become a single Ministry. Nevertheless, detailed consideration of important diplomatic areas has been excluded:

- The effect on our foreign relations of increasing charges for, and creating a two-tiered system of, educational services offered to Asia, and perhaps beyond (Walford 1988 and Welch 1986 document effects in the UK);
- The possible negative trade side-effects should the nations affected so choose;
- The future of the subsidised overseas student programme once full cost recovery has been established as a principle;
- The notion that we are 'aiding' Asia by establishing courses, predominantly for their rich, which, determined by market forces, need bear no relationship to their governmental and social needs and priorities. It has been stated as a justification for the

new developments that previous programmes did not best "meet the needs" of the sending countries. How this is so is not specified, though research consistently indicates that enhanced individual rather than social rates of return are common results of overseas study, and that that study is often in areas inappropriate to the needs and level of technological and socio-economic development of the countries involved (Hetland 1984). It it may yet be that Australian involvement in training and institution-building in those countries would be a better, and even a more 'profitable' direction for 'exporting' of Australian educational expertise.

- With many of the foregoing problems in mind, a fee-charging system with presumably mainly private students may be further creating wealth and public/private splits in those countries.
- An exception, and one which already exists, is the contract-based provision of 'training packages' for particular countries. Do we have a competitive advantage in the development of a market-oriented and low-cost, largely private alternative?

3. *Who calls the tune?*

The examination in this chapter of the interest structure of education could be used to argue that the inside and outside views of education, especially over the last five years in Australia, are locked into non-intersecting trajectories, operating on different and irreconcilable principles. Insiders have participated in the reviews and discussions that have shaped current policy, although the Minister for Employment, Education and Training reduced that input for the finalisation of his 1988 Policy Statement.

A joint Australian Vice-Chancellors' Committee (AVCC) and Business Council of Australia working party, established by the Prime Minister and reporting in 1986, states:

> Australia needs to create more wealth in order to lift employment and living standards, and to do this it needs to foster the conditions that will allow industry to perform. To help achieve this, Australia must have an appropriate business and investment

> environment, and in the area of the application of new technology and manpower planning, a much greater involvement between business and university sector will assist in the attainment of these goals. (Report of the Joint Working Party 1986: 1)

In addition to measures already undertaken, through new university-based consulting companies, prototype venture capital companies and the like, the joint working party explored greater representation by business at all levels of university decision-making (but not the reverse!), more consultancies, joint staff appointments, broad-based degrees especially research degrees (current ones are considered too specialised, narrow and mostly 'pure' rather than mission-oriented or applied), special fellowship and teaching company schemes along lines similar to recent developments in the UK, and collaborative projects (3–7).

The Commonwealth Tertiary Education Commission (CTEC) Review of Efficiency and Effectiveness, which took an intermediary-protective view, provoked the following responses. AVCC (i) saw the 'overall thrust of the report as perceptive and analytical'; (ii) 'endorses the review committee's analysis of the growth in demands placed on institutions since 1975 and the expressed view that the capacity of institutions to cope with additional curtailment of real funding is exhausted'; (iii) 'shares the review committee's scepticism about proposals for making tertiary education more marketable and supports its analysis of the place of fees and vouchers'; (iv) welcomes 'the approach which the review committee has adopted towards the use of performance measures to determine financial allocations to institutions'; but (v) 'is concerned at the detail of some of the suggestions, believing that they imply an undue intervention in the affairs of autonomous institutions' (AVCC 1987: 1).

The Federation of Australian University Staff Associations (FAUSA), was more critical, not only of the industrial proposals but also of the proposals to 'rationalise' research funding, postgraduate studies and external studies (FAUSA 1987: 1–3). Both supported a stress, subsequently abandoned by government with its Unified National System of Higher Education introduced in 1989, on the continuation of the binary system, the expansion in the number of institutions, backlog funding for equipment and maintenance, and recommendations for greater inter-institutional cooperation.

The business community, perhaps trading on crisis, has the attentive ear of both government and opposition. The main differences between the parties is in the degree of regulation and the lip-service paid to non-monetary social goals. CTEC and the institutions could at best fight a rearguard action.

Some insiders welcome the privatisation push, others the general emphasis on responsiveness and accountability. Whether they like it or not, change is happening. Along with confused argument and lack of logic, research is notably absent from Australian approaches to this and other areas of social change. Insiders and outsiders debate on ideological grounds about critical aspects (education and research) of the nation's future.

CONCLUSION

It is suggested that the Australian situation, while having local features, is an example of wider change. Writing a decade ago, Altbach listed teaching, research, leadership training and general national, cultural and governmental participation as areas in which the qualifications and morale of academics have an effect (1980:13). He maintains however that academics have tended merely to resist change, implying a downward spiral of poor morale-lowered performance-less participation.

In examining change, the non-participation and resistance of academics and of educational institutions is one factor to be taken into account, especially in looking at the nature of change. The absence of research on the subject in countries like Australia, and the almost-total exclusion of comparative research from its funding agendas, is another factor, leading inter alia to ignorance of the relative roles of endowments and fees in generating surpluses in institutions in the UK and US.

It is therefore difficult to escape the conclusion that the commodification of education has two functions. The first is to legitimate the decrease in public spending by opening avenues for private payment. However, the profit to the institutions is not proven; it is merely to attempt to maintain existing resources through diversification of the sources of funds. The second is to de-legitimate non-economic bases for educational activities, or at best to relegate them to some idealistic realm awaiting spare resources or better times for their realisation.

The effects are to de-legitimate alternative approaches to the role of education. Even the normative instrumental difference is disappearing. 'Service has come to mean the indeterminate adaptation of the university to every demand that interests in the general public could imagine making' (Roszak 1968: 8).

> The multiversity is the institution of the future, for all over the world, including Europe, universities are being inevitably forced to change themselves in this direction. The reason is that the multiversity is a complex of institutions that can together fulfil all the diverse educational and research requirements of the state, industry and society in general . . . What needs to be explored in greater detail is how the multiversity in the service of this symbiosis has expanded into a knowledge complex which holds a near monopoly of all knowledge in society. (Redner 1987: 52–3)

Equity and popular participation certainly appear to be the losers. This is not only because the reproduction of the work-force has achieved primacy (Carnoy 1986: 212). Changes in economic activity, with the shift from 'the politics of hegemony to the politics of empirical rivalry' (Camilleri 1986: 50) and attendant changes from investment to non-productive international and national stock market games, have changed the nature of the world economy. Habermas argues that the nature of economic growth under capital (I would add state or private) is crisis-ridden, but that conflicts of interest are increasingly displaced to the level of the steering system, so that 'systems crises gain an objectivity rich in contrast. They have the appearance of natural catastrophes that break forth from the center of a system of purposive rational action'. (1973: 30)

If this is the case, then the commodification and privatisation of the education system is inevitable as alternative views are subordinated to the crisis-based economic discourse. It may not be simply a case of political acumen and continuing to apply known principles for democratisation (Carnoy 1986: 213) in order to re-assert alternative views. We are faced, rather, with a cultural project in the broadest sense of the term culture. Stretton's advice to social scientists can be more broadly applied to define the cultural dimensions of the task:

> Basically we should educate more and better social democratic intellectuals—but not by trying to replace a conservative version of the one true science with a socialist version of it. True to our free-thinking democratic values we should educate social scientists [I would extend this to all students] in ways which encourage them to think for themselves, seriously, about their social values; to understand the role of values in their science; and to serve their chosen values, or those of the clients they choose to represent, with the best available theories and methods for the purpose. (1987: 207–8)

And while working within economic 'realities', such a project is not costly in monetary terms, though the space in which to act may be diminishing.

ACKNOWLEDGMENTS

A substantial part of the research on which this chapter is based was undertaken with assistance from a grant from the School of Education, La Trobe University in 1987. Richard Barcham, my assistant, proved a stimulating and helpful research partner during that year.

REFERENCES

Altbach, Philip G. (1980) 'The Crisis of the Professoriate'. *Annals, AAPSS*, 448: 1–14.

Anwyl, John (1987) 'Sliding Towards Anarchy in Higher Education Planning'. *The Australian*, Higher Education Supplement, April.

Australian Science and Technology Council (ASTEC) (1987) 'Improving the Research Performance of Australia's Universities and Other Higher Education Institutions. A Report to the Prime Minister'. Canberra, Commonwealth Government Printer.

Australian Vice-Chancellors' Committee (1986) 'AVCC Response to the Commonwealth Tertiary Education Commission Review of Efficiency and Effectiveness in Higher Education'. Canberra, November (mimeo).

Barber, Elinor G., Altbach, Philip G., and Myers, Robert G. (1984) *Bridges to Knowledge. Foreign Students in Comparative Perspective*. University of Chicago Press.

Barlow, Kerry (1989) 'The White Paper and Restructuring the Academic Labour Market'. *Australian Universities' Review* 32(1): 30–7.

Bates, Inge (1984) 'From Vocational Guidance to Life Skills: Historical Perspectives on Careers Education'. In I. Bates et al., loc. cit.: 170–219.

Bates, I., Clarke, J., Cohen, P., Finn, D., Moore, Robert, and Willis, P. (1984) *Schooling for the Dole*. London, Macmillan.

Ben-David, Joseph (1977) *Centers of Learning*. New York, McGraw-Hill.

Bessant, Bob (1986) 'Privatisation and Academic Freedom'. *Australian Universities' Review* 29(2): 11–15.

Bessant, Bob (1988) 'Corporate Management and the Institutions of Higher Education'. *Australian Universities' Review* 32(2): 10–3.

Buckingham, David (1986) 'Education as an International Commodity. The Policy Context'. Canberra, Ministry of Education (mimeo).

Buckingham, David (1988) 'The Full Fee Overseas Student Program—the Move Forward'. Paper presented at the National Centre for Development Studies symposium, 'Full Fee Courses in Australian Education: the Australian Experience', Canberra, October 21 (mimeo).

Burns, Robin (1981) 'Process and Problems in Educational Reform in Sweden'. *Compare* 11(1): 33–44.

Burns, Robin (1986) 'Implications of the Accelerated Commercialisation of Higher Education And research'. In R.R. Gillespie and C.B. Collins (eds.) loc. cit.: 145–162.

Camilleri, Joseph (1986) 'After Social Democracy'. *Arena* 77: 48–73.

Carnoy, Martin (1986) 'Educational Reform and Planning in the Current Economic Crisis'. *Prospects* 16(2): 205–214.

Cheit, Earl J. (1971) *The New Depression in Higher Education*. New York, McGraw-Hill.

Clarke, John, and Willis, Paul (1984) 'Introduction'. In I. Bates et al., loc. cit.: 1–16.

Committee of Vice-Chancellors and Principals (1985) *Report of the Steering Committee for Efficiency Studies in Universities* (The Jarratt Report). London, HMSO.

Commonwealth Ministry of Education (1985) 'Guidelines for Full Fee Overseas Students in Courses Provided by Commonwealth Funded Higher Education Institutions'. Canberra (mimeo).

Commonwealth Tertiary Education Commission (CTEC) (1986) *Review of Efficiency and Effectiveness in Higher Education.* Canberra, AGPS.

Connell, R.W., Ashenden, D., Kessler, S., and Dowsett, G.W. (1982) *Making the Difference: Schools, Families and Social Division.* Sydney, Allen and Unwin.

Crossley, Michael (1983) 'Strategies for Curriculum Change with particular reference to the Secondary Schools Community Extension Project in Papua New Guinea'. Unpublished PhD dissertation, Bundoora, La Trobe University.

Curriculum Development Centre (1980) *Core Curriculum for Australian Schools.* Canberra, CDC.

Dalyell, Tam (1983) *A Science Policy for Britain.* London, Longman.

Dawkins, Hon. J.S. (1988) *Higher Education. A Policy Statement.* Canberra, AGPS.

Department of Education and Science (1987) 'Higher Education: Meeting the Challenge'. The Government's White Paper on Higher Education, Cmnd. 114, London, HMSO.

Department of Employment, Education and Training (1988) *Higher Education Funding for the 1989–91 Triennium.* Canberra, AGPS.

Federation of Australian University Staff Associations (1987) 'Review of Efficiency and Effectiveness in Higher Education'. Response by FAUSA. Melbourne, FAUSA (mimeo).

Finn, Chester E. (1978) *Scholars, Dollars and Bureaucrats.* Washington, D.C., The Brookings Institute.

Gillespie, Roselyn R., and Collins, Colin B. (eds.) (1986) *Education as an International Commodity.* Brisbane, ANZCIES.

Goldring, J., comp. (1984) *Mutual Advantage. Report of the Committee of Review of Private Overseas Student Policy.* Canberra, AGPS.

Habermas, J. (1975) *Legitimation Crisis* (trans. T. McCarthy). Boston, Beacon Press.

Harman, Grant, and Meek, V. Lynn (eds.) (1988) *Australian Higher Education Reconstructed?* Armidale, University of New England Department of Administrative and Higher Education Studies.

Hetland, Atle (ed.) (1984) *Universities and National Development.* Stockholm, Almqvist & Wiksell.

Husen, Torsten (1974) *The Learning Society*. London, Methuen.

Jackson, G., comp. (1984) *Report of the Committee to Review the Australian Overseas Aid Program*. Canberra, AGPS.

Karmel, Peter, comp. (1985) *Quality of Education in Australia. Report of the Review Committee*. Canberra, AGPS.

Mangan, J.A. (1981) *Athleticism in the Victorian and Edwardian Public School. The Emergence and Consolidation of an Educational Ideology*. Cambridge University Press.

Marginson, Simon (1987) 'Foundations of the Free Market Disourse'. Melbourne, Australian Teachers Federation (mimeo).

Marginson, Simon (1989) 'The Decline and Fall of Equality of Opportunity'. Paper presented to the Australian and New Zealand Comparative and International Education Society (ANZCIES) conference, Melbourne, December (mimeo).

Marklund, Inge (1981) 'The Sectoral Principle in Swedish Research Policy'. Uppsala University, Department of Education (mimeo).

Marklund, Sixten (1981) 'The Post-comprehensive Era of Swedish Education'. *Compare* 11(2): 185–190.

Maslen, Geoff (1990) 'Campus Crisis as Too Few Dons for Students'. *The Age*, 29 March.

McCulloch, Grahame and Nicholls, Jane (1986) 'The Privatisation of Higher Education'. Paper presented to the ANZCIES Conference, Brisbane, December (mimeo).

McLean, Martin (1988) 'Educational Reform in Industrial Market Economies: Corporatist and Contract Strategies. Recent British policies in Comparative Perspective'. Paper presented to the Comparative and International Education Society conference, Atlanta Georgia, March (mimeo).

The National Commission on Excellence in Education (1983) *A Nation at Risk: the Imperative for Educational Reform*. Washington, D.C., US Government Printing Office.

Noble, D. (1977) *America by Design. Science, Technology and the Rise of Corporate Capitalism*. New York, OUP.

Ong, B.K. (1986) 'Towards a New Internationalism'. Paper presented to the ANZCIES Conference, Brisbane, December (mimeo).

Orivel, Francois (1986) 'Economic Crisis and Educational Crisis: Looking Ahead'. *Prospects* 16(2): 197–204.

Palmer, M.S. (1986) 'Market for Education Services, Malaysia'. Kuala Lumpur, Australian Trade Commission (mimeo).

Price, Geoffrey (1984/5) 'Universities Today: Between the Corporate State and the Market'. *Universities Quarterly* 39(1): 43–58.

'Report of the Joint Working Party on University/Business Co-operation to Business Council of Australia and Australian Vice-Chancellors' Committee' (1986) (mimeo).

Redner, Harry (1987) 'The Institutionalization of Science: A Critical Synthesis'. *Social Epistemology* 1(1): 37–59.

Roszak, Theodore (1968) *The Dissenting Academy*. New York, Pantheon.

Ryan, Susan (1985) 'Higher Education Institutions' Full Fee Courses for Overseas Students'. Canberra, Ministry for Education News Release m80/85.

Sivard, Ruth Leger (1985) *World Military and Social Expenditures* 1985. Washington, D.C., World Priorities Inc.

Smart, Don (1986) 'The Financial Crisis in Australian Higher Education and the Inexorable Push towards Privatisation'. *Australian Universities' Review* 29(2): 16–21.

Staples, Peter (1986) 'The Charge of the Fees Brigade'. *Australian Universities' Review* 29(2): 9–10.

Stretton, Hugh (1987) *Political Essays*. Melbourne, Georgian House.

Topsom, R.D. (1987) 'Government Spending on Research'. *La Trobe University Research Bulletin* 3, February.

Walford, Geoffrey (1988) 'The Privatisation of British Higher Education'. *European Journal of Education* 23(1/2): 47–63.

Welch, A.R. (1986) 'For Sale, by Degrees'. Paper presented to the ANZCIES Conference, Brisbane, December (mimeo).

Welch, A. R. (1988) 'For Sale by Degrees: Overseas Students and the Commodification of Higher Education in Australia and the U.K.', *International Review of Education*, 34, 3.

Willis, Paul (1977) *Learning to Labour*. Hampshire, Gower.

Knowledge, Culture, and Power: Educational Knowledge and Legitimation in Comparative Education

ANTHONY R. WELCH

School of Social and Policy Studies in Education
Faculty of Education, University of Sydney, New South Wales

The notion of legitimation in relation to educational knowledge has developed into a significant theme within comparative research over the past decade or more. This chapter reviews important developments within this literature, and analyzes some of the intellectual underpinnings of this recent work. The debate is seen as a development from older work in comparative education, which often employed a more restricted focus, consisting of explanations of knowledge-changes in education and society, sometimes from a broadly functionalist, positivistic perspective; and the work of more recent scholars, many of whom have been influenced by more conflict oriented approaches, including Max Weber, elements of the Marxist tradition, and the work of critical theorists such as Jürgen Habermas.

Some newer currents of work within comparative education havc embraced a far more socially critical conception of knowledge, and are far less dominated by natural scientific definitions of knowledge. Even within this developing stream of scholarship, however, distinctions can be made. Within the work of comparative authors of the last decade or so, the notion of legitimation has altered from a concern with the specific processes whereby educational knowledge becomes legitimate, including changes in the hierarchy of educational knowledge, to a wider concern with the dialectical relationship between the legitimation of educational knowledge and the legitimacy of the modern state.

Conceptions of knowledge and culture are both argued to have changed, leading to a new formulation of educational change.

EARLY SCHOLARSHIP: 1930–1970

The study of curriculum change has been a significant motif within the annals of comparative education for several decades at least. Leading figures such as I. Kandel (1935), N. Hans (1931, 1951, 1963), O. Anweiler (1964), and B. Holmes (1958) have all examined processes of curriculum change from empirical and theoretical perspectives. Some of these studies have stood the test of time better than others. Kandel's work on Nazi education, and Hans' work on the eighteenth century and on Soviet education, are perhaps two more notable examples. But there are important theoretical shifts noticeable when one compares this earlier work with some more recent work of comparative scholars, who, in line with theoretical developments in other areas of educational research, have largely redefined the field. It has not been the case, then, that curriculum and change have been neglected as a recognizable focus of interest for scholars of comparative education. Rather, the perspective has altered. In older comparative accounts of curriculum change, curriculum was not seen so much as socially organised knowledge in educational settings, but more like 'what was taught in schools'. Curriculum then, it has been argued, was largely seen as an unproblematic category in these accounts: consensual, unitary knowledge. This view, it is argued, was largely in accord with dominant functionalist[1] accounts of social science of the pre- and postwar era. More recently, however, notions of how knowledge becomes legitimate, and the connection between the legitimation of knowledge in educational settings, and the maintenance of overall system legitimacy by the modern state, has become an increasingly important focus for research within comparative education.

Clearly, however, not all accounts of changes to curriculum by comparative educationists of an earlier time were inspired by broadly functionalist visions of society and social change, in which the structures and institutional definitions of knowledge were seen as unproblematic. Kandel's (1935) account of the dramatic changes to

German education following the rise to power of the Nazis is an example of work uninspired by functionalist principles. Kandel makes no pretense at value-neutrality when describing the transformation of the German secondary curriculum:

> Physical Education has been reorganized as a part of military training; Geländesport and Wehrsport are militaristic in character; history teaching is revised to imbue the youth with the conquering spirit of the race; the Hitlerjugend, which now embraces virtually all youth organizations, is the junior branch of the Sturm-Abteilung (Storm troops, S. A.) and the Schutz-Staffel (Special guard, S.S.); the labor camps devote as much time to military training as to labor; and, finally, brawn will in future play a greater part than brain in securing admission to higher education and the liberal professions, including teaching. (1935: 13)

Equally in Kandel's more detailed account of the changes to the German secondary and higher educational curriculum, his portrayal of the introduction of military subjects as "evidence of the widespread cult of the militaristic spirit" (1935: 16) is hardly a sign of the acceptance of functionalist tenets of objectivity and value-free analysis. Neither is his trenchant critique of the concept of Gleichschaltung, or the coordination of all aspects of German life so as to be in accord with Nazi policies. Gleichschaltung can be seen as an extreme form of the unifying and integrative dimension of functionalist theory, which emphasizes the organizational importance of a single value system that is held consensually by all individuals, and underlies the operation of all subsystems of action. Within functionalism, the subsystem of education has, like others in society, the responsibility to impart this value system. Kandel's equally strident critique of the Nazi principle of the necessity of the subordination of individual life in the face of the common need ('Gemeinnutz geht vor Eigennutz') constitutes a further rejection of functionalism, in particular the argument that values are passed down unproblematically from larger and more significant systems of action to smaller and less significant ones, including, ultimately, individuals.

Kandel's work on curriculum changes under the Nazis, then, does not conform to functionalist principles; indeed it views that educational knowledge-frame as a particular political construct, at a specific point in history, explained by a series of specific social, economic and political events. This is much more in accord with the methodological orientations of later theorists of the 1970s. Hans' (1951) work on educational reform in the eighteenth century also does not bear out this point regarding the dependence upon functionalist principles entirely. Basically, Hans' analysis is a solid historical account of pressures, or 'motives' as he terms them, for educational change in England in the eighteenth century. Of these, Hans emphasised three 'motives': religious, intellectual, and utilitarian. In identifying these three, however, Hans eschewed, perhaps unconsciously, the principal tenets of functionalism, in particular the static, integrative, and formal nature of the analysis. On the contrary, Hans points to the influence of specific historical chapters on the reform of the school curriculum in the eighteenth century. The "struggle for religious freedom which flared up in a civil war" (1951:14), and movements for freedom which began on a purely intellectual basis, but were transformed into social and economic movements for reform by events such as the anti-slavery campaign and the industrial revolution, were two to which Hans pointed.

There is an interesting contradiction here, however. It is clear that Hans' work on major educational reforms of the eighteenth century and, in particular, revisions to the curriculum, did not conform to the oft-argued criticism by more recent scholars that all research on educational knowledge prior to the publication of Michael Young's (1971) *Knowledge and Control* was predicated on functionalist social and methodological principles. Nonetheless, Hans was not unaware of the growing influence of functionalism upon educational research, and there is evidence to suggest that he tried to accomodate to it to some degree at much the same time that he was writing his work on the eighteenth century. Equally clear, however, was the fact that Hans' understanding of functionalism was somewhat misconcieved. Indeed, Hans, perhaps due to his methodological orientation as an historian, partly confounded functionalist analysis with the historical mode of research, and argued that functionalism was to be contrasted with statistical forms of analysis: "Comparative education is based on history and should be dealt with functionally, which is another way of saying historically" (1964: 94).

Not all work by comparativists on the theme of changes to educational knowledge, then, were predicated upon functionalist principles, in the period before the flowering of the 'new sociology of education'. But some were. Holmes' (1958) outline of the connections between social change and the curriculum contained no critical commentary on values within or outside the educational system. The thrust of the analysis was largely in accord with functionalist procedures: that is to simply accurately describe and explore theoretical relationships between areas of change in society—

> ". . . since educational change is bound up with the general social pattern, it is desirable to be in a position to be able to predict the trend of events which will follow any social innovation." (1958: 375)

—within a framework of taken-for-granted values, especially the system-imperative of stable maintenence of that society being analysed.

Neither evolutionary nor revolutionary forms of social change were analysed critically in terms of either the relations between the structuring of educational knowledge and the structuring of power relations in society, or an overall set of human values which were open to debate and critical scrutiny. Further, one of the principal values which was not open for debate but simply uncritically assumed within Holmes was that of positivism, which again reveals the connection to functionalist concerns with devising a technologically efficient 'social science'. For Holmes, a technicist preoccupation with transforming comparative education into a social science modelled upon the physical sciences was axiomatic.

> ". . . sociological laws . . . bear to man's social environment the relationship that 'natural laws' (of science) have to his physical or natural environment. For those who wish to study the mechanics of curriculum development the importance of studying modern opinions on the main characteristics of scientific laws is thus obvious. (1958: 373)

Holmes' employment of Popperian analysis[2], itself based upon the positivist assumption that the model of investigation for the social sciences must be identical with, and derived from, the form used for investigation in the physical sciences, was a further illustration of his dependence upon positivist precepts. Equally his reliance upon theoretical analysis, rather than detailed empirical analysis, was also redolent of functionalist influence, in particular its tendency towards an abstract, formal style of explanation. This dependence upon positivist traditions, including a broadly functionalist notion of social science and social change, was both Holmes' crowning glory in comparative education, and his fatal flaw. It permeated all his work, including the analysis of curriculum change.

INFLUENCE OF THE 'NEW' SOCIOLOGY OF EDUCATION: THE 1970s

In the next phase of comparative scholarship on connections between knowledge and society, it was Young's suggestive work of 1971 which provided an important catalyst for a reconceptualization of the problem of knowledge and schooling. Young's effort to redirect sociology of education largely took as its focus the connection between patterns of power in society and the patterning of knowledge within institutions of education. Although the suggested reorientation of sociology of education from one based on fuctionalist assumptions of consensus to more conflict oriented approaches was, as has been implied above, perhaps drawn too starkly[3] nonetheless the volume can be seen as something of a watershed for future work in the field. No longer was it possible to write of any particular structure of educational knowledge as representing an assumed social consensus. Sociological enquiry, by contrast, was now to inquire into the institutional establishment of any educational form or construct, no matter how admired or historically legitmated. It therefore became the task of sociological enquiry, according to this brief, to treat these categories not as absolutes but as constructed realities realized in particular institutional contexts.

Prevailing conceptions of order were being challenged on two fronts by Young's work and those of his co-authors. Firstly, conventional functionalist conceptions of order in society, based upon an assumed social consensus in regard to norms and the operation of institutions in society (Welch 1985, 1991) were largely rejected in favour of approaches which focused on the operation of power and conflict in society. In particular, both connections between educational institutions and other sources of power in society, and forms of ideological domination in education, became major guiding principles by which the 'new' sociology of education investigated the process of the legitimation of educational knowledge. Knowledge was now to be seen as representing a particular selection from culture, one of many possible selections. Thus, questions of how any particular selection came to operate in a given cultural context became a matter of explaining the specific ideological and institutional forces in society which brought this selection into being, or combined to sustain it, at times even after the original reasons for its inception had long passed. Equally, the re-emphasis upon the notion of power in educational explanation did not just connote structural relations of power in the wider society, but also a concern with the power of knowledge itself, and an examination of why certain subjects occupied positions of privilege within a specific knowledge hierarchy at certain times. A critical concern with the power of scientific knowledge, and the rise of positivistic reasoning, with its potential to add to social control, was an important illustration of this concern, and again formed a connection to the work of figures such as Habermas and Marcuse. Young was one of the first to link science and social control in the context of the critical analysis of educational knowledge in society:

> Much . . . social criticism, and the alternatives implicit in it, has been based upon a new absolutism, that of science and reason. Today it is the commonsense conceptions of 'the scientific' and 'the rational', together with the various social, political and educational beliefs, that are assumed to follow from them, that represent the dominant legitimizing categories. (1971: 3)[4]

Secondly, the taken-for-granted order of the school, and assumptions about school-knowledge, and the operation of power and control (including the control of knowledge) within the environment of the school, was also opened to increasing scrutiny. Day-to-day routines of school governance, teachers' work practices, and forms of pedagogy were subjected to detailed analysis, in an effort to uncover messages and forms of knowledge which were being conveyed to students, often implicitly, by the so-called hidden curriculum. The way in which such knowledge was passed to students, and the implicit messages conveyed by teachers in their quotidian practices, stimulated research by comparative scholars such as Richard Heyman, who argued that ethnographic, or specifically ethnomethodological, forms of inquiry in schooling provided a new basis for research in comparative education (1979a, 1979b, 1980, 1974). Not until the process whereby the basic structures of producing and legitimating knowledge in schools was laid bare by ethnomethodological accounting practices could one begin to ground an adequate explanation of the phenomenon of schooling, according to Heyman, who also went on to criticize the contemporary IEA studies for failing to ground their analyses in the study of the lived experience of the pupils and teachers studied.[5]

For comparative educationists in particular, then, the differing contributions in Young's anthology could be seen as mapping out unusually fertile territory for further exploration. For not only did the authors invoke a much more critical stance towards previously taken-for-granted categories in education, but there were also several chapters which broadened the Anglocentric nature of the debate considerably, and brought international perspectives into clear focus. Robin Horton's (1971) work on traditional African thought brought into question, at the same time, the legitimacy of traditional and largely unquestioned accounts of western science, a stance which would also prove suggestive to some comparative scholars. And Pierre Bourdieu's astringent account of the ossified French intellectual tradition (1971), and the ways of thought it has legitimized, revealed starkly the connections between knowledge hierarchies and power. The analysis of curriculum was being transformed into a branch of the sociology of knowledge with an overtly comparative dimension:

> A comparative study of the commonest subjects of academic essays or treatises and of lectures in different countries at different periods

> would make an important contribution to the sociology of knowledge by defining the necessary frame of problematic reasoning, which is one of the most fundamental dimensions of the intellectual programming of a society and a period. (1971:191)

Explanations of the ways in which particular forms of organization of educational institutions (including particular configurations of knowledge) reflected, and perhaps reinforced, wider patterns of power and privilege in various societies at different times, inspired a new generation of researchers in comparative education. Connections between power and knowledge came to be seen as increasingly central to explanations of educational change in societies, and the study of knowledge-changes in societies at different times, acquired an increasingly concrete, historical character. What passed for knowledge at any time in particular societies came to be seen as one possible response to the problem of cultural transmission, and hierarchies of knowledge came under increasing scrutiny:

> . . . what is a 'topical question' largely depends on what is socially considered as such; there is at every period in every society, a hierarchy of legitimate objects for study, all the more compelling . . . since it is lodged in the instruments of thought that individuals receive during their intellectual training. (Bourdieu 1971: 195)

During the 1970s then, largely due to the influence of a widespread and critical reorientation in many fields of educational research, comparative scholars began to take a fresh look at explanations of the issue of knowledge-changes in education, and the connections between these and changes in relationships of power within society. Did particular, powerful groups in society have the capacity to press for changes in the status of certain subjects within the overall knowledge-hierarchy operating in educational institutions? Equally, could these same groups resist successfully the pressure for changes from more assertive groups in society, concerned with enhancing their access to the elite? Under what specific social circumstances, then, do changes in the structure and status of knowledge change?

A number of scholars took up the challenge to explore the theoretical and empirical possibilities offered by the legitimation of educational knowledge, in relation to comparative educational research. Robert Cowen, one of the first to examine this motif, argued that research into the legitimation of educational knowledge had been neglected within comparative education, although he did point to at least one "brilliant early sketch" (Cowen 1975).[6] As part of his attempt to define the field, Cowen posed three central questions with respect to the processes underlying the legitimation of educational knowledge:

> how does it, in particular forms become valued and sustained; in what circumstances does it become changed; and what does a cross-national comparison of such processes and contents suggest about the reciprocal relationship between educational knowledge, social change, social consensus, mobilization, and the division of labour? (1975: 282)

Overall, Cowen's argument reinforces the dialectical connection between a society and its form (s) of educational knowledge:

> The legitimations and forms of educational knowledge stand in reciprocal relationship to the society in which the educational knowledge is located: such legitimations reflect certain major characteristics of the society and the educational knowledge creates nationally differentiated, and in certain circumstances, subnationally differentiated, reality-definitions among educands. (1975: 283)

Cowen went on to develop several thumbnail sketches of changing national models of education, all of which exemplify his central point that educational knowledge is an important political index of cultural transmission. Focussing on the contest for control over the model of educational knowledge in England in the nineteenth century, for example, Cowen argued that this still operated within "self consciously class-based" (1975: 283) notions of society, which still valued elite education above all. In France at the same time, a similar attachment to a class based education, and especially the education of the elite, was acompanied by a piece of Napoleonic Realpolitik which saw the primary schools revert to the control of the Church. In both countries, he suggested, it was education for the masses, rather than for the elite, which was contentious. On the other hand, in both revolutionary China and Cuba the political rationale was different: priorities here were literacy for all, and there was also a much wider definition of educational knowledge, which embraced people and institutions well outside the traditional confines of the school.[7] Educational knowledge, especially if gained within formal educational settings, was not the only or necessarily the principal means of gaining prestige or advancement.

> The conclusions which Cowen draws from the preceding discussion are in terms of the potential pluralization of knowledge: it is not 'knowledge' that is rendered problematic in this perspective, he suggests, but 'knowledges'. Cowen argues that further case studies could illuminate the central problem of how particular groups are (or are not) "able to legitimate and institutionalize their specialized versions of educational knowledge" (1975: 294). Such case studies could be illuminating at both the level of practical policy formation, and at the level of promoting our understanding of concrete school-society interrelations.

THE DEBATE WIDENS: THE LAST DECADE

The period to approximately 1980 had begun to establish legitimacy as a topic worthy of comparative investigation. The work of Cowen, and Heyman, had shown how the 'new' sociology of education could be used by comparativists in both macro and micro contexts, as a basis for making educational knowledge problematic. In both cases, much the same question came to be posed, ultimately: how did this particular knowledge-frame come into being? In both cases too, the result was much the same; a corroding of the previously more monolithic notions of knowledge.

The next stage was to employ, and expand upon, questions of the relationship between power and knowledge, through the development of case-studies of educational change. In so doing, several comparative scholars engaged in fruitful dialogue with two developing, and critical, European research traditions, which were not entirely separate. The first was a revitalized version of Max Weber's work, made available principally through the work of Margaret Archer and, to a lesser extent, Michalina Vaughan. The second was a powerful reinterpretation of a current of Western Marxism, largely in the form of the principal contemporary exponent of 'Critical Theory': Jürgen Habermas. Comparative scholars working within the latter approach, in particular, raised and began to explore connexions between the legitimation of educational knowledge and the legitimacy of the modern state.

Some of this newer group of authors drew upon the social and natural sciences to develop their case studies in the legitimation of educational knowledge. Institutional and ideological forces for and against the incorporation of science into higher education in England and Germany around the nineteenth century was the focus of one such study, which proposed two major forms of analysis upon which studies in the legitimation of educational knowledge could be based.

The first drew upon a critical social scientific tradition originating in figures such as Karl Marx and C. Wright Mills, and including some of the more contemporary educationists such as Michael Young and Michael Apple. What was common to these diverse thinkers was a critical sociology of knowledge, that is, an acceptance of "a theory of mind . . . that conceives social factors as intrinsic to mentality" (Welch 1981: 72, Mills 1939) as well as a commitment to changing those circumstances and structures in society which yielded and sustained social inequities. A principal focus of these inequities was education and, in particular, the operation of knowledge hierarchies within institutions of education. High status knowledge, from this point of view, marks out social divisions in society largely irrespective of its utility, and it is this ability to maintain social divisions that, as Apple argues, which means that an

> attempt to make substantive alterations in the relationship between high status and low status knowledge by, say, making different knowledge areas equal, will tend to be resisted. (Apple 1979: 39)

The second form of analysis was drawn from the annals of contemporary philosophy of science, particularly the theories of Karl Popper and T.S. Kuhn. Popper's formulation of the stages of problem solution[8] was applied to the process of curriculum change, whereby any particular curriculum could be seen as one possible solution to the problem of cultural transmission. This tentative solution, however, may be subsequently modified in the light of further relevant evidence. When combined with a revised account of Popper's critical dualism (a dualism of facts and decisions, or norms and institutions), which allowed for a more political account of knowledge and knowledge change, Popper's stages of problem solution, it was argued, provided a basis for studies in the legitimation of educational knowledge: both a model for curriculum change and a taxonomy for its analysis.

Kuhn, too, was examined in terms of his potential for explaining changes in the legitimacy of knowledge. Kuhn's theory of paradigm change is seen as a powerful tool with which to analyze the process, in that political dimensions are admitted to have a role to play in the process of change. No longer are changes in knowledge seen as a uniqely rational process, in which successive theories triumph because of their demonstrated logical or empirical superiority (a superiority which is often evident only in hindsight, and which is largely a matter of agreement in any event). On the contrary, rather than being defined in some teleological sense whereby, like Whig history, scientific knowledge unfolds as a process of remorseless, if uneven improvement, Kuhn revealed the process of change in science (or knowledge) to be a form of crisis resolution, whereby a challenge to the orthodox, or conventional, scientific explanation is often fiercely resisted by defenders of the older paradigm, although the genesis of the contender may have been inspired by anomalies discovered in the old paradigm. Adjustments to the old form of explanation are accompanied by vigorous political activity within scientific communities, which is designed to help sustain the legitimacy of the old form. According to this analysis, replacements to the old knowledge paradigm are as much a matter of specific political changes (such as key adherents of the new paradigm gaining key posts, writing key texts, or older adherents dying out), as the specific ways in which the new paradigm for the field is seen by its adherents to be a superior form of explanation. Indeed the two are by no means entirely separate.

From this point of view, then, changes in knowledge must be explained in concrete and social terms, rather than as an illustration of the onward march of an abstract reason. This meant that adequate explanations of particular episodes of changes to knowledge could no longer continue to be a matter of a simple appeal to a universal model of abstract rationality to which the specific illustration was supposed to conform, but rather had to take into account a whole new range of historical and sociological data, which had to be seen in its own terms, rather than interpreted with hindsight. A more anthropological or case study approach to changes in knowledge was one possible consequence of this view. The critique of value-free, positivistic accounts of knowledge, which were both monolithic (or perhaps mono-logical) and rooted firmly in an objectivistic view of the natural sciences, was an implicit part of this account of knowledge legitimation.

In the above study, therefore, a subsequent empirical examination developed a case study of the legitimation of science in higher education in England and Germany around the nineteenth century, in terms of the particular interaction of ideological and institutional forces in each culture. The different constellation of ideological and institutional pressures for change and conservation in the two countries were argued to have led to different responses, and rates of response, to attempts at changing the definition of legitimate knowledge in the eighteenth and nineteenth centuries, in particular the desire to introduce science as a legitimate arena of investigation into higher education.

According to other comparative researchers, however, Weberian analytic techniques, in this case the idea of the contest for educational control applied to specific socio-historical situations, provided the basis for explanation. In particular, the work of Margaret Archer and her sometime co-author Michalina Vaughan, who have been foremost in demonstrating the utility of a less bowdlerized conception of Weber, with an emphasis on the struggle for control over state systems of education, proved suggestive to some younger scholars. For Archer (1979) and Archer and Vaughan (1971a), educational control, including the control of educational knowledge, was akin to educational ownership. Indeed historically, in many cases, this was literally the case, since those who controlled education also owned its physical resources and supplied its teachers. Monopolization of these resources by a dominant group in society could maximize educational control, at least for a time. Archer, and Vaughan and Archer, sought to investigate particular educational settings wherein this educational control was vested in a small group of powerful individuals in society. Although this control resided in different groups (political or religious elites, for example, in different cultural settings), in each case Archer argues that the suppliers of education could, through the use of sanctions, exert more control over education than that which education could exert over the other spheres. "Educational change could not be initiated endogenously" (1979: 63), which is to say that educational change is often a product of the actions of the dominant group to achieve ends which are by no means limited to education. Archer gives as one example the pressure for change centred upon the restrictive and outmoded nature of the, largely religious, knowledge-frame which was dominant at the time of Peter I's accession, and which she argued restricted the efficiency of the army, commerce, accounting, and the bureaucracy, as well as inhibiting the prospects for the Russian nobility gaining acceptance among the French-speaking nobility from other European nations.

Robin Burns (1979, 1981a, 1981b) largely used ideas developed by Archer, as well as some of Habermas' concepts, to investigate the more contemporary question of how development education came to be legitimated in both Australia and Sweden.[9] Beginning with an outline of two central questions raised by the notion of legitimacy—

1. What is the basis of legitimacy for an institution or group of institutions?
2. What are the limits of that legitimacy in terms of the range of individuals and groups by whom and/or for whom jurisdiction is claimed? (1979: 25)

—Burns pointed to Habermas' work as revealing both the psychological and empirical dimensions of the legitimacy claims of a particular order. From Habermas' point of view, mere belief is an insufficient basis for the establishment or maintenance of legitimacy claims. There is also an empirical aspect of claims to legitimacy, which reveals, at the same time, a rational validity claim which "can be tested and criticized independently of the psychological effect of these grounds" (Habermas 1976: 97). This central but contentious claim of Habermas rests upon the ability of the ruling group to maintain social consensus in the face of apparent inequalities. Indeed a central concern for Habermas, here, is attempts by the state to rationalize the distribution of the social product, unequally, yet legitimately. The education system is an important arena of social distribution whereby the state attempts to mobilize and maintain that uneasy consensus, and thereby substantiate its legitimacy claims.

But in examining the case of Development Education, Burns argues that it is the formation and content of the ideology of the dominant group in society which is of principal importance, an insight which while consonant with Habermas, she derives from the Weberian scholars Vaughan and Archer (1971b). The Habermasian connection between legitimation and domination is also recognized in Vaughan and Scotford Archer's work. For these authors, an ideology which "legitimat (es) the the monopolistic claims of a group and justif (ies) pressures for the maintenance of its domination" (1971b: 64) is part of three major interrelated factors involved in the successful continuing dominance over an education system by a group: monopoly, constraint and ideology. Ideology is of particular importance in that, if universally accepted, it has the capacity to transform a system of control into one of legitimate authority. Monopoly (the control of scarce resources) consists of either the control over human and material resources to impart instruction or, in a situation where education is integrated with other sub-systems, monopoly will not be so specifically educational. Constraints may be either legal and economic, or coercive and repressive. Again, forms of constraint will be more generalized if education is more integrated into other social institutions. Of these three factors, ideology can form a very important means of sustaining the parameters of what is acceptable knowledge in a pluralist society, since not only does it seek to gain assent for the control by the dominant group itself, but also the methods it uses. Challenges to the legitimacy of the dominant group consist of instrumental activities, bargaining power, and an alternative ideology. If these factors are directed by an assertive group at the existing form of institutional domination, it is ideology which weakens first, since the very existence of the challenge indicates that the old legitimating ideology is no longer completely successful.

Ideology, and the processes by which it changes, however, can be explained in the language of the natural sciences too as, inter alia, Kuhn has shown. Kuhn's description of the process whereby an older scientific theory is increasingly challenged by a new contender is again seen by Burns to be an interesting illustration of the legitimation of educational knowledge. Indeed, the question of legitimacy is seen to be at the centre of this mode of explanation, given that in Kuhn changes only become possible when alternative paradigms bring about a crisis of confidence in the older form. The process of change to a new paradigm, or worldview, is likened by Kuhn to that of a Gestalt switch, or conversion, rather than a process of the rational replacement of an inferior explanation with a superior form. The paradigm itself functions normatively, specifying how the research ought to be carried out, and the tests and interpretations which are integral to it. The political function of paradigms is revealed for Burns in their capacity to legitimate scientific practice, especially in the realm of human affairs.

Burns' argument clearly shows the centrality of power and conflict to an understanding of the legitimation of educational knowledge. She, too, delves into Critical Theory, reviewing Habermas' argument that knowledge is distorted when not rooted in the a priori of autonomy and responsibility. In so doing, she shows the limits of the positivistic account of knowledge, revealing it as static, and as unrelated to the notion of culture or the quotidian practices and concerns of people's lives. The more critical conception of knowledge, by contrast, does not separate the operation of a particular knowledge paradigm from the ongoing struggle to realize the good life.

And Burns makes more explicit the connection between science, especially in its more positivistic form, and social control. She cites Lindblom's argument that scientific positivism has produced the current paradigm for development in the industrialized world but that this paradigm has largely run its course; indeed

> this development seems to have reached and passed its optimum and has now become counterproductive as far as man's liberation and growth is concerned . . . (Lindblom 1978)

As opposed to positivism's emphasis on efficiency, objectivity, and a strict separation of theory and practice, Burns argues for "equity for and the emancipation of the individual, and a just and liberated society" (1971: 338) as the goals for educational practice. The argument here is about educational and social reform ('the practice of educational and social change'), and thus the problematic of the role of knowledge and the processes whereby it is made legitimate, as also the ways it can lend legitimacy to particular programmes of educational and social reform, is something which is seen in concrete historical terms, rather than the abstract, remote conception of knowledge characteristic of positivism. In other words, knowledge is conceived here as malleable, and, in particular, able to be used by the powerful in society for their own ends. From a Habermasian perspective, it can be argued that knowledge is not only something which is produced under particular social conditions, but is often used to sustain the state's continual quest for legitimacy. Knowledge, then, is subject to particular interests, and can be used for technical, hermeneutic, or practical/emancipatory ends (Habermas 1978, Hesse 1980, Held 1980, McCarthy 1978). Knowledge and rationality are not value free, as the positivistic paradigm presupposes, but rather are used in particular ways by particular social forces; the results of this tend towards more, or less, liberating social directions.

By the end of the 1970s, the concept of legitimation had substantially begun to replace the work of earlier theorists of curriculum change in comparative education, in whose eyes knowledge had often been conceived in object-like terms. By contrast, the work of a newer generation of theorists substituted a more dynamic concept of knowledge, and its relation to social change and social control. In particular, they argued, knowledge was not neutral, or unrelated to political and economic change. On the contrary, some of the case studies, and much of the analysis, pointed to the potential for social domination of various forms of knowledge, including those affected by the positivist knowledge paradigm. Australia's development paradigm during the 1970s is characterized by Burns as much more simply technocratic, and less critical, than that of Sweden at the same time. For example, while Sweden disputed the role of research which was not appraised by indigenous people, Australia's position was based on the uncritical production of skilled personnel, especially in the areas of science and technology which were thought to be crucial for development, but inhibited because of factors such as lack of management skills and capital. More recently, Toh and Farrelly, in an interesting analysis of a group of students from the Third World who were studying at an Australian university, has argued that the position has not changed all that much with respect to Australia's production of technocrats for the Third World (Toh and Farrelly 1991). In the case of both Burns, and Toh and Farrelly, there is a rejection both of the monolithic nature of knowledge, and the technocratic basis of Australia's aid programme to the Third World.

The 1970s, then, was a decade in which links between knowledge and power, in both schools and the wider society, began to be explored more systematically. The understanding of legitimacy, however, was still largely in terms of paradigms within the sociology of knowledge, or at least did not usually make specific links between the legitimation of knowledge and the legitimacy of the modern state.

EDUCATION, LEGITIMATION AND THE STATE

The 1980s has seen an even greater emphasis on the notion of legitimacy by scholars in comparative education. As before, one of the key figures whose work has inspired much of this research is Habermas. Habermas' emphasis on the key concept of legitimacy within his vast and impressive work contains two elements which have proved particularly suggestive for comparative researchers in education in the 1980s.

As we saw above, Habermas has argued, along with others such as Claus Offe (1975), that the modern capitalist state operates with a continuing legitimacy deficit (Habermas 1976) and is therefore constantly searching for new sources of legitimation, in a failing effort to secure ongoing assent, by the populace, to state control. Education is one important arena wherein the state seeks to shore up its falling stocks of legitimacy, which endanger its survival. Without ongoing legitimacy, the state has no authority and cannot continue to rule. Thus it seeks to use the education system as a means of disseminating ideology, which it perceives as one means whereby it can compensate for its failing legitimacy claims.

Secondly, Habermas' central use of the concept of ideology has been seen as having important implications both in terms of school-society relations, and within the school. Habermas' argument on ideology transforms the older Marxian notion from simply being evidence of the dominance of ruling class ideas and ideation in areas of social activity such as philosophy, law, and implicitly in education, to an in-depth understanding of the particular role of rationality in modern society and its power to replace systems of ethical practice. Habermas, building partly on the work of others before him, such as Marcuse (1968) and Horkheimer and Adorno (1979), has argued that Western society, from at least the time of the Enlightenment, has been made increasingly subject to processes of rationalization which tend to place practical-moral questions in parentheses, and strive to extend a more strategic form of rationality into all phases of human existence. The dominance of such a means-ends ethic for decision-making is, according to Habermas, at the loss of personal and social autonomy and liberation, and is not independent of the rise of technological and scientific thought and associated systems of social control in societies over the last few centuries (Habermas 1971: 81–122). This argument, exemplified in comparative educational research by the gradual supplanting of the traditional modernization paradigm by more critical theories (Welch 1985), has involved Habermas in a sustained and critical engagement with the Weberian theory of rationalization, which has been characterized as a major index of the modernization of societies (Habermas 1984, 1987, Bernstein 1985). If, according to Habermas, the extension of science and technology and associated purposive-rational systems of action have yielded a net increase in forms of social control in society, then we may need to scrutinize much more closely and critically the impact of science and technology upon society, especially in legitimating a form of decisionistic rationality which inhibits the development of personal autonomy and social development, because of its power to supplant systems of action based upon ethics. Further, we need to examine the role of the modern state, which is now often subject to a crisis of legitimacy.

Weiler has been perhaps the principal researcher in comparative education who has explored the implications of these ideas during the 1980s. In particular, Weiler has identified three major responses by the state in attempting to deal with the ongoing problem of a legitimacy deficit, via education (Weiler 1983a, 1983b, 1982, 1989).

Beginning with the generally identified crisis of late capitalist states—which has been either characterized as a 'crisis of governability' by conservative theoreticians (Crozier et al. 1975), or as a crisis of legitimacy by more critically oriented theorists—(Offe 1975, Habermas 1976) Weiler discerns particular major institutional strategies by which the state tries to pursue its strategy of 'compensatory legitimation' through education, attempting to retrieve lost authority.

As the state broadens its activities into more and more areas, its need for legitimacy increases, which then leads it into still wider areas of activity, seeking yet more legitimacy. Contradictions arise between different imperatives, and the state, having lost its claim to normative legitimacy, can only compensate for that loss through particular strategies. But the two principal forms which Offe points to—increased material gratification or coercive repression—contain within them the potential for adding fuel to the fire, rather than stemming the flames.

Part of this problem, it is argued, lies in the class structure of the capitalist state, which generates increasing contradictions, which the state must solve for its continuing survival, but increasingly is unable to achieve:

> Because the reproduction of class societies is based on the appropriation of socially produced wealth, all such societies must resolve the problem of distributing the surplus social product inequitably and yet legitimately. (Habermas 1976: 96)

In education, this can mean that reformist policies generate expectations which the capitalist state, given its limited power to tolerate genuine social change, cannot fulfil. The sphere of politics becomes 'overloaded' (Rose 1980). This problem has been explored before within comparative education, for example in the contexts of the limits of reform in Western European education. Levin's acount of the contradictions inherent in trying to satisfy the demands of capitalist labour markets while at the same time trying to use education, in particular the newer comprehensive school structures in several parts of Europe, as a means to promote greater mobility and equality than had been the case under the earlier bipartite or tripartite schooling system, is one example of this argument (Levin: 1978).

Given that these tensions exist in societies, what does this imply for the role of knowledge in societies, and in particular the legitimation of educational knowledge? Here we begin to discern the more specific connections betweeen the legitimation of educational knowledge and the process of political legitimation. Weiler argues that when the state wishes to use education as a response to the erosion of its legitimacy, that there are three principal forms which this response takes. Each of these forms has the capacity to increase the legitimacy of state-run education, while at the same time largely blunting any genuine prospect of significant reforms. 'Legalization' or 'judicialization' embraces the increasing role of the judicial process in framing educational policy. 'Expertise' involves the use of experts in framing or legitimating policy options, through the use of experiments or forms of planning. 'Participation' includes the strategies of employing and incorporating forms of participatory decision making in education.

Weiler demonstrates that each of these forms of compensatory legitimation have been adopted in paricular instances. Both in the US and the Federal Republic of Germany, courts and the judicial process have intervened substantially in the process of shaping educational policy and running schools. Education, health, transport, and energy are all fields which bear witness to this trend. In the Federal Republic, Weiler points to the increasing intrusion of legal norms into the educational process, through four specific forms:

- Increasing legal specifications (rules and regulations) governing educational reform.
- Greater use of court cases to determine educational policies, or decisions in school.
- Increasing use of legislation to provide educational norms.
- More use of legal arguments in political debates over educational policy.

Weiler argues that one of the principal reasons for the West German Federal Constitutional Court (Bundessverfassungsgericht) to become more involved in the determination of educational policy was its perception of a 'legitimacy deficit' in methods of arriving at educational policies. Weiler sees the increasing intrusion of the (BVerfG) Court in the Federal Republic as an attempt to compensate for the loss of legitimacy on the part of executive and legislative branches of state power. In other words, the increasing interventions themselves reflect an overall loss of legitimacy by the State.

If the above reaction by an arm of the State reflects an attempt to redefine educational knowledge, or at least who has the power to determine educational knowledge, the form of 'legitimation by expertise' relates more closely to the overall argument regarding legitimation in this chapter. In this form, the interaction between knowledge and decision-making is the primary focus. In particular, Weiler examines the ways in which experimentation can play a role in the legitimation of educational knowledge. More simply we can talk of the desire by planners in education to give what Janet Weiss has called "a patina of scientific respectability" (Weiler 1981: 17, Weiss 1979: 448)[10] to policy decisions, which in some cases precede the experiment. At certain times, '. . . social science research becom (es) increasingly necessary to legitimate institutional action' (Weiss 1979: 446).

The prospect is an attractive one for educational planners. For Weiler, the notion of 'reform as experiment' raises the "prospect of being able to say with scientific conviction and credibility, that one social programme was 'better' than another, that advocates of a given policy were 'right' and its opponents 'wrong'" (Weiler 1983a: 269), or the other way around, as the case or data may be. Examples of the introduction of comprehensive schooling models in Sweden and, later, into the Federal Republic of Germany are examples of this form of legitimation. For Weiler, it is the legitimacy of the process (i.e that of experimentation) which provides legitimacy, rather than that of the specific results. In at least one case which Weiler cites, the experiment was fallacious *ab initio*, an attempt to compare like with unlike, since the two schooling systems being compared had fundamentally different goals (Weiler 1983a: 271–2).

The other element of experimentation which has utility for the state is argued by Weiler to be that of conflict resolution. Sex education classes, particular programmes of study such as MACOS and SEMP in Australia (Scott and Scott 1980, Smith and Knight 1978, 1981), or the implementation of a desegregationist school policy, can all give rise to significant levels of dispute among different sectors of the populace. One means whereby this conflict can be 'managed' is through the use of selected experiments. Again, Weiler cites the example of attempts to evaluate the comprehensive school form as a competitor for the traditional differentiated secondary school pattern in West Germany. Although the use of a 'scientific experiment' gave the veneer of rationality to this choice, the comparison was misconceived, as was argued above. But, not only did the scientificity of the experiment lend credence to decision-making, but the experiment also helped to defuse a very heated political dispute, which, partly because of the party-political affiliations of the protagonists, threatened to destabilize the West German state.[11]

> This potential conflict was effectively moderated and defused by the device of the experimental program, . . . the 'cooling out' condition which allowed the system to tolerate the conflict between two fundamentally different philosophies of education. (Weiler 1983a: 271)

What we have in the use of experimentation cited above is the attempt to manage conflict through the control of knowledge. The legitimacy of scientific knowledge has significant political potential, as was argued by Young above. Recognizing this, the state can use this potential to compensate for the erosion of legitimacy in other areas of policy development, while at the same time appearing to show some commitment to reform. In a sense then, the State can manage conflict by managing knowledge, appealing to the power of the scientific paradigm to defuse potentially damaging conflicts.

The final strategy which Weiler points to is that of the management of participation, which again has relevance for the legitimation of educational knowledge. Citizen participation, like the other forms of legitimation strategies, can also demonstrate a commitment by the State to reform, while at the same time securing further legitimation for its activities. Equally, the careful selection of which citizens are to participate in the process allows these people to be defined as having legitimate knowledge, and the views of other, perhaps more critical elements, to be de-legitimized. It has been argued by some critics that the multicultural debate in Australia, including in education, has been 'managed' in this way.

Weiler uses the example of curriculum planning and reform to show how the state can "experiment with the participation of those affected" (Habermas 1976: 72), although he recognizes that the strategy is a risky one for the State:

> The more planners place themselves under the pressure of consensus-formation in the planning process, the more likely is a process that goes back to two contrary motives: excessive demands resulting from legitimation claims that the administration cannot satisfy under conditions of an asymmetrical class compromise; and conservative resistance to planning, which contracts the horizon of planning and lowers the degree of innovation possible. (Habermas 1976: 72–3)

Thus it may well be that the State encourages selected forms of educational participation as a means of defusing some of the significant educational conflicts which can emerge around curriculum reforms, but that if these forms of participation lead to significant effects, state educational structures may well feel threatened and react accordingly.

Recent research dealing with the re-conservatization of the debate on education, equity, employment and the like bears out some of the conclusions reached above on the extension of the role of legitimation with respect to educational knowledge. Indeed, we have seen in recent years, the development of a significant literature dealing with movements to legitimate particular versions of knowledge about education in society, especially with respect to the so-called 'basics' of literacy and numeracy.

As the crisis of the modern capitalist state deepens, more and more stringent and widespread efforts are undertaken to legitimize the explanation in terms of the failure of education. The crisis of the State is being transformed into the crisis of education. Perhaps this marks a further stage of the process, whereby the State no longer sees education as a site of legitimacy compensation, except in a negative sense: by delegitimizing (mass) education it can direct attention away from its own crumbling legitimacy.

Major recent educational reform efforts in several states have been based on campaigns to focus the blame away from the economy and onto the education system. In the US the document *A Nation At Risk* (Gardner et al. 1983) was of precisely this sort, and played on increasing national paranoia with respect to the loss of US competitiveness vis-à-vis its current international competitor, Japan. Comparativists have not been the only ones to point out similarities with an earlier era when, in the late 1950s, the US became equally concerned that its assumed technological lead was being overtaken, on that occasion by the Soviet Union (Altbach, Kelly and Weiss 1985). The response on that occasion was broadly similar to the current one: to blame its own education system, to assume that the competitor's educational system was much more efficient, and to invest large sums of money into scientific and technological forms of education, on the assumption that this would somehow cure the international economic or technological gap which was perceived (Luke 1988: 1). The legitimacy of the social and economic system was threatened, and the response was to look to education as as means to solve the wider problem of perceived economic and technological deficiency. The major difference, however, is that in the 1950s, as Altbach points out, not only was the system undergoing massive expansion, but substantial sums were invested in "improving science education, reforming the preparation of teachers, building schools, supporting libraries and the like" (Altbach, Kelly and Weiss 1985: 15), a situation which is no longer the case today, and which arguably allows less room for the shoring up of failing legitimacy claims.

Michael Apple has been one of a number of contemporary critics (Apple 1987, Aronowitz and Giroux 1986, Welch and Freebody 1990, 1991) to point out this process of redirecting the public's attention away from wider and deeper system problems, as in his recent introduction to a comparative work on the politics of literacy:

> . . . by shifting the public's attention to the problems of education, the real sources of the current crises are left unanalyzed. That is, the crisis of the political economy of capitalism is exported from the economy to the state. The state then in turn exports the crisis downward onto the school. Thus whenever there is severe unemployment, a disintegration of traditional patterns of authority, and so on, the blame is placed upon students' lack of skills, on their attitudes, on their 'functional illiteracy'. (Apple 1987: vii)

In sum, then, what has been argued is that in comparative educational research into the legitimation of educational knowledge, substantial changes have occurred with respect to several dimensions of the debate. Firstly, a broadening has occurred in regard to the interpretation of the key concept of legitimation. In earlier stages of the research into legitimation, the research was directed to the examination of institutional and ideological processes whereby knowledge was rendered legitimate within educational settings. This involved greater scrutiny of theoretical and empirical connections between the operation of power in education and the operation of power in the wider society. This research reinforced the view that knowledge can convey power, and that this insight related to hierarchies of knowledge/status both within educational institutions and the wider society. Later, the debate on legitimation widened to include the whole notion of the ways in which education relates to the state's continual need for legitimacy, in particular viewing the education system as a site for the state to seek to re-establish its failing legitimacy claims.

Notions of knowledge and culture were politicized during the course of this research. No longer could knowledge or culture be seen as either monolithic or neutral, as with some of the earlier comparative research. On the contrary, knowledge and culture tended now to be seen as arenas of contest, with classes, gender groupings or ethnic groups vying for control, and with different aspects of knowledge and culture as having more or less power and status, and as being connected to the distribution of power in society in particular ways. The notion of 'cultural capital' (Bourdieu 1971) or 'cultural power' (Livingstone 1987)[12] has been another means used to express this relationship. One's differential access to cultural capital, or particular varieties of knowledge, had much to do with one's ultimate location in the power/status hierarchy in society, it was argued.[13]

To some extent too, however, moves away from the monolithic conception of culture have parallelled, and perhaps licensed, a move away from the concentration upon the nation-state as the prime or sole unit of analysis in comparative education. Further explorations in the legitimation of educational knowledge, and the connexions to political legitimacy, may yield yet more insights into the role of education in the production and reproduction of educational and social order.

NOTES

1. While it is not possible to explicate functionalism here fully, and give an account of its mainsprings and methodological consequences, see Welch, A.R. (1985) 'The Functionalist Tradition in Comparative Education', *Comparative Education* 19 (2), and 'The Sedative Science: Functionalism as a basis for Research In Comparative Education', in Schriewer, J., and Pedro, F. (1991) *Educación Comparada: Teorías, Perspectivas, Investigaciones*, Herder, Barcelona.

2. For Holmes' application of Popperian analysis, in particular the notion of Critical Dualism, to curriculum change, see p. 375 et seq.

3. See Bernbaum, G. (1977) *Knowledge and Ideology in the Sociology of Education,* London, Macmillan, for the view that functionalism was neither the whole nor sole mode of educational research in the period of the 1950s and the 1960s. The work of earlier British theorists committed to some form of social egalitarianism in education, such as Tawney, R.H.(1931, 1964) *Equality*, London, Allen and Unwin; Floud, Jean, Halsey, Alex, and Martin, F.M. (1958) *Social Class and Educational Opportunity*, London, Heinemann; and Jackson, Brian and Marsden, Denis (1966) *Education and the Working Class*, Penguin, lends some credence to this view.

4. For the implications of Young's concern regarding the rise of this new absolutism, that of scientific reason, see Young, p. 3. Young, of course, also was also part of the editorial collective responsible for producing *Radical Science Journal*. The works of relevance by Habermas and Marcuse include Habermas, J. (1971). 'Technology and Science as Ideology,' *Toward a Rational Society*, London, Heinemann, and Marcuse, H. (1968) *One Dimensional Man,* New York, Sphere.

5. For a critique of the ethnomethodological position, see Welch, A.R. (1986) 'Sociology without Society? A Critique of Quotidian Reason in Comparative Education.', *Journal of International and Comparative Education* 1 (1).

6. The earlier research Cowen alluded to was Lauwerys' Opening Address in *General Education in a Changing World*, The Hague, Martinus Nijhoff, 1967.

7. It is important to remind ourselves here that Cowen was writing towards the end of the period of Cultural Revolution in China.

8. Popper's stages of problem solution were as follows: P1 —> TT —> EE —> P2, where P1 represents the initial formulation of the problem, TT the tentative solution, EE the stage of error elimination, and P2 a later version of the problem, revised in the light of the evidence provided by the test of the earlier hypothesized solution. See Popper, K. (1972) *Objective Knowledge*, Oxford, Oxford University Press, p. 144, and for their application to processes of the legitimation of educational knowledge, see Welch, 'Curriculum . . .', p. 72.

9. See, for example, Burns' case study of development education in both Australia and Sweden, where she points to the way in which the international skills and knowledge of Swedish scholars was used to sustain Swedish domination of Norway in the period after 1905. Equally in the case of Australia, Burns cites the incorporation of a significant number of officers from the former Department of External Territories (formerly responsible for colonial administration) into the Australian Development Assistance Bureau, a move which she argues perpetuated colonial styles of thought and administration.

10. Another current example which Weiss cites is that of unemployment and inflation rates, which have largely been analysed within the language of economists, at the expense of questions of equity and fundamental human values.

11. The two major political parties in West German politics in the postwar period were the Social Democrats and the Christian Democrats. Each had very different attitudes to the introduction of the comprehensive school, and in fact the implementation of comprehensive schools largely depended, ultimately, on which group held power in the various Länder.

12. The notion of cultural power has been connected to the failing legitimacy of the modern state by Livingstone, in his recent work: "Cultural power involves the capacity of social groups to convey notions of actual, possible and preferable social beliefs and practices to their own groups and throughout society as a whole. While declining sentiments of confidence in established institutions of advanced capitalism are now substantial among overlapping groups of working class people, women, racial minorities and the

young or old, the cultural power of such subordinated groups generally remains limited and fragmented." Livingstone, D. (1987) *Critical Pedagogy and Cultural Power*, South Hadley, Bergin and Garvey, p. 7.

13. Although this too has been subjected to critique, notably by Archer, who has pointed out that the assumption of cultural capital does not always explain sufficiently how the process of exclusion works in practice, thus rendering the analysis somewhat ahistorical. See Archer, M. (1983) 'Process Without System'. *Archive Europeenne Sociologique*, xxiv (1), and Archer, M. (1981) 'Educational Systems', *International Social Science Journal*, xxxiii (2).

BIBLIOGRAPHY

Altbach, P., Kelly, G., and Weiss, L. (1985) *Excellence in Education*. Buffalo, Prometheus.

Anweiler, O. (1964) *Geschichte der Schule und Pädagogik in Rußland*. Heidelberg, Quelle und Meyer Verlag.

Apple, M. (1987) 'Foreword'. In C. Lankshear and C. Lawler, *Literacy, Schooling and Revolution*, Sussex, Falmer Press.

Apple, M.W. (1979) *Ideology and Curriculum*. London, Routledge and Kegan Paul.

Archer, M., and Vaughan, M. (1971) 'Domination and Assertion in Educational Systems'. In E. Hopper, *Readings in the Theory of Educational Systems*, London, Hutchinson.

Archer, M. (1983) 'Process Without System'. *Archive Europeenne Sociologique* xxiv (1).

Archer, M. (1981) 'Educational Systems', *International Social Science Journal* xxxiii (2).

Archer, M. (1979) *The Social Origins of Educational Systems*. London, Sage.

Aronowitz, S., and Giroux, H. (1986) *Education under Siege: The Conservative, Liberal and Radical Debate over Schooling*. South Hadley, Massachusetts, Bergin and Garvey.

Bernbaum, G. (1977) *Knowledge and Ideology in the Sociology of Education*. New York, Macmillan.

Bernstein, R. (ed.) (1985) *Habermas and Modernity*. Cambridge, Polity Press.

Bourdieu, P. (1971) 'Systems of Education and Systems of Thought'. In M. Young, *Knowledge and Control*. London, Collier Macmillan

Bourdieu, P., and Passeron, J-P. (1977) *Reproduction in Education and Society*. London, Sage.

Bourdieu, P. (1971) 'Systems of Education and Systems of Thought'. In E. Hopper (ed.), *Readings in the Theory of Educational Systems*. London, Hutchinson.

Burns, R. (1981) 'Development Education and Disarmament Education'. *Prospects* 11 (2).

Burns, R. (1981) 'Process and Problems in Educational Reform in Sweden'. *Compare* 11 (1).

Burns, R.J. (1979) 'The Formation and Legitimation of Development Education with particular reference to Australia and Sweden." Unpublished PhD dissertation, Latrobe University.

Cowen, R. (1975) 'The Legitimation of Educational Knowledge: a Neglected Theme in Comparative Education'. *Annals of the New York Academy of Sciences*. New York.

Crozier, M., Huntington, S., and Watanuki, J. (1975) *The Crisis of Democracy: Report on the Governability of Democracies to the Trilateral Commission*. New York, New York University Press.

Floud, J., Halsey, A. and Martin, F. (1958) *Social Class and Educational Opportunity*, London, Heinemann.

Gardner, D.P., et al. (1983) *A Nation at Risk. The Imperative for Educational Reform. An Open Letter to the American People. A Report to the Nation and the Secretary of Education, United States Department of Education, by The National Commission on Excellence in Education*, April.

Goody, J., and Watt, I. (1962) 'The Consequences of Literacy'. *Comparative Studies in History and Society* 5 (3).

Habermas, J. (1978) *Knowledge and Human Interests* (2nd rev. ed.). London, Heinemann.

Habermas, J. (1976) *Legitimation Crisis*. London, Heinemann.

Habermas, J. (1971) 'Technology and Science as Ideology'. *Toward a Rational Society*. London, Heinemann.

Habermas, J. (1987) *The Philosophical Discourse of Modernity*. Cambridge, Polity Press.

Habermas, J. (1984) *The Theory of Communicative Action*. Boston, Beacon Press.

Hans, N. (1964) 'Functionalism in Comparative Education'. *International Review of Education* 10.

Hans, N. 1964 (1931) *History of Russian Educational Policy*, 1701–1917. New York, Russell and Russell.

Hans, N. (1951) *New Trends in Education in the Eighteenth Century*. London, Routledge and Kegan Paul.

Hans, N. (1963) *The Russian Tradition in Education*. London, Routledge and Kegan Paul.

Held, D. (1980) *Introduction to Critical Theory Horkheimer to Habermas*. London, Hutchinson.

Hesse, M. (1980) 'Habermas' Consensus Theory of Truth'. Hesse, M., *Revolutions and Reconstructions in the Philosophy of Science*. Brighton, Harvester.

Heyman, R. (1979) 'Comparative Education from an Ethnomethodological Perspective'. *Comparative Education*, 15 (3).

Heymann, R. (1979) 'Toward a Non-Science of Comparative Education'. *Comparative and International Education Society*, March.

Heymann, R. (1980) 'Ethnomethodology. Some Suggestions for the Sociology of Education'. *Journal of Educational Thought* 14 (1).

Heymann, R. (1974) 'Knowledge, Schools and Change'. *Comparative Education Review* 18 (3).

Holmes, B. (1958) 'Social Change and the Curriculum'. In G. Bereday, and J. Lauwerys (eds), *The Yearbook of Education. The Secondary School Curriculum*. London, Evans Brothers.

Horkheimer, B., and Adorno, T. (1979) *The Dialectic Of Enlightenment*. London, Verso.

Horton, R. (1971) 'African Myths and Western Science'. In M. Young, *Knowledge and Control*. London, Collier Macmillan.

Jackson, B., and Marsden, D. (1966) *Education and the Working Class*, Penguin.

Kandel, I. (1935) *The Making of Nazis*. New York, Bureau of Publications, Teachers College, Columbia University.

Kozol, J. (1985) *Illiterate America*. New York, Anchor and Doubleday.

Lauwerys, J. (1967) 'Opening Address'. In *General Education in a Changing World*. The Hague, Martinus Nijhoff.

Levin, H. (1978) 'The Dilemma of Secondary School Comprehensive Reforms in Western Europe'. *Comparative Education Review* 22 (3)

Lindblom, S. (1978) 'Our Paradigm for Development and the Cultural Crisis. *Internationale Entwicklung* 3 (10).

Livingstone, D. (1987) *Critical Pedagogy and Cultural Power*. South Hadley, Massachusetts, Bergin and Garvey, p. 7.

Luke, A. (1988) *Literacy, Textbooks and Ideology*. Sussex, Falmer.

Marcuse, H. (1968) *One Dimensional Man.* London , Sphere.

Mc Carthy, T. (1978) *The Critical Theory of Jürgen Habermas.* London, Hutchinson.

Mills, C. W. (1939) 'Language, Logic and Culture'. *American Sociological Review* 4(5).

Offe, C. (1975) *Strukturprobleme des kapitalistischen Staates. Aufsätze zur politischen Soziologie*, Frankfurt, Suhrkamp.

Popper, K. (1972) *Objective Knowledge.* Oxford, Oxford University Press.

Rose, R. (1980) *Challenge to Governance: Studies in Overloaded Politics.* Beverly Hills, California, Sage.

Scott, A., and Scott, R. (1980) 'Censorship and Political Education in Queensland'. *International Journal of Political Education* 3.

Shor, I. (1986) *Culture Wars. School and Society in the Conservative Restoration 1969-84.* Boston, Routledge and Kegan Paul.

Smith, R., and Knight, J. (1981) 'Censorship in the Teaching of the Social Sciences'. *Australian Journal of Education* 25 (1).

Smith, R., and Knight, J. (1978) MACOS in Queensland'. *Australian Journal of Education* 22 (3).

Tawney, R.H. 1931 (1964) *Equality.* London, Allen and Unwin.

Toh, S-H., and Farrelly, T. (1992) 'The Formation of Third World Technocrats for Rural Development: A Critical Perspective on Australia's Role in Study Abroad'. In R.J. Burns and A.R. Welch, *Contemporary Perspectives in Comparative Education.* New York, Garland.

Vaughan, M., and Archer, M. (1971) *Social Conflict and Educational Change in England and France 1789–1848.* Cambridge, Cambridge University Press.

Weiler, H. (1982) 'Education, Public Confidence and the Legitimacy of the Modern State'. *Phi Delta Kappan* 64(1) September.

Weiler, H. (1983) 'Legalization, Expertise, and Participation: Strategies of Compensatory Legitimation in Educational Policy'. *Comparative Education Review* 27 (2).

Weiler, H. (1989) 'Why Reforms Fail: The Politics of Education in France and the Federal Republic of Germany'. *Journal of Curriculum Studies,* 21 (4).

Weiler, H. (1983) 'Education Public Confidence and the Legitimacy of the Modern State: Is there a Crisis Somewhere?' *Journal of Curriculum Studies* 15 (2), April–June.

Weiss, J. (1979) 'Access to Influence: Some Effects of Policy Sector on the Use of Social Science'. *American Behavioural Scientist,* January/February.

Welch, A., and Freebody, P. (1991) 'Alfabeticizacion, Cultura y Estado'. *Revista De Educacion* 293.

Welch, A., and Freebody, P. (1992) *Knowledge, Culture and Power: International Perspectives on Literacy Policies and Practices.* London, Falmer, U.K.

Welch, A.R. (1981) 'Curriculum as Institution and Ideology'. *New Education* 2 &3 (1).

Welch, A.R. (1985) 'The Functionalist Tradition in Comparative Education'. *Comparative Education* 19 (2).

Welch, A. (1991) 'La Ciencia Sedante: El Funcionalismo como Base para la Investigacion en Educacion Comparada'. In J. Schriewer and F. Pedro, *Educacion Comparada: Teorias, Investigaciones, Perspectivas.* Barcelona, Herder.

Welch, A.R., and Freebody, P. (1990) 'Literacy, Culture and the State'. Comparative Education Society of Europe, Madrid, July.

Welch, A.R. (1986) 'Sociology without Society? A Critique of Quotidian Reason in Comparative Education.'. *Journal of International and Comparative Education* 1 (1).

Young, M. (1971) *Knowledge and Control. New Directions in the Sociology of Knowledge.* London, Collier Macmillan.

Young, M., et al. *Radical Science Journal.*

Comparative Education Redefined?

RONALD F. PRICE

Centre for Comparative and Policy Studies
School of Education,
La Trobe University, Victoria

The outsider, looking at comparative education, is perhaps surprised at the extent to which the insiders have been worried and have indulged in self-criticism and soul-searching during the past decades. The anxiety to be recognised by the rest of the academic community[1] as a real social science with a recognised methodology has resulted in a considerable literature. One example was the volume of *Comparative Education Review* devoted to 'The State of the Art: Twenty Years of Comparative Education' (1977: 21, 2 & 3). More recently we have had Erwin Epstein's plea for the recognition of 'ideology' by practitioners, first as the Presidential Address to the US Comparative and International Education Society's annual meeting of 1982 and then again in *Compare* of 1987 on the occasion of honouring Brian Holmes. This is to cite a only a handful of the large literature devoted to the genre. While adding to this literature is not to my taste I am compelled to do so by the concern I feel, not so much with comparative education but with the state of the world in general and education in particular, and by the desire I feel that the work to which I have devoted a considerable slice of my life should be of more than personal satisfaction. This would certainly classify me among those whose aim Epstein regarded as 'practical' (he comments that 'we display almost an obsession over the need to achieve some practical benefit from comparative study' [1983: 6]) and I freely confess to being 'ideological' in some of the rather many meanings he gave that term (cf. Holmes 1983: 42).

I am encouraged to write in this vein by two things. Firstly, during the last seventeen years I have found a majority of students taking comparative education courses have done so in the hope that they will learn about a better way of living and learning. Many have chosen to study China, Sweden or the USSR with that hope in mind. Of course they have been naive and their ideas have been ill-defined and diffuse. But they have been sincere and anxious, as young teachers-to-be, to do a better job than was done to them. They have been altruistic! That their study of comparative education has only served to disillusion them is a sad comment on our predicament, but it is also a challenge I have sought to take up.

Secondly, I am encouraged by a long tradition of writers in comparative education who have put before us the need to contribute to solving, in the words of a recent writer, 'the great problems of our epoch' (M. Pecherski in Dilger et al. 1986: 147). Of course, all too many writers in the field have followed too narrowly the precept put forward by Jullien in 1817, that 'education should become a positive science' and that 'facts and observations... should be ranged in analytical tables, easily compared, in order to deduce principles and definite rules' (cit. in Hans 1958: 1). Nicholas Hans himself, writing in London in 1947, saw his book as being of interest not only to teachers, but also to 'the general reading public' because he considered 'educational reforms' (i.e. reform of schooling) to be 'intimately connected with politics, with problems of race, nationality, language and religious and social ideals' (Hans ix), i.e. 'the great problems'. He chose as case studies England, the US, France and the USSR because 'both in the past and in the present' he considered they had been 'leaders of humanity in building up a new democratic society and supplied the ideas which later became the property of all nations and all races' (324). His book looks to the past as a means of understanding his present and and as a guide to the future. That his ideal was, as he put it, 'that grand ideal of culture générale' (325) rather than a recognition of the real problems of the liberal democracies he admired, does not detract from the value of his general approach. He was concerned with values and the possibilities of human life and accepted it as a function of the educated to see life whole and to make judgements rather than to adjust to narrow interest and temporary political or economic order. A recent writer from the same European Enlightenment tradition is Bogdan Suchodolski of the University of Warsaw. Writing in a Festschrift for the German Comparativist, Oskar Anweiler, he calls for 'a vision of a new, a "different" future'. Recognising that schooling is largely a conservative and adaptive force he invokes organisations like UNESCO and the Club of Rome as providers of an alternative vision (Dilger et al. 1986: 19–20). He refers to the 'growing threat of total catastrophe', both through irreversible pollution of the environment and through the consequences of the unprecedented level of arms production (Dilger et al. 1986: 18). Other writers in this Festschrift look in a similar direction. I have already referred to Mieczyslaw Pecherski who, like Suchodolski, refers to the Club of Rome's 'no limits to learning' and to the 'creation of a new and rational society' (Dilger et al. 1986: 156). He counterposes 'the destruction of the world' and 'the improvement of life on earth' (ibid) but does not offer us any real guidance in how comparative education might help. A number of contributors to the Festschrift, however, do offer, either explicitly or implicitly, a focus for comparative education studies which I believe could help, and there are other similarly directed writings to which I shall refer. But first let me define what I see as the 'threat' and the alternative.

Like many others I am, as Epstein might say, 'obsessed' with the contrast between the wealth devoted to war and the profit of big corporations and the poverty and unemployment which afflicts so many human beings. I am 'obsessed' by the threat to human and other life posed by polluting industries which put short-term profit before the social good. Put differently, how can we establish a genuinely democratic, co-operative society which would finally eliminate the absurdity of poverty in the midst of plenty (which has been the general lot of humankind) and solve the ecological crisis: the threats of soil depletion, water poisoning, destruction of the ozone layer, loss of genetic variety and the like. In my 'ideology' there is a direct connection between a political economy which puts commodity exchange and the accumulation of monetary capital first and the widely recognised threats to human, and an ecologically sustaining, life. The educational problem is not so much that the problems are not recognised, nor even that the connection I have just stated is not widely made. It is that problems are perceived in isolation and the means for their solution are not clear. It is, perhaps, here that comparative education could make a small contribution.

There is a previous question to any consideration of comparative education, which is the way in which academia fosters the exploration of what is and the extrapolation of future trends rather than the consideration of questions of what might or what ought to be. The various disciplines, therefore, too often become a rationalisation, a justification of the status quo, rather than a critical exploration of the problems which face humankind. This is particularly so where the institution and/or the discipline is closely linked with particular interests. The links may be administrative, where the research school is government-funded and controlled, with, perhaps, the research topics determined in more or less detail by the government. Governments may say, as does the Australian government in its 1988 White Paper on Education, that it wants a higher education system which will not fail to 'criticise the society in which it operates' (Dawkins 1988: 7). But when it comes to it few will pay for radical criticism, and it would be naive to expect otherwise. Comparative education, in seeking to become a tool of government advising is forced into a conceptual framework where criticism is unlikely to be radical and, I would add, where the focus is likely to be on the wrong problems. However, it is more a question of internal definition of disciplines and the methodologies they employ than of external influence. The 'great problems' find themselves divided, and lost, between the disciplines of Philosophy, Psychology, Economics, Physics, to mention but a few. It is here that comparative education, drawing on all of these disciplines but bound by none of them, offers the opportunity to discuss the real world as the whole that it is. To those who have argued the difficulty of being familiar with more than one or a few disciplines I would counter with the difficulty of breaking out of conceptual frameworks once learned and the identification and avoidance of the game-playing nature of so much of academic disciplinary activity.

The search by Comparative Educators for an ideal methodology faces another problem which the destructive nature of much of modern technology is bringing increasingly to the fore. A broad range of people are expressing doubts about the attempt to apply universally the methodology developed by Newtonian Physics. This narrow mechanism, or reductionism as it is referred to by such writers as Steven Rose, is seen as unsuitable for the natural sciences today, as well as for the so-called social sciences and humanities.[2] Therefore I consider much of the discussion which has diverted comparative educators over the years, in part an attempt to fit our discipline into that mechanistic frame, to be doubly unhelpful. Not only has the object been too narrowly conceived, but the methodological debate has been one-dimensional.

There are other common features of academia which make the handling of the 'great problems' difficult. Within the institutions the ladders to the clouds to a great extent predetermine what kind of research and teaching is done. The constraints of examinations is an old story, often retold. The concept of what a master's or a doctoral thesis is; the difficulties of accepting group research reports; the problems of finding examiners for genuinely new topics; all these factors make for a conservative pattern and encourage the careful treading of already marked-out paths. There is a rhetoric of new, creative and critical, but the reality is somewhat different. Promotion and tenure, increasingly a problem for younger staff, depend on acceptance of traditions rather than critical excursions into the unestablished. These last two are also often dependent on relations outside the institution. Then it is necessary to 'publish or perish', and this again requires conformity to existing patterns. The established, and therefore acceptable, journals draw their referees from those established in the discipline and have an established editorial set. It may be difficult to find a publisher for an unusual topic or for an approach radically different to the norm. A socially significant example of this is the difficulty which those working on the danger of low radiation for human health have in getting their papers published in mainstream journals (Chowka 1980: 30–2). An example in comparative education is one from my own experience. With a colleague I am currently studying the teaching of science in Chinese schools. But comparative education journals and journals of Chinese Studies tend to publish broad, policy-type articles. Journals specialising in science education tend not to publish papers on foreign curricula problems. Papers which attempt to illuminate wider problems through detailed examination of curricula and school textbook materials are hard to place. This has, of course, been said many times. The knowledge is widespread, but the will to solve the problems is vitiated by particular interest.

TOWARD A NEW FOCUS

In 1981 Ludwig Liegle of the University of Tübingen made a number of suggestions for a change of perspective in comparative education which anticipated those I made in my *Marx and Education in Late Capitalism* in 1986. These were: (1) the shifting of central attention from the schools and pedagogic ideas to the subjects of education, children and youth; (2) putting in the foreground out-of-school groups like the family, adults, neighbours, the local community, the work-world and the learnings of freetime and from the media; (3) thematising this 'environment-education': learning through participation and action, through interaction and communication, through observations, etc.; (4) studying the effects of the 'hidden curriculum' of competition and striving for achievement, of feelings of anxiety and aggression and of the expression of youth cultures and generation-conflicts; and (5) the shifting of focus from only cognitive education to the development of values and political culture, and to those psychological structures on which the reproduction and change of society depend (Dilger et al. 1986: 103–04). Liegle's account of developments in the study of socialisation in the USSR in his Festschrift contribution, where these suggestions were repeated, and where I first read them, fails to bring out the real value of his proposals (Dilger et al. 1986: 109–18). To me this lies especially in where he speaks of 'the development of those psychological structures which serve the reproduction (or also the change and putting in question) of society' (Dilger et al., 104). I would only remove the brackets!

It is, of course, not new to recognise that learning, and important learning, takes place outside the school, and that this has important consequences for the learnings which occur within the school. What is new is the attention being given to these processes by educators who in the past have devoted their attention too one-sidedly to the schools and to teaching within them. A nice example of this is the Eighty-fourth Yearbook of the National Society for the Study of Education which was devoted to *Education in School and Nonschool Settings* and had chapters devoted to such 'other educational settings' as families; workplace; museums; religious institutions; youth-serving agencies; media and technology (Fantini and Sinclair 1985). However, we must distinguish here those who look at the whole range of teachings and learnings which occur in these different, but interacting agencies, and those who concentrate on their role as intentional teachers. An example of the latter is the book, *Maverick of the Education Family: Two Essays in Non-Formal Education*, a book which describes the diverse teaching provided by organisations of many kinds in Botswana (Townsend Coles 1982). So far as 'the great problems' are concerned, the unintended learnings and teachings are at least as important as the intended, and, of course, much more difficult to theorise.

Let us try to put these aspirations and suggestions for a change of focus together and see what it might mean for comparative education. Taking first the suggestions of Liegle, I would not restrict the shift of focus to 'children and youth', his first point, but include people of all ages. My focus change would be on the content of the learning-teaching processes in which they are involved, a content which includes knowledge, skills, beliefs, values, attitudes and feelings. I agree completely with his second point, that the focus needs to be shifted to the out-of-school situation, and with his third point, the need to thematise this. But I would like to do this through clarification of 'the great problems' as identified by significant groups in different societies. In *Marx and Education in Late Capitalism* I particularly discussed the women's movement, the peace movement and the trade unions as significant educational groups. The ecology movement should certainly be added to that list. But my point is that comparative education studies could reveal which groups were significant, where, in what ways, to what numbers and kinds of people. Thematisation through 'great problems' would bring together learnings and teachings in and by different groups. For example, the important questions of the use of nuclear fission processes, whether 'for war' or 'for peace', are differently expressed in the peace movement and the ecology movement. A holistic understanding requires that the teachings of both these movements are considered, as well, of course, as the more obvious governmental, industrial and academic sources. Such examination requires careful analysis of the logical skills taught: of question formulation, the selection of evidence and its evaluation; the clarification of values involved; and the clarification of the interests of the parties concerned.[3]

What does this all mean for the aims of comparative education? It is not suggested that it should become a political movement! It will continue to be an academic discipline, a study of, among other things, political movements. The aim, as I believe it should be of all studies, will continue to be understanding. But that understanding will be more clearly focussed on those learning-teaching processes within which, as I put it elsewhere, 'human beings learn the lessons which determine their being and their becoming' (Price, 1986: 279). With that focus the school will find its rightful place, central for some people and peripheral or absent for others. Such a focus I would expect to assist us by clarifying the visions which different groups have of 'a new and different future' (Suchodolski) and the means by which it might be achieved. More than that an academic discipline cannot hope for. More requires practice, but practice in part guided by the understanding which comparative education could help provide.

I would like to conclude this essay by examining some comparative education and other studies in the light of the focus I have been outlining. I shall suggest that there already exist many studies which can be built upon.

WORK WORLD AND WORLD VIEW

One way or another educators of all persuasions have seen work in some form as important for education. Writing in 1929, Pinkevitch, then President of the Second State University of Moscow, outlined the ideas of educators towards 'labour in the school'. He classified educators on a scale ranging from 'reactionary bourgeoisie' (Neuendorf) to 'Proletarian-communists' (Kalashnikov, Blonski) (Pinkevitch 1929: 165). Naturally he gave John Dewey careful attention. The interesting Soviet contemporary of Pinkevitch's, Shul'gin, is cited as saying: 'To us labour . . . is the best method of teaching children how to live the contemporary life' (Pinkevitch 199; Fitzpatrick 1979: 139–44; Price 1984). Today governments and employers are looking to the schools to solve problems of unemployment or to help with 'modernising' the economy, as in China. The difficulty of looking at the work world in a different way is shown very clearly in the contribution of Marvin Feldman, President of the Fashion Institute of Technology, NY, to the already cited book on *Education in School and Nonschool Settings* (Fantini and Sinclair 1985: 102–13). Writing about "The Workplace as Educator' Feldman begins: 'The modern corporation does everything schools do, and more' (Fantini and Sinclair 1985: 102). He mentions instructing, motivating, athletics and other 'interest groups', medical treatment and prevention, and (in Japan) company songs! When he writes 'Clearly the experience of working is itself a learning experience' (Fantini and Sinclair 1985: 102) one's hopes are raised, only to be dashed when one quickly finds he is speaking of employers' requirements of work experience. Feldman is not talking about learning a world view. Again one's hopes are raised when he goes on to speak of 'unresolved ethical, political, and pedagogical questions' and to ask 'to what extent should schools shape students to the requirements of the workplace and to what extent should educators ignore the requirements of the workplace (thus, perhaps, making their graduates less employable) and insist on a more balanced and broadly liberal learning experience?' (Fantini and Sinclair 1985: 107–08). But he does not spell out what he sees as value contradictions or just what these ethical, etc. problems are. As for the possibility of a different type of economic system, this appears to be unthinkable? We are only told: 'The school, however, is the steward of a community's larger educational responsibility. The school must bring to contractual arrangements a sense of the noncommercial values that must nourish any true educational effort' (Fantini and Sinclair 1985: 108). Above all, like so many other writers today (Jones 1982) he gives a very misleading impression of the general economic trend. He sees 'our whole economy [as] converting to a new, dramatically different technological base' in which 'everybody in the system' is going to be 'pushed up a notch' in the social hierarchy (Fantini and Sinclair 1985: 110). Far from understanding the capitalist nature of current technological developments, i.e their function in furthering the production of surplus value and capital accumulation rather than the social good, he sees it in abstract technological-social terms, in terms of a change of skills for which schools and industry alike must train people. For a more realistic view of modern capitalism, indeed the whole current world economy, one must turn to such writers as Joyce Kolko (1988). The volume edited by Rachel Sharp (1986) is also valuable for its attempt to answer the question:

> whether there are common elements in the structuring and restructuring of the forms of capitalist schooling which relate to the underlying logic and dynamic of the capitalist mode of production as analysed by the framework of historical materialism. (Sharp 1985: xxiii)

The accounts of the various national economies and the changes in schooling provide a basis for the kind of examination I am suggesting, even though the version of Marxism Sharp et al. offer is inadequate for that task. For realism about the so-called 'information society' Webster and Robins (1986) are also helpful.

For an understanding of the work world in terms of teachings and learnings there already exists a large data base in sociology. Some of the seminal papers have recently been collected together by R.E. Pahl under the title *On Work: Historical, Comparative & Theoretical Approaches* (1988). Studying this topic with education in mind might help to more usefully relate questions about conceptualising the economy,[4] conceptualising work (Pahl ch. 32, 33), and the actual experience of work of different kinds. Studies of workshops from the inside like those of Burrawoy give some insight into learnings as well as teachings (Pahl ch. 8, 9; cf. Pfeffer 1979). Others, particularly those which give an overview of the ongoing changes in the nature of the workforce, throw light on teachings. Important here are the division between the so-called 'permanent' labour force and the 'flexible' (Pahl, 602–03) and the redivision of societies with the dirty, dangerous and usually lowest-paid jobs going to 'women, the young, and migrants' (Murray in Pahl 266, speaking of Italy, cf. Davis 1986: 304–05 for the US). Accounts like that of Wallraff, who posed as a Turkish worker in Germany in order to expose conditions there, present a close-up of one of these migrant groups (1988). But what should one expect of an examination of the work world in terms of education? To many it may appear a lesson in disillusionment, in defeated aspirations and retreat into cynical individualism: 'I'm all right Jack!' No doubt for many that is the lesson learnt. But examination of the needs and aspirations of people in the concrete conditions of their working lives (including the conditions of those denied work by the present system) and comparison of these with the possibilities offered by the present technical-scientific knowledge available, I believe, suggests disillusionment is a partial picture. A more thorough understanding of the present distribution of knowledge, beliefs and values, and of the barriers to its wider distribution could help change this, preparing the way for practical change.

Returning to a consideration of the school, the question of what is taught by and learnt within the real world of work is a very different one from that of the teachings/learnings that have occurred in the various experiments known variously as Radical Education or Open Schooling. Comparative education has not yet usefully evaluated these experiments, either by conceptualizing them or locating them in the social contexts in which they took place. One of the few recent Comparative writings on more general aspects of 'radical education' is that by Knaup and Wompel on 'Openness as an educational-political category in centralised systems: Poland and France' (Dilger et al. 1986: 441–75). While they testify to the persisting interest in the concept of 'openness', to recognition and use of teachings and learnings in and through other institutions than the school in both Poland and France, they do not explore the nature of these in any depth. But they make the interesting point that in Poland, where the concept has been part of official educational policy for longer, out-of-school institutions are used to reinforce official 'socialist' teaching, whereas in France, where the school has traditionally been cut off from society outside, openness takes more varied forms and pays more attention to changing relations on a personal-social level (Dilger et al. 1986: 474). The authors appear to recognise the need to relate their study to the wider out-of-school situation, but it is not clear in what sense they would do this.

At the beginning of this section I referred to Pinkevtich and Shul'gin and the latter's ideas on labour as teacher. The arguments of Soviet educators and Communist Party officials over 'polytechnical education' have been often told.[5] In the more recent past the term became simply a halo word (Price 1977: 184–219). My attempt to categorize the various uses of this term and the wider concept of 'linking education with productive labour' as used in the USSR and China in a way which could be used to evaluate different experiences has not been followed up. Writers continue to accept current Soviet usage unanalysed. Muckle's very useful recent study makes the mistake of regarding Khrushchev's reforms as 'making (polytechnical education) compulsory again', when the essence of them was monotechnical; and he fails to distinguish between the Marx-Krupskaya tradition in which polytechnical education was to teach a critical understanding of society, and that of Stalin-Gorbachev which is that of adjusting the student to the current social norms and work world (Muckle 1988: 35–6). In any case, what is needed is studies which show the relation between what is taught and the lessons of the world of work outside the school.

The concepts polytechnical education and 'combining education with productive labour' belong to the wider concept of moral-political education, and to this I will now turn.

MORAL-POLITICAL EDUCATION

One recent definition is that of Roberta Sigel: moral-political education is 'the process by which people learn to adopt the norms, values, attitudes and behaviours accepted and practised by the on-going system' (cit. Price 1986: 164–5). But this is to neglect the problem posed by the gulf between what is accepted in words and in deeds, or by different groups within a society, and the equally important learning, the rejection or simple ignoring of those norms. In many cases one might wish to argue the need for the last! Have not our present set of values come about historically through people rejecting the teachings of their times? But the schools and those studies based on them do not often discuss this, confining themselves to conformity and adaptation. One clear example of this is the set of common themes prepared by the International Civic Education Committee for the IEA Civic Education study (Torney and Oppenheim in Price 1986: 172). Under 'Behavioural Content' we find 'willingness to obey the law, pay taxes' and the like, propositions which seem at variance with society's real problems.

In the school it is widely recognised that moral-political education takes place in all subjects, being especially explicit in literature, history and the social sciences. Muckle notes that for Soviet educators '[p]olytechnism is a spirit which is meant to permeate the whole of education' (36). At the same time there is a long tradition of special subjects in schools. If one goes back to beginnings, whether in China or Christian Europe, one must recognise that the early curriculum was almost entirely moral-political in subject matter. But in modern times, while occupying a less overt position and putting aside religious teaching, there have been many varieties of moral-political courses (Price 1986: 173–82). Most recently a number of new courses have appeared with names like Peace Studies, Women's Studies, Global Education, the Humanities Curriculum Project (Schools Council/Nuffield), or World Studies. These have led to a new controversy about Controversial Issues in the Curriculum, to use the title of a recent book (Wellington 1986). But the discussion appears to revolve around problems of 'indoctrination' and the best methods of teaching such subjects, if they are to be taught, rather than around the substantive nature of the issues and the skills required for judgements. Two expressions of this kind are:

> Pike and Selby: 'There remains, for instance, something essentially 'unpeaceful' about the teacher who lectures on peace issues from the front of the class'. (Wellington 49)

> Aspin: 'the teaching methods adopted will be, one imagines, much less likely to succeed if they are predicated upon the confrontational or the heavily authoritarian model still favoured by some teachers in this area'. (Wellington 145)

One of the promising lines of study for our purposes is that of content analysis. Because of the overt nature of moral-political teaching in the USSR, and more recently China, there have been a number of studies of the content of teaching in the schools of these countries. Some of these, like *The Making of a Model Citizen in Communist China* (Ridley, Godwin and Dooley 1971) and the more recent *Was Maos Erben in der Schule lernen* (Bos and Straka 1987) attempt to be 'scientific' by the use of elaborate attempts at 'objectivity', counting and statistical juggling. In the process the content of the teaching is reduced to banalities like the number of times something is referred to, or complex passages are reduced to vague terms like 'order', 'patriotism' or 'friendship'. Better are such 'subjective' accounts as *What Ivan Knows that Johnny Doesn't* (Trace 1961), or T. Scrase in this volume, where the approach is clear but the detail provided allows readers to make their own judgement.[6] More studies along these lines, combined with the approach of Bronfenbrenner's (1974) *Two Worlds of Childhood (US and USSR)* might bring us nearer the goal I am suggesting. But one further step is required. Bronfenbrenner's world is that of childhood. Much more attention needs to be given to the adult world, the world of work and unemployment, and the ongoing and inter-acting teaching-learning processes of adults, youth and children.

CONCLUSION

I have tried to argue two things in this essay: that the focus of research and teaching in comparative education should be shifted more towards the learning and teaching about the 'great problems' which humankind faces today; and that comparative education, because of its embracing the various disciplines is in a unique position to do this. I have shown that I am not alone in making this call for a shift of focus, and that there is already a precedent for it. I have also drawn attention to the existing demand for such a focus from many who choose to study comparative education at the post-graduate teacher training level. Such a reorientation could pave the way for a similar and much-needed reorientation in schooling at other levels.

So far as teaching is concerned, it is not difficult to show what is taught, where, how and to whom (by class and number). What is difficult is to say anything worthwhile about learning. Here we are faced with definitional and psychological problems: the nature and interrelations of knowing, understanding, believing, and, a jump, behaving. The last is what is visible but is it congruent with intentions, feelings, beliefs? What about the possibilities, perceived and real? It is doubtful to what extent comparative education can help us in these difficult areas. But it may at least be able to clarify some of the questions.

NOTES

1. Community is a much misused word. In reality, the academic world is more often mean and competitive than it is cooperative and supportive.

2. Needham's position has been often repeated. Best seen in his *Science & Civilisation in China,* it is also shortly expressed in his contribution to Hilary & Steven Rose, *The Radicalisation of Science.* See also Rose, Lewontin & Kamin, *Not in Our Genes,* and Levins & Lewontin, *The Dialectical Biologist,* Musschenga & Gosling, *Science Education & Ethical Values.*

3. Much of the heart-searching about impartiality and neutrality would be unnecessary if there was more clarity about what is meant by a value, and more attention were paid to the logical skills I have outlined. It should not be a question of 'support[ing] alternative points of view equally' (Bridges in Wellington, 1986, 31), but of making judgements about the evidence presented in favour of this or that proposition.

4. Gershuny's 'formal and informal economies' and his calculations of a time-based system of accounts (Pahl, 579–97), discussions of the limitations of the measurement of Gross National Product and alternative ways of measuring the contribution of economic activities (Ekins, 128–66) and Marxist approaches which focus on concepts of exploitation and the form of production and appropriation of a surplus are useful here.

5. Perhaps the best is that by Oskar Anweiler (1964). Fitzpatrick is excellent. Regrettably Zepper's study of Krupskaya does not appear to have

been turned into a book and there remains a dearth of good studies of, or even translations into English of her writings.

6. I recently completed a study of Moral-Political Education in Chinese Schools (1988, manuscript) which cites heavily from Chinese textbooks and teachers' materials.

REFERENCES

Anweiler, Oskar (1964) *Geschichte der Schule und Pädagogik in Russland vom Ende des Zarenreiches bis zum Beginn der Stalin-Ära*. Heidelberg, Quelle and Meyer.

Bos, Wilfried and Straka, Gerald A. (1987) *Was Maos Erben in der Schule lernen: Ergebnisse einer vergleichenden Inhaltsanalyse von Grundschult-extbüchern der VR China*. Münster, Waxmann.

Bronfenbrenner, Urie (1974) *Two Worlds of Childhood: US and USSR* (1970). Harmondsworth, Penguin Books.

Chowka, P.B. (1980) 'A Tale of Nuclear Tyranny', *New Age*, August, pp. 26–35, 68–9.

Davis, Mikc (1986) *Prisoners of the American Dream: Politics and Economy in the History of the US Working Class*. London, Verso.

Dawkins, J.S. (1988) *Higher Education: A Policy Statement* (The White Paper). Canberra, Australian Government Publishing Service.

Dilger, B., F. Kuebart and Schäfer, H-P. (eds.) (1986) *Vergleichende Bildungsforschung: DDR, Osteuropa und interkulturelle Perspektiven (Festschrift für Oskar Anweiler zum 60. Geburtstag)*. Berlin, Arno Spitz.

Ekins, Paul (1986) *The Living Economy: A New Economics in the Making*. London, Routledge and Kegan Paul.

Epstein, Erwin, H. (1983) 'Currents Left and Right: Ideology in Comparative Education'. *Comparative Education Review* 27 (1): 3–29.

Epstein, Erwin, H. (1987) 'Among the Currents: a Critique of Critiques of "Ideology in Comparative Education"'. *Compare* 17 (1): 17–28.

Fantani, M.D. and Sinclair, R.L. (eds.) (1985) *Education in School amd Nonschool Settings* (84th Yearbook of the National Society for the Study of Education). Chicago, University of Chicago Press.

Fitzpatrick, Sheila (1979) *Education and Social Mobility in the Soviet Union, 1921–1934*. Cambridge University Press.

Hans, Nicholas (1958) *Comparative Education: A Study of Educational Factors and Traditions*, 3rd ed. (1949). London, Routledge and Kegan Paul.

Holmes, Brian (1983) 'Commentary on Epstein', *Comparative Education Review* 27 (1): 42–5.

Jones, Barry (1982/86) *Sleepers, Wake! Technology and the Future of Work.* Melbourne, Oxford University Press.

Kolko, Joyce (1988) *Restructuring the World Economy.* New York, Pantheon Books.

Levins, Richard and Lewontin, Richard (1985) *The Dialectical Biologist.* Cambridge, Mass., Harvard University Press.

Muckle, James (1988) *A Guide to the Soviet Curriculum: What the Russian Child is Taught in School.* London, Croom Helm.

Musschenga, B. and Gosling, D. (1985) *Science Education and Ethical Values.* Washington, D.C., Georgetown University Press.

Needham, Joseph (1954–ongoing) *Science and Civilisation in China* (especially vol. 2). Cambridge University Press.

Pahl, R.E. (1988) *On Work: Historical, Comparative and Theoretical Approaches.* Oxford, Basil Blackwell.

Pfeffer, Richard M. (1979) *Working for Capitalism.* New York, Columbia University Press.

Pinkevitch, Albert P. (1929) *The New Education in the Soviet Republic* (ed. George S. Counts; trans. Nucia Perlmutter). New York, John Day.

Price, R.F. (1977) *Marx and Education in Russia and China.* London, Croom Helm.

Price, R.F. (1984) 'Searching for a Marxist Education: the Soviet Union and China', *Slavic and European Education Review* 1982 (2)–1984 (1, 2): 7–20.

Price, R.F. (1986) *Marx and Education in Late Capitalism.* London, Croom Helm.

Price, R.F. (1988) *Moral-Political Education in Chinese Schools* (manuscript, p. 253).

Ridley, C.P., Godwin, P.H.B. and Doolin, D.J. (1971) *The Making of a Model Citizen in Communist China.* Stanford, The Hoover Institution Press.

Rose, Hilary and Rose, Steven (1976) *The Radicalisation of Science.* London, Macmillan.

Rose, Steven, Lewontin, R.C. and Kamin, Leon J. (1987) *Not in Our Genes: Biology, Ideology and Human Nature* (1984, Pantheon). Harmondsworth, Penguin Books.

Sharp, Rachel (ed.) (1986) *Capitalist Crisis and Schooling: Comparative Studies in the Politics of Education.* Melbourne, Macmillan.

Townsend Coles, Edwin K. (1982) *Maverick of the Education Family: Two Essays in Non-Formal Education*. Oxford, Pergamon Press.

Trace, Arthur S. (1961) *What Ivan Knows that Johnny Doesn't*. New York, Random House.

Wallraff, Günter (1988) *Ganz unten. Mit einer Dokumentation der Folgen* (1985). Köln, Kiepenheuer and Witsch.

Webster, Frank, and Robins, Kevin (1986) *Information Technology: a Luddite Analysis*. Norwood, New Jersey, Ablex Publishing Corporation.

Wellington, J.J. (ed.) (1986) *Controversial Issues in the Curriculum*. London, Basil Blackwell.

Zepper, J.T. (1960) 'A Study of N.K. Krupskaya's Educational Philosophy'. Unpublished PhD thesis, University of Missouri.

Education in the Third World: Present Realities and Future Prospects

M.K. BACCHUS

Centre for International Education and Development
Faculty of Education, University of Alberta
Edmonton, Alberta, Canada

Before attempting to discuss the current educational situation in the developing countries and speculate about its future it would be useful to examine the historical realities within which these systems developed. This should provide a better understanding of both the current and possible future role which education plays and is likely to play in these societies. The developing countries have nearly all been colonies at one time or another and even though a few of them might not have been formally colonized their development was strongly influenced by a relationship which was essentially colonial in character. Their educational systems have therefore largely emerged out of this context and were essentially part of the institutional infra-structure of the colonial state.

One can roughly identify three broad phases in the development of education in most ex-colonies (Bacchus et al. 1988). The first was during their period of "primitive accumulation" prior to their colonization. Their traditional educational systems were largely non-formal though some more formal institutions, such as Koranic schools, also existed. The education which was provided in these pre-colonial days was directed mainly at the development in the young of the skills, knowledge, attitudes and values which were necessary for the economic survival and social cohesion of the groups. This was largely achieved through the transmission of their traditional practices, values, and beliefs including their rituals and myths. It was not focussed on fostering economic development or providing opportunities for individual social mobility. One of the major functions of these early educational systems, therefore, was to assist in ensuring social stability rather than in producing social change. In other words, it was geared primarily at preparing the young to grapple with those realities of life which they were going to face in their transition to full adult status. But such realities were usually those which were created by the groups themselves, or were influenced by the physical conditions under which they lived, and not the result of conditions imposed on them by an outside group of colonizers.

The next phase can be referred to as the "middle period" during which the establishment of the colonial state became a reality. Modern colonialism started around 1500 and occurred in two major spurts. The first began with the colonization of the West Indies and the Americas in the late fifteenth and early sixteenth century while the second period started from about the mid-nineteenth century and saw the rapid expansion of the Europcan colonial empire. The initial efforts were primarily directed at establishing control over the colonized and developing an infrastructure of 'law and order' as defined by the colonizers. This period was usually referred to by early colonial historians as one of "pacification" and it was often achieved by the raw use of force over the colonized (Oliver and Fage 1962). In some colonies the state functions were initially carried by private companies such as the East India Company, the Royal Niger Company, the British South African Company but by the mid-nineteenth century they were increasingly taken over directly by the metropolitan governments.

There were two major goals of these early colonial enterprises. The first was the exploitation of the wealth of the colonies and the second was to provide for the settlement of the excess population of Europe. In other words the object of colonization was, in some cases, simply to establish "colonies of exploitation" while in other cases it was to be "colonies of settlement" and "exploitation" (Maunier 1949). The education which developed in these different types of colonies had some of their own special characteristics.

Once the new colony was established the major problem which was faced by the colonizers was the maintenance of social order and stability which were necessary for effective economic exploitation. Different strategies were used to achieve this goal such as the introduction of indirect rule by the British which gave a facade of power and control to the accepted traditional sources of authority. Another approach was to attempt to "educate" or socialize a few of the local population to accept the values, beliefs and assumptions of superiority which the colonizers had of themselves, and to use these individuals both as models for others who were aspiring to improve their conditions of life and to establish some links with the masses. As Lloyd pointed out in referring specifically to Africa "the official aim" of the colonizers was to produce some individuals "to staff the growing bureaucracies and provide a cultural bridge between the expatriates and the African masses" (Lloyd 1967).

Therefore the education provided for the indigenous population during these early years was aimed at developing among the colonized a loyal group who would undertake some of the routine administrative functions of the state. A few of these individuals were also needed to carry out the menial and unskilled jobs which became available in the European dominated sector of these economies.

The education which was provided usually comprised:

(a) language skills which equipped some of the colonized to understand thereby becoming more effective links with the masses. It also made it possible for them to follow more easily the instructions which they received.

(b) 'technical' skills which the colonized needed for the more efficient performance of their new economic roles and

(c) an introduction of the colonized to the values of the colonizers. This was often provided mainly through religious education. The colonized were in essence taught to be subservient and loyal to their imperial masters and to addept willingly their own positions at the lowest levels of the social and economic hierarchy of these societies.

In the case of colonies of settlement there was a somewhat different attitude to the establishment of schools and other educational institutions. For example, many North American colonists established schools for their children, largely on the pattern of those that existed in their countries of origin. Their goal was to transmit to the young the culture and beliefs of the parents and "to keep up Learning and all Helps of Education going, lest degeneracy, Barbarism, Ignorance and irreligion doe by degrees breake in upon us" (Mitchell 1972). By the mid-seventeenth century, laws were even passed in the New England colonies which made mandatory the establishment of "a reading and writing school" in every settlement of fifty families or more. In the Spanish colonies the emphasis was somewhat different since the educational provisions were initially directed at meeting the needs of the elites. This was obvious in the early emphasis placed on the establishment of universities in the Spanish colonies. This emergence of a dualistic educational structure in the early colonies of settlement was later repeated in Canada, Australia, and East, Central and Southern Africa where efforts were made to provide a different type of education for the indigenous population.

During the second period of colonial expansion which came in the mid-nineteenth century the control by the metropolitan power of the colonial state became more firmly established. The colonies were initially regarded simply as sources of raw materials but later, the ability of the colonized to purchase products from the metropole also became an important concern. The State therefore began to direct efforts at getting the colonized to work as labourers in the cash sectors of the economy or to grow cash crops which would allow them to earn money to purchase these imported commodities.

For those who could not find positions within the "modern" economic sector attempts were made, partly through education, to get them to improve their levels of living and their standards of health. Therefore, an education which stressed the skills needed for community development was provided along with lessons in hygiene. These early educational efforts at community development were geared towards preventing the large percentage of the population, who remained in the traditional sector, from becoming too frustrated at not being able to improve their circumstances by securing an academic education which might lead them to the better paid white collar employment in the modern sector.

THE FOCUS OF EDUCATION IN A COLONIAL STATE

The underlying assumption of this article is that the major purpose of the colonial state was the exploitation of the colonies and the colonized, not the development of educational opportunities for the masses in these societies. Admittedly, there were also some liberal minded individuals who had a humanitarian concern for the colonized but their activities were only permitted if they were compatible with the interest of the colonizers, or at least not perceived as in any way presenting a challenge to the colonial state.

The role of an institution and the diverse and specific social practices which characterizes it in any setting, including a colonial one, can only be fully understood if it is examined within the context of the means of production and the relations of individuals in the production process. From this perspective one can see that the development of colonial eduction systems was influenced by both the dynamics of the capital accumulation process and the need to maintain the power relations between different economic, political, and social groups in the colonies. A study of education in this setting therefore requires one to focus on the dynamic interaction between the State and the population and the efforts made both to foster capital accumulation and to reduce destabilizing influences in this process. But, because power relations among groups are expressed in increasingly important ways through a society's political structures, and more specifically through the State, any political economy analysis of the educational system must be based on some implicit or explicit analysis or theory of the purposes or functioning of the state (Carnoy and Levin 1985).

The liberal democratic state, as O'Connor noted, was faced with two important and sometimes contradictory functions (O'Connor 1973). They were (a) to foster capital accumulation and (b) to develop a certain degree of social harmony and consensus in society as part of its legitimation function. Such challenges were obviously also confronted by the colonial state. But while O'Connor's dual challenges of the state might be quite adequate for analyzing and explaining the social and economic policies of a liberal-democratic state, it needs a somewhat different orientation if it is to be valuable in analysing the policies of the colonial or, in many cases, the post-colonial state.

The colonial state was inherently autocratic, unrepresentative and coercive. Therefore it was much less concerned with the so-called legitimation function and its educational policies were not as heavily influenced by an attempt to balance the often contradictory demands of capital accumulation and legitimation. Instead, the capital accumulation function was the major concern of its overall policies including its educational policies. Nevertheless, since the total dependence on the use of physical control mechanisms of the State was likely to be expensive, even the colonial state had to attempt to meet certain minimal requirements in terms of creating some degree of social consensus in society. So, even though the attempt to balance the two functions was not as crucial as in a liberal democratic state, the colonial authorities increasingly tried to use the educational system to help create this minimal consensus. In other words the administrative-coercive capacity of the colonial state apparatus was increasingly supported by the nature of the education provided for the colonized.

THE OUTCOMES OF EDUCATION UNDER COLONIAL RULE

As indicated above, the colonial state was less concerned with the process of legitimation than with economic exploitation and capital accumulation. One outcome of this was that the education provided for the colonized was geared towards meeting the economic need for suitable manpower in the colonies. Since all managerial, technical and supervisory personnel tended to be recruited from the metropole, partly to ensure social control of the population, the job opportunities for highly educated local personnel in either the European dominated sector of the economy or the public service were limited. The economy mainly required individuals to fill some lower level positions such as messengers, office assistants, janitors and later postmen, letter carriers, telegraph messengers, lower clerical positions and even police constables. For these relatively few individuals, a primary education was all that was considered necessary and therefore there was some limited provision for this level of education, especially in the urban areas. For the majority of workers, who were employed as agricultural labourers in resource extraction and the production of raw material, a formal education was often regarded as unnecessary even though later, education was gradually provided for most of those working in the modern sector of these economies.

As the colonial state continued to extend its activities there began to be a need for more individuals with basic literacy and numeracy skills. Further, it was also becoming increasingly obvious that, if the colonies were to achieve the goals of the metropolitan governments by becoming financially self-supporting and increasingly profitable, there had to be a substitution of local workers for some of the highly-priced expatriates who were occupying lower level positions in the occupational hierarchy. But while reducing the costs of administering the colonial state was important it was also necessary to increase the moral support from the colonized for the State, especially from those who helped in its administration or were receiving reasonably high incomes under the present political system. Therefore, the education of these individuals was partly directed at preparing them for this supportive role and the political socialization function of such education became very important. The songs which students sang, the poems which they learnt by heart, the geography which they studied, the text-books which they used and the festivities which their schools celebrated all contributed towards developing this loyalty among the colonized.

Initially, the colonizers unilaterally decided that the type of education which would be provided for the colonized masses would be "practical" and religious in nature, with the Gospel and the Plough being the two symbols which were sometimes used to describe the nature of this education. The early educational efforts were therefore usually undertaken by missionary societies and although they often provided some practical training for their students their over-riding concern was with the "spiritual upliftment" of the "natives". They therefore pursued their own educational agenda, almost regardless of the consequences for the structure of relationships which existed among the local population as Achebe has so strikingly portrayed in his novel

"Things Fall Apart" (Achebe 1977). Nevertheless, they had operated within the colonial framework and their activities were often usually congruent with the interests of the colonial state.

The focus on practical training dominated these educational concerns. For example, in the 1890s the Secretary of States of the Colonies perceived the major need for education in the West Indian colonies to be an improvement in the quality of the labour force available for colonial agricultural enterprises. He therefore encouraged West Indian Governors to give attention to the topic of agricultural education in schools and even sent out a copy of the agricultural syllabus then used in the schools in rural France. The suggestion was that the instructional approaches to the subject in the French rural schools should prove a suitable model for West Indian schools also.

The education for those individuals who were to occupy higher level positions within the occupational structure was aimed at socializing them, not only to accept the superiority of the colonizer, but also to make them even more familiar with his culture and his ways of thinking. It was therefore usually the same type of classical secondary education which was provided in the metropole. In the French colonies it was also noted that "strict copies of metropolitan schools" were created and by 1960 "African students could feel confident that their schools offered the same curriculum available in any French town" (Gifford and Weiskel 1971). A limited number of these schools were established in the colonies and the prestige which they were expected to enjoy was often reflected in their names—Queen's College, Georgetown; Queen's Royal College, Trinidad; King's College, Lagos; Royal College, Mauritius; which hinted at some royal connection.

The British colonial government tended to maintain a secondary school in each colony which was "a showpiece bestowing great prestige on all those who passed through it". Consequently, despite the limited funds expended on education, a substantial proportion of it was spent on this one secondary school. In 1938, for example, the expenditure on Achimota secondary school in Ghana was about 25 percent of the total education budget for the colony (Lloyd 1967). One of the objectives of these schools was to impress on those locals who attended them the superiority of the colonizer. This could, for example, be seen in the observations made by the Attorney General of Trinidad who, when proposing a bill to establish a Government Secondary school—the Queen's Royal College—on the island in the 1850s, observed:

> There is . . . no training equal to that (given by) the great English public schools. . . . It may be that Providence has seen fit to make us Englishmen with such a breadth of pelvis, both physical and intellectual, that the love of freedom is a law of our being. Be that as it may, there is no doubt that Eton, and so in their order the other public schools, do produce the men who, whether in the State, or at the Bar, or in the field, in the House of Commons, or in Westminster Hall, or in the Crimea, are the leaders in the world. (Govt. of Trinidad, 1857)

In some cases when it was considered necessary to provide additional education for these local individuals in the metrople this overseas experience was expected to make them better prepared to carry out their role as mediators between the colonizers and the masses. Governor North who very early introduced such a program in Sri Lanka (then Ceylon) suggested that the education of these young men would help to ensure that while they remained

> attached to their country by birth and relations (they would become attached) to England by their education. (This will put them) in a situation in which they will be respected and without envy . . . they would . . . become the most effectual preservers of contentment, tranquility and morality among their countrymen and a means of connection between them and us. (Governor North, 1799)

The colonizers were always aware of the potential danger of having the output from schools reaching a point where there might be more educated individuals than the number of lower level jobs available for them. To prevent such a development the colonial authorities severely limited their expenditure on education. In the 1930s for example, only 4 percent of the total revenues of Nigeria and the French African colonies was being spent on education. In addition the British formulated an educational policy which stressed the need for the type of education that would deemphasize the preparation of students for these few white collar jobs. The education which was to be provided within this policy was to focus on improving the quality of life of the local population through their improved performance in their traditional social and occupational roles. The purpose was

> To make the school the means of improving the condition of the peasantry, by teaching them how health may be preserved by proper diet, cleanliness, ventilation and to give them a practical training in household economy, and in the cultivation of cottage garden, as well as in those common handicrafts by which a labourer may improve his domestic comfort. (Shuttleworth 1847)

By the end of World War I the African colonies were also already beginning to reach the point in their educational development at which it was considered that there might soon be an over-supply of school-leavers with a primary education, in relation to the number of white collar jobs that were likely to be available to them. Further, individuals from the metropole were migrating to the colonies of settlement in East, Central and Southern Africa and these migrants wanted to ensure exclusivity of the schools which their children attended and the jobs for which they were being prepared. In such a situation efforts were made to strengthen the dualistic division in the education offered in the schools—with a different type being provided for the potential elites or the white settlers and a more "practical" or "useful" type provided for the black masses.

The British Government tried to find a model for its colonial educational policies for the masses, and the education then being provided by some black communities in the southern United States was considered to be ideal for this purpose. This was because the education offered there provided the blacks with little chance of mobility into the white dominated sectors of this society and at the same time it did not seem to result in much discontent among those being educated. The British colonial authorities therefore decided to shape its educational policies, especially for its colonies in Africa, along these lines and in 1922 and 1924 it invited two Commissions, funded by the Phelps Stokes Foundation of the United States, to go out and report on education for Eastern, West, Southern and Equatorial Africa. The commissions were headed by Thomas Jesse Jones of the Hampton

Institute of North America which was a well-known educational institution for blacks.

Their focal concern of the commission was to relate education to the "needs" of the local communities so that the youngsters, after attending school, would not try to move elsewhere in search of jobs but would instead try "to fill the shoes of their parents" (Hailey 1938). Therefore in addition to agriculture, subjects like village crafts, health, hygiene and home improvement were taught. Even the academic subjects were to be related to the "living consciousness" of the population which meant that the arithmetic which was to be taught in schools was to be 'relevant' for farmers and that the teaching of vernacular languages was to be stressed. Teacher training was to have the community orientation and the adoption of Jeanes Teacher training model was proposed for this purpose. Further, the establishment of "out-schools" in rural communities which were deprived of permanent school facilities—similar to those tried out among the blacks in the Southern states of the US—was recommended.

These reports formed the basis of the 1925 *Education Policy in British Tropical Africa* which stated that:

> Education should be adapted to the mentality, aptitudes, occupations and the tradition of the (Africans) . . . , conserving as far as possible all sound and healthy elements in the fabric of their social life . . . Its aim should be to render the individual more efficient in his or her condition of life, whatever it might be, and to promote the advancement of the community as a whole. (Govt. of Great Britain 1925)

Malinowski's functional theory of society which focussed on the contribution which each institution made towards overall social equilibrium also had much influence on this development. Educating youngsters with knowledge and values that were foreign to those shared by their parents was seen as likely to have a functionally disequilibrating effect on traditional societies and therefore something had to be done, through education and other institutions, to reduce this potential source of conflict. Further, the new policy recognized the fact that the responsibility for decision making in these communities rested with the adults. Therefore much of the education given to the young aimed at changing attitudes and beliefs, such as those pertaining to health and hygiene, was likely to be ineffective or to take a long time to produce results because children attending regular schools had so little influence on change. This led to the development of a strong interest in community adult education which was seen in the 1944 report on Mass Education in African Society. The rationale advanced for this approach was that:

> The progress of a backward community will be greater and more rapid if the education of the adults is taken in hand simultaneously with that of the young, . . . efforts to educate the young are often largely wasted unless a simultaneous effort is made to improve the life of the community as a whole. (Govt. of Great Britain 1944)

While many of these policies were implemented through tribal schools, trade schools and Jeanes Teacher training programmes, they virtually failed to achieve the social and educational goals which the colonizers considered important for the colonized. So when the late Dr. G.B. Jeffrey, as former Director of the Institute of Education, did his Survey of Education in West Africa in 1951 he continued to criticize the educational systems of these countries

> for providing too superficial an education . . . for being too much bound by external examinations; for being too bookish and unpractical; for producing too many clerks and too few farmers; . . . and for utterly failing to stop the drift to towns; . . . for the break up of tribal society, and the loosening of moral standards. (Jeffrey 1953)

Incidentally, many of the perceived failures of the system were often considered achievements by the colonized. The main point here is that the colonizers had suggested that the educational developments were being pursued because they would be valuable for the masses within the emerging needs of their societies. But in reality they stemmed largely from the colonizers' perceptions of their own interests. In writing on educational developments in Africa, Lord Hailey candidly admitted that, despite all the practical and theoretical reasons which were advanced for these educational programmes,

> Conceptions as to what is best in education are . . . coloured by political objectives; indeed . . . what at times has been put forward by administrations as a policy of education has in truth been only the expression of a political determination, or an effort to implement the view held of the place which the African should occupy in the social economy. (Hailey 1938)

After the Second World War many of these colonies began to clamour for and gradually move towards self government and independence and this was accompanied by a number of new developments both in their economies and in their education. But the economic policies pursued during the post-independence years were geared towards sustaining and extending the infrastructural complex which was originally developed in these societies and they were geared to further the expansion of capitalism by keeping intact the social and economic structures which existed under colonial rule.

EDUCATIONAL POLICIES IN THE POST-COLONIAL STATE

After the Second World War the role of the colonial state began to be expanded. It became concerned not only with law and order but also with "development" issues and this led to a substantial increase in its activities. Further, with the movement towards self-government and independence in some colonies there was an increase in the number of jobs which were being vacated by the metropolitan civil servants and therefore local individuals had to be trained to fill them. All these developments led to a continued need for an expansion of the educational systems in these societies, especially at the secondary, technical and university levels which together often necessitated an increase in the provision of primary education also.

The increase in educational facilities after the mid-1940s was therefore an outcome of

(a) the fact that production in the colonies was becoming more capital intensive, especially as the import substitution policy was being implemented.

(b) the attempts to "modernize" these economies which were fuelled by the demands of the anti-colonial movement of the time and which also demanded an expansion of educational facilities beyond the primary level.

(c) the attempts of the colonizing powers to expand or develop an intellectual infrastructure in these colonies which would help to ensure the emergence of comprador elites who would continue to serve the interests of the colonizers after they had withdrawn from the local scene. In the British colonies this was seen in the establishment after the mid-1940s of University Colleges attached to the University of London, in the West Indies, West Africa, East Africa, Sri Lanka, Malaysia, and Hong Kong. This began just prior to the period when independence was being granted to the colonies.

The political decision makers in the newly independent nations began to be faced with the dual problems relating to the need to increase capital accumulation to ensure further economic growth and to maintain the legitimacy of the State. In the eyes of the newly enfranchised masses this was largely dependent on what the new states could provide for them. They therefore continued to demand an education which would provide increased opportunities for social and economic mobility for their children. This meant that the State had to ensure that there was continued economic growth which would open up new job opportunities, and at the same time, it had to provide increased access through education to these jobs. For the local propertied and professional classes the demand was largely for an expansion of traditional secondary and university or technical education which would prepare them to fill the top level jobs which the expatriates had left or which were being created in the public and private sectors.

Initially, the locally elected representatives were quite responsive to the demands of the masses and therefore tried to meet the demands for more education which led to further expansion of educational facilities. Because of the new developments which were taking place in these societies a substantial number of those who began to graduate from schools were able to secure jobs as a result of their education. But as their numbers increased competition for jobs became keener and this fuelled the demand for even more education at the higher levels.

However, the cost of this education was quite substantial. For example, in some African countries the provision of higher education for one student was equivalent to the cost of educating 283 of them at the primary level (Todaro 1981). The expanded provision of education services therefore soon began to put a strain on the process of capital accumulation in these countries, especially since the local entrepreneurs were looking for opportunities to benefit from the new economic policies such as import substitution which seemed to open up new opportunities for investment.

But once the infrastructure needed to sustain the new political and economic order was in place the structural constraints which are inherent in the process of dependent development came into play. It not only blocked or slowed down further educational expansion but also created an important source of discontent and instability in these countries. The popular pressures for the expansion or improvement of educational facilities continued while at the same time the State was continuing to experience financial difficulties in meeting the additional costs. In other words the State now began to face problems which resulted from the conflicting demands of capital accumulation and legitimation and this created further problems in these societies. Attempts were therefore made to slow down the rate of educational expansion partly to ensure that the need for capital accumulation was maintained. But in many cases the cost in terms of social disruption over education was heavy, as was seen in such countries as Sri Lanka and Mauritius.

Many developing countries attempted to grapple with this problem through different means. One was to permit the privatization or increased privatization of education by allowing various individuals and groups to provide educational facilities for fee-paying students. This even took place in socialist Tanzania which for a long time resisted such a development. Another was to encourage community involvement in the provision of education services. But laudable as some of these developments might have been, in terms of providing increased access to education by some sectors of these societies, they often resulted in the strengthening of the dualistic structure of the educational systems in these countries. For example, in comparing the

Harambee schools in Kenya which were provided largely through community efforts and the traditional Government schools one observer noted that

> the lucky students who live in communities with a government school have access to highly qualified teachers, sophisticated equipment and plenty of text books. On the other hand the students who attend Harambee schools usually have only one trained teacher (the rest being recent graduates of secondary schools themselves), little or no science equipment, and a few books if they are lucky. This inequity virtually ensures that students of government schools will be the ones who get the valued places in university. Kids begin secondary school on unequal terms, and it is almost impossible for the students of the poor Harambee schools to catch up. (Connell p. 10)

To help cope with the demands for more education some developing countries have sought aid from the economically developed countries or loans from the World Bank. But such external funding has only accentuated the fiscal crisis of the State in these countries in their efforts at ensuring the availability of capital to further their economic development while, at the same time, using available funds to expand education in an attempt to prevent social unrest from erupting. The outcome was that the post-colonial states continued to face growing financial problems in their efforts to strengthen or prevent an erosion of their legitimacy among the general public. Partly as a result, they turned towards shoring up the state control mechanisms of the army and the police to ensure law and order were being maintained, the outcome of which has been the authoritarian governments in so many developing countries. Many of them seemed to have been in a "Catch-22" situation because the more they need to borrow funds to provide facilities like education, the greater becomes the problem of their external debt; more local efforts then have to be geared towards production for export; the more local needs remain unsatisfied, the more the local discontent spreads, and the more the State has a problem of legitimacy and resorts to shoring up its physical control mechanisms to crush any signs of disorder.

Despite their financial difficulties these states cannot remain entirely unresponsive to popular demands for facilities such as education, if they want to retain some shred of legitimacy. This has resulted in the keen interest shown by some developing countries in the provision of educational services which are considered less expensive or are thought to have more immediate economic pay-off. Hence the growing interest in non-formal education (Stromquist 1992), distance education, education of women and girls, vocational education and in some cases even universal primary education. This, however often continues to put pressure on the capital accumulation process which has repercussions on the rate of growth of their GNPs. The failure of the economy to provide the goods and services demanded by the population in turn makes it difficult for the legitimacy of the State not to be challenged. So while the elected post-colonial governments were somewhat more responsive to the demands of the population for educational services and have tried to expand educational services, they are caught in a bind between the dual concerns of the State for capital accumulation and legitimacy which, as indicated above, tends to be affected by what the population sees their governments doing to help them to cope with the harsh realities of life which they face.

One issue which arises is whether the contribution of these expanded educational services could have contributed more to economic development and therefore helped with, rather than detracted from, the problem of capital accumulation. One might begin to examine this issue by first asking the question "What changes in education occurred which increased its contribution to the development of these countries?" For many reasons, including the speed with which most of these countries wanted to expand their educational services, they did not generally develop the kind of educational programme which they would require as an independent nation state, as Tanzania attempted to do. Instead, they tended to continue using the metropolitan models of education as the basis for expanding their own services. The result was that, despite the massive increases in educational facilities which took place in these ex-colonies, the type of education provided remained virtually unchanged. This can partly be seen in the case of the University Colleges which were established in the British colonies after 1945 and which offered programs of study that were often identical with those found in the metropolitan universities.

Such curriculum changes did occur with, say, local history and geography gradually taking the place of history and geography of the metropole and some new approaches to mathematics and science teaching were introduced. But the whole purpose of the education provided tended to remain essentially unchanged. In addition, the influence of the metropole on the nature of the education offered in the ex-colonies was continuously strengthened by the large numbers of students from the periphery who came to the centre to do their postgraduate or high professional studies. Even more inescapable was the continued influence on the developing countries of Western intellectual ideas, including theories of development and how education can contribute to the development process—all of which were crucial factors that influenced development strategies and educational policies in the Third world during their post independence years.

But probably the most important reason for the persistence of the crucial elements of the previous educational programs was the fact that they were geared towards sustaining and extending the infrastructural complex which was developed in these societies to further the expansion of capitalism by keeping intact the social and economic structures of these societies which existed under colonial rule. For example, the export oriented production which was a characteristic of colonial economic policy continued to be their main development thrust after independence. Later it was accompanied by the import substitution strategy advocated by Prebisch. But these approaches did not essentially change the dependency nature of the relationship between the metropolitan centres and their colonies. Nor were the strategies geared towards meeting the needs of the total population since, for example, the imports substituted were generally those which the middle class and the relatively small sections of the population employed in the modern sectors of these economies could afford.

These appoaches to development set the conditions for the ready acceptance of the human capital theory and the manpower planning approach which became popular in these countries. This was later followed by the assessment of the contribution which specific educational inputs were making to learning outcomes and the rates of return analysis which was used to determine educational priorities. But these developments only resulted in an expansion of the educational structures developed under colonial rule with very little modification.

In addition, the rapid expansion of educational services which occurred in these ex-colonies since the emergence of the post-colonial state has often been accompanied by greater inequalities in income distribution, more urban migration, an increase in the number of those who are living, not only below the poverty but also below the destitution line, and an increase in unemployment among the educated. While it would be rash to assume a causal relationship between these indices of underdevelopment among the masses and the expansion of educational services, these outcomes helped us overcome our innocence in assuming, as educational advisers such as Harbison, Myers, Ashby and others had earlier done, that expansion of educational services in the developing countries would somehow automatically contribute to their overall development.

In view of the fact that many of the structural elements of thesc ex-colonial societies have remained basically unchanged, except that their local ruling class is now made up of indigenous elites, the question needs to be re-considered as to whether, and if so how far, the function of education in the developing societies has changed since independence. In fact, it seems that the educational experiences of the LDCs have provided strong evidence to support social reproduction theory, since education in these countries has largely continued to consolidate the power of the ruling elites, as it did under colonial rule. Further, in many of these countries the ruling elites have not only become compradors of their metropolitan counterparts and useful links for most ex-colonial governments but are increasingly less dependent on the general public for their political legitimacy, even minimally through the ballot box. Many of them simply look after their own interests at the expense of the masses and consolidate their power base by the use of the physical control mechanisms of the State, with the assistance of arms which are increasingly supplied to them by their metropolitan connections. As a result they are now in a better position to ignore some of the earlier commitments to provide universal primary education for the masses.

The educational systems of these developing countries have also become less of an instrument of social mobility, as they temporarily were in the immediate pre- and post independence years, and as indicated above, more a means of consolidating and even extending social inequalities in these societies. In fact, in some countries, for example Bangladesh, funds which were originally earmarked in the development plans for the expansion of primary education for the masses were consistently shifted towards university education largely for the children of the elites (Chowdhury 1984). This indicates that education in the LDC's might be becoming a means of further impoverishing the poor and aiding the economically better off sections of these societies.

If education in the LDCs is becoming more a means of reproducing the elitist social order and increasing social inequalities, educators might probably need to re-examine their role in this process—those who teach, do research, administer and are responsible for making decisions about funding education in the developing countries. They need to ask whether they have any responsibility, as professionals, to play a part in helping to reverse this trend or whether they should simply take comfort in the belief that, as professionals, they should not be involved in what are essentially matters for the governments of the developing countries. A related question is "Should they be worried about the possibility that they might be helping to train other professionals who would, by their mere technical efficiency, help to prop up an increasingly unfair and elitist system, thereby eventually adding to the political unrest in the developing countries without even having any doubts raised in their minds about what they are doing?" Or conversely "Should they regard the present situation as a challenge to develop counter hegemonic educational strategies which might help to correct this situation?"

It is increasingly becoming obvious that those involved in the education of the developing countries cannot seek cover in the fact that, because their mandate does not arise from the poor in these countries, but from the governments, they can absolve themselves from involvement, even indirectly, in these obviously political issues. Whether they recognize it or not, educators working in this field are already involved on one side of the fence or another. The kind of knowledge and training which are often provided for students in education from the developing countries will be used politically, either to sustain the present inequitable systems or help to change them. The main issue is the type of involvement which educators should have, that would be consistent with their role as academics, policy makers or administrators. And here the suggestion is that those involved in education in the developing countries must begin to examine the weakness of the very knowledge basis with which they currently operate.

TOWARD A NEW APPROACH TO EDUCATION IN THE DEVELOPING COUNTRIES

Educators, like other social scientists, have tended to be guided by the assumption that the study of their subject should be based only on the use of rational empirical knowledge. But this, in many ways, has tended to provide support for the continued use being made of the educational systems in the LDCs by the local elites to serve their own interests, at the expense of the masses.

Here, it might be useful to look at the basic types of knowledge interests which it has been suggested ought to guide the concerns of educators and others in their approach to their work. Habermas, in one of his earlier books, has identified three knowledge guiding interests for the human sciences including education (Habermas 1986). While he has changed his terminology somewhat this paper will adhere to the earlier ones which seem to be a little more comprehensible, although some personal interpretation of what falls into each of his categories will also be attempted.

Each of these areas of knowledge interests has its own objectives and dominant research methods which influence the type of knowledge which it makes available as a basis for developing policies or programs. First, there is an interest in empirical-analytical knowledge which is essentially geared towards producing information that can lead to the rational technical solution of problems. Methodologically, it involves the kind of research approach which one associates most closely with the natural sciences and is not geared primarily towards producing an understanding of phenomena within particular settings. Rather, it tends to be focussed on establishing causal links between phenomena and seeks explanations which are generalizable. It therefore does not provide a sound enough basis for developing policies to grapple with problems within particular social contexts where it is often necessary to take into consideration the motivations and concerns of the various groups of human actors involved.

The knowledge produced by this approach is also ideally suited for the maintenance of a relationship dominated by the expert who decides the kind of educational policies which should be implemented, based on the available "scientific" evidence. In other words it provides an excellent basis of control by technically competent individuals whose loyalties are usually with the dominant groups. Those who are at the receiving end of these policies are expected to take comfort from the fact that their lives, at least as far as the education of their children is concerned, are in the hands of these experts. This, in some ways, reminds us of the process of policy making which occurred during the colonial days in which decisions were made on the basis of bureaucratic expertise with little, if any, consultation of those for whom these policies were being drawn up. This technical knowledge also does not provide any clear ideas about the desired goals towards which it should be used.

Secondly, there is the "practical" knowledge guiding interest which is related to historical hermeneutic knowledge, the objective of which is to increase understanding of, and to give a deeper insight into, particular social phenomena. This approach is more likely to throw light on the factors which influence the human actors and actions within given cultural settings. But it can also be used, as it was in colonial days, for the purpose of social control. The misuse of Freirean approach has shown how a more in-depth understanding of the masses and their concerns might be used not to liberate them but to enhance their domestication. The Project Camelot was another outstanding example of how an increase in our knowledge and understanding of peoples is sometimes sought for the purpose of manipulating them.

Thirdly, there is critical emancipatory knowledge, the objective of which is not simply to increase comprehension of a phenomenon but also to sharpen awareness of the relationships of dominance and submission which underlie it. Because of this it can help individuals increase and transform their consciousness about these social phenomena, and where necessary, make them better prepared to transform this reality. This is an area of concern which has been very much neglected in education generally, since educators have tended to become more technicist in their orientation. This can be seen, for example, in the increased importance attached to psychometrics in education which followed the decline in popularity of progressive education after the 1940s. Further, it must be noted that even the educational goals towards which the technical experts were working and which they might have helped to define were essentially political in nature, whether they dealt with more efficient means of selecting students for secondary schools or defining objectives for the various subjects in the curriculum.

To be more effective in their work in education and development educators in the Third World countries need to be guided by all three areas of knowledge interests. But, to a large extent they have tended to focus their attention on the acquisition of empirical analytical and to a lesser extent historical hermeneutic knowledge. One of the crucial weaknesses of the present approach is therefore a virtual neglect or lack of interest in critical emancipatory knowledge as a means of helping to increase the effectiveness of education in the development process, especially among the poorest sections of these societies.

If educators realize the importance of critical emancipatory knowledge interests in their work they might begin to see the need to construct a whole new agenda for their field of activity. Such a perspective was characteristic of the work of Dewey, Counts and others in the progressive education movement. It also later appeared in the writings of Freire whose efforts were directed at the education of adults and has been explored more fully by the critical theorists such as Giroux, Apple and others.

Once the importance of critical emancipatory knowledge is accepted by educators, then they would be in a position to ask such questions as to "How can the sensitivity or consciousness of educators about the importance of the political and other constraining factors in education be increased so that they can become more aware of them, in their role as educational planners, curriculum developers, and teacher educators?" And "how can educators help to break down or reduce the influences of these barriers which interfere with the emancipatory possibilities of education?" At a more macro level they would also become concerned with such issues as "How can education contribute to social transformation in these societies, not simply prepare individuals to fill slots in the existing occupational hierarchy, as a first step towards improving the socio-economic levels of the population as a whole, and not only the more privileged sections?"

While some attempts have been made in this paper to throw light on how the metropolitan countries have constrained the development of their satellite ex-colonies by continuing to dominate their social, economic and educational structures, no attention has been directed here to the ways in which the internal political structures of these societies have resisted all efforts to make education contribute more effectively to the development outcomes of the LDCs. As a result, much of the time spent by educators in these countries has been directed at trying to arrive at answers about how curriculum reform can best be achieved, the correct balance between "practical" and "academic" subjects and the instructional strategies which are likely to increase certain desired learning outcomes. Ignoring the issue of the emancipatory possibilities of education seemed to have left these educators grappling with the more technical and more peripheral issues in education in the LDCs.

As previously indicated, such an interest in the emancipatory possibilities of education was strongly shared by the Progressive Education Movement in the 1920s and 1930s. But this has since subsided considerably, if not entirely disappeared from the concerns of most educators. At that time the progressivists saw the future of democracy in the US being threatened by the rise of new large scale industrial enterprises, and called on their fellow educators to help tackle the problem of revitalizing or even reconstructing the basis of their democracy. For this task it was suggested that educators should develop a critical awareness or a vision of the type of society which they should be involved in helping to construct.

It was

> a vision of society in which the lot of the common man will be made easier . . . A society (which will) combat all forces tending to produce social distinctions . . . ; manifest a tender regard for the weak, ignorant and the unfortunate; . . . strive for genuine equality of opportunity . . . ; regard as paramount the abiding interests of the great masses of the people (Counts 1978).

This belief in the power of education to transform society was no doubt unrealistic but it was the vision of its emancipatory possibilities which those involved in education for development need to re-kindle, if they are not to become just highly skilled technical experts who have no concern for the outcomes of their work, and little compassion for those in whose education they should be primarily interested. If they are to pursue this concern then they would need to become more involved with the experiences of the poor and oppressed in these countries.

At this point one is reminded of the message which the peasants of Guatemala sent to the Roman Catholic bishops who were meeting in Puebla, Mexico in 1978. If one was to take poetic licence with the words and maintain the sentiments expressed in the letter to the bishops, the message would read something like this:

> "We the peasants of Guatemala know that you are about to discuss our problems after which you would give us documents to serve as guides as to how we should educate our children. But we are fully aware of our own realities and we, on our part, would like to share these with you. We would therefore invite you to come down from your ivory towers or from your association only with the elites of our countries and be involved with the peasants in an effort to understand them and their concerns more fully. We would like you to enter into dialogue with the exploited and suffering people in order to better understand their reality and thereby fulfil more effectively your role as educators" (Open Letter 1978).

In other words, they would be challenging educators to think about exploring the emancipatory possibilities of what they were attempting to do. This can only be achieved if the educators are willing to search for knowledge from, and share theirs with, those who probably benefit least from their current efforts, i.e. the poor and the oppressed. This, it is believed, will help the educators to increase their contribution to the overall development process. If this challenge was accepted, then educators would have to re-think the kinds of topics and issues on which they focus their attention and on the way in which they conduct research on education in the developing countries.

REFERENCES

Achebe, Chinua (1977) *Things Fall Apart*. London, Heinemann.

Bacchus, M. Kazim, Rajinder S. Pannu and Carlos A. Torres (1988) 'The Sociology of Educational Expansion and Development Revisited'. Paper presented at the Mid-Term Conference of the Sociology of Education Research Committee, International Sociological Association held in Salamanca, Spain, August 23–27, 1988.

Carnoy, M. and Levin, H. (1985) *Schooling and Work in the Democratic State*. Stanford, Stanford University Press.

Chowdhury, K.P. (1984) *Efforts in Universalization of Primary Education: The Case of Bangladesh*. Buffalo, New York, Comparative Education Center, Faculty of Educational Studies, State University of New York at Buffalo.

Connell, Meg (1989) "Kenya's Other Schools." In *Crossworld Winter* 15(3); 10. Toronto, Canada by Canadian Crossroads International p.10.

Counts, George (1978) *Dare The Schools Build a New Social Order?* Carbondale, Southern Illinois University Press, 38–57.

Gifford, P. and Weiskel, T.C. (1971) "African Education in a Colonial Context—French and British Styles." In P. Gifford and Wm. R. Louis (ed.), *France and Britain in Africa*. New Haven, Yale University Press, p. 672.

Govt. of Great Britain, Advisory Committee on Education in the Colonies (1925) *Education Policy in British Tropical Africa*, Cmd. 2374 London, HMSO.

Govt. of Great Britain, Advisory Committee on Education in the Colonies (n.d.) *Memorandum on the Education of African Communities*, Col. No. 103, London, HMSO.

Govt. of Trinidad (1857) Report of the Legislative Council, September 2.

Habermas, Jürgen (1968) *Knowledge and Human Interests* (trans. Jeremy Shapiro). Boston, Beacon Press.

Hailey, Lord (1938) *An African Survey*. London, Oxford University Press.

Jeffrey, G.B. (1953) *A Study of Educational Policy and Practice in British Tropical Africa*. Oxford, Nuffield Foundation and the Colonial Office.

Letter from Governor North (1799) to the Court of Directors, February 26, 1799. Quoted by J.E. Jayasuriya in *Educational Policies and Progress During British Rule in Ceylon*.

Lloyd, P.C. (1967) Africa in Social Change. Harmondsworth, England, Penguin Books.

Maunier, R. (1949) *The Sociology of Colonies* (ed. and trans. E.O. Lorimer). Routledge and Kegan Paul.

Mitchell, Jonathan (1972) "Harvard College Records 111". CSM Pubs. XXXI: 311. Quoted in C. and R. Bridenbaugh (1972), op. cit.

O'Connor, J. (1973) *The Fiscal Crisis of the State*. New York, St. Martin's Press, 1973.

Oliver, Roland and Fage, J.D. (1962) *A Short History of Africa*. Baltimore, Maryland, Penguin Books.

Open Letter by a Group of Guatemalan Peasants to the Third General Conference of Roman Catholic Bishops in Latin America Meeting in Puebla, Mexico (1978), *Come to the Fields and Struggle with the Peasants*.

Shuttleworth, K.B. (1847) *Brief Practical Suggestions on the Mode of Organizing and Conducting Day Schools of Industry, Model Farm Schools and Normal Schools, as part of a System of Education for the Coloured Races of the British Colonies*, CO/318/138.

Stromquist, N. (1992). Empowering Women Through Knowledge: International Support for Nonformal Education; Burns, R., and Welch, A., *Contemporary Perspectives in Comparative Education*. New York, Garland Publishing, Inc.

Todaro, Michael P. (1981) *Economic Development in the Third World* (2d ed.). New York, Longman, Inc.

Welch, A. (1988). 'Aboriginal Education as Internal Colonialism: The Schooling of an Indigenous Minority in Australia'. *Comparative Education* 22 (2).

The Formation of Third World Technocrats for Rural Development: A Critical Perspective on Australia's Role in Study Abroad

TOH SWEE-HIN AND TERRY FARRELLY

Department of Social, Cultural, and Curriculum Studies, Faculty of Education, Nursing, and Professional Studies, University of New England, Armidale, New South Wales

•

Mt. Hagen Teachers College, Mount Hagen, New Guinea

INTRODUCTION

Principally after the Second World War, and in the wake of colonialism, most independent Third World nations eagerly sent many students abroad to be trained and educated at all levels and diverse disciplines or professions. It was deemed essential to have well educated and qualified locals to fill positions formerly or still occupied by expatriates. Backed by "human capital" theory and related investment concepts propagated by emergent economists of education (Harbison and Myers 1964), Third World leaders and bureaucrats believed in educational expansion as a virtual passport to economic growth (Cerych 1965). Study abroad served as a quick, cheaper method of producing middle- and high-level personnel when local universities, colleges and institutes were still scarce. Not least, the advanced industrial states offered the carrot of thousands of scholarships as part of their educational aid programs (Carter 1973). This was an incentive difficult to refuse by Third World governments, not only for the above reasons but also their widespread faith in the "superiority" of overseas qualifications, especially those from the West.

Hence, over the period 1950 to 1978, tertiary students (including a majority from the Third World) studying and training in both advanced capitalist- and state socialist-bloc regions increased eightfold, from over 107,00 to nearly 843,00 students (Cummings 1984: 241). For Australia, overseas student enrolment has quadrupled between 1965 and the early 1980s (Goldring 1984: 65). However, it is clearly Western powers like the United States, United Kingdom and a few European ex-colonial states like France and West Germany who dominate the study abroad market in sponsored as well as private students. With the advent of the Colombo Plan, Australia and New Zealand also opened their doors to increasingly larger numbers of overseas students, notably those from the Southeast and East Asian regions. The latest UNESCO statistics indicate that some 920, 547 Third World post-secondary students studied abroad in 1980, with at least 65 percent in major Western countries (Jones 1986: 67). By 1982, Australia's overseas student population from the Third World totalled about 22,00 distributed as follows: 74 percent (tertiary) and 26 percent (secondary); 84 percent (private) and 16 percent (sponsored) (Fraser 1984: 283). At the end of the eighties, these numbers had grown considerably largely due to the encouragement of full-fee paying students, notably in short-term nonformal courses (e.g. English as Second Language). In 1988/89, the overseas student population in Australia was comprised of some 17, 992 subsidised students (82 percent tertiary, 18 percent secondary), which included about 1000 students on awards of the Australian International Development Assistance Bureau (AIDAB), and 38,35 full-fee students (17.8 percent higher/post-secondary; 11.1 percent secondary; 71.1 percent other), which included approximately 13,00 students from the People's Republic of China predominantly on short-term English-language courses (Joint Committee on Foreign Affairs, Defence and Trade 1989: 98; Dept. of Employment, Education and Training 1989: 63, 298). In 1988, Australian institutions had enrolled about 1500 AIDAB-sponsored overseas students (mostly postgraduate), and 42, 562 private overseas students, including those on their own government's scholarships and self funding students (Jones 1989: 13).

Among host and donor countries, at both official and private levels, it is easy to find praise for study abroad programs. The Third World obtains a ready source of highly qualified personnel with advanced technological knowledge and skills deemed "beneficial" to development in all its dimensions. Host institutions and societies gain from the presence of citizens from diverse cultures which contribute to "international understanding". Nationally, rich world nations build up a store of "goodwill" among overseas students who upon return, are favourably disposed to their former hosts' economic, commercial, and political-strategic interests. In the Australian context, such positive views are echoed by politicians and civic leaders, and are commonplace in various governmental reports including the findings of the Harries(1979) Committee and the Jackson (1984) Committee on Australian aid policies, the Morrison (1984) parliamentary committee report on Australian-ASEAN relations, and the Goldring(1985) Report focusing on private overseas students. Similar arguments have been employed in the recent push to "export" Australian education, including a proliferation of courses/programs requiring overseas students to pay full-cost fees (Chong 1985; Dept. of Trade 1985).

While a few stated benefits of study abroad seem logical enough (e.g. supply of advanced skills not yet available in Third World contexts; intercultural exchanges between student and host society/institution), a critical analysis cannot avoid asking in-depth questions about what are taken-for-granted assumptions and beliefs not just among politicians and entrepreneurs, but also within the academic community. Is it the case, as one former Australian Minister of Education stated, that the "overseas student program makes a significant contribution to the economic and social development of the source countries"? (Ryan 1985). In what ways do the qualifications, skills, knowledge and values acquired by Third World students benefit the poor majorities in their countries?

This paper seeks to clarify such questions both conceptually and empirically. To begin with, a review of available writings on study abroad in the advanced industrialized West, which has hosted the bulk of overseas students, will highlight a glaring deficiency in conceptual and methodological emphasis. Specifically, it is argued that a valid evaluation of study abroad must bring into consideration which paradigm(s) of Third World development is or are emphasized in the education and training received. This conceptual framework is then applied to an empirical study of the curriculum received by a sample of Third World students in four Australian universities. Mostly sponsored by Australian official aid programs, these students were during 1985 acquiring postgraduate qualifications in agricultural science, extension and economics, fields which all relate to "rural development". The paper concludes by drawing some critical implications for the problem of study abroad in general, and the ethical responsibilities of Australian educators, institutions and policy-makers in providing Third World students with knowledge, skills and value-orientations which are relevant to just and equitable development.

RESEARCH AND DISCUSSIONS ON STUDY ABROAD

The substantial postwar (1945) increase in Third World citizens studying abroad was accompanied, notably in the United States, by research and analyses of various aspects of such "educational exchanges". A number of bibliographies in the sixties reflected the burgeoning scholarly interest in study programs and experiences of overseas students (Crabbs and Holmquist 1967; Giacalone and Davis 1967; Spencer and Awe 1968; Spaulding and Flack 1976; Spencer and Stahl 1983; Lulat and Cordaro 1984). The bulk of this research and analysis, however, was cast in an administrative mould, rather than on substantive probing of the underlying assumptions and conceptual rationale of study abroad. Thus, concern has been raised in the US, Canada, Western Europe and Australia on the following issues and problems:

(i) Selection: What criteria and procedures are "best" for selecting overseas students into courses and programs of study? Studies relate to the "quality" and assessment of Third World educational qualifications (Murphy 1960; Dremuk 1967); the

English-language proficiency of overseas students (Lesser and Peter 1957: 177; Gue and Holdaway 1973; Strain 1973), and collaboration between Third World officials, donor government agencies, and accepting institutions (Henry 1960; Wilcox 1966).

(ii) Orientation: Are there adequate orientation programs for overseas students to overcome "culture shock" and facilitate socio-psychological and academic adjustment to often very different cultural and educational milieus? (Cormack 1963; NAFSA 1964; Klineberg 1970; Klein et al. 1971). Conversely, analysts and researchers have been equally concerned about the re-entry problems students encounter prior to and upon return to their home societies (Lesser and Peter 1957: 181; Cormack 1963; Livingstone 1964; Hodgkin 1966; Sinauer 1967: 18; Gama and Pedersen 1977; Bochner, Lin and McLeod 1980; Radford 1984: 47ff.).

(iii) Student Problems and Services: Many studies look at the diverse academic and non-academic problems overseas students face during their sojourn, and suggest possible coping strategies. These include English-language difficulties and adjusting to different teaching-learning styles and expectations (Beck 1962; Selltiz et al. 1963: 124ff; Bloom 1969; Deutsch 1970: 79; Benson and Kovach 1974; SELMOUS Group 1980; Bradley and Bradley 1984); personal-social problems in diet, customs, racial discrimination, gender relationships, climatic differences, absence of family ties/support, status diminution, and loss of self-esteem (Singh 1963; P.E.P. 1965; Leeper et al. 1967; Klein et al. 1968; Deutsch 1970; Bochner and Wicks 1972; Pruitt 1977; Noesjirwan et al. 1979; Klineberg 1980; Dunnet 1981); adequacy of provision of appropriate foreign student advising, counselling and other support services, including cross-cultural interactions with the wider host society (Bang 1961; NAFSA 1966, 1967a, 1967b; I.I.E. 1969; Deutsch 1970; Jenkins 1973; Klineberg 1980); and unwillingness to return to home societies after completion of studies, or intentions to join the "brain drain" at some future opportunity (Lundstedt 1963: 7; Davis 1964; Lavergne 1969: 45; Rao 1976).

(iv) Institutional Structures: Much less researched have been issues related to the degree of institutional support and planning accorded to study abroad programs. These included analysis of the

behavioral influence of academic staff, especially their capacity to communicate effectively with students from other cultures (Lesser and Peter 1957: 187; Livingstone 1964; Deutsch 1970: 157); whether university and foreign aid agency administrations are geared to meeting the special demands of overseas student programs (Neal 1964; Gardner 1964; Humphrey 1967; Richardson 1969; Deutsch 1970: 167ff; Goodwin and Nacht 1983; Radford 1984); and of late, the question of fees which have been increased by many host governments as part of a profit-maximization thrust in tertiary educational planning (Commonwealth Secretariat 1982; Fraser 1984; Williams 1984). In Britain, the overseas student question was scrutinized by a collection of well-known scholars including Mark Blaug, and Peter Williams (1981). The major thrust of this report basically upheld the mutual benefits of study abroad to Third World countries and to Britain, including commercial and foreign policy interests and the training of high-level expertise.

Undoubtedly, the kind of research and studies highlighted above does help to improve the organization and operation of study abroad programs. At least overseas students, upon arrival, are not left to fend for themselves in strange environments, and their chances to succeed in host institutions/programs improved. The goals of international understanding and intercultural exchange are also better met when the presence of overseas students is organizationally recognized and utilized as a valuable asset. In the Australian context, a rather belated appreciation of such administrative complexities/responsibilities in study abroad was recently expressed by the Australian Vice-Chancellors Committee (1988) in its "ethical guidelines" for universities interested in attracting more overseas students to their campuses. However, an administrative approach to analyzing study abroad issues fails to tackle the substantive and important question raised earlier, viz., is the education/training of overseas students really contributing positively to Third World development and thereby meeting the basic needs of the poor majorities? We turn now therefore to studies and discussions which perhaps could help answer this question, namely analyses of curriculum relevance and broader evaluation research on the impact of study abroad.

It is difficult in the fifties and sixties to find much concern with issues of curriculum relevance. Occasional reports suggested that academic programs for overseas students may not be preparing them for their roles back in home cultures and societies (Dresden 1955; Michie 1968). A two-year U.S. study of the Committee on the Professional School and World Affairs (1965: 324) concluded that many schools and fields pay little attention to helping foreign students relate "American doctrines and techniques to the quite different backgrounds of their own countries". This view is echoed in more recent writings (Baron 1979; Owen 1981). Such analyses of "relevance, " however, still beg the question of what it means for curriculum to be "relevant" to the students' societies, since there is no in-depth examination of Third World development realities. Without this examination, how is it possible to assess if the home "backgrounds" and the returned students' "roles" referred to are indeed appropriate for achieving the fundamental goal of development, namely meeting the basic needs of the poor majorities? A similar deficiency characterizes evaluation case-studies, such as Scott's (1966) assessment of the foreign graduate program of the University of Michigan Graduate School of Business Administration. Questions asked of a sample of returned Asian alumni used status-quo criteria to measure success (e.g. meeting needs of employers, "satisfactory progress in assuming increasing responsibility and leadership, " furthering personal careers). Nothing was asked about how the graduates might be applying their skills and knowledge in the service of the Asian poor and underprivileged. The same criticism applies to Suskind and Schell's (1968) positive assessment of University of California (Berkeley) foreign postgraduate engineering returnees, who mostly expressed "satisfaction" with the relevance and utility of their masters and doctoral degrees. Gue's (1972) report on the University of Alberta-Thailand Comprehensive School Project likewise had no independent critical framework for relating the training to structures of underdevelopment in Thai society, as was the case for Toh's (1974) largely administrative assessment of the University of Alberta's Ugandan teachers training program. A similar weakness characterizes the Australian study of Keats (1969) who surveyed

500 returned Colombo Plan-sponsored scholars from Southeast Asia. While the returnees reported that their training programmes had been fairly successful, the question " who benefited from that success" deserved in depth analysis. Another Australian study by Hodgkin (1972), looking at Malaysian and Singaporean tertiary returnees, is somewhat more thoughtful, raising issues of possible curriculum irrelevancies and difficulties in adapting skills and ideas learnt in Australia to different cultural contexts at home. However, her conceptual emphasis upon returned students acting as "innovators" for "development" takes for granted the assumptions of modernization upheld by the students' national governments and elite sectors. Recently, the official Jackson (1984: 92) Committee which reviewed Australian aid did admit that

> Australian courses are not always suitable for developing country conditions . . . Australian agricultural courses are biased towards mechanised techniques and engineering skills, and frequently lean towards the latest, rather than the most appropriate technology.

Regrettably, the report fails to elaborate on this promising criticism, and goes on to argue for expansion of the overseas student programme without further discussion of the important issue of curriculum relevance.

In recent times, there is regrettably still not much evidence of analysis of the impact of study abroad programs which holds up for critical examination their implicit or explicit assumptions about what "development" means. For example, Jones' (1986) review of Australia's international relations in education, while providing a useful description of evolving policies, activities and programs, inadvertently leaves the general impression that educational exchanges have been beneficial to the Third world, despite an early acknowledgment of the existence of alternative paradigms of development. It would have been important to analyze what paradigmatic emphases, if any, underlie Australia's contributions to study abroad. The special issue of *Comparative Education Review* on "foreign students in comparative perspective" (Barber, Altbach and Myers 1984) is another telling case in point. Except for one explicit analysis by Weiler (1984), and some arguments of another article (Moock 1984), the remaining five contributions are marked by deficiencies of commission or omission.

For instance, Coleman (1984) evaluated the Rockefeller Foundation's institution-building efforts in Thailand and Zaire, whereby Foundation fellowships enabled Thai and Zairean university staff to obtain PhDs abroad. Coleman's criteria of success in the case of Thailand's Mahidol University were the high return rate, professional performance of returnees (e.g. publications, research) and the institutional performance of the life-sciences departments in the Faculty of Science (e.g. own postgraduate training). Although noting his awareness of the criticisms that life-sciences training in Western industrialized contexts is elitist and often fails to meet the health needs of the masses (Donaldson 1976), Coleman dismisses such views rather casually by arguing that the "elite-mass dichotomy in medical education tends to distort, if not falsify, reality. Both approaches have a degree of validity and necessity". By then further stating that "four" Mahidol faculty members had initiated a community health program and pointing to the post-Mao shifts in Chinese medical education towards basic high-level knowledge, Coleman urges us to believe that the Rockefeller-Mahidol program had been a "seemingly faultless investment" in study abroad. This verdict, however, is problematic, since Coleman does not provide concrete evidence that the life-sciences PhDs trained on Rockefeller fellowships are systematically serving the primary health and medical needs of the poor Thai majorities, and most importantly contributing to the radical transformation of the Thai health system, vital for development based on social justice and equity. It is also apposite to note here that Coleman makes no reference to Berman's (1979) critique of the educational aid role of US foundations to Africa between 1945 and 1975. In his systematic analysis, Berman shows how the foundations' motivations for their philanthropic activities, such as institution building of African universities (which includes training of Africans in elite US schools), are related to corporate interests in maintaining African political, economic and cultural dependency upon the West.

Likewise, in his global empirical assessment of study abroad, Fry (1984) attempts to be even-handed by suggesting that although study abroad can reinforce cultural and political dependency, it also helps expose Third World citizens to new ideas, including radical ones conducive to social change. Granted, while the latter may happen, Fry's analysis nevertheless should have looked more carefully at the curriculum offered to Third World students in most advanced industrial institutions, and enquire how likely the students would be formally educated to think and to apply alternative critical concepts and methodologies relevant to grassroots development. Indeed, his qualitative exemplars of "successes" via study abroad, mostly in the Thai context, could well be queried by local and external observers concerned about the entrenched inequities and oppressive nature of military/bureaucratic/economic structures in contemporary Thailand. Amidst the current environmental crisis, it is good to know that Costa Rica has benefited ecologically from the training of two national park managers in the US. But to really convince us, Fry should have more systematically investigated what proportion of economists, political scientists, public administrators and other Third World technocrats educated abroad have been/are being systematically infused with environmentalist values and hence are now actively trying to save the Amazon, other rainforests and natural resources of the Third World from the plunder of profit-maximizing growth strategies, instead of buttressing the latter.

Another three articles in the *Comparative Education Review* special issue similarly provide no departure from the dominant approach to examining study abroad (Cummings 1984; Williams 1984; Fraser 1984). Only Weiler (1984), in part Moock (1984) and Lulat and Cordaro (1984) in briefly introducing their post-1975 bibliography, raise what constitute for us crucial issues and criteria for evaluating the costs and benefits of educating Third World students in the advanced industrial world. Essentially, they point out that curricula and values/attitudes formation of these students are predominantly steeped in the knowledge-technology paradigms and the cultural superstructure of transnational capitalism. This intellectual and cultural dependency in turn pose questions about the ability and willingness of returned students to work for social justice and equity policies, and the growth of endogenously-centred institutions and ideas. Elsewhere, other critical educational analysts, such as Carnoy (1974), Goonatilake (1975), the earlier mentioned Berman (1979), Altbach (1977) and Arnove (1982), have also raised parallel concerns about the cultural and intellectual imperialism exercised through educational aid programs, including study abroad. In our view, however, such critiques are more clearly understood by a systematic consideration of the paradigm (s) on development which are implicitly or explicitly embodied in study abroad programs. Thus, prior to reporting on an empirical study of Third World postgraduate students enrolled during 1987 in "rural development" fields in Australian universities, it is useful to concisely contrast two major paradigms of understanding the root causes of underdevelopment, and suggesting strategies to overcome problems of hunger, poverty and basic-needs deprivation of the poor majorities.

PARADIGMS OF UNDERDEVELOPMENT AND DEVELOPMENT

The era of political independence for many Third World countries after 1945 also heralded a growth in interest among social scientists in "underdevelopment" and "development". Why are poor countries "underdeveloped"? How have the affluent nations risen to their present conditions of economic and social "progress"? How can the Third World develop? What relationships between rich and poor countries might be conducive to the latter's "development"? Conducted by scholars from a gamut of disciplines, notably economics, sociology and political science, this initial concern laid the basis of what is still the dominant paradigm about issues/problems of underdevelopment and development (e.g Lerner 1958; Hoselitz 1960; McLelland 1961; Millikan and Blackmer 1961; Krause 1961; Weiner 1966; Hoogvelt 1976: 50–64; Little 1982). Often labelled the modernization paradigm, this worldview finds its ubiquitous expression in the "development" strategies and plans of most Third World governments, the policies of advanced industrialized countries towards poor nations, and the activities of official bilateral or multilateral aid organizations such as USAID (US Agency for International Development), AIDAB (Australian International Development Assistance Bureau) and the World Bank, as well as some private agencies (e.g. major US foundations, child-sponsorship non-governmental organizations).

Modernization advocates conceptualize the end-goal of "development" in terms of poor nations emulating the path taken by, and becoming like, advanced industrialized mass-consuming societies. Underdevelopment is attributed to a lack of prerequisite and sustaining factors, including financial capital, infrastructure, sophisticated technologies, educated/trained human resources, "achievement" or other entrepreneurial values/attitudes, and modern social structures. In turn, the industrialized world can foster "development" by diffusing those necessary factors of modernity to the Third World through trade, foreign aid, investments, technology-transfers, and political support. Modernization requires a strong emphasis on economic growth, whose benefits are expected to flow down to all members of Third World societies.

Concrete expressions of the modernization paradigm in the Third World since the fifties include the much vaunted "Green Revolution", based on developing high-yielding seeds so as to produce an abundance of food for the world's hungry millions; the extensive presence of transnational corporations in the Third World in cheap labour "free trade zones, " export-oriented agribusiness and marketing/service sectors; the growth, catalyzed by foreign aid, of modernized educational systems initially transplanted under colonialism; infrastructural expansion (e.g. dams, highways, ports) to meet the needs of export-oriented growth and vigorous exploitation of Third World natural resources and environment; political/strategic support (e.g. military aid) to sustain an investment-attractive climate of "stability"; an emphasis on population-control programs to cope with "overpopulation, " a perceived primary cause of underdevelopment; the pervasive presence of "development experts", mostly from the rich countries, who advise Third World governments, bureaucrats and technocrats on modernization projects/programmes; and the phenomenal growth of external debt in order to fund such modernization policies and plans (e.g. Borlaug 1980; Ehrlich 1968; Harbison and Myers 1964; Drucker 1974; Ghertman and Allen 1984; Krueger 1982; Yudelman 1977; Eicher and Staatz 1984; Psacharopoulos and Woodhall 1985).

The prevailing dominance of the modernization paradigm in Third World development theorizing and practices does not, however, necessarily imply "success". Depending upon which criteria are used to assess "successful development, " serious questions can be raised about the validity of modernization principles. Indeed, as successive decades of modernizing strategies were implemented, the continuing and even worsening problems of poverty, deprivation of basic needs and abuse of human rights afflicting the majority of Third World populations have inspired the emergence of alternative critical perspectives about underdevelopment and development. Such views are clustered under what has been referred to as the "dependency" or "structuralist" paradigm. Essentially, this worldwiew queries the ethnocentric bias of "modernity" concepts, and of viewing "development" as a unilinear goal and path with the advanced industrialized free-enterprise societies as the pinnacle of achievement. Rather than blaming deficiency of internal factors for underdevelopment, the dependency/structuralist paradigm emphasizes the explanatory role of global political-economic relationships (past and present) and the power-structures of Third World societies, as well as the linkages between these external and internal determinants (e.g. Frank 1970; Bernstein 1971; Hoogvelt 1982; Trainer 1985; Foster-Carter 1985; Toh 1987).

Thus, important exemplars of the underlying roots of world hunger and poverty include international economic inequalities favouring advanced industrialized states (e.g. terms of trade, protectionist barriers against Third World manufactured goods, control of world finance); socially unjust structures and systems of use, production and distribution of resources, wealth and income within Third World societies (viz "structural violence" based on exploitation, oppression and gross rich-poor gaps); promotion by "development experts" and modernization aid agencies of programs that tend to benefit the elites at the expense of the poor majorities (e.g. "Green Revolution, " large infrastructures, agribusiness, over-capital intensive technologies); the "debt trap" and debt "management" programmes of the IMF and private creditors (e.g. structural adjustments, conditions) which impose the heaviest burden upon the poorest and marginalized; the denial of meaningful participation of poor peoples in planning and control of "development" programmes; the additional oppression borne by women due to culture-based patriarchialism and sexism embodied in modernization strategies; transfers of technologies inappropriate for Third World employment, social and cultural needs; the super-profits extracted from Third World cheap, repressed labour and natural resources by transnational corporations; political-strategic support of Third World allies by rich countries, notably in military assistance which contributes to repression, human rights violations, and the growth of dictatorships and authoritarianism; the expansion of modern formal education systems that reinforce inequalities, political hierarchies, inappropriate curricula, and the "diploma disease"; and the escalating environmental destruction aggravated by profit-maximizing export-oriented and growth-first exploitation of land, water and air, which makes it even harder for the poor to obtain their basic needs (e.g. George 1976, 1987; Hayter and Watson 1984; Payer 1974, 1983; Mass 1976; Timberlake 1985; Barnet and Muller 1974; Burbach and Flynn 1980, 1984; Hill 1983; Eckholm 1982; Chomsky and Herman 1979; Crough and Wheelwright 1982; Carnoy 1982; Bacchus 1981; Dore 1976; Freire 1985; Arnove 1980; Toh 1987). Consequently, dependency and structuralist analysts argue for alternative development strategies based on principles of participation, grassroots democracy, social justice, gender equity, conscientization, appropriate technology/values, environmental care and self-reliance.

The existence of these competing paradigms for explaining and overcoming problems of underdevelopment provides an important yardstick for assessing study abroad. What paradigmatic emphasis can be found in the academic training and curriculum of Third World students who receive their education in advanced industrialized countries? Given that emphasis, if discernible, how relevant for participatory, equitable and basic-needs development will the graduates be when they return to their home environments?

Alternatively, will the mode of education and training perhaps largely add to the stock of Third World technocratic expertise functional to modernization strategies? In the concluding section of this chapter, we report on a study conducted by Farrelly (1987) on Third World postgraduate students in the field of agricultural science/extension/economics at several Australian universities. Although limited to one curriculum field, the investigation yielded findings which hold significant implications for assessing the value of study abroad in general. The choice of agricultural science/economics was also purposive, given the centrality of rural development to the lives of a majority of Third World populations.

RESEARCH METHODOLOGY

Qualitative in orientation, the study primarily sought to find out what views were held by a sample of Third World post-graduate students in four Australian universities (Queensland, Melbourne, LaTrobe, New England) on general and specific issues and problems of development. However, partial data were also obtained which clarified aspects of the curriculum of the students as well as the development orientations of some academic personnel responsible for the students' training.

Sampling: In 1985, the year during which the research was undertaken, there were about 20,00 overseas students enrolled in Australian tertiary institutions (Overseas Student Office 1985). The sample of students for this study were enrolled in agricultural science, extension or economics, and in the four selected universities, there were around 140 of such students. The sampling procedure comprised (i) organizing a meeting at each institution where students were informed of the goals and nature of the research, (ii) requesting students to volunteer to be interviewed. As Table 1 indicates, a total of 34 interviewees constituted the final sample, distributed fairly equitably across the four universities and reflecting 13 different nationalities. While there was no means of ascertaining how this "voluntary" approach to sampling might be biased in particular directions, it was felt that (i) the neutral non-threatening explanation of the research probably reduced the incidence of non-volunteering on the criterion of paradigmatic orientation, (ii) the broad spread of countries represented promised more generalizable findings, and (iii) data gathered from the academic personnel responsible for the total population of students as well as aspects of curriculum content provided some corroborative evidence.

In addition to the students, a total of eight academic personnel of the four universities were also interviewed. They were selected because of their involvement in the students' academic programs either as lecturers of the courses and/or thesis supervisors.

Interviewing: Conducted during July and August, 1985, the interviews with both students and academic personnel were based on schedules of open-ended questions. For students, information was sought on personal background (i.e. socio-economic status, family); knowledge and attitudes about Third World development issues/problems (including causes of lack of development and rich-poor nation gap, social inequalities, Green Revolution, land reform, industrialization, transnational corporations, foreign investment, trade, aid, education, preferred solutions to problems); motivations for study abroad; and future plans for their careers in development. For academic personnel, the interviews focused on their perception of the relevance of the academic programmes of the students for future contributions to national development, and their paradigmatic orientation towards understanding underdevelopment and development.

TABLE 1:-COUNTRY OF ORIGIN AND UNIVERSITIES OF STUDENTS SAMPLES

Country of Origin	*No. of Students*	*Universities*	*No. of Students*
Bangladesh	6	La Trobe	8
Burma	1	Melbourne	10
Ethiopia	2	New England	7
Fiji	1	Queensland	9
India	2	*Total*	34
Indonesia	3		
Malaysia	1		

Table 5 (cont'd)

Nepal	5
Nigeria	1
Philippines	4
Sierra Leone	1
Sri Lanka	6
Thailand	3

FINDINGS

Students' Background: Based on Niles' (1979) prestige scale for Sri Lankan occupations, virtually all the students come from at least middle-class families. Sixty-five percent of the interviewees had more than half of their brothers and sisters with tertiary qualifications, while 35 percent had university-educated spouses. This middle-class and high educational background coincides with a largely urbanized lifestyle. Only four (12 percent) of the students had spent their childhood or presently resided in a rural village environment. Little identification with rural communities was apparent, and over half of the interviewees admitted they could not give any opinion on how the rural poor felt since they had never talked to any of them. Most had no desire to live in rural areas, noting that the main reason for urban residence was to benefit from the better services available there. Almost all their parents had been wage earners and therefore would have difficulty in identifying with the outlook of subsistence farmers. Virtually all students interviewed came to Australia from established careers in government departments, universities and other public organizations. In sum, the students' family and personal contexts have already predisposed them away from an active concern and identification with grassroots rural development, even before they commenced their Australian studies. It is pertinent to note that for 31 students in the sample, their visit to Australia constitutes their first experience in study abroad.

Knowledge of Development Issues: It was found that 57 percent of the interviewed students had been exposed to development issues via a course on economic development. However, another 30 percent professed to have no knowledge at all of theories of development. Overall, among those with some awareness about development, the majority (60 percent) clearly espoused an understanding based upon the modernization paradigm. Only 10 percent could be said to have some or a partial appreciation of dependency and structuralist perspectives. Most significantly, when causes of underdevelopment were discussed, no less than 32 out of 34 interviewees identified factors which are usually raised by modernization analysts.

A common response blamed the agricultural system for being ineffective. Students from Bangladesh and India tended to emphasize the cause of "over-population, " while the Sri Lankans, Thais and Indonesians saw lack of capital, infrastructure and human resources as barriers to development. Seventy percent of respondents assessed the Green Revolution as successful, and 90 percent mentioned inadequate irrigation as a serious inhibition on agricultural development. The culture of rural people in resisting change was also criticized by some students, especially the Bangladeshis. When political factors were mentioned as in Thailand and the Philippines, most emphasis was placed on corruption, mismanagement and wastage, but these internal problems were deemed capable of being resolved through greater democratization along Western lines and application of educated expertise. Thus, the tendency to blame internal deficiencies in Third World societies for underdevelopment was very strong among the students.

The external factors of underdevelopment such as distortions introduced by colonialism or the contemporary political-economic dominance of rich nations were invariably unmentioned. For instance, while two respondents did not welcome transnational corporations, and seven registered some reservations about lack of government regulation of TNC activities, most of the students argued, consistent with modernization thinking, that TNCs brought investment, employment, goods and technology essential to their countries' development. Only a few interviewees expressed concern over low wages for factory workers and unhealthy working conditions, but 80 percent saw urban factory workers as better off than rural labourers due to more secure work conditions. Hardly any criticism was made of the dependency generated by TNCs, as well as their excessive profits, exploitation of cheap repressed labour, and use of inappropriate technologies.

Similarly, with regard to foreign aid, a large majority of students interviewed generally saw aid (except food aid) as playing a positive role in development. Only three mentioned that aid could be used by donors as leverage on recipient governments, while one argued strongly for rejecting aid so as to avoid further economic dependency. However, for those welcoming aid, some concerns were raised about the need to stop corruption in management of aid funds (which is not inconsistent with modernization thinking) and 90 percent of respondents did recommend against World Bank loans, which partially reflects dependency paradigm analysis. Significantly, however, of hardly any systematic critique was raised about the modernization bias of World Bank strategies and other official aid organizations.

It should not be inferred from the above that the students were totally unaware of issues and problems in a way which might lead towards understanding based on the dependency/structuralist paradigm. However, such awareness usually embodied contradictory elements and ultimately was limited by a basic allegiance to modernization perspectives. This is shown most clearly in the responses on agricultural development, where only three students expressed the need for involvement of poor farmers in rural development planning, production for local needs, reversal of the urban bias in power structures, and authentic land reforms which reach the poorest. The remaining students did mention the desirability of such tactics as providing credit for subsistence and low-income production, developing plant/livestock varieties suited to local conditions, small-scale irrigation, and cooperatives, all of which in theory should benefit the rural poor. Some admitted that existing banks, transport systems and marketing institutions tended to support large-scale agriculture. Nevertheless, these insights are not extended into a critical analysis of the structures of internal and external structural violence which deny the poor and marginalized equitable access to resources and decision-making power. Instead, when asked how the desirable services would be provided, most respondents could only point to the "responsibility of governments", and did or would not countenance radical redistribution of political and economic power to bring about social justice and equity.

This elite-centred approach to political change is consistent with modernization perspectives, which in the case of most students interviewed was confirmed by responses to questions about social stratification in their countries. While many acknowledged rural-urban disparities, the major causes cited were to blame the poor's culture and religion, their inability to afford modern inputs, and the lack of rural services (which are really more symptoms than causes). The idea of a significant devolution of power to the poor majorities was invariably rejected. A further reflection of modernization orientation among most of the students was apparent in their conception of education's role in development. Education has to fulfil manpower requirements of a modernizing economy. It helps modernize attitudes and cultural change, especially among the rural poor so that they can better adopt modern techniques of production. And an educated elite is essential to overcome ignorance and corruption. Only two students who argued for dependency/structuralist ideas envisioned a conscientization role for education.

It was only in the area of trade where many respondents could be said to be somewhat more consistent with the dependency paradigm. Thus some 60 percent argued for self-reliance on the part of Third World countries, especially in basic food production. The reality that some rich nations use food supply as a political weapon is recognized by some students, while most did not see much prospect of advanced industrialized states agreeing to changes embodied in the New International Economic Order proposals. Nevertheless, this recognition of international trading inequalities is still not based on an in-depth understanding of global political-economic relationships that are, as earlier noted, vitally linked to internal structural violence.

The overall picture then is that almost all the students interviewed, whilst professing concern about the directions of development in their countries in particular and the Third World in general, are predisposed towards the modernization paradigm. Partial awareness is shown on a few issues and problems, but the lack of a coherent integrated framework for critically analyzing relationships of centre-periphery dependency, inequalities and uneven development means that their preferred strategies for implementing development would not readily benefit the marginalized poor majorities.

Motivations and expectations: With regard to the reasons for studying abroad, some 70 percent of the students identified the lack of advanced facilities (e.g. laboratories, computers, scholarly journals) to pursue their desired research topics at home. Another major factor behind seeking Australian training was the access to academic personnel who could trasmit to them knowledge, skills and methodologies apparently not so available in their countries. Little concern was demonstrated as to how relevant that expertise available in Australian faculties of agricultural science/economics/extension might be for meeting the basic needs of poor communities. The overriding ethos projected by the students interviewed, with very few exceptions, is that study abroad will yield technocratic solutions to the problems of underdevelopment. It was difficult to discern interest in or knowledge of alternative strategies for grassroots development based on authentic peoples' participation, structural redistribution and self-reliance.

On the topic of future plans after completing their Australian studies, five students claimed not to wish to return to their home countries. Twenty-nine students (80%) intended to return and work in the public sector, although since many of the interviewees were on ADAB scholarships, this was obligatory anyway. What is significant from the perspective of this study is that the major areas of future work would be in the modern economic sector in senior levels of research, tertiary teaching and administration, invariably in urbanized contexts. No student explicitly expressed a commitment to work in situations where they would be directly helping the poor meet their basic needs in participatory and just development programmes. Juxtaposed with the above predominant knowledge and attitudinal preference for the modernization paradigm, it is reasonable to expect that most respondents will likely return to their countries as technocrats well trained, by commission or omission, to reinforce and promote the theory and practice of modernization.

Curriculum and Lecturers: Although the scope of the study did not permit an indepth look at the curriculum and pedagogy received by the students, partial data were obtained which lent weight to the major findings. Thus, apart from one special masters programme in "agriculture in developing countries" which enrolled ten of the interviewed students and attempted to focus on problems of small-farm management and techniques at the University of Queensland, the remaining 24 students in the sample were in mainstream postgraduate programmes. The latter usually comprised courses also undertaken by Australian students, although two universities (Queensland, New England) claimed to have a few courses more relevant to the needs of "developing countries" (e.g. tropical agriculture, rural sociology, agricultural extension, natural resource sector planning). However, despite these claims to "relevance, " a separate analysis of curriculum and pedagogy of at least one of these universities' offerings in agricultural economics indicates a predominant emphasis on the modernization paradigm.

Frequently, Third World students with prior awareness of dependency/structuralist ideas have privately expressed frustration at the academic barriers to pursuing issues outside modernization views in their coursework and thesis research. Even in the above mentioned University of Queensland's special masters course, the methodological and conceptual thrust is to equip students with skills in quantifying relationships between agricultural policy and social and economic outcomes. This approach largely neglects the political dimensions of rural underdevelopment which the dependency/structuralist paradigm argues must be integrated into the training and socialization of potential contributors to self-development efforts of marginalized communities.

All ten doctoral students in the sample, and five at masters level, were engaged in full-time research, usually employing use of computers or sophisticated laboratory equipment. Most importantly, only two of these were working with data which had been gathered in their home countries, which raises the issue of relevance of the research programme for Third World development. Furthermore, a perusal of some past theses submitted by returned students, and discussions about 1985 research projects with the students concerned revealed a bias towards concepts and methodologies based on microeconomic models of adoption of new technologies/processes, highly specialized technical studies on aspects of agricultural or natural resources use/management, and elaborate statistical manipulations of quantifiable factors (e.g. LaTrobe University 1984; University of New England 1985; University of Queensland 1985; Towett 1983; Tungu 1983; Karim 1983). The bibliographies of the theses examined indicated no reference to theorists and researchers from outside modernization circles. From the dependency/structuralist paradigm, what is problematic about such a research orientation is that students are being inducted into very narrow, technical views and procedures about problems of underdevelopment and potential solutions. This is not to deny the possible utility of scientific skills and techniques in helping to resolve problems confronting the Third World's poor majorities. But the essentially depoliticized training received by the students, compounded by a lack of exposure to non-modernization analysis, makes them into functional technocrats helping to preserve existing social, economic and political status quos. Conversely, their Australian educational experience would have done little to catalyze a commitment to research and development work grounded in principles of conscientization, social justice and participation.

The latter conclusion is bolstered by the data obtained from interviewing eight lecturers involved in teaching and/or supervising the sample of students. From Farrelly's (1987: 86–97) detailed findings, the following generalizations can be drawn. To begin with, the modernization paradigm was overwhelmingly favoured by the lecturers although they were aware of dependency and structuralist ideas. Two explicitly stated that dependency theory could not be taken seriously since it is based on unprovable "anecdotal evidence and conspiratorial factors". While two lecturers admitted to it being a possible useful alternative analysis, they felt unable, as academics, to be involved in any political implications of the theory. The primary thrust of their research and consultancies (e.g. AIDAB, World Bank) in Third World development is to design models and frameworks for efficient diffusion of modern agricultural techniques to increase production (Wilson and Woods 1982; Dillon and Hardaker 1980; Ongkili and Quilkey 1982; Crouch and Chamala 1982). Although many insisted that their efforts were directed to helping small farmers, it was clear that proposed strategies were conceived in a modernization framework within existing political and economic structures. No proposals were provided, as required by the dependency and structuralist paradigm, to empower the rural poor to transform their oppressive realities.

Indeed, the lecturers' general "apolitical" ethos translates into their expectations of their training of Third World students. One noted that " we are training analysts—not people who can effect social change, " while another claimed that "lecturers are not citizens of Third World countries and therefore have no right to influence political outcomes in those countries by forcing students to study sociological issues or show them political strategies for change". From the dependency/structuralist paradigm, such views reflect an inability or unwillingness to recognize that the seperation of "technology" and "scientific practices" from their political-economic contexts is not possible, and a seemingly "apolitical" or "neutral" approach to training Third World students is no less political in theory and practice than if students had been also exposed to dependency/structuralist analysis. Furthermore, World Bank or other aid consultants cannot escape from bearing a political responsibility by their "expert" contributions to development plans and processes. Despite professed concern for the Third World poor, the lecturers' attempted distinction between "expertise" and political influence allows them to avoid considering that technocratic knowledge has unavoidable political impact, often deleterious to the marginalized, in the context of structural violence.

In short, both the curriculum and training received by Third World students of agricultural science/economics/extension in the four sampled universities are basically embedded in assumptions, values, attitudes, content, methodology and strategies of the modernization paradigm. While more detailed research into pedagogical aspects of the training would be useful and interesting, it is reasonable to conclude on the basis of the above documented data that the sampled students' development thinking is invariably congruent with their education, training and research apprenticeships obtained in Australia. While it is likely that prior to their Australian studies, the students may already prefer the modernization paradigm, their training in this country evidently socializes them further into this paradigm.

CONCLUDING REMARKS

This chapter has sought to (a) critically review the state of scholarly thinking and research on the education/training of Third World students in advanced industrialized countries; (b) suggest the utility of evaluating the worth of study abroad programmes on the basis of paradigms of Third World underdevelopment and development; and (c) report on the major findings of a research investigation into the formation of Third World agricultural scientists/economists/extension personnel in four selected Australian universities. With regard to the first objective, it is clear that there are important conceptual, methodological and empirical shortcomings in much analysis and research of issues/problems of study abroad over the past three decades. Most significantly, the bulk of scholars have focused on narrowly administrative and technical dimensions of training Third World students abroad. Where wider concerns are raised in the context of relevance of that education to Third World societies, the approach tends to make implicit or explicit assumptions about "benefits". Such assumptions in turn tend to be derived from the modernization paradigm of explaining underdevelopment and suggesting strategies for development.

The chapter then went on to argue that a systematic and objective analysis of study abroad programmes needs to consider the existence of competing paradigms of understanding underdevelopment and development. In contrast to the dominant worldview of modernization, the dependency/structuralist paradigm is posited as a valuable framework for assessing the relevance of the training and education Third World students receive overseas as in Australia. It was consequently demonstrated, using findings from a research investigation into Third World students studying in agricultural science/economics/extension postgraduate programmes in four selected Australian universities, that serious questions can and should be raised about how our tertiary institutions are helping to produce highly qualified personnel for Third World development. The sample of students investigated reflects an overwhelming predisposition towards modernization ideas and principles, while their curriculum and teachers in the Australian faculties concerned are no less embedded in the modernization paradigm. Although, of course, the research reported focuses only on one specific field of study abroad, and a selection of Australian universities, it is nonetheless a crucial sector of this country's contribution to training of high-level skills for the Third World. After all, the graduates would be returning to fulfil public roles in agricultural development, which relates directly to the lives of the poor majorities in their home countries. Indeed, we would hypothesise reasonably confidently that similar results would obtain for parallel assessments of study abroad programmes in other fields like economics, medicine, engineering, public policy, and educational administration. The results of this study have also provided complementary empirical evidence to reinforce the critical assessment of educational aid and exchange issues by earlier cited analysts like Carnoy, Arnove, Altbach, and Berman.

In sum, we ask administrators and colleagues in Australian tertiary institutions, as well as government officials concerned with the study abroad programme, to seriously consider if current training of Third World students, along the lines we have elucidated, is likely to make the graduates useful to basic-needs development of the poor? Our view is that education/training in Australian universities can contribute more effectively and authentically to rural development if Third World students also have substantive opportunities to explore ideas, values, skills and methodologies drawn from the dependency/structuralist paradigm. While there is no guarantee that a particular curriculum results in expected outcomes of a graduate's personal/social practice, at least Third World students will have been exposed to principles of conscientization, justice, structural violence, self-reliance and participation. The obstacles to revising Australian tertiary curriculum and pedagogy in those critical directions are admittedly weighty (e.g. most academics and many Third World students are often unwilling to contemplate paradigmatic shifts; the resistance from Third World governments to their students receiving alternative ideas and skills which can be threatening to existing power-structures; the commercial/strategic imperatives of Australian foreign policy which makes it more important to fulfil Third World governments' expectations about study abroad). Nevertheless, a failure of concerned comparative and international educators to raise such issues and lobby for change can only mean that Australian universities will continue, wittingly or unwittingly, to help in the formation of Third World technocrats irrelevant or even inimical to the basic rights of poor peoples for just, equitable, participatory and humane development. This prediction bears even more weight in the context of emergent political, economic and institutional pressures in Australia towards exploiting education as an "international commodity" for sale to the Third World (Gillespie and Collins 1986).

REFERENCES

Altbach, Philip G. (1977) 'Servitude of the mind? Education, Dependency and Neocolonialism'. *Teachers College Record* 79 (2): 187–205.

Arnove, Robert F. (1989) 'Comparative Education and World-Systems Analysis'. *Comparative Education Review* 24: 48–62.

Arnove, Robert F. (ed.) (1982) *Philanthrophy and Cultural Imperialism.* Bloomington, Indiana University Press.

Australian Vice-Chancellors' Committee (1988) *Code of Ethical Practice in the Provision of Full-Fee Courses to Overseas Students by Australian Higher Education Institutions.* Braddon, AVCC.

Bacchus, M. Kazim (1981) 'Education for Development in Underdeveloped Countries'. *Comparative Education* 17 (2): 215–227.

Bang, Katherine C. (1961) 'The Community's Role in Cross-Cultural Education'. *The Annals of the American Academy of Political and Social Science* 335: 54–65, May.

Barber, Elinor, Altbach, Philip G., and Myers, Robert G. (eds.) (1984) 'Special Issue: Foreign Students in Comparative Perspective' *Comparative Education Review* 28 (2).

Barnet, R.J., and Muller, R.E. (1974) *Global Reach*. New York, Simon and Schuster.

Baron, Marvin (1979) *The Relevance of US Graduate Programs to Foreign Students from Developing Countries*. Washington, D.C., National Association for Foreign Student Affairs.

Beck, Robert H. (1962) 'The Professional Training in Education of Foreign Students in the United States'. *Journal of Teacher Education* 13: 140–149.

Benson, August, and Kovach, Joseph (eds.) (1974) *A Guide for the Education of Foreign Students*. Washington D.C., National Association for Foreign Student Affairs.

Berman, Edward H. (1979) 'Foundations, US Foreign Policy and African Education'. *Harvard Education Review* 49 (2): 145–184.

Bernstein, Henry (1971) 'Modernization Theory and the Sociological Study of Development'. *Journal of Development Studies* 7: 141–160.

Bloom, Judith M. (1969) 'The Foreign Student as a Student Teacher'. *Supervisors Quarterly* 5 (1): 13–17.

Bochner, Stephen, Lin, A., and McLeod, B.M. (1980) 'Anticipated Role Conflict of Returning Overseas Students'. *Journal of Social Psychology* 110 (April): 265–272.

Bochner, Stephen, and Wicks, P. (eds.) (1972) *Overseas Students in Australia*. Sydney, University of New South Wales.

Borlaug, N. (1980) 'The Green Revolution and Beyond'. *Foreign Agriculture* 15–18, January.

Bradley, D., and Bradley, M. (1984) *Problems of Asian Students in Australia: Language, Culture and Education*. Canberra, AGPS.

Burbach, R., and Flynn, P. (1980) *Agribusiness in the Americas*. New York, Monthly Review.

Burbach, R., and Flynn, P. (eds) (1984) *The Politics of Intervention*. New York, Monthly Review.

Carnoy, Martin (1974) *Education as Cultural Imperialism*. New York, David McKay.

Carnoy, Martin (1982) 'Education for Alternative Development'. *Comparative Education Review* 26 (2): 160–177.

Carter, William D. (1973) *Study Abroad and Educational Development*. Paris, UNESCO.

Cerych, Ladislav (1965) *Problems of Aid to Education in Developing Countries*. New York, Frederick A. Praeger.

Chomsky, Noam, and Herman, Edward S. (eds.) (1979) *The Political Economy of Human Rights*, Vols. 1 and 2. Boston, South End.

Chong, Florence (1985) 'Australia's Latest Export Commodity'. *Business Review Weekly*, August 16.

Coleman, James S. (1984) 'Professorial Training and Institution Building in the Third World: Two Rockefeller Foundation Experiences'. *Comparative Education Review* 28 (2): 180–202.

Committee on the Professional School and World Affairs (1967) *The Professional School and World Affairs*. Albuquerque, University of New Mexico.

Commonwealth Secretariat (1982) *Educational Interchange: A Commonwealth Imperative*. London, Commonwealth Secretariat.

Cormack, Margaret (1963) 'Three Steps to Better Orientation' *Overseas* 3: 11–15, September.

Crabbs, Richard F., and Holmquist, Frank W. (1967) *United States Higher Education and World Affairs: A Partially Annotated Bibliography*. New York, Frederick A. Praeger.

Crouch, B.R., and Chamala, S. (1981) *Extension Education and Rural Development*. Brisbane, John Wiley.

Crough, G.J., and Wheelwright, E.L. (1984) *Transnational Corporations and the Pacific*. Sydney, University of Sydney, Transnational Corporations Research Project.

Cummings, William K. (1984) 'Going Overseas for Higher Education: the Asian Experience'. *Comparative Education Review* 28 (2): 241–257.

Davis, James M. (1964) 'Some Trends in International Educational Exchange'. *Comparative Education Review* 8: 48–57.

Department of Employment, Education and Training, Australia (1989) *Annual Report 1988/89*. Canberra, AGPS.

Department of Trade, Australia (1985) *Report of the Australian Government Education Mission to Southeast Asia and Hong Kong*. Canberra, AGPS.

Deutsch, Steven E. (1970) *International Education and Exchange*. Cleveland, Case Western University.

Dillon, J.E., and Hardaker, J.B. (1980) *Farm Management Research for Small Farmer Development*. Rome, FAO.

Donaldson, Peter J. (1976) 'Foreign Intervention in Medical Education: A Case Study of the Rockefeller Foundation's Involvement in a Thai Medical School'. *International Journal of Health Services* 6 (2): 265–266.

Dore, Ronald (1976) *The Diploma Disease*. Berkeley, University of California.

Dremuk, Richard (ed.) (1967) *Report of the Training Workshop on the Evaluation of Asian Educational Credentials*, Honolulu, November 26–December.9. Washington, D.C., National Association for Foreign Student Affairs.

Dresden, Katherine (1955) 'Weaknesses in International Exchange Programs'. *Journal of Teacher Education* 6: 200–204.

Drucker, Peter (1974) 'Multinationals and Developing Countries: Myths and Realities'. *Foreign Affairs* 53 (1): 521.

Dunnet, S. C. (1981) *Factors Affecting the Adaptation of Foreign Students in Cross-Cultural Settings*. Buffalo, Council of International Studies, State University of New York.

Eckholm, E.P. (1982) *Down to Earth*. New York, W.W. Norton.

Ehrlich, Paul (1968) *The Population Bomb*. New York, Ballantine.

Eicher, C.K., and Staatz, J. M. (eds.) (1984) *Agricultural Development and the Third World*. Baltimore, Johns Hopkins University.

Farrelly, Terry (1987) *Technocrats for Rural Development?: A Study of Third World Students in Selected Australian Universities*. Unpublished MEd thesis, Armidale, University of New England.

Foster-Carter, A. (1985) *The Sociology of Development*. Lancaster, Causeway.

Frank, A. Gunder (1970) 'Sociology of Development and Underdevelopment of Sociology'. In *Latin America: Underdevelopment or Revolution?* New York, Monthly Review.

Fraser, Stewart E. (1984) 'Overseas Students in Australia: Governmental Policies and Institutional Programs'. *Comparative Education Review* 28 (2): 279–299.

Freire, Paulo (1985) *The Politics of Education*. London, Macmillan.

Fry, Gerald W. (1984) 'The Economic and Political Impact of Study Abroad'. *Comparative Education Review* 28 (2): 203–220.

Gama, E.M.P., and Pedersen, P. (1977) 'Readjustment Problems of Brazilian Returnees from Graduate Studies in the United States'. *International Journal of Intercultural Relations* 1 (4): 46–59.

Gardner, John W. (1964) *AID and the Universities*. New York, Education and World Affairs.

George, Susan (1976) *How the Other Half Dies*. Ringwood, Penguin.

George, Susan (1987) *A Fate Worse than Debt*. Ringwood, Penguin.

Ghertman, Michel, and Allen, Margaret (1984) *An Introduction to the Multinationals*. London, Macmillan.

Giacalone, C. a Davis, D. (1967) *Research in International Education—Research in Progress and Research Recently Completed. 1966–67 Survey*. Washington, D.C., National Association for Foreign Student Affairs.

Gillespie, Roselyn R., and Collins, Colin B. (eds.) (1986) *Education as an International Commodity*. St. Lucia, Australia and New Zealand Comparative and International Education Society.

Goldring, J. (chairperson) (1984) *Mutual Advantage: Report of the Committee of Review of Private Overseas Student Policy*. Canberra, AGPS.

Goodwin, C.D., and Nacht, M. (1983) *Absence of Decision: Foreign Students in American Colleges and Universities*. New York, Institute of International Education.

Goonalatilake, S. (1975) 'Development Thinking as Cultural Neo-Colonialism: the case of Sri Lanka'. *IDS Bulletin* 7 (1): 4–10.

Gue, L. R. (1972) *Thailand Comprehensive School Project*. Edmonton, University of Alberta, Faculty of Education.

Gue, L.R., and Holdaway, E.A. (1973) 'English Proficiency Tests as Predictors of Success in Graduate Studies in Education'. *Language Learning* 23 (1): 89–103.

Harbison, F.H., and Myers, C.A. (1964) *Education, Manpower and Economic Growth*. New York, McGraw-Hill.

Harries, O. (chairperson) (1979) *Report of the Committee on Australia's Relations with the Third World*. Canberra, AGPS.

Hayter, T., and Watson, C. (1984) *Aid: Rhetoric and Reality*. London, Pluto.

Henry, David D. (1960) 'The 1960 Nigerian-American Scholarship Program'. *Institute of International Education News Bulletin* 36 (3): 17–25.

Hill, Helen (1983) 'The Impact of Development Policies on Women'. In J. Langmore and D. Peetz (eds.) *Wealth, Poverty and Survival*. Sydney, Allen and Unwin.

Hodgkin, Mary C. (1972) *The Innovators: the Role of Foreign Trained Persons in Southeast Asia*. Sydney, Sydney University Press.

Hoogvelt, A.M. (1976) *The Sociology of Developing Societies*. London, Macmillan.

Hoogvelt, A.M. (1982) *The Third World in Global Development*. London, Macmillan.

Hoselitz, B.F. (1960) *Sociological Aspects of Economic Growth*. Glencoe, Free Press.

Humphrey, Richard A. (ed.) (1967) *Universities and Development Assistance Abroad*. Washington, D.C., American Council on Education.

I.I.E. (Institute of International Education) (1969) *English Language and Orientation Programs in the United States*. New York, Institute on International Education.

Jackson, G. (chairperson) (1984) *Report of the Committee to Review the Australian Overseas Aid Programme*. Canberra, AGPS.

Jenkins, Hugh M. (1973) 'NAFSA and the Student Abroad: A Silver Anniversary Review'. *International Educational and Cultural Exchange* 6 (4): 1–13.

Joint Committee on Foreign Affairs, Defence and Trade, Parliament of the Commonwealth of Australia (1989) *A Review of the Australian International Development Assistance Bureau and Australia's Overseas Aid Program*. Canberra, AGPS.

Jones, Phillip W. (1986) *Australia's International Relations in Education*. Hawthorn, Australian Council for Educational Research.

Jones, P. W. (1989) 'Overseas Students in Australia: Who Benefits?' *Current Affairs Bulletin*, 66(2): 12–15.

Karim, R. (1983) *A Multisectoral Model for Agricultural Policy Analysis in Bangladesh*. Unpublished PhD thesis, Bundoora, LaTrobe University.

Keats, D. (1969) *Back in Asia*. Canberra, Australian National University.

Klein, M.H., et al. (1971) 'The Foreign Student Adaptation Program'. *International, Educational and Cultural Exchange* 6 (3): 77–90.

Klineberg, Otto (1980) 'Stressful Experiences of Foreign Students at Various Stages of Sojourn: Counseling and Policy Implications'. In G.V. Coelho and P.I. Ahmed (eds.), *Uprooting and Development*. New York, Plenum.

Krause, W. (1961) *Economic Development*. San Francisco, Wadsworth.

Krueger, A.O. (1982) 'Newly Industrializing Economies'. *Economic Impact* 40: 26–32.

La Trobe University (1984) *Annual Report 1984: School of Agriculture*. Bundoora, La Trobe University.

Lavergne, D.C. (1969) 'University and Government: Two Views of the Foreign Graduate Student'. In *University, Government and the Foreign Graduate Student*. New York, College Entrance Examination Board.

Leeper, M. H., et al. (1967) 'Schools of Public Health and World Affairs'. In Committee on the Professional School and World Affairs (ed.) *The Professional School and World Affairs*. Albuquerque, University of New Mexico.

Lerner, D. (1958) *The Passing of Traditional Society*. New York, Free Press.

Lesser, S.O., and Hollis, P.W. (1957) 'Training Foreign Nationals in the United States'. In R. Likert and S.P. Hayers. Jr. (eds.), *Some Applications of Behavioral Research*. Paris, UNESCO.

Little, I.M.D. (1982) *Economic Development*. New York, Basic Books.

Livingstone, A.S. (1964) *The International Student*. Manchester, University of Manchester.

Lulat, Y.G-M., and Cordaro, J. (1984) 'International Students and Study-Abroad Programs: A Select Bibliography'. *Comparative Education Review* 28 (2): 300–339.

Lundstet, Sven (1963) 'An Introduction to Some Evolving Problems in Cross-Cultural Research'. *Journal of Social Issues* 19 (3): 1–9.

Mass, B. (1976) *Population Target*. Toronto, Latin American Working Group.

McClelland, D.C. (1961) 'The Achievement Motive in Economic Growth'. In Ness, G. (ed.) *The Sociology of Development*. New York, Harper and Row.

Michie, A.A. (1968) *Higher Education and World Affairs*. New York, Education and World Affairs.

Millikan, M.F., and Blackmer, D.L. (eds.) (1961) *The Emerging Nations*. Boston, Little, Brown.

Moock, Joyce L. (1984) 'Overseas Training and National Development Objectives in Sub-Saharan Africa'. *Comparative Education Review* 28 (2): 221–240.

Morrison, W.L. (chairperson) (1984) *Australia and ASEAN: Challenges and Opportunities. Report from the Joint Committee on Foreign Affairs and Defence*. Canberra, AGPS.

Murphy, E.J. (1960) 'African Exchange Problems'. *Institute of International Education News Bulletin* 36 (3): 11–16.

NAFSA (1966) *Academic and Personal Advising. Guidelines*. Cleveland, National Association for Foreign Student Affairs.

NAFSA (1967a) *American-Foreign Student Relationships. Guidelines*. Cleveland, National Association for Foreign Student Affairs.

NAFSA (1967b) *Housing of Foreign Students. Guidelines*. Cleveland, National Association for Foreign Student Affairs.

Neal, Joe W. (1964) 'Developing the International Office'. *Overseas* 3 (8): 7–10.

Niles, F.S. (1979) *School Achievement in Sri Lanka*. Bundoora, LaTrobe University, unpublished Ph.D. thesis.

Noesjirwan, J.A., Anderson, A.M., and Kelleher, B.M. (1979) *Culture Shock of Overseas Students at Hawkesbury College*. Sydney, Ethnic Affairs Division, NSW Government Premier's Office.

Ongkili, M.J., and Quilkey, J. (1982) 'Some Considerations in Modelling the Adoption Decision Processes of Traditional Farmers'. In *Proceedings of 26th Annual Conference of the Australian Agricultural Economics Society*. Parkville, University of Melbourne.

Overseas Student Office (1985) *Australia's Overseas Student Policy*. Canberra, Ovwerseas Student Office.

Owen, W. (1981) 'Higher Education in Economics: Major Trends and Dimensions'. In W. Owen, et al., (eds.) *Higher Education in Economics*. Boulder, Economics Institute.

Payer, Cheryl (1974) *The Debt Trap*. Ringwood, Penguin.

Payer, Cheryl (1983) *The World Bank: A Critical Analysis*. New York, Monthly Review.

P.E.P. (Political and Economic Planning) (1965) *New Commonwealth Students in Britain*. London, George Allen and Unwin.

Pruitt, F.S. (1977) *The Adaptation of African Students to the USA*. New York, Council on International Studies.

Psacharopoulos, G., and Woodhall, M. (1985) *Education for Development: An Analysis of Investment Choices*. Oxford, Oxford University Press.

Radford, M., Ongkili, D.J., and Toyoizumi, M. (1984) *Overseas Students in South Australia*. Adelaide, Flinders University, International Students Association.

Rao, G.L. (1976) *Overseas Students in Australia*. Canberra, Australian National University.

Richardson, J.M. (1969) *Partners in Development*. East Lansing, Michigan State University.

Ryan, S. (1985) 'New Policy on Overseas Students'. *News release: Minister of Education*. Australia, Commonwealth Dept. of Education.

Scott, James D. (1966) *Educating Asian Students for Business Careers*. Ann Arbor, Graduate School of Business Administration, University of Michigan.

SELMOUS (Special English Language Materials for Overseas University Students) Group (1980) *Study Modes and Academic Development of Overseas Students*. London, British Council.

Selltiz, C., et al. (1963) *Attitudes and Social Relations of Foreign Students in the United States.* Minneapolis, University of Minneapolis.

Sinauer, E.M. (1967) *The Role of Communication in International Training and Education.* New York, Frederick A. Praeger.

Singh, A.K. (1963) *Indian Students in Britain.* New York, Asia Publishing House.

Spaulding, S., and Flack, M.J. (1976) *The World's Students in the United States: A Review and Evaluation of Research on Foreign Students.* New York, Praeger.

Spencer, R.E., and Awe, R. (1968) *A Bibliography of Research on Foreign Student Affairs.* Urbana, University of Illinois, Urbana Office of Instructional Resources.

Spencer, C.S., and Stahl, V.R. (1983) *Bibliography of Research on International Exchanges.* Washington, D.C., US Information Agency.

Strain, W.H. (1967) 'Some Doubts About Educational Exchange'. *College and University* 42: 141–146.

Susskind, C., and Schell, L. (1968) *Exporting Technical Education.* New York, Institute on International Education.

Timberlake, L. (1985) *Africa in Crisis.* London, Earthscan.

Toh, Swee-Hin (1974) *A Study of the Administrative Process in the Uganda-Canada Primary Teacher Training Project, 1964–66.* Unpublished M.Ed. thesis, Edmonton, University of Alberta.

Toh, Swee-Hin (1980) *The Overseas Development Council.* Unpublished Ph.D. thesis, Edmonton, University of Alberta.

Toh, Swee-Hin (1987) 'Survival and Solidarity: Australia and Third World (South) Peace'. *Social Alternatives* 6 (2): 59–66.

Toh, Swee-Hin (1987) 'Education for Participation: Third World Perspectives'. *WCCI FORUM: Journal of the World Council for Curriculum and Instruction* 1 (1): 20–43.

Towett, N.C. (1983) *The Organization and Operation of Group Ranches, Narok District, Republic of Kenya.* Unpublished MAgricSt thesis, St. Lucia, University of Queensland.

Trainer, F.E. (1985) *Abandon Affluence.* London, Zed.

Tungu, L.S.M. (1983) *A Study of Adoption of Block Farming and its Relationship to Ujamaa Village Policy in Bangani District, Tanzania.* Unpublished MAgricSt thesis, St. Lucia, University of Queensland.

University of New England (1985) *Dept. of Agricultural Economics and Business Management, 1985 Postgraduate Handbook.* Armidale, University of New England, Dept. of Agricultural Economics and Business Management.

University of Queensland (1985) *Extension: Dept. of Agriculture*. St. Lucia, University of Queensland, Dept. of Agriculture.

Weiler, Hans W. (1984) 'The Political Dilemmas of Foreign Study'. *Comparative Education Review* 28 (2): 168–179.

Weiner, M. (ed.) (1966) *Modernization: The Dynamics of Growth*. New York, Basic Books.

Welch, A.R. (1986) 'For Sale by Degrees: The Commodification of Higher Education in Australia and the U.K.' Brisbane, ANZCIES, University of Queensland.

Welch, A.R. (1988) 'For Sale by Degrees: International Students and the Commodification of Higher Education in Australia and the U.K.' *International Review of Education* 34(3).

Wilcox, Lee (1966) 'A Prediction Study of African Students Selected through the African Scholarship Program of American Universities'. In M. Sasnett and I. Sepmeyer (eds.), *Educational Systems of Africa*: 1494–1505. Berkeley, University of California.

Williams, Peter (ed.) (1981) *The Overseas Student Question*. London, Heinemann.

Williams, Peter (1984) 'Britain's Full-Cost Policy for Overseas Students'. *Comparative Education Review* 28 (2): 258–278.

Wilson, R.K., and Woods, C.S. (1982) *Patterns of World Economic Development*. Melbourne, Longman Sorrett.

Yudelman, M. (1977) 'Integrated Rural Development Projects: the Bank's Experience'. *Finance and Development* 14 (1): 15–18.

Education and Developing Countries: A Framework for Analysis

COLIN E. HINDSON

Univeristy of South Australia, South Australia

"... the educators were mesmerised by the economists's use of funny numbers" (Dore 1976: 84).

INTRODUCTION

The period of the 1960s and 1970s was one of rapid educational growth in countries of the developing world. As new nations emerged and gained independence, the need for a trained administrative and technical elite became more pressing and Third World countries allocated large sections of their budgets to education at all levels.[1] The need for some planned approach was imperative, and the influence of Western economists and educationists was great. Much has been written about this period of development, both from a formal descriptive viewpoint and from a more critical stance, and comparative educationists have applied their methodologies to particular case studies as well as cross-country analyses.

There has been little written, however, on development in the small island states, such as those found in the South Pacific. Some attention has been paid to their economic vulnerability (e.g. Brock 1983), but research on educational development has been relatively neglected. Brock (1983: 132) has suggested that 'It is . . . only through the informed involvement of the human population of small countries that the changes necessary for survival and meaningful occupation can be affected'. The peculiar economic and social circumstances of small island states have implications for the general development of education. Case studies of the small islands may address some of the theoretical and methodological problems in comparative education (Alladin 1987: 14). This applies particularly to the South Pacific region, an area under close scrutiny in the latter part of this century, and certainly relatively neglected in terms of educational research. It is argued in this chapter that further research on education and its role in developing countries is essential. However a consideration of education and development in the context of established planning models can be misleading, and a revised approach is necessary. Accordingly, this chapter examines the debate over the role of educational planning in development throughout the Third World, with particular reference to the South Pacific. Doubts are expressed about the application of the formal Western educational planning process, and an alternative framework is proposed to assist further research, particularly into education in small island states.

ECONOMIC DEVELOPMENT PLANNING: A PERIOD OF OPTIMISM

The emergence of a more organised approach to modern development planning began in the late 1950s and early 1960s. During this optimistic period, it was widely believed that high levels of economic growth would result in economic development, measured largely by per capita gross national product. It was argued, albeit naively, that rapid gains in this area would trickle down to the masses in the form of jobs and other economic opportunities (Sharp 1982: 16–21). 'Modernisation theory' of the 1950s suggested that a society could not hope to develop until the majority of its population held modern values (Fägerlind and Saha 1983: 16), and this tied in with views of the proponents of economic growth and 'trickle-down' theory. The economists also formulated their own theory of development which centred upon the productive capacity of the human manpower process and in doing so played down the social implications of development issues and treated the improvement of the workforce as a form of capital investment. This 'human capital' theory focused heavily on the provision of manpower for specific purposes.

While this faith in the rational nature of linear human progress was not borne out by later analysis of the period, it nevertheless profoundly influenced educational planning. The rapid expansion of education in developing countries was strongly motivated by a number of factors. Concern for human rights was one of these, including the desire to see greater equality of access to schooling. This concern soon became entangled, however, in the mechanics of the drive to expand education for economic purposes. Modernisation theory certainly influenced many educational planners, but so too did human capital theory, and the two became closely linked. Other contributing factors included the provision and financing of cducation by the state and the role played by bilateral and multilateral agencies of international assistance, notably the World Bank, in introducing models of educational planning into developing countries.

Economists thus began to exert an influence on the emerging field of educational planning. Dore (1976: 84) asked, in terms still appropriate today, whether it was:

> . . . due to the fact that it was the economists who commanded the money, or whether the educators were mesmerised by the economists' use of funny numbers, or whether they were just over-awed by the superior professional status of the economic profession.

Modern education was equated with enlightenment. So strong was the belief in the power of universal literacy and numeracy that it developed into something akin to a faith which the early missionaries would have envied. Access to knowledge would enable the masses of the Third World to gain greater economic independence. Literacy would facilitate informal participation in politics and provide access to modern communications media. This, in turn, would generate modern-sector development skills thereby enhancing economic benefit both to the individual and the nation.

In practice, human capital theory and modernisation theory affected educational planning by giving rise to two closely linked planning approaches: 'international comparisons' and 'manpower planning'. The basic tenet of manpower planning and the associated cost benefit analysis was that education's role in development was to create a suitably skilled and viable workforce. The education planner's job was primarily to provide the number and type of skills 'required' by the various economic sectors. Manpower planning dominated educational thought in most developing countries, and the majority of Asian and African development plans of the 1960s and 1970s used some form of this approach (Oxenham 1984). This same rationale was also extended to the Pacific area in the 1970s, as Bray's (1984) analysis of educational planning in Papua New Guinea demonstrates.

Further studies of education and development suggested some broad international trends which could guide decision-making and the 'international comparisons' approach had great influence during the 1960s, possibly because most developing countries lacked domestic data. Harbison and Myers (1964) constructed a so-called 'composite index of human resource development' and suggested that for a country to reach a high level of national income it must first increase its score on this index. This led to the regarding of particular areas of education as essential for economic 'take-off'. As a result a heavy emphasis was placed on secondary school and university expansion in educational planning (Psacharopoulos 1986: 561). Manpower planning was based firmly on economic criteria and on the perceived role of education in generating economic development. Little attention was given at this time to the education process itself.

REACTIONS AGAINST RATIONAL PLANNING IN ECONOMICS AND EDUCATION

It is argued here that the rational economic planning model is not a useful one to use when examining educational development in Third World countries, nor is it applicable to the South Pacific region. This is because the model was based on false premises and raised more problems than it solved. This judgement was initially made by Western educational theorists, but they were soon joined by local critics in the developing countries themselves as they sought a more relevant education for their own contexts.

A basic criticism of the 'human capital' approach is that any success has to be measured by increased access to economic wealth and the perceived benefits of Western development. Judged solely by income increases in Third World countries the development process was successful in the 1960s—Third World countries experienced higher levels of growth than at any other time in the past (Sharp 1982: 16–21). The growth, however, did not automatically trickle down to less fortunate Third World groups—the standard of living for a large proportion of the population remained unchanged and in some cases declined absolutely (Sharp 1982). By the end of the 1960s, economic growth was starting to be seen as a mixed blessing. The decreased quality of life for many, and the realisation that planning and development was *not apolitical* gave rise to further approaches to development planning. The use of measures such as inequality, unemployment and a lack of provision of basic needs was proposed by many critics of the growth approach such as Seers (1969) and Todaro (1981).

The emergence of these problems threw real doubts on the validity of the 'education leads to economic growth' thesis. What became obvious through the experience of a number of developing countries, including those in the South Pacific, was that massive educational investment was not leading to *sustained* economic growth and, more importantly, the goal of equality was not being reached. The fact that gaps still existed between rich and poor *despite education* caused many educators to revise their thoughts (Curle 1973). Todaro (1981: 312) suggested that rather than being a general force for equality, the educational systems of most developing nations acted to increase rather than to decrease income inequalities. Carnoy (1975) and Carnoy and Levin (1976) suggested that this is particularly so when those who gained secondary and tertiary education tended to be from middle-class or upper-class backgrounds, mainly urban, and often children of the new elites. The conclusion was that economic growth could not be equated with development, and access to education did not lead necessarily to equity.

Various aspects of modernisation and human capital theory and their practical applications also came under attack in the 1970s. The very basis of modernisation theory was questioned, i.e., whether development in the Western sense was even desirable. The role of education was seriously questioned, particularly as it appeared to create and indeed exacerbate rather than reduce inequalities, thus contributing to disjunctions which adversely affected socio-economic development. The very ethnocentricity of the concept of modernisation and its ideological basis precluded consideration of alternatives. Fägerlind and Saha (1983: 49) pointed out that 'To the extent that education for modernisation shares this bias, as an institution and process its effects may be unintended and its efficiency less than economical or tolerable'. (See also Simkin 1981.)

The rush to modernisation by expanding Western formal education had some disturbing consequences. As the decade of the 1970s passed it became obvious that there had been an over-investment at particular levels. This in turn further stimulated the desire for more schooling to provide better opportunities of employment. As a result, both the educational level and average age of the unemployed rose (Bacchus 1981: 217). This so-called 'Diploma Disease' rapidly became a serious problem in most developing countries during the late 1960s and 1970s. Dore referred to the 'endless escalation of costs as rising enrolments are compounded by the consequences of high birth rates and falling infant mortality' (Dore 1976: 4). The maintenance of burgeoning educational systems also became an increasing burden on the public purse of Third World countries attempting to cope with a range of social and economic problems in the world recession of the late 1970s.

The application as well as the theoretical basis of human capital theory also came under question. Dore (1976: 87–93) summarises the major criticisms of manpower planning in education. The basic assumption that manpower planning *can* change education and that education systems *will* respond to plans, and that resulting social change *will* occur, has already been queried. A more fundamental criticism is that manpower planning, particularly in education, has often been dramatically wrong in its forecasts. While the exercise of manpower planning may have helped in identifying the problems and enabling discussion about education's role in social and economic change, many educational plans have not been put into practice for a variety of reasons.

The international comparisons approach has also been discredited. The causal link between further education and income has been shown to exist, but the *direction* of causation is doubtful. The validity of indices supposed to work across countries is extremely doubtful, particularly with the volatile political and economic environments of the developing world. This is stressed if one accepts the bases and implication of dependency theory (see below). As Dore (1980) has emphasised, the debate about education and development has too often been conducted as if it was about *the* role of *the* school system in *the* economy—as if the whole world were the same.

MORE RECENT APPROACHES TO THE ROLE OF EDUCATIONAL PLANNING

What approaches remain for making some sense of the search for educational direction? While most comparative educationists and academics have based their research on structural-functional and human capital notions, these had lost credibility during the 1970s as competing approaches claimed more attention. Simkin (1981: 429) points out that, in general terms, modernisation theories have never provided comparative educationists with clear guidelines about the relationship between educational and economic development. 'The poor educational and economic situations of many Third World countries have made it increasingly difficult for comparative educationists to continue to write enthusiastically about educational planning'.

From the doubts about human capital theory an even more trenchant criticism has arisen, namely the long absence from the debate of consideration of the fundamentally political nature of educational planning. Julius Nyerere said that 'to plan is to choose' (quoted in Weiler 1981: 152) and it is the political implications of educational planning that have become more recognised in recent times. Dissatisfaction with the 'technocratic' approach of the 1960s and early 1970s and acknowledgement of the political nature of educational planning resulted in two interlinked approaches—those of the 'search for relevance' and of the application of dependency theory to education.

(a) The search for relevance

This has been an ongoing part of the educational scene since the 1930s in Africa, but re-emerged in various forms in Asia and the Pacific during the 1970s and 1980s. The desire for relevance has generally involved acknowledgement that not all that is Western and modern is necessarily good; that not all school-leavers can find modern-sector employment; and that the social and cultural, as well as the economic nature of education has to be recognised. The influence of writers such as Paulo Freire (1972) and Ivan Illich (1971) was of importance during the 1970s. Their writing led to various attempts to 'diversify', both in the actual structure of the school-system itself and in the nature of the curriculum. Part of the argument was that the school system should be made more relevant to the world of work, which largely meant an emphasis on vocational-technical and agricultural education. Traditional academic education was thought to be dysfunctional at the secondary level because there were too many educated unemployed. A more 'practical' curriculum would surely be more relevant to countries' needs for middle-level technicians. A community-oriented curriculum would also enable early school-leavers and the unemployed to re-enter the traditional or village sector, taking with them skills of practical use.

Not all educationists have favoured this approach. In the 1960s Philip Foster (1965) pointed out the 'vocational school fallacy' of regarding this type of schooling as the solution for matching education with manpower needs. He argued that schools alone could not solve manpower problems in the less developed countries, and indeed were clumsy instruments for doing so. Crossley and Weeks (1986) examined twelve such attempts to reform secondary education but found that most of the examples had been unsuccessful, or adapted well beyond their original concept. Their conclusion that 'The international transfer of educational innovations is also a complex issue and one that hides in many different disguises' (Crossley and Weeks 1986: 427), supports the author's contention that the established planning models are of little use when considering education in developing countries.

During the 1970s educational research focused more on non-formal education, with particular reference to rural and literacy programmes, and the role of traditional cultural values in attempts to 'modernise'. The early 1970s saw either strong support or cautious optimism towards non-formal education alternatives. This period, also, was not one of lasting value to comparative educationists. Problematic links were soon discovered between non-formal education, literacy and agricultural development, and the lack of practical success of many programmes raised further doubts about this approach.

(b) Dependency theory and education

The emergence of neo-Marxist dependency theory in the late 1960s and early 1970s provided a rationale for the criticisms of human capital theory, and gave some ideological structure to the arguments for moves away from formal Western education. Comparative educationists began to see the possible relevance later in the 1970s. In economic terms, dependency theory stated that underdevelopment is a man-made phenomenon of exploitation of the Third World periphery by the capitalistic nations of the First World. Development is not seen as a linear transition from tradition to modernity, and obstacles to development are not traditional cultures but exploitative capitalism (Simkin 1981: 436). Both personal and national *self-esteem* and *independence* are seen as fundamental to the concept of development. According to dependency theory, the essence of development is *self-reliance* or *development without dependency.*

It is in this context that educational critics took a new look at the role of education, and the concept of 'cultural imperialism' became widespread. The nature of education systems was now queried. Despite over two decades of independence the education systems of most developing countries are still modelled on former colonial patterns and, as Keith Watson (1985: 84) points out, 'because many still use international languages, foreign textbooks, foreign-set examinations, employ expatriate staff, etc., the educational process is bound to perpetuate dependency'. The ever-present and currently controversial topic of the role of international aid is seen in many cases as deepening the dependency of the poor countries on the rich for more goods and services (Zachariah 1985; Hindson 1987). Carnoy (1982: 170–1) argued that educational conflict over the nature of Third World education systems and changes in education are dependent on the course of transnational rather than national development. He poses the key question—how can education contribute to fundamental, structured change when it is part of an overall restrictive development?

Dependency theory, while providing for a much more coherent and critical analysis of education and development, presents problems as a structural framework for the examination of educational planning. These include the accusation that it is itself 'Western' in character and derivation, and is, therefore, also a form of cultural imperialism. Simkin (1981: 438) suggests that 'dependency theories are essentially as linear and teleological as modernisation theories. They also, in their neo-Marxist varieties, represent the imposition of a Western intellectual tradition onto the Third World'. The approach often taken by comparative educationists of single-nation case studies does not allow for genuine examination of global dependency. The problems of subsuming a whole range of variables within dependency theory itself have confused educational analyses. More importantly for this work, dependency theory does not cater fully for the complex internal factors and influences which may affect underdevelopment.

AN ALTERNATIVE APPROACH TO CONSIDERATION OF EDUCATIONAL PLANNING IN DEVELOPING COUNTRIES

Comparative research in the 1980s into the role of schooling in the Third World has tended to polarise around adapted modernisation or dependency views and there is no single reliable and acceptable theoretical framework. It is argued that the use of any of the established models, including dependency theory, fails to take into account the now generally-accepted complexity of the interaction between education and development. There is always a danger, in Knapman's terms (1987), of developing 'the tunnel vision of the paradigmatically myopic, who squeeze the evidence into a preferred model'. Any framework tends to be general in nature, and as such cannot take into account the total range of local factors and tensions that emerge in the complex socio-political milieu of educational decision-making. The logical rational planning process has thus often been subverted by the impact of local tensions based in local cultural contexts, and resultant educational direction has not been determined by the Western rational model. These tensions have acted as persistent resistances to educational planning and have hindered the coming of enlightenment promised by the traditional Western model. It is argued here, however, that a framework can be developed which takes into account the particular experiences and local situations of the developing countries. This will recognise the fact that much closer attention needs to be paid by educational analysts to the local situation and the nature of the local tensions. Such a framework will take into account the particular circumstances of the country and its cultural and socio-political context, and can be used to examine how major tensions operate in particular cases. This will avoid the generalisations that occur in the planning models and allow for more specific conclusions.

Educational policy-making on the ground, it is argued, has generally proceeded in an apparently *ad hoc* fashion in response to specific local influences. This is not to say that there is an absence of direction in the process, but that educational policy-making has proceeded through its own impulsion in response to the push/pull of particular tensions. This gives the appearance of 'ad hoc-ery'[2] from the viewpoint of the Western rational planning model.

The traditional approach and the approach developed in this chapter can be represented diagrammatically as shown in Figure 1. The adapted approach illustrates how educational development proceeds in response to specific local tensions, rather than as a direct consequence of rational planning.

The South Pacific and Education

The search for educational direction in the South Pacific region illustrates the difficulty underlying the formal planning processes, particularly during the the period of the 1970s when so many countries moved toward independence. The small island situation raises questions that derive from the disappearance of traditional self-sufficiency and the ever-decreasing possibility of attaining economic independence in a modern world. The political nature of planning becomes even more complex in such a situation. The tensions that emerged during the 1970s in South Pacific countries prevented the rational planning process from working effectively. It is the nature of these tensions and their particular operation in specific local contexts that is under scrutiny here.

FIGURE 1. EDUCATIONAL DIRECTION—AN ALTERNATIVE APPROACH.

A. Traditional view

Traditional model	—> Enlightenment	—> Educational
of Western rational planning	through education	direction

B. Adapted view

Traditional model	—> Tensions provide	—> Specific	—> Educational
of Western rational planning	resistance/doubt over process	responses to tensions (ad hoc-ery)	direction

Educational planning during the 1970s was dominated by the formal Western rational planning processes outlined above. South Pacific countries accepted the Western model of education, partly because it had been imposed by the colonial powers, partly because national leaders and new emerging elites were products of such systems, and partly because political leaders and parents alike believed it would provide the 'cargo' of Western economic materialism. The acceptance of the role of schooling in economic growth boosted the importance of this type of education, justifying even more the faith of parents and planners in its ultimate value. The development of these attitudes occurred later than in Afro-Asian countries because political and economic changes took longer to mature in the South Pacific region.

Tupeni Baba (1985: 28) claims that the preparation of manpower for independence was an outstanding success, but 'the outcome of schemes designed to bring about the (schools' broader role in development) were not encouraging'. However, the fact that planning was taking place somewhat later in the Pacific than elsewhere meant that some of the doubts being raised by the critics did have some impact in the region. The queries about the validity of human capital theory and the debate about relevance were important in the South Pacific but the surge of nationalism and the drive to economic progress did not allow them to influence educational policy.

There was little influence on educators from the neo-Marxists or from dependency theory, though the 'search for relevance' was high on the rhetorical agenda. There was an ongoing discussion over what constituted a relevant curriculum, and what could be done for those who could not find employment in the modern sector. The issues raised by Foster, Illich and Freire clearly coloured educational debate throughout the 1970s. It is interesting to note, for example, that Illich and Freire both visited Papua New Guinea during the early 1970s, at about the time when locals began to play a more important role in educational planning and when there was much discussion about the community role of schooling as independence approached. The various programmes of curriculum development and the attempts at structural change and diversification were a combination of both the desire to find a more 'Pacific' type of schooling and a reaction to the dominance of human capital theory. The 'vocational school fallacy' was also evident in South Pacific countries. Nevertheless, most educational planning in the 1970s took place in the context of modernisation, human capital theory and manpower planning.

James Johnstone (1987), focused attention on policy-making in education in general in the South Pacific. His conclusions were similar to those already outlined:

> Very often the policies in many Pacific countries are not stated at the normative level so that there is only an implied overall direction for the development of education. (Johnstone 1987: 90)

> To date these problems (of what kind of education) have not been fully recognised. Education is provided without identifying its real purpose, and it is likely that this situation will continue at least with the primary and junior secondary levels for quite some time. (Johnstone 1987: 94)

SPECIFIC TENSIONS IN THE DEBATE IN THE SOUTH PACIFIC

As educational planners tried to decide between conflicting policy objectives, tensions were created. A study by the author of the education planning process in the South Pacific area during the 1970s which included case studies of Fiji and Kiribati identified four main areas of conflict which, incorporated in the adapted model, provide a useful structure for the analysis of education in particular countries (Hindson 1988).

1. The potentially adverse effects of the expansion of schools and enrolments on the quality of education was under constant discussion. This concern with the impact of growth was often expressed in rather vague, ambiguous terms, and the nature of these were often difficult to define. There appeared, however, to be four main criteria used by the critics and planners to judge quality during the 1970s:

a. Sufficient numbers of trained teachers,
b. adequate physical conditions in schools (e.g. small classes, comfortable buildings, etc.),
c. curriculum revision, and
d. maintenance of academic standards as measured by results in examinations.

Where any or all of these were not met, or were affected by unplanned growth, a drop in quality was often perceived. While not unique to the region in question, they were centrally important in the countries studied.

2. A major area of conflict occurred in the debate about the 'relevance of education', though this was often confused by lack of

definition. Writers were often vague in their use of the term, and were not specific in their criticisms, but their concerns seem to have expressed themselves in two ways. There was constant discussion about whether the Western formal academic model of schooling was appropriate for the South Pacific, whether there were any alternative models, and how much local culture and traditions should be part of school life. This conflict between 'colonialist' and 'traditionalist' development models as they affected education in the South Pacific, or 'local' and 'Western' as Francis (1978) prefers, was the second issue examined in the case studies.

3. A third area of conflict arose over the relative merits of academic and vocational education. Few job opportunities were available for young Pacific school leavers who were finishing academic schooling. The alternatives were schools or curricula that provided education with a technical bias leading to employment in the semi-skilled sector of the economy, and/or an agricultural emphasis which would lead back to employment in the rural sector. The two aspects of relevance were often interwoven. For example, the terms 'Western' and 'academic' often were used synonymously, but can be seen as separate concerns. Within the Western model there is a choice between academic or vocational curricula in which the role of traditional culture is not an issue.

4. The fourth issue which led to tensions was the attempt to find a balance between economic and social objectives. Many South Pacific countries had begun economic planning in the 1960s before independence. By the early 1970s Fiji, the Gilbert and Ellice Island Community, Samoa, the British Solomons Islands Protectorate and Tonga had all incorporated educational aims into their economic development plans. The desire for Western-oriented economic development and the perceived need for an educated elite to serve this often led to development plans perceiving schools primarily as suppliers of manpower, downgrading other aspects of education's social role.

INCORPORATION OF SPECIFIC TENSIONS INTO THE FRAMEWORK

The first major conclusion of the author's study was that rational education planning in the South Pacific did not result in enlightened educational decision-making due to the resistance of specific local tensions. An examination of the public documents which outlined educational aims revealed internal inconsistencies and contradictions. Shifts in direction occurred as attitudes changed and some tensions were eased by agreement or compromise. The existence of these tensions in the educational debate was not in itself negative, but in fact often led to positive action to resolve difficulties, thus generating new educational goals. This often occurred outside the formal planning process and, given the complexities of the rapidly-changing South Pacific situation, there are no grounds for assuming that the Western-oriented planning model would have achieved any more desirable outcomes. The case studies of Fiji and Kiribati demonstrated that there was a range of factors involved confusing the planning process. While dependency theory provides some insight into the education debate in the South Pacific, it does not take such tensions wholly into account, and would need further elaboration before it could be used as a basis for analysis. As proposed in the introduction, Figure 1. B outlines an alternative framework, and the application of this to particular case studies will help educational researchers to analyse the search for educational direction.

The second conclusion derived from the author's study was that the identification of the four particular sources of tension proved useful as an analytical tool and these can be incorporated into a framework which is helpful when considering the education debate in other South Pacific countries and in developing countries generally. Many of the problems that existed were attributable to the differing backgrounds and peculiarities of local contexts, and this factor needs to be given greater consideration in such studies. While accepting that the educational operation and problems of other developing countries should be considered, it is also argued that they should not necessarily be used as models unless background circumstances are very similar. For example, there may be advantages in looking more closely at school operations in small island states in other parts of the world. This can be represented diagrammatically:

FIGURE 2. EDUCATIONAL DIRECTION THROUGH RESPONSES TO TENSIONS.

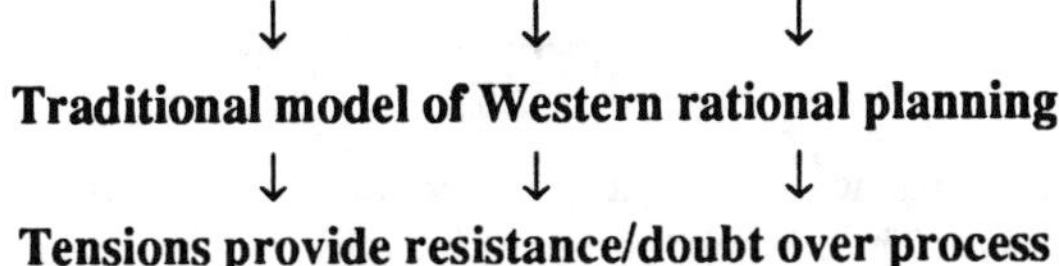

a. Concerns about the possible adverse effects of growth on the quality of education.

b. Moves to a more local form of education and pressures to retain the Western model.

c. Unease with the academic nature of schooling and desires to see a more vocational/practical emphasis.

d. Attempts to establish a balance between economic and social aims in education.

↓ ↓

Specific responses to tensions

↓ ↓

Educational direction

This chapter has argued that the past has not been a good teacher, that each country still sees its educational problems as being solved by the application of established models. The operation of international agencies and aid organisations certainly works to reinforce this view. This is partly, as Dore (1981: 57) pointed out, because the debate is often conducted as though the whole world were the same. This is, of course, not so. Circumstances do differ, and the situation of African countries in the 1960s was different to that of the South Pacific in the 1970s and 1980s. Experience can provide guidelines, but, as Crossley and Weeks (1986: 426) point out: 'Insights can be gained from the experience of others, but specific educational projects must also be economic levels of society and at the micro level of local community, school and classroom conditions'. It is the 'actualities of context' that need to be given far more attention in educational analysis, and the proposed alternative framework gives comparative educationists firmer guidelines for their research.

NOTES

1. In keeping with current practice the terms 'less-developed', 'developing' and 'Third World' are used interchangeably, though there are problems with all the terminology.

2. The term, though awkward, is deliberately used. Consideration was given to such terms as 'random selection', 'convenience' or 'reactive thinking', but they did not convey the sense intended.

BIBLIOGRAPHY

Alladin, I. (1987) 'Educational Development in 'Small' Island Economies: an Area for Further Enquiry'. *ANZCIES Newsletter* 4 (2).

Baba, T. (1985) 'Education in the Pacific Islands in the Year 2000'. in R. Kiste and R. Herre (eds.), *The Pacific Islands in the Year 2000*. Honolulu, University of Hawaii.

Bacchus, M. (1981) 'Education for Development in Underdeveloped Countries'. *Comparative Education* 17 (2): 205–227.

Bray, M. (1984) *Educational Planning in a Decentralised System: The Papua New Guinea Experience*. Sydney, University of Sydney Press.

Brock, C. (1983) 'Education, Environment and Economy in Small Commonwealth Countries'. In K. Watson (ed.), *Youth, Education and Employment, International Perspectives*. London, Croom Helm.

Bude, U. (1983) 'The Adaptation Concept in British Colonial Education', *Comparative Education* 19 (3): 341–355.

Carnoy, M. (1974) *Education as Cultural Imperialism*. New York, David McKay.

Carnoy, M. (1978) 'Can Education Policy Equalise Income Distribution?' *Prospects*, 8 (1): 3–18.

Carnoy, M., and Levin, H. (1976) *The Limits of Educational Reform*. New York, David McKay.

Carnoy, M. (1982) 'Education for Alternative Development'. *Comparative Education Review*, 17 (2): 160–177.

Crossley, M., and Weeks, S. (1986) 'Curriculum as an International Commodity: Dilemmas of Relevance and Change'. In R. Gillespie and C. Collins (eds.), *Education as an International Commodity*. Brisbane, Australian and New Zealand Comparative and International Education Society.

Curle, A. (1973) *Education for Liberation*. London, Tavistock.

Dore, R. (1976) *The Diploma Disease*. London, Allen and Unwin,.

Dore, R. (1980) 'The Diploma Disease Revisited', *Institute of Development Studies Bulletin* (Sussex).

Fagerlind, I., and Saha, L. (1983) *Education and National Development: a Comparative Perspective*. Oxford, Pergamon Press.

Foster, P. (1965) 'The Vocational School Fallacy in Development Planning'. In C. Anderson and M. Bowman (eds.), *Education and Economic Development*. Chicago, Aldine Publishing.

Francis, R. (1978) 'Either Way You've Still Had It, Education and Development in the South Pacific'. In D. Davis (ed.), *Education and the Economy*. ANZCIES, Macquarie University.

Freire, P. (1972) *Pedagogy of the Oppressed*, New York, Herder and Herder.

Harbison, F., and Myers, C. (1964) *Education, Manpower and Economic Growth*. New York, McGraw Hill.

Hindson, C. (1987) 'Educational Aid in the South Pacific: a Look at Priorities', *Directions: a Journal of Educational Studies*, University of the South Pacific, 9 (1): 26–41.

Hindson, C. (1988) 'The Education Debate in the South Pacific During the 1970s'. PhD Thesis, Flinders University, Adelaide.

Illich, I. (1971) *Deschooling Society*. London, Calder and Boyars.

Johnstone, J. (1987) 'Policy Dilemmas Facing Education in the Pacific'. In C. Throsby (ed.), *Human Resources Development in the Pacific*. Canberra, National Centre for Development Studies, Australian National University.

Knapman, B. (1987) *Fiji's Economic History: 1874–1939*. Canberra, ANU, 1987. Quoted in Book Reviews, *Pacific Island Monthly*, September, p. 48.

Lillis, K., and Hogan, D. (1983) 'Dilemmas of Diversification: Problems Associated with Vocational Education in Developing Countries', *Comparative Education*, 19 (1): 89–107.

Oxenham, J. (ed.) (1984) *Education Versus Qualifications?* London, Allen and Unwin.

Psacharopoulos, G. (1986) 'The Planning of Education: Where Do We Stand?' *Comparative Education Review*, 30 (4): 560–573.

Seers, D., (1969) 'The Meaning of Development'. *International Development Review*, December.

Sharp, R. (1982) 'The Meaning of Economic Development'. *Integrated Development Centre Bulletin* 3: 16–21.

Simkin, K. (1981) 'Comparative and Sociological Perspectives on Third World Development and Education'. *International Review of Education* 27: 427–447.

Simmons J. (ed.) (1980) The Education Dilemma: Policy Issues for Developing Countries in the 1980s. Oxford, Pergamon.

Todaro, M. (1981) *Economic Development in the Third World* (2nd ed.). New York, Longman.

Watson K. (ed.) (1982) *Education in the Third World*. London, Croom Helm.

Watson, K. (1985) 'Dependence or Independence in Education? Two Case Studies from Post-colonial South-East Asia'. *International Journal of Educational Development* 5: 2.

Weiler, H. (1981) 'The Uses of Educational Planning: Some Further Thoughts'. *Prospects* 11 (2): 149–153.

Zachariah, M. (1985) 'Lumps of Clay and Growing Plants: Dominant Metaphors of the Role of Education in the Third World, 1950–1980'. *Comparative Education Review* 29 (1).

Collaborative Research, Ethnography and Comparative and International Education in the South Pacific[1]

MICHAEL CROSSLEY

Department of Education, Bristol University, England

INTRODUCTION

The South Pacific region has assumed increased economic and strategic importance in world affairs in recent years. Academic interest in the development of the region has, in turn, increased, with analysts from many disciplines being attracted and motivated by the implications of the spectacular economic growth of the Pacific Rim countries, the rise of Japan and China as regional superpowers and the strategic manoeuvrings of Russia and America to strengthen footholds within the island nations. Related to the latter issue is notable growth in the number of small independent Pacific island states during the last two decades: nations such as the Solomon Islands, Vanuatu and Kiribati that are perceived with increasing respect from outside.

Within the Pacific Islands, which are a main focus of the present analysis, shifting perceptions of developmental options and of the role of the Pacific in the world at large are also increasingly apparent (Stratigos and Hughes 1987). Pacific leaders recognize the emergence of their international importance at the same time as they seek to play a stronger role in determining the course of regional development.

> There is a new Pacific. The parts which constitute its whole may be the same, but I feel that the way they are now put together and perceive each other could be different. To start with there has been a re-appraisal of how the world itself now sees the Pacific . . . the

> increasing strategic importance of the Pacific is directly related to the growing economic dominance of the Asia-Pacific region—the emergence of the Pacific Century as it has been tagged. (Chan 1988)

A second, but less economically oriented, standpoint taken by Ieremia Tabai, President of Kiribati, draws attention to the ethical and cultural concerns of those involved in development within the Pacific.

> For us in Kiribati development is not only concerned with increasing the material and social welfare of the people. While that is certainly very important, we view development primarily as a process by which we expect to be able to live a viable and dignified way of life. By that, I mean development is not dependence on others; development is the ability to make a free decision, a free choice, in pursuit of one's interest. I believe it is possible for even a small country like Kiribati to achieve that. (Tabai 1987: 49)

Similarly, in the academic world Pacific writers are making an increasingly significant impact on the development of ideas and knowledge, both building upon already well articulated critiques of colonialism and dependency (Hau'ofa 1987) and challenging the international transfer of critical theory itself (Meleisea 1987).

In this chapter the development and application of comparative and international education in the Australia-Pacific region is explored in the light of the contemporary social (and research) context outlined above, and of the methodological and ethical dilemmas faced by those working within the field. Particular attention is paid to the potential of ethnographic research methods as a way of promoting genuinely collaborative research of increased value to policy makers and practitioners, in addition to enhancing the vitality and future potential of the field of study throughout the region.

EDUCATIONAL DEVELOPMENT AND EDUCATIONAL RESEARCH IN THE PACIFIC

Interest in educational development within the Pacific has grown as in other fields of study. With the onset of the decolonisation process the potential for educational reform has attracted much attention, investment in new developments by outside agencies, such as the World Bank, has increased and formalised evaluations of educational policy and practice have become increasingly common. Furthermore, as the study of small countries has emerged as a worldwide pre-occupation of social scientists (Bray 1987), the study of education in small island states—notably those of the Pacific—has found a place in the international literature (Bacchus and Brock 1987).

The involvement of educational researchers in the Pacific takes many forms ranging from independent studies based upon the personal interests of the researcher to formalised consultancies related to specific projects or participation in the work of international aid agencies. In this activity foreign researchers have considerable influence, either through the impact of their published work and theoretical perspectives or by direct involvement.

At the governmental level the tone of Australian involvement in Pacific educational development is reflected in the 1984 Report of the Committee to Review the Australian Overseas Aid Program (The Jackson Report, Commonwealth of Australia 1984: 10) which said:

> Assistance for education within developing countries should be emphasised in bilateral aid programming. More support should be given to curriculum development and teacher training for primary, secondary, and vocational schools. Support for national and regional post secondary education should be continued with a strong emphasis on the involvement of Australian colleges of advanced education, and technical and further education institutions.

Looking at the Jackson Report from within the Pacific, Baba (1987) argues that such statements betray former Australian policy that better stressed the importance of developing the research, consultancy and teaching capacity of Pacific regional and national tertiary institutions. As Baba points out, it is obviously to Australia's advantage to adopt recommendations which boost its own tertiary institutions 'at a time when these institutions were experiencing falls in enrolment and when some were threatened with closure' (1987: 5).

COMPARATIVE AND INTERNATIONAL EDUCATION

For the purposes of the present volume Baba's paper is of specific interest because it was first presented at the Fourteenth Annual Conference of the Australian and New Zealand Comparative and International Education Society (ANZCIES) on the topic of 'Education as an International Commodity' (Gillespie and Collins 1986). As the title of the conference indicates, comparativists in the region were keenly aware of the dilemmas of international aid to education and of a growth in the marketing of educational services. The proceedings of previous ANZCIES conferences (e.g. Welch 1981; Sheehan 1983; Maddock and Hindson 1985) further demonstrate that while studies relating to education in the Pacific have been well represented, an uneasy ambivalence with respect to the ethics of practical involvement in the process of educational development in less developed countries has also characterised much comparative and international research within the region.

Intellectual tensions resulting from this critical reflection are a healthy sign for our field of study since many derive from recognition of the dangers and ethical dilemmas of the international transfer of educational policy and practice. Such issues have long distinguished the work of comparative educationalists, alongside concern for the study of socio-political factors at the macro-level of contextual analysis.

THEORETICAL PERSPECTIVES

Over the last decade some of the most significant and challenging work of ANZCIES members has, for example, focussed upon an evolving critique of positivism in both theory and methodology (Jones 1979; Burns 1981; Welch 1985), upon the application of dependency theory to educational issues of regional and international concern (Simkin 1981) and upon the role of international development assistance in education (Jones 1986). Central to much of this work is recognition of the role of cultural values and ideology in the legitimation of educational knowledge and research paradigms, combined with an emphasis upon the generation or further refinement of critical theory.

On the other hand, as with all fields of study, the advancement of theoretical perspectives has much to gain from insights derived from involvement in the field and from the study of practice. Without this reference point theory has a tendency to become divorced from reality—particularly in the social sciences where the wisdom of a search for causal relationships, universal laws or generalisations is so strongly challenged (King 1977, 1985; Kemmis 1984; Welch 1985). Dependency theory, for instance, has faced significant criticism for generating overly negative analyses that undermine the very real achievements in educational development worldwide. Theoretical perspectives, we should remember, also transfer across international boundaries and this may be just as unwarranted and inappropriate as the transfer of policy and practice that more generally receives critical attention. With this in mind the former editor of *Compare*, the journal of the British Comparative and International Education Society, pointedly notes that there has as yet been little empirical testing of dependency theory at work in education in the Third World (Raggatt 1983).

To return to the Pacific, the international transfer of theoretical perspectives has recently been raised in the social sciences and humanities by writers such as Meleisea (1987), Hau'ofa (1987) and Wendt (1987). Writing from an islands perspective they mount an impassioned critique of the pervasive influences of the transfer of fashionable ideological and theoretical perspectives by Western academics—the 'Marxist' or 'new intellectual missionaries'. Significantly theirs is not a total rebuttal of dependency theory or its predecessors but a subtle critique of the more fundamental imposition of Western middle class values and intellectual modes of thought upon their own island cultures. Their plea is for increased recognition and respect for Pacific values and intellectual perspectives in the analysis of the problems and development of their region.

Applied Research in Education

In an ever-tightening world economic climate, where educational researchers are increasingly called upon to demonstrate the practical or policy relevance of their work (Lewin 1987), the need for comparative and international education to combine theoretical advances with developments of an applied and more practical nature is now particularly apposite. The influence of educational research upon policy and practice may indeed be difficult to discern (Keeves 1987), but worthwhile impact can certainly be improved, as Parkyn (1977) pointed out more than a decade ago, if determined efforts are made within our field to bridge the theory practice gap. Indeed Parkyn is widely supported when he argues that comparative educationalists should begin with real problems as the starting point for research, because such analyses also generate the best theory (e.g. King 1977).

For their distinctive perspective, comparative and international educationalists are clearly in a strong position to contribute to both the intellectual debate and the process of educational development within the Pacific without falling prey to the dangers of international transfer. Without their influence in both arenas educational development in the region and its disciplined study will surely be impoverished. The impact of the influential 1986 ANZCIES conference is perhaps indicative of the nature of the present challenge and of the potential of the comparativists' response (Gillespie and Collins 1986; Williamson 1987).

Collaborative Research

Looking to the future of comparative and international education within the Pacific, it is argued here that the nature of contemporary theoretical and methodological debate points towards the need for more genuine collaboration between metropolitan and indigenous scholars—between researchers from both the developed and the less developed countries of the region.

If we are really to challenge dependency relationships the views of those within less developed countries must come more to the fore. As the Brazilian educator Benno Sander points out, we cannot:

> . . . question seriously the transplantation, transfer or unidirectional adaption of theories and methodologies and of educational forms and contents from the dominant society to the dependent society without a detailed study of the needs and aspirations of the dependent society from its own perspective. It is in this context that having assumed a commitment to the dependent society, comparative education should assume the role of mediator, at once critical and autochthonous, emancipated and emancipating. This mediation, conceived of here as a concrete category based on the perspective of the dependent society, denies the unidirectional or vertical determination of the dominant society over the dependent society. It assumes that the dominant and dependent societies limit one another reciprocally and construct one another dialectically. (Sander 1985: 201)

In supporting collaboration, scholars from the South such as Salmi (1985) recognise the value of critical analysis and the comparativists' traditional defence of the outsiders' perspective. But the issue is one of balance and as Bacchus (1983) argues, the emphasis needs to shift in favour of the Third World. A shift towards such collaborative research is emerging in the work of some British comparativists (Watson and Oxenham, 1985), although as King (1985) points out, much remains to be done and the nature and form of collaboration could certainly be diversified to the benefit of our field of study. King's argument is especially relevant to the debate within the Pacific since it parallels Baba's concern with the increasingly dominant consultancy mode of evaluative research tied to foreign aid projects. In this model collaboration is rarely that of equal partners if, as Baba fears, it exists in substance at all. So often the legitimacy of the evaluation depends upon the standing of accredited researchers from the funding nation (Salmi 1985). For example, in Papua New Guinea work by Gannicott (1987) into the financing of education has been conducted and well disseminated to funding agencies and decision-makers via the prestigious sponsorship of the Australian National University's National Centre for Development Studies.

In brief, Gannicott's work is highly critical of the 'internally inefficient' funding of education within Papua New Guinea—especially at the university level. This overtly economic and cost-benefit perspective reflects similar World Bank analyses undertaken elsewhere in less developed countries (Psacharopoulos and Woodhall 1985), and draws attention to important aspects of the financing of education within the country. Recommendations stemming from the study emphasise the need for reduced spending, economies of scale and the redirection of funds from tertiary to primary education. Implicit in the analysis, however, is an assumption that while Papua New Guinean universities should limit their activities to 'a small core of mainstream commerce and technology disciplines' (1987: 152), Australian institutions could build new strengths and provide higher level programmes for Papua New Guinean nationals overseas. Without denying the potential of many of Gannicott's findings, the indigenous response to his recommendations has been less than enthusiastic. From within the country Gannicott's analysis is seen by many to undermine local university development and to generate an over-critical tone, partly through inappropriate international comparisons with vastly different Asian educational systems and economic circumstances. Perhaps even more significantly for the present discussion, the accuracy of some of Gannicott's local data is questionable, and economic analyses alone do not adequately deal with the cultural and political dimensions of educational development that so often dominate the aspirations and perceptions of those involved within country. Had indigenous perspectives been more carefully built into the study, had collaboration with Papua New Guinean scholars been more strongly featured, and had disemination and discussion within the country been pursued more carefully, this particular research may have been more realistically useful for policy makers and more readily received. In a sense the unacknowledged and externally oriented politics and ideology of the study detract from the impact of an otherwise worthwhile and incisive analysis.

How then can a more equal partnership of educational researchers be facilitated within the field of comparative and international education? Kenneth King (1985) usefully provides three options for consideration which all hold considerable potential within the Pacific region. The first of these is the better promotion of non-contracted projects involving independent researchers from developed and less developed nations. The second is the establishment of stronger academic linkages and collaboration between institutions within the region. The Educational Research Unit (formerly of the University of Papua New Guinea, now a constituent part of the new National Research Institute), for example, has long maintained informal contacts with external research bodies, and visiting researchers have made major contributions to ongoing studies co-ordinated by national staff within Papua New Guinea. This brings multiple advantages to Papua New Guinea; strengthening the research effort, contributing to staff development and boosting indigenous research capacity and institutional development. Contacts between other Pacific research bodies and selected overseas universities could perhaps become more systematised and so further strengthen institutional ties and international collaboration.

King's third option is that of encouraging greater direct funding of collaborative research, within and for the benefit of less developed countries, by external and independent research councils. Finally, and this is especially pertinent here, King argues for greater diversification in research paradigms in less developed countries, particularly in the field of evaluative research.

Qualitative Research in Less Developed Countries

Underlying King's call for a diversification of research methods in less developed countries is recognition of the present dominance of the quantitative paradigm, a dominance that is increasingly causing concern within the research community, a concern that echoes many of the contemporary challenges to the conduct of research in comparative and international education. To cite Shaeffer (1986: 5), Associate Director of the Canadian International Development Research Centre (IDRC):

> In much of the developing world, educational research is largely empirical and quantitative, characterized by the development of standardized tests and questionnaires, the production of data from

> large samples of schools and individuals, and the analysis of these data by a variety of statistical methods. There are good reasons for such an approach to research. Policymakers wish to know how well their system of education is performing vis-a-vis that of an earlier period of time or those of other nations, or whether a particular reform or innovation is succeeding. Ministry or university researchers assigned the task of gathering this information, usually with a short deadline, are acquainted and comfortable with empirical, quantitative research from their own (often North American) training, and such research is efficient. It lends itself to a division of labour among a number of individuals with various skills and levels of competence. As a result of these factors, the world of educational research, especially in the developing world, continues to be dominated by research traditions and paradigms that emphasize quantitative, empirical, and statistical methods.

We shall return to the work of the IDRC later for Shaeffer and his colleagues have been instrumental in supporting alternative research paradigms in the Third World context. Moreover it is a central thesis of this chapter that a methodological broadening of scope—notably in the realm of ethnography—is especially appropriate for educational research carried out in less developed countries and for a strengthening of comparative and international education in the Pacific.

In articulating support for ethnographic research methods it should not be assumed that this is to advocate a rejection of more firmly established paradigms and procedures. Following Epstein (1983), the concern is to help broaden the methodological repertoire of comparativists and, as argued elsewhere (Crossley and Vulliamy 1984), to encourage the combination of different research methods, where appropriate, in detailed and multi-faceted case studies.

Nor should this be seen as a further example of the simplistic international transfer of Western research methodologies for, as explained below, in many respects ethnographic enquiry may be singularly more appropriate for less developed countries and local researchers than it is for their richer colleagues in the developed world.

Ethnographic Research Traditions

Having qualified our argument in this way it is appropriate and useful to acknowledge how the emergence of modern ethnographic research in education is related to contemporary developments in the social sciences, educational research and evaluation and comparative and international education in developed nations such as Britain and America.

In North America anthropological and sociological studies of education featuring ethnographic enquiry have a distinguished, though not mainstream, tradition dating back to the 1930s and the work of the Chicago School (Delamont and Atkinson 1980). As in Britain, however, later developments in the new sociology of education, and the emergence of education evaluation as a major field of activity, have inspired a new generation of qualitative researchers and their own methodological literature. School case studies by Hargreaves (1967) and Lacey (1970) exemplify early British sociological research of this nature which emphasises the multiple perspectives of those involved in the educational process. More recent research has received significant attention, and Willis (1977), Woods (1979) and Ball (1981) make more explicit attempts to relate micro-studies of schools and classrooms to broader concerns with the structural features of society.

Common to the methodological foundations of such work on both sides of the Atlantic is support for:

> . . . those research strategies such as participant observation, in-depth interviewing, total participation in the activity being investigated, fieldwork etc, which allow the researcher to obtain first hand knowledge about the empirical social world in question. (Filstead 1970: 6)

Delamont and Atkinson (1980) provide a more detailed comparative account of the British and American research traditions in this genre, but Gibson's (1988) recent study of the response of immigrant Punjabi Sikhs to the opportunities offered by public high schools in California is a good example of the American anthropological perspective which typically focuses upon ethnic minority issues. This is a thorough and challenging analysis of the relative success of an immigrant minority and of the relationship of this success to the preservation of group values and culture within the broader host society. As such it is an example of ethnographic research that holds considerable potential for the development or refinement of theory and an informed re-assessment of educational policy and practice.

Similar concerns and intellectual perspectives underpin the 'new wave' or qualitative evaluation movement that sprang up on both sides of the Atlantic during the 1970s. In Britain, the work of Parlett and Hamilton (1972) on 'illuminative evaluation' perhaps best exemplifies the paradigmatic shift in evaluation literature, while that of Stake (1967) is regarded as of seminal influence in the American context. Reflecting and stimulating the challenge to quantitative and positivistic research in education, such qualitative evaluators emphasised the importance of context (at the micro-level) upon the processes of learning and evaluation. They also challenged the dominance of Ralph Tyler's (1949) objectives model of curriculum development and evaluation drawing attention to the unanticipated (and neglected) effects of educational innovation. Highlighting the need for the study of educational processes and context, in addition to measurable outcomes, Parlett and Hamilton outline their alternative model by suggesting that:

> The aims of illuminative evaluation are to study the innovatory programme; how it operates; how it is influenced by the various school systems in which it is applied; what those directly concerned regard as its advantages and disadvantages; and how students' intellectual tasks and academic experiences are most affected. It aims to discover and document what it is like to be participating in the scheme, whether as teacher or pupil; and in addition to discern and discuss the innovation's most significant features, recurring concomitants and critical processes. In short, it seeks to address and to illuminate a complex array of questions. (In Hamilton et al. 1977: 10)

With respect to contemporary developments in the field of comparative and international education, the future potential of qualitative research methods, and ethnography in particular, is considerable. This stems as much from the epistemological foundations of such work as it does from the more obvious methodological characteristics. With its concern to elicit the multiple perspectives of those engaged in educational processes, combined with respect for the importance of cultural values and the politics of research (Simmons 1987), comparativists should be among the first to recognize how ethnography could contribute to the ongoing challenge to positivism within their field of study.

Just as comparative education has traditionally stressed the importance of contextual variables at the national and international levels, so too ethnography displays a central concern with context at the micro-level. As sociological studies of schooling have begun to draw out broader implications relating to the structural features of society, the potential for fusing micro and macro level studies in comparative and international education also becomes clearer (Crossley and Burns 1983). This is a particularly significant line of development for theorists within the field for, as we have already argued, the refinement and development of theory benefits considerably from the generation of sound empirical data. For the educational ethnographer this necessitates the detailed study and documentation of practice by disciplined observation in the field. The product of such research is regarded as especially strong in 'ecological validity' (Bracht and Glass 1968). Stenhouse, for example, argues that:

> . . . comparative education will miss making an important contribution to the understanding of schooling if it does not participate in the current development of case-study approaches to educational processes and educational institutions. (1979: 9)

Reflecting Glaser and Strauss's (1967) thesis for the 'discovery of grounded theory', Stenhouse went on to suggest that we 'develop in our field a better grounded representation of day-to-day educational reality resting on the careful study of particular cases' (1979: 10). Masemann (1982) usefully takes the argument further into the realm of critical theory and comparative education.

Qualitative research does not claim to identify universal laws for the social sciences, as the positivists seek, but improved knowledge and understanding can lead to powerful insights into educational issues and dilemmas with value beyond the confines of the specific case. The findings of Gibson's (1988) study of the Sikh response to the pressures of assimilation in American society, for example, have a strong theoretical dimension that holds potential for broader comparative analysis elsewhere where immigrant issues are foremost. Relationships between island migrants and Australia and New Zealand as metropolitan centres are obviously relevant in this respect—with the link between indigenous perspectives and the immigrants' educational experience already being sensitively portrayed in Pacific literature by observer/participants of the calibre of Albert Wendt (1973).

By focussing upon 'foreshadowed problems' as opposed to fixed questions or pre-specified hypotheses the line of enquiry in ethnography remains flexible at the outset. This characteristic further assists in avoiding the potential tyranny of theory, be it of the modernisation or dependency mode, that is inappropriately transferred from one context to another.

This brings us back to our central issue and the distinctive potential of ethnography for comparative and international education in less developed countries and the Pacific region in particular.

THE POTENTIAL OF ETHNOGRAPHIC METHODS IN THE PACIFIC REGION

A first factor that enhances the potential of ethnography in educational research in less developed countries concerns the qualitative nature of many of the most crucial problems in such contexts. As Beeby points out, the quantitative methods and assumptions of positivistic science that dominate the Third World have 'proved of limited value in attacking the peculiar qualitative problems in the classroom that are now the main worry of educators in these countries' (1978: 139). Qualitative research techniques, on the other hand, having strength in ecological validity combined with sensitivity to educational processes and the various perceptions of those involved, have demonstrated greater responsiveness to contextual factors and to barriers facing successful change and innovation (Crossley 1984). The explanatory power of qualitative studies of practice can thus be of considerable assistance to practitioners and policy makers.

While few well known qualitative studies have as yet been conducted in less developed countries, work by Avalos and her associates (1986) in Latin America is instructive in this respect. Moreover this is an excellent example of collaborative ethnographic research involving scholars from developed and less developed countries utilising financial support from the IDRC. This study explored reasons for the scholastic failure of poor children in four South American countries (Chile, Bolivia, Colombia and Venezuela) linking the analysis to the school-effectiveness literature and aspects of neo-marxist theoretical frameworks. In concluding that the quality and nature of teaching given to the poor does indeed make a significant impact upon the quality of learning, the study holds much to commend it to educational decision makers and practitioners—should they choose to make use of it.

At the theoretical level this research also demonstrates how ethnography can play an important role. In this case findings from the four country studies add to the school effectiveness debate, and to our knowledge of cultural reproduction processes in schooling, while challenging 'the determinist assumptions behind a number of theoretical and empirical studies about educational opportunities that, in practice, led to the neglect of the schooling process as such' (Avalos 1986: 12). These are valuable contributions for the research community interested in the role and quality of education in less developed countries.

A second major advantage of qualitative research relates to its presentation form and mode of dissemination. Ethnographic research and evaluation is both descriptive and analytic—often reporting the direct words of key informants in the field to illustrate or defend points of special significance. The narrative style of such reporting has a number of advantages over quantitative and statistically oriented studies, especially in systems where practitioners, administrators and policy makers are unlikely to have the benefit of advanced higher education or research training to assist them in interpretation. Ethnographic reports speak more plainly to the reader and are more likely to reflect a social construction of reality that is recognisable and understandable to an experienced practitioner.

In terms of effectively communicating the results of research to those who might use it, this can be a distinct advantage, especially in view of the fact that research is widely believed to influence policy makers largely through informal, interpersonal contacts and a 'percolation' effect (Oxenham 1985; Dove 1985).

To this should be added the drawbacks to valid quantitative research in less developed countries where the statistical data base is often unreliable and the trained personnel and computer technology necessary for effective analysis is frequently lacking (King 1985).

The third major theme that is of special significance here returns us to the notion of collaborative research. Just as illuminative evaluators have moved to involve practising teachers in aspects of their work through action research models stressing participation and collaboration (Kemmis 1984), so too ethnography has the potential to facilitate more equal collaboration between practitioners and researchers and—more importantly in the present context—between scholars from developed and less developed countries. The work coordinated by Avalos exemplifies this well, but, within the Pacific, research into the international transfer of school-based curriculum development by the present writer (Crossley 1984), and by other personnel associated with the Educational Research Unit (ERU) coordinated evaluation of the Secondary Schools Community Extension Project in Papua New Guinea, is of this nature (Vulliamy 1985; Weeks 1987).

A number of papers presented to the more recent conferences of the ANZCIES indicate further support for ethnographic perspectives or collaborative research (Williamson 1987) and, within Papua New Guinea, ANZCIES members are also involved in new large-scale collaborative research, incorporating observational methods, that is designed to assist in fundamental changes to the policy and practice of primary sector teacher education.

If support for this line of development is forthcoming from metropolitan scholars and institutions it will surely be welcomed within the Pacific communities where critics such as Baba believe improved collaboration is long overdue. Indeed, expressing the standpoint of the

Institute of Pacific Studies at the University of the South Pacific, Crocombe maintains that 'a double benefit is gained if the researcher is the researched—or at least is part of the researched community' (1987: 133). Reflecting long personal experience, he continues: 'This is not to say that outside perceptions should be excluded but it is to say that a grossly disproportionate share of the studies of islands and island communities have been done from external perceptions'. (1987: 133)

CONCLUSION

Collaboration, then, is a significant and timely avenue of development that holds considerable potential for the future of comparative and international education in the Australia-Pacific region and beyond. The challenge is considerable however, for valid qualitative research requires careful training and rigorous efforts both in design and execution. International collaboration adds further cultural and practical difficulties in itself, and a broadening of what is regarded as acceptable research data may meet resistance in some quarters.

Here the support of academic journals and regional publishers for the dissemination of qualitative educational research and of ordinary practitioners' perspectives—especially as interpreted by Pacific writers—will be helpful in broadening intellectual sensitivities and horizons, even if the variety of commentary may not meet traditional academic expectations. Understanding the views, the perceived realities, of those involved in educational processes is, after all, at the heart of this matter (see for example, Crossley, Sukwianomb and Weeks 1987).

Other more popularised means of disseminating research findings also deserve attention. As Thompson (1985: 232–233) points out with reference to the evaluation of educational projects in less developed countries:

> . . . an evaluation which is not designed for, accessible to and intelligible to our clientele is of little value . . . For much of the time we appear to be addressing each other and wondering why no-one else is listening. Often we use the echo principle—if our own voice

comes back to us we are content. We have much to learn about effective dissemination.

The problems encountered in supporting these dimensions of comparative and international education will be many, but if the voices of Pacific scholars and practitioners can be better represented as we study contemporary educational issues and problems, the strengths and value of our field of study within our region will surely be enhanced for the benefit of all.

NOTE

1. This chapter, originally written for the present volume, has also been published in the *International Journal of Educational Development* 10(1), 1990.

REFERENCES

Avalos, B. (ed.) (1986) Teaching Children of the Poor. An Ethnographic Study in Latin America. *Ottawa, IDRC*.

Baba, T. (1987) 'Academic Buccaneering Australian Style: The Role of Australian Academics in the South Seas'. *Directions* 9(1): 3–11.

Bacchus, M.K. (1983) 'Towards a Development Strategy for Education and Educational Research in Third World Countries'. *International Journal of Educational Development* 3(2).

Bacchus, M.K. and Brock, C. (1987) *The Challenge of Scale*. London, Commonwealth Secretariat.

Ball, S.J. (1981) *Beachside Comprehensive: A Case Study of Secondary Schooling*. London, Cambridge University Press.

Beeby, C.E. (1978) 'Teachers, Teacher Education and Research'. In R. Gardner (ed.), *Teacher Education in Developing Countries: Prospects for the Eighties*. University of London Institute of Education: 135–157.

Bracht, G.H. and Glass G.V. (1968) 'The External Validity of Experiments'. *American Educational Research Journal* 5: 437–474.

Bray, M. (1987) 'Small Countries in International Development'. *The Journal of Development Studies* 23(2): 295–300.

Burns, R.J. (1981) 'Knowledge or Propaganda? The Politics of Learning about the World'. In A.R. Welch (ed.), *The Politics of Educational Change.* University of New England/ANZCIES.

Chan, J. (1988) 'It Is a New Pacific'. *The Times of Papua New Guinea,* September 15–21.

Commonwealth of Australia (1984) *Report of the Committee to Review the Australian Overseas Aid Program* (The Jackson Report). Canberra, Australian Government Publishing Service.

Crocombe, R.G. (1987) 'Studying the Pacific'. In A. Hooper, et al., loc. cit.: 115–139.

Crossley, M. (1984) 'Strategies for Curriculum Change and the Question of International Transfer'. *Journal of Curriculum Studies* 16(1): 75–88.

Crossley, M. and Burns, R. (1983) 'Case-study in Comparative and International Education: an Approach to Bridging the Theory-Practice Gap'. In B.A. Sheehan (ed.), loc. cit.

Crossley, M., Sukwianomb, J. and Weeks, S.G., eds (1987) Pacific Perspectives on Non-Formal Education. Suva and Port Moresby, *Institute of Pacific Studies and University of Papua New Guinea Press.*

Crossley, M. and Vulliamy, G. (1984) 'Case-Study Research Methods and Comparative Education'. *Comparative Education* 20(2): 193–207.

Delamont, S. and Atkinson, P. (1980) 'The Two Traditions in Educational Ethnography: Sociology and Anthropology Compared'. *British Journal of Sociology of Education* 1: 139–152.

Dove, L.A. (1985) 'Educational Policy, Planning and Research: A Global Reassessment'. *Comparative Education* 21(1): 91–94.

Filstead, W.J. (ed.) (1970) *Qualitative Methodology: First Hand Involvement with the Social World.* Chicago, Markham.

Gannicott, K. (1987) 'The Evaluation of Human Capital in Papua New Guinea'. In C.D. Throsby, *Human Resources Development in the Pacific.* Canberra, National Centre for Development Studies, The Australian National University.

Gibson, M.A. (1988) *Assimilation Without Accommodation. Sikh Immigrants in an American High School.* Ithaca, Cornell University Press.

Gillespie, R.R. and Collins, C.B., eds (1986) *Education as an International Commodity.* University of Queensland/ANZCIES.

Glaser, B. and Strauss, A.L. (1967) *The Discovery of Grounded Theory.* Chicago, Aldine.

Hargreaves, D. (1967) *Social Relations in a Secondary School.* London, Routledge and Kegan Paul.

Hamilton et al. (1977) *Beyond the Numbers Game. A Reader in Educational Evaluation*. London, Macmillan.

Hau'ofa, E. (1987) 'The New South Pacific Society: Integration and Independence'. In A. Hooper, et al., loc. cit.: 1–15.

Hooper, A., et al. (eds.) (1987) *Class and Culture in the South Pacific*. Centre for Pacific Studies, University of Auckland, and Institute of Pacific Studies, University of the South Pacific.

Jones, P. (1979) 'Pluralism and Education: Some Implications'. In N. Bricknell, and R. Hunter, eds. *Education: Planning and Process in Plural Societies*. Mount Gravatt College of Advanced Education/ANZCIES.

Jones, P. (1986) Australia's International Relations in Education. *Australian Education Review* No. 23. Melbourne, Australian Council for Educational Research.

Keeves, J.P. (1987) *Australian Education: Review of Recent Research*. Sydney, Allen and Unwin.

Kemmis, S. (1984) 'Educational Research Is Research for Education'. *Australian Educational Researcher* 11(1): 28–38.

King, E. (1977) 'Comparative Studies: An Evolving Commitment, a Fresh Realism'. *Comparative Education* 13 (2): 101–108.

King, K. (1985) 'North-South Collaborative Research in Education'. *International Journal of Educational Development* 5(3): 183–191.

Lacey, C. (1970) *Hightown Grammar: The School as a Social System*. Manchester, Manchester University Press.

Lewin, K. (1987) *Planning in Austerity: Options for Planners*. Paris, IIEP, Unesco.

Maddock, J. and Hindson, C. (eds.) (1985) *Quality and Equality in Education*. Flinders University/ANZCIES.

Masemann, V.L. (1982) 'Critical Ethnography in the Study of Comparative Education'. *Comparative Education Review* 26(1): 1–15.

Meleisea, M. (1987) 'Ideology in Pacific studies: a personal view'. In A. Hooper, et al., loc. cit.: 140–152.

Oxenham, J. (1985) 'Transpositions from Research into Policy and Practice: Possibilities for Foreign Researchers'. *International Journal of Educational Development* 5(3): 193–202.

Parkyn, G.W. (1977) 'Comparative Education Research and Development Education'. *Comparative Education* 13(2): 87–93.

Parlett, M. and Hamilton, D. (1972) Evaluation as Illumination: A New Approach to the Study of Innovatory Programmes. Occasional Paper No.

9, *Centre for Research in the Educational Sciences, University of Edinburgh.*

Psacharopoulos, G. and Woodhall, M. (1985) *Education for Development: An Analysis of Investment Choices*. Washington, World Bank.

Raggatt, P. (1983) 'One Person's Periphery'. *Compare* 3(1): 1–5.

Salmi, J. (1985) Educational Research on the Third World or with the Third World: A View from the South'. *International Journal of Educational Development* 5(3): 223–226.

Sander, B. (1985) 'Education and Dependence: The Role of Comparative Education'. *Prospects* 15(2): 195–203.

Shaeffer, S. (1986) 'Foreword'. In B. Avalos (ed.), loc. cit.: 5–6.

Sheehan, B.A. (ed.) (1983) *Comparative and International Studies and the Theory and Practice of Education.* University of Waikato/ANZCIES.

Simkin, K. (1981) 'Comparative and Sociological Perspectives on Third World Development and Education'. *International Review of Education* 27(4): 428–447.

Simmons, H. (1987) *Getting to Know Schools in a Democracy*. London, Falmer Press.

Stake, R.E. (1967) 'The Countenance of Educational Evaluation', *Teachers' College Record* 68: 523–548.

Stenhouse, L. (1979) 'Case Study in Comparative Education. Particularity and Generalisation'. *Comparative Education* 15(1): 5–10.

Stratigos, S. and Hughes, P.J. (eds.) (1987) *The Ethics of Development. The Pacific in the 21st Century*. Port Moresby, University of Papua New Guinea Press.

Tabai, E. (1987) 'The Ethics of Development: A Kiribati View'. In S. Stratigos and P.J. Hughes (eds.), *loc. cit.*

Thompson, A.R. (1985) 'Evaluation in Overseas Education: Some Parameters and Priorities'. *International Journal of Educational Development* 5(3): 227–234.

Tyler, R.W. (1949) *Basic Principles of Curriculum and Instruction*. Chicago, University of Chicago Press.

Vulliamy, G. (1985) *A Comparative Analysis of SSCEP Outstations*. ERU Report 50, Waigani, University of Papua New Guinea.

Watson, K. and Oxenham, J. (eds.) (1985) Research, Co-operation and Evaluation of Educational Programmes in the Third World. Special Issue of the *International Journal of Educational Development* 5(3).

Weeks, S.G. (1987) 'Education for Village Life? What Has Happened to Grade Ten Leavers from the Five SSCEP High Schools?' *International Journal of Educational Development* 7(1) 33–48.

Welch, A.R. (ed.) (1981) *The Politics of Educational Change*. University of New England/ANZCIES.

Welch, A.R. (1985) 'The Functionalist Tradition and Comparative Education'. *Comparative Education* 21(1): 5–19.

Wendt, A. (1973) *Sons for the Return Home*. Harmondsworth, Penguin.

Wendt, A. (1987) 'Novelists and Historians and the Art of Remembering'. In A. Hooper, et al. (eds.), *loc. cit.*: 78–92.

Williamson, A. (ed.) (1987) *Educational Exchanges and their Implications. Challenge and Response*. Sydney, ANZCIES.

Willis, P. (1977) *Learning to Labour*. Farnborough, Saxon House.

Woods, P. (1979) *The Divided School*. London, Routledge and Kegan Paul.

Comparison and the Limits of Comparison in Working Toward Non-Sexist Education

LYN YATES

La Trobe University, Victoria

A comparative experience has been at the heart of contemporary Western understandings of the situation of women. It has been fundamental to our recognition that there is a problem with the education of girls, to our investigation of this, and to many of the strategies which have been proposed and developed to produce non-sexist education.[1] This chapter is an attempt to analyze some of the ways in which comparative method and knowledge have been used by those concerned with sexism in education, to indicate some of the distinctive forms of the development of research in this area as well as the way comparative strategies have informed developments within the field of curriculum reform, and to point to some of the tensions inherent in these dynamics.

One thrust of this chapter is an argument that 'comparative' perspectives in education should not be taken as synonymous with cross-cultural comparison. The discussion will show how new comparisons relating to gender have shaped cross-cultural comparative research as well as being shaped by it. A second concern will be to show that while comparison has been important in relation to concerns about the education of women, so too has been a critical attention to the frameworks within which comparisons are developed.

COMPARISON AND INSIGHT ABOUT WOMEN, GIRLS AND EDUCATION

In education discourse, a 'comparative' approach is usually identified with international and cross-cultural comparisons. What is suggested in this section is that, over the last two decades, the women's movement and the focus on girls, women and education have added some new and important dimensions to the comparative exercise. There has been a new emphasis on gender comparison (both of women with women and of women with men) and the development of new modes of undertaking this. Moreover, the development of new questions and some new substantive concepts relating to girls and women has revitalized a number of traditional types of educational research.

(i) New Concepts of Comparison

The activities of the women's movement and theorizing by feminists have been a growing phenomenon in Western social life in the last decade. These activities are not homogeneous in their approach, and one might go about characterizing their core characteristics in a number of ways. The two types of comparative insight discussed here are one way of understanding characteristics which are found very widely as part of feminist theory and action, though the degrees to which they are consciously recognized in that way will vary widely.[2] In terms of new concepts of comparison, one widely recognized distinctive practice of the contemporary women's movement has been 'consciousness raising'. In 'ideal type', consciousness-raising might be described as a meeting where women share their experiences in a setting that is formally egalitarian and unstructured. There is no teacher or leader, and the sharing of experiences becomes the basis of new understandings for those involved. The 'new understandings' referred to here are taken to encompass both a new insight or passive knowledge and, more actively, a new structuring of perception and outlook. The 'comparison' based in consciousness-raising then is not comparison with a contrasting group, but with a like group. It focusses on the characteristics each has in common, for example, their situation as women, wives, mothers.

Nevertheless, the form of this comparison allows a new perspective on the original experience:

> [Consciousness-raising] involves seeing the same reality differently . . . women's understandings of our lives are transformed so that we see, understand and feel them in a new and quite different way, at the same time as we see them in the 'old' way . . . women come to understand the . . . contradictions present within life . . . this 'double vision' of reality and our involvement in it is essential to the idea and the actuality of 'feminist consciousness'. (Stanley and Wise 1983: 54)

In some ways the processes here are similar to those Paulo Freire has described as 'conscientization' (Freire 1972a, 1972b). It is a form of comparison where those experiences which are shared and deemed important within the group are being used as a basis for what is to be taken seriously, in contrast to forms of teaching and research which pre-formulate the terms in which the experience of participants is to be understood. 'Consciousness-raising' extended or changed Freire's approach in two ways. Gender rather than class or colonized status was taken as the substantive focus, the basis on which the 'like' group was formed and (self-)examined. And, even more than in Freire's exposition, the understanding of oppression was to come from within the group rather than (via a 'dialogical' teacher) from outside 'more powerful' knowledge. The point of significance here for comparative method is that some forms of comparison compare different groups, countries or sexes, but do so in terms which are pre-formulated and do not adequately represent the groups under examination. (cf. Wilson 1974; Hamilton 1980) The contribution of the type of comparison described above (that is, among a like group which has previously been taught and researched, at least in part, in terms alien to it) is that it gives a basis for reformulating the terms or categories in which future research and comparison might proceed. (It is true that in recent times academic feminist theory would seem to have moved in many cases to very high levels of intellectual abstraction, which appear to be a long way indeed from the consciousness-raising model of practice just outlined. But even this, I would suggest, owes some debt to this form of comparison internal to the oppressed group, to the new naming of a problem 'which had no name' (Friedan 1963) or which had previously been named only by others in terms of otherness (that is, from a male perspective). The legacy of this new comparison among women is sometimes made explicit in the autobiographical introductions and interjections of theorists who otherwise stand as representatives of more abstracted and intellectual forms of theorizing women's state.[3] We might note too, somewhat ironically, that as feminist theorizing seems to have moved away from consciousness-raising as an adequate source of insights, strategies for girls in schools in Australia have often been eager to embrace it.[4])

Notwithstanding such asides, the new concept of comparison represented by 'consciousness-raising' is an important reminder of an ongoing problem for comparative method. Whatever the limitations of the approach discussed above, the new comparison of women with other women about their situation as women has had a powerful effect on new practices of research and educational strategy related to non-sexist education. In research on science education for example, one important approach to understanding in a fresh way why girls were less likely to continue with science has been based in listening to what present and past female students said about their experiences (cf. Kelly 1981). Research on girls and science using pre-existing categories tended to focus on correlations of success with types of assessment, IQ, topics, etc. Using the reflections of female students however, researchers were led to some subtle qualitative reflections about the nature of the problem. They found, for example, that the female students were upset by the 'banter' which male students and previous researchers had seen as light-hearted and engaging; or they confronted the problem that the girls felt they were not 'taken seriously' as future scientists. Through such reflections, researchers gained some understanding of the nature of the marginalization of the girls in these classes, the way in which they were placed as 'the other' in a pedagogy and curriculum which constructed science and the science classroom as masculine (see also Kelly 1987).

In terms of new educational strategies concerned with gender, the interest in insights to be gained from comparisons within the group can be seen in the 1987 *National Policy for the Education of Girls in*

Australian Schools. The earlier Australian policy report in this area (*Girls, School and Society* 1975) had mounted the case concerning the inequality of girls and women by comparisons with boys and men (as to outcomes and treatment) and by cross-cultural comparisons (to demolish explanations in terms of biological inevitability). The 1987 National Policy took a different path and presented a major part of its case in a chapter entitled 'Being a Girl in an Australian School', where it tried to show how girls themselves saw that experience. As in the case of the science research referred to above, this different starting-point produced new emphases, new interpretations of what was significant and what was at issue. (In particular, it found that girls were more affected by the physical environment of the school than had previously been recognized.)

Another Australian report, spanning both action research and policy recommendations, was even more clearly framed within the new form of comparison. *Educating Voula* (Tsolidis 1986) was a project designed to listen to girls of non-English speaking background (NESB), carried out by a researcher who shared this background. It argued that some of the categories in which NESB girls were commonly framed needed to be reversed. These girls, the report argued, were not a deficit group, but a group with more knowledge than their fellow students; the problem for them was not that they could not measure up to the demands of the school, but that the teachers were not serious enough in the demands they made on the students.

But possibly the most far-reaching effect of the attempt within educational theory to re-think comparison by devising new frameworks from within the group has been in discussions of knowledge and rationality. In some widely discussed writings, Gilligan (1977, 1982), Martin (1982, 1984, 1986) and Belenky, Clinchy, Goldberger and Tarule (1986) have argued that aspects of the core of the educational enterprise itself need to be rethought. They have suggested that the 'development of the mind' which has been a widely accepted framework for the structuring of Western education has been in fact derived from comparisons among males, and that other ways of seeing the development of the mind (and emotions, and morality) are built when women are taken as the source of the study within which comparisons are made. It is true that all these writers begin and to some extent make their case by a comparison of women's writing and thinking to that which has been written about men. But central to what they do is not simply this comparison of women to men, but a new comparison among women. They seek to understand the thinking of women not in terms of how far it measures up to existing definitions of what is important but in terms of new definitions of what is important and valuable derived from the comparisons made within a group of women.[5]

> This repeated finding of developmental inferiority in women may, however, have more to do with the standard by which development has been measured than with the quality of women's thinking *per se*. . . . The systematic exclusion from consideration of alternative criteria that might better encompass the development of women indicates not only the limitations of a theory framed by men and validated by research samples disproportionately male and adolescent but also the effects of the diffidence prevalent among women, their reluctance to speak publicly in their own voice, given the constraints imposed on them by the politics of differential power between the sexes. In order to go beyond the question, "How much like men do women think, how capable are they of engaging in the abstract and hypothetical construction of reality?" it is necessary to identify and define in formal terms developmental criteria that encompass the categories of women's thinking. (Gilligan 1977: 489–90)

Finally, however, while the comparison among women gave rise to new questions and concepts for the investigation of education, and a criticism of some of the categories through which the educational experiences of women had been researched, in more recent times a similar process has been used to draw attention to racism and cultural differences among women, and to raise critical questions about the categories being used in research on gender. Arguments have been made that the voices of black women, women of non-English speaking background, ethnic minority women need to be heard and need to have some scope to define themselves what is the nature of the problem. Mainstream feminist research has been criticized for repeating the processes which they had criticized in male-based research: that is, for making the existence of the groups of minority women invisible, or for stereotyping and painting as victims the groups of different ethnic and racial origin.[6] A second lynchpin of feminist theoretical work and of action for non-sexist education has been the comparison of girls and women with boys and men, and the comparative (questioning) perspective on existing structures of education and knowledge and power. Fundamental to both is a recognition that there is likely to be something different about women's experience, that this should be taken seriously, and that the difference may well be a problem, that is a likely source of oppression or discrimination for women.

It might be objected here that the points I am making apply only to some lines of the activities related to non-sexist education. Certainly there are important differences in the assumptions and strategies being pursued. In the early stages in particular, and among 'liberal' rather than 'radical' feminists more recently, it might seem that that basic assumption is to deny that women and girls are different from men and boys, and to use this as the basis for objecting to different outcomes. More recently there has been what might seem an opposite approach, one which asserts the differences pertaining to women, and questions why schools are not formulated more in those interests.[7] Although the differences here are important, and will be discussed further below, in practice both approaches have drawn on the new concepts of comparison being discussed in this section. The 'liberal' approach of assuming no basic difference among women and men has raised new criticisms about differential educational outcomes in the present period in part at least because of the comparisons among women (that is, the contemporary women's movement) which declared these to be a problem with an educational and social basis, not simply the sum of individual free choices. Concepts about women's specific oppression which once might have been associated with the concerns of consciousness-raising and other radical feminist groups are now part of what government-constituted Equal Opportunity Boards try to deal with in terms of cases of sexual harassment and in devising affirmative action plans. And on the other hand, in the educational context, the 'radical' approaches which are most interested in developing new women-centered forms of education, nevertheless use evidence of how girls fare compared with boys in the traditional classroom as one starting point of demonstrating a new problem to be addressed.

Educational research has, of course, often used sex as a category when gathering data—although, too, research has surprisingly often been undertaken by males on male subjects, with a tacit assumption that these stood for everyone (cf. Spender 1981). However, before the period discussed here, the use of sex as a category was comparative only in the most limited sense. Different achievements might be collated and presented, but they were not taken as a subject for further investigation and critical interpretation. By contrast, in a period when women began to compare their experiences with each other, to take these experiences seriously, and to acknowledge unhappiness about the paths they had taken, we began to see a different type of research on girls and boys in education. This gave more emphasis to the significance of collating and comparing what happened to girls as compared to boys, and it had new concepts for extending investigation into why education processes might be working as they were.

A central element of feminist theory and non-sexist activity, then, has been to be conscious of and to utilize the idea that women have an inbuilt comparative situation: they have experiences which can give critical insight into existing institutions and existing structures of knowledge which have been dominated by men. From a variety of fields we might begin to analyze why comparative experience of this particular type might be enlightening and powerful. The arguments mentioned earlier of Stanley and Wise, and of Paulo Freire, show how activist-theoreticians have posited that knowledge for change depends on both knowing an experience, and knowing it differently. In a different type of case, Hugh Stretton, a philosopher of the social sciences, has argued that the very process of gaining knowledge in social sciences (knowledge of causes and influences, judgements of significance, and so on) depends on being able to test situations against what he refers to as 'imagined alternatives'. (Stretton 1969). Taking up the same theme from a different basis, Marcia Westkott suggested that Women's Studies was important in a curriculum for just such a process: to work on a 'vision' so that 'critical judgement' of the present is possible (Westkott 1983).

A more sociologically-based approach to reflecting on the sources of comparison which women were now able to use is the idea that 'muted groups', because of their situation, need to, and do, obtain greater knowledge of the dominant groups as well as themselves than do dominant groups of the muted. Both sociological and fictional treatments of slavery in the US for example have shown how slaves learned to understand the perspectives on the world through which the slave-owners operated and their own place as slaves within that and to understand the meaning of their own behaviour within that perspective. But as well, the slaves lived and knew another reality, a perspective on their own lives and traditions which was not known to the owners.[8] Similarly, it has been suggested that women as wives, as secretaries, as conversational help-meets to men, need a sensitivity to men's needs and concerns which is not reciprocated equally by the men whom they support, and they also know an alternative reality of the work required to maintain the form of femininity and availability through which they appear to those men.[9]

Again, looking to a parallel example which might be a source for further investigation as to the ways in which inculcation in opposing 'worlds' can be a source of development, we might look at the relation between traditional forms of Catholic education in Australian society and the citizens they produced. Here Eileen Haley has suggested that the production of many strong and feminist women by the Catholic system might be attributable less to the single-sex nature of the schools these women attended than to the content of their education, wherein, at every point, they were inculcated with an ideal, values and even facts which were at complete odds with the mainstream society (Haley 1973). That is, although the overt message of much convent education might be concerned with teaching women to be obedient and submissive, it also preached disdain for worldly goods in a society oriented to commodity consumption; it was organized by nuns as single women, devoted to their work and powerful within the institution, in a society where most women were expected to require a man and were lacking in such power.

(ii) Gender Comparison and the Development of 'Comparative' Research

What I have been trying to suggest to this point is that the new attention to girls and women which grew so rapidly from the mid-70s, although superficially taking the form of an 'adding-on', was likely to be more significant than this. Because of its source (its social basis) it was likely to be both comparative and critical. That this is so is most readily illustrated by the large body of empirical, quantitative 'mapping' research concerned with sex differences, which has grown enormously in the contemporary period. The research includes both formal, published research and also a very large amount of research carried out at school level by teachers engaged in action research projects (see Yates 1987). Research activities such as checking male and female illustrations in text-books, charting resource allocation, subject-choices, career paths of girls and boys, even counting who speaks in the classroom with attention to gender, might all seem methodologically simple and unoriginal. But, because of the social base which gave rise to them, these studies have had a considerable impact. First, in terms of the acknowledgement of gender as a problem for education, these studies were not simply documenting a problem that was already generally recognised by teachers (cf. Evans 1983), but were showing that the absence of girls and women in 'hard' terms was far greater than anyone recognized. Secondly, because the knowledge gathered was not seen as a merely 'academic' exercise, but was posed as a problem, such research was the basis for opening up some new types of reflection on classroom processes and institutional structures.

In some respects the developments here are something like the paradigm changes in research described by Thomas Kuhn, where the process of filling out old theories is replaced by attention to new ones (Kuhn 1970). In Kuhn's terms, a 'paradigm' is the body of theory and assumptions which guide the particular research projects which scientists carry out: these define the problems to be addressed, the factors deemed to be 'relevant' in terms of controlling conditions, the assumptions which are made in interpreting results. According to Kuhn, after a period of time, when a particular paradigm is ceasing to provide sufficient progress in solving problems, it is replaced by an alternative one which generates its own research agenda. In the case of education and gender, what I have been suggesting is that the new attention to gender and sex equality as a problem represents something of a paradigm change of this sort. However, in comparison with Kuhn's theories about science, I am suggesting that the source of this new paradigm for education was not in problems thrown up from previous educational research paradigms, but was a new social movement which raised new issues for educational researchers.[10]

What has all this meant in terms of that field of educational research we usually call 'comparative'—that is, cross-cultural and international research? Cross-cultural research and international comparisons have been an important form of data, both in the initial explorations of gender and education, and in the continued re-definitions and refinement of it—but it is data interpreted according to a new vision which assumes women's rights to equality, and which is interested in finding social and cultural sources of women's inequality. Both evidence of similarity of girls' achievements and participation in different countries and evidence of difference have been enthusiastically taken up by researchers in this area. Initially, inquiries such as the Australian government report, *Girls, School and Society* (1975) used evidence of differences as important. They used cross-cultural studies to dispose of some of the shibboleths concerning the biological bases of certain characteristics deemed feminine and masculine in this particular culture. But in the period since then, evidence of some cross-cultural similarities in the experiences of girls and women in education (such as their relatively lower participation and achievement in certain subject areas) has been used not to resurrect biological explanations but as a basis for some further theorizing about gender (cf. Kelly 1981; Kelly 1987; Kelly 1989). Such research has been used to extend the significance of gender as an explanatory concept in research, in the sorts of ways that 'class' has been developed.

In terms of international comparative research, it should be noted too that the paradigm shift which was posing new questions and suggesting new interpretations for educational researchers was also reshaping the raw data itself. As Gail Kelly recently comments in a reflection on a large volume of international research:

> Over the past twenty years, educational access for women has widened dramatically. In 1960, it would have been a truism to state that everywhere women were undereducated relative to men . . . Worldwide, gender was the single greatest predictor of educational access. Today, this is not necessarily the case. The number of females in school in the 1980s is higher than in any period in history. The proportion of girls in primary, secondary and higher education has risen in almost every country in the world . . . (Kelly 1989b: 547)

The ongoing use of international and cross-cultural comparative research over the past twenty years, however, has been useful in extending and refining understandings about sexual inequality as an issue relative to education. It is one means of deriving pointers to the possibilities for education and educational systems. In the IEA studies of science achievement for example, although the lower achievement of girls relative to boys is found consistently within each particular country, the absolute achievement varies enormously between countries, so that girls in one country may achieve far higher than boys in another.[11] Research on particular countries can suggest too how the forms in which education is offered may contribute very significantly to what is made available to girls, in a way we can distinguish from the general influences of the culture itself. For example, Cunningham, writing about Scotland, traced ways in which the structure and content of education in that country produced quite different results for women than its near neighbour, England (Cunningham 1984). Elliot, writing about India, suggested that some forms of offering education to women in that country have been very successful, as compared with other attempts to achieve similar ends which have proved quite unsuccessful (Elliot 1984).

As well, studies of education in different countries can be of interest in suggesting some of the constraints we are likely to face when trying to produce change in the direction of counter-sexist ends. Here the statistical comparisons of achievement in different countries would seem to show some similarity in the pattern of science and mathematics achievement among many different countries, and the difficulty of theoretically accounting for the persistence of these patterns (Kelly 1981b). As well, studies of particular countries which have been prominent in attempted interventions in education designed to combat sexist processes, raise food for thought regarding many signs of lack of success. Sweden, for example, has had a history of reform in this area and official commitment to the equality of women and men which has been of longer duration, more extensively supported and more carefully monitored than most other countries. Despite this, researchers report considerable lack of success in achieving intended goals:

> Although women's access to secondary education has increased as a result of reform, secondary education remains sex segregated, despite intensive efforts to encourage girls to enter non-traditional fields of study . . . Girls who enter courses of study that have traditionally excluded them on the secondary level have a higher dropout rate than do girls who pursue study in traditional fields . . . In higher education, the pattern of sex segregation also holds . . . The average income in 1985 was SEK 62,000 for women and SEK 95,500 for men.[12]

From their review of the Swedish experience, Andrae-Thelin and Elqvist-Saltzman raise questions about the adequacy of the assumptions guiding Swedish government sexual equality policies. In particular they question the emphasis on identical treatment of girls and boys, on career counselling, and on shifting women to 'non-traditional' areas as sufficient strategies in working towards equality. They draw new attention to the significance of domestic life and responsibilities in shaping participation in the paid workforce, and new attention to general curriculum messages about this.

International comparisons too are one way of trying to test theories of what is significant in relation to sexual equality and education. Gail Kelly, for example, comparing reports on women's education in 23 countries, notes that there is some broad correlation of women's educational experience with the wealth, religion, and political form of a country (Kelly 1989b: 558). But she finds too that none of these factors are definitive determinants. For example, she notes examples of poorer countries (Kenya, Sri Lanka, China) which give more equal access to girls than richer countries (Saudi Arabia, Oman); of poorer Islamic countries (Tunisia, Iraq, Syria) which give greater access than richer Islamic countries (Saudi Arabia); of countries where socialist revolutions lead to girls gaining more equal access to primary education (China, Vietnam, Tanzania), and of those which do not (Laos, the People's Republic of Yemen, Yugoslavia) (Kelly 1989b: 558–9). As well, while countries that provide relatively equal access of women to higher education are all industrialized societies, the extent of the differentiation in access between men and women in other countries does not reflect simply either wealth or degree of industrialization (Kelly 1989b: 568).

Finally, in terms of gender and comparative educational research, I would suggest that two key issues have emerged. One is a problem for comparative research; the other is a problem for education and sexual equality which comparative research has helped to define more clearly.

The problem for comparative research stems from challenges by black women and ethnic minority women concerning the racism of feminist theory, and criticizing the practice of any academic mainstream which defines on their behalf what categories are of concern and what is the nature of the problem.[13] This problem goes beyond acknowledging that in some countries access to education may be a central issue for women, while in other countries it is not; and beyond repeating criticisms of the distortions necessary to calculate achievement data in widely different contexts on a common scale (cf. Hamilton 1980). It relates to the 'imperialism' involved in producing international encyclopaedias, handbooks and comparative collections where the comparisons that are made and the general theory and frameworks that are developed are done from the perspective of the dominant group.

The recent *International Handbook of Women's Education* (Kelly 1989a) demonstrates something of this problem. Although the individual chapters on different countries indicate something of the distinctive concerns within each country, it is clear that the framework overall is one which is interested in questions of access, of formal provision and legislation, of outcomes in terms of women's participation in paid work and in politics. It is less interested for example in comparisons to be made about curriculum and its effects, or about the relationship between education and changes in the domestic division of labour, or in tracing differences in the ways different countries conceptualize the issues. Nevertheless, to acknowledge this problem is not to accept that the data produced here are of no value. Indeed this collection does produce some interesting insights for considering strategies towards non-sexist education in a country like Australia.

For one thing, though the authors were asked to focus on data on access, participation, achievement, employment and politics, the editor notes that the various writers make clear that the problem cannot be addressed through taken-for-granted categories:

> Although the chapters in this volume are not explicitly theoretical, they are guided by implicit feminist theory. They all look at education in the context of women's oppression. None presumes that women's subordination is determined solely by the economy and easily remedied by "quick fixes" like a socialist revolution or a mass entry of women into paid labor. None presumes that society or the schools are gender-neutral . . . (Kelly 1989a: ix–x)

More importantly, the data overall raises new questions about what in fact is the relationship between education and sexual inequality more generally:

> differences in the proportion of women educated and the amount of education they receive have resulted in few changes in their rate of entry into the workforce for a wage, the degree of gender segregation in the workforce, women's income relative to men's (although education does appear to relate to women's income relative to other women), and women's access to political power. (Kelly 1989b: 560)

The argument in this section has been that the development of the women's movement and the movement for non-sexist education have transformed educational research in a number of ways. Both in research within one country and in cross-cultural comparisons, it has led to the collection of some new sets of data, and also to the treatment of data from a new comparative base, so that it is interpreted and used in some new ways. I have emphasized here the new values and insights through which the research was being conducted, but have not been trying to suggest that research is simply ideological. Rather, by the references to the mapping activities and by the examples of some ways in which cross-cultural comparative research might contribute to our understandings of sexism and the processes of education, I have been trying to show that research into empirical reality can provide some important checks and extensions to the values and theories with which we begin. What was also suggested throughout this section is that the valuable developments have been of a form that makes research a dynamic process, that treats data as a source for further questions and investigation rather than as a body of inert fact.

(iii) Comparative Strategy Within Curriculum

To date, the discussion in this chapter has largely focussed on the contributions comparative study might make to our knowledge about education. But Australian strategies concerned with non-sexist education have also raised some interesting matters about the way in which comparative study should be part of the school curriculum.

The 1975 report, *Girls, School and Society* took a comparative approach to be a central curriculum strategy for a good liberal education. In that report, 'comparison' was taken to mean an awareness of and reflection about 'alternatives', in contrast to allowing behaviour and attitudes to be dictated by custom. Thus, in a much quoted accusation about the ways in which schooling in Australia was restricting and distorting the life-paths of girls, the report claimed:

> Sexism is a process through which females and males not only progressively learn that different things are required and expected of them because of their sex, but learn those things in an unexamined way. Good education is incompatible with such a process; central to it is the examination of assumptions and the rational consideration of alternatives. Hence 'sexist education' is a contradiction in terms . . . [14]

In the concluding section of the report, when dealing with 'principles for 'action in schools', the theme of the importance of a comparative basis for knowledge is continued:

> action should be designed to extend the capacity of both girls and boys to make considered choices on the basis of relevant knowledge and within a considered value framework. In the fluid situation existing in our society at present custom is inadequate as a guide in the choices facing young people. There are options available which may be exercised intelligently only in the light of knowledge of alternatives open, and the consequences of particular choices. These options and choices need no longer be regarded as limited by the sex of the person operating them.[15]

More recently, an extensive curriculum package designed for schools, the *Social Literacy Project* also uses comparison as a central basis by which students can be led to see the social construction of gender and sexism and the forms it takes in particular cultural contexts, including contemporary capitalist Australia.[16]

Nevertheless, comparison of this type has not been a dominant thrust of curriculum strategy for non-sexist education in Australia. Rather it has been overtaken by a concept which might also be said to be comparative, but in a quite different way, the concept of 'inclusiveness'.[17] The 'comparison' in this case concerns the comparison among women, and the attention to the specificity of previously silenced groups referred to earlier in this chapter. The principle is that school practices should not assume a pedagogy and curriculum framed as if all students were the same as the dominant group, but it should be 'inclusive' of the different groups that make up the classroom and that make up Australian society.

Both of the strategies have their problems. The Swedish experience would seem to suggest that a strategy based on some 'rational' consideration of alternatives which 'makes no assumption about sex differences' founders on the reality of the non-rational pressures and sex differences in life histories of men and women. The strategy of 'inclusiveness' however tends to lose the critical comparative questioning by which changes in the relations of the groups to be included might come about.[18]

DILEMMAS OF COMPARISON

Both in research and in curriculum practice, new comparative approaches have been developed by those concerned about sexual inequality and education. In the case of research, the approaches have produced new insights about the nature of this problem, and in the case of school practice have led to strategies that seem a useful corrective to some taken-for-granted forms of discrimination and channelling that research on gender had charted in the education system. But the discussion has also made clear the complexity of what is involved in the act of comparison. In discussing developments and dilemmas faced by work within this particular field, it is clear that researchers and teachers are also contending with problems of positivism, relativism and power.

First of all, it may be useful to repeat (again) some of the earlier points about how the situation of women came to be seen in a new way, and how education came to be seen as sexist. The lines of research and action concerning sexism in education did come about in part because of comparative experience: the data that such and such was the case with girls and something else was the case with boys; or information that the feelings of frustration of the suburban housewife were not just an idiosyncratic emotion but a shared experience which could be analysed and interpreted in relation to its context. But the recognition that the situation of women or the education of girls was a problem, was a system of disadvantage or oppression, did not come about simply because of the availability of different information. It depended on the ways that information was interpreted and judged. And, in any case, it is not a simple one-way process. We might ask what led to the production and collation of the information: why, for the first time, did someone see that girls were rarely speaking in the classroom, when before this had been invisible? In terms of feminism and the women's movement, the starting point was to 'value women' in a certain way, to say that the experience of girls and women, their feelings, were to be seen as legitimate, a subject to be explored and taken seriously rather than ridiculed or explained away. In terms of the education system and national governments, the new starting point was that different outcomes for girls and boys were to be taken as a problem, an issue to be dealt with, rather than an appropriate function of the education system. Both of these moves represent certain values and political positions—as do any decisions taken in an education system. As Popkewitz has explained it:

> The work of science [that is, educational research] is a work of people who are striving to understand and improve our social conditions and institutional patterns. The competing assumptions, questions and procedures of research contain values that represent deep divisions within American society about principles of authority, institutional transformation and social order . . . Social inquiry emerges from a communal context in which there are norms, beliefs and patterns of social conduct. These patterns are not static and involve continual debate. The debate evolves around differing assumptions about the nature of social life and the purpose of a science . . . (Popkewitz 1984: vii)

Of course the issue of the value-ladenness of research is not new; it has been discussed extensively, in many different ways in many different theoretical frameworks.[19] Nevertheless, these extensive discussions stand alongside rather than replacing similarly extensive commitments to and beliefs in positivism within educational research. These beliefs assume that the facts and statistics presented do represent an objective truth which tells a story regardless of the purposes and beliefs of the researcher. Such beliefs particularly pervade what I earlier called 'mapping' research, and confront us in research which attempts to gain some 'international' picture.

As this chapter has made clear, the work on gender and education has been characterized both by a critique of 'positivism' but also by an attempt to use mapping and cross-cultural comparisons as solid hard data. Although values are involved in seeing the education of girls as a problem, and although these are clearly discussed in writings about women's studies and feminist methodology, especially in the critique of existing research[20], in writings and policies concerning girls and education the acknowledgement that values are involved has often been relatively hidden. Even *Girls, School and Society*, for example, most often used the approach that the facts (of girls' different educational patterns or of cross-cultural research or of changes in the Australian social fabric) 'spoke for themselves', in relation to what education should be doing.

One reason why attempted reforms in relation to girls and education have shied away from addressing the issues of what is to be valued, is that the dominant discourse about education that is acceptable in Australia (and other Western industrial countries) is generally one that is both liberal and positivist. It is liberal in that the continued rhetoric of the system is one based on notions of 'equality', 'fairness', 'fulfillment' or 'development' of the 'individual', etc.[21] It is positivist in that both the rhetoric of policy documents and the research which is done rarely acknowledges the different interpretations which may be made of these terms, or the different significance that may be ascribed to the 'facts' that a research project uncovers.[22]

Another reason for the reluctance by researchers to give up the use of comparative data and to leave everyone to define their own categories of concern, is that such relativism is at odds with a movement which is seeking to change women's position.[23] In this context, it is appropriate that reports and projects which aim to produce change in government policies and school action in education make their case within the forms that are dominant and acceptable. But such an approach is also likely to produce tensions in relation to girls/women and education, in that the making of a case based on 'the facts' will be at odds with the attempt to maintain a continued critical perspective as a basis for understanding how girls and women are not treated fairly. Here what Popkewitz has said about the 'contradictory character' of educational research in general, applies even more sharply to those engaged in research projects seeking to change dominant assumptions and practices:

> The researcher acts as an expert-in-legitimation, creating symbolic canopies that make the interests of few seem the interests of the society as a whole. At the same moment, there is a criticizing and probing attitude towards human society and its particular situations in time and place. (Popkewitz 1984: viii)

Dilemmas of negotiating comparison with a group who are oppressed, and of negotiating relativism and dogmatism in doing so are also seen in some lines of action in schools attempting to work towards non-sexist education. For example, following *Girls, School and Society*, a number of courses were developed which were committed to presenting the types of alternative relationships that may be found in the community in the area of human relations and sexuality, with the aim of having students reflect on them so that they would make 'considered choices' about their own behaviour and life-patterns.[24] Yet, as one writer notes, the 'rational consideration of alternatives' should not be the only guiding framework of such programs:

> values clarification is not always the most appropriate [technique]. If you want to convince or persuade, then don't use values clarification. For example, do not use it when trying to convince a group that rape is wrong.[25]

This is a useful reminder that the starting point of concern about sexism in education was, as suggested earlier in the chapter, not some free-floating relativism, but based on a commitment to certain core values. It is also an implicit recognition that the basis of students for assessing alternatives may not be the same as the women in the consciousness-raising group.

On the other hand, the commitment to certain values has led to strategies in danger of developing an alternative dogmatism ('women can do everything', 'boys and men treat girls and women badly'). This approach may be seen in some alternative careers teaching kits, especially videos, and some of the material on classroom dynamics. The problem here is not that the content of these propositions is necessarily wrong. Rather, the problem is when such issues are treated as facts rather than subjects for investigation and reflection, when the basis of an educated, adult, middle-class, feminist teacher for seeing them as facts is by no means the same as that of the male and female, adolescent, working-class students. The problems become particularly apparent when a dogma of non-sexism confronts a dogma of multiculturalism.[26]

These examples point to some of the concerns expressed in the initial points of departure of the movement for non-sexist education discussed at the beginning of this chapter. Firstly, criticism of existing structures in education and in existing research was often based on a claim that what appeared to be value-free detached comparison in fact embodied assumptions of those who had held power in the society, in this case men. In terms of teaching, then, we should not expect that issues of power and control can be done away with by processes of abstracted rationality, such as 'values clarification'. At the same time, we need to remember the protests about the suppression of women's reality by the imposition of categories of those in power, and to be careful that the same thing is not happening in relation to students in the presentation of a non-sexist message (cf. Greenberg 1982).

In the examples I have given, I have tried to point to some tendencies of action which might be issues of concern, and not to suggest that the tendencies I have isolated represent the whole or even the most dominant aspects of teaching in this area. What has been attempted has been to suggest some of the complexities (tensions, contradictions) at work in how we come to recognize the nature of the problem of sexism and education, how we develop knowledge about it, and how we develop teaching in the area. I have also been trying to suggest how the insights of feminist research and theorizing have been making some valuable contributions to the methodology and subject-matter with which comparative researchers should be concerned

NOTES

1. This chapter is a revised version of a paper originally given to the ANZCIES annual conference held at La Trobe University in November 1984. If I had been writing it today, rather than revising it, it would have had a different form, and would have more centrally addressed some of the tendencies of post-structuralist theorizing which have become important both in feminist theorizing and in anthropology. Nevertheless, the prominence of that discourse in contemporary writing does not persuade me of the irrelevance of arguments of the type presented in this chapter. Indeed I would want to argue that this contemporary critique and deconstruction (in relation to feminism at least) is only made possible because of the 'new concepts of comparison' discussed in the first part of this chapter. My position concerning this is discussed further in Yates (1990).

On terminology: I most commonly use the term 'non-sexist' rather than either 'feminist' or 'education for girls', because the movements in education to which I refer are not confined to those who describe themselves as feminists (they include men, for example) and are not restricted to those whose attention is confined to girls (they include those who want to work towards an education system which is better for all students). However 'non-sexist' here refers not only to those whose aim is to remove some discriminations or to ignore gender in education (cf. Dugdale 1983), but also to those whose aim is to work towards a system which is good for both girls and boys. Where I use 'feminist' in the paper, it refers to writings or actions of those who identify themselves as such. More recently, and partly because of the findings of comparative research on the effects of strategies for 'non-sexist' education (cf. Kelly 1989a), I think the area is better described as concerned with sexual inequality and education.

2. For example, I would see such forms of comparison as one of the 'conditions of possibility' for analyses such as those of Kristeva and Irigaray. So, where Davies (1989) draws a typology of feminist theory in terms of liberal feminism (the comparison with men), radical feminism (the comparison among women), and post-structural feminism (going beyond gender as a category), I would suggest that all do draw, at least as a starting point, on some of the new concepts I discuss here.

3. See, for example, Walkerdine and Lucey (1989, preface), and Spivak (1987).

4. See, for example, Taylor (1989). The development is 'ironic' not only in terms of timing, but because of questions concerning whether the situation of students is parallel (Greenberg 1982, Yates 1983).

5. The approaches discussed here have also been subject to considerable criticism. My concern here is not to judge their adequacy, but to note that they have been highly influential, and to say something about the form these approaches take.

6. See, as examples of the general debate, Amos and Parmar (1984); Barrett and McIntosh (1985), and the varied responses to this latter article in *Feminist Review* 22 (February 1986). In terms of the debate regarding school strategies in Australia, see the various discussions in WOW Project, *Including Girls* (1987); Tsolidis (1984); and Kalantzis and Cope (1987: 7). Some further discussions of the political spectrum of feminist strategies within education are Middleton (1984); Yates (1985); Weiner and Arnot (1987); and Davies (1989).

7. This emphasis is reflected in the *National Policy for the Education of Girls in Australian Schools* (1987), in the Victoria-based McClintock project on girls and science education (McClintock Collective 1989), and in articles in Kelly (1987).

8. The point is strikingly illustrated in the novel *Beloved*, by Toni Morrison. Anyon (1983) and Walkerdine and Lucey (1989) both draw on some parallels with slavery in discussing the situation and actions of girls.

9 Cf. Spender (1980); Pringle (1988); Anyon (1983).

10. This is discussed further in Yates (1990).

11. See Comber and Keeves (1983). Note that similar comparative pointers need not be based on 'international' comparison. In the Australian context, some similar evidence is produced by comparisons between States (Moss 1982), and between schools within a State (Brown and Fitzpatrick 1981).

12. Andrae-Thelin and Elqvist-Saltzman (1989). Similar points are made by Scott (1984).

13. See above, note 6.

14. *Girls, School and Society, Report of a Study Group to the Australian Schools Commission*, Canberra 1985: 2.30.

15 Ibid. 14.6.

16. See a discussion of the assumptions informing this project by Kalantzis and Cope (1987). The framing of the comparisons in this project assumes a materialist perspective.

17. See the articles on 'Inclusive Curriculum' in *Curriculum Perspective* 1987, 7 (1) , especially those of Vale and Roughead, and Suggett; also Foster (1989).

18. This is discussed further in Yates (1988). See also Kalantzis and Cope (1987) and Suggett (1987).

19. See, for example, Hamilton et al. (1977); Popkewitz (1984); Roberts (1981).

20. See, for example, Spender (1981); Bowles and Klein (1983); Stanley and Wise (1983).

21. I have discussed further the nature of liberal assumptions and the radical critiques of these in Yates (1987), and see also the useful discussion of the contemporary uses of 'liberal' in Williams (1976). For the purposes of the discussion here, the main point is that the liberal social theory within which government institutions operate is one which refuses to acknowledge a structured and group-based opposition of interests within the State (for example, between workers and employers, or between women and men), and sees the State as the sum of individuals. The institutions of the State are understood as neutral rather than constituted to further the power of particular groups, and, if this is shown (by a government inquiry, for example) not to be the case, it is seen as the result of oversight and inadequate knowledge, and able to be reformed without radical change to the form of the society.

22. D. Bennett's (1982) discussion showed how the idea of 'independence' and freedom from values and particular interests made possible the considerable influence of the Australian Council for Educational Research (ACER), and he

also showed how the agendas of this body re-shaped to a considerable degree the questions it had been asked to investigate. Until the 1982 conference the Australian Association for Research in Education (AARE) was also dominated by positivist assumptions. That conference for the first time included a symposium on ideology in research.

23. This problem was acknowledged in the debate over racism within feminism (*Feminist Review* 1986, 22), and also in a number of criticisms that have been made of the implications of post-structuralist analysis.

24. Two published examples of such courses are *Taught Not Caught* (the Clarity Collective, Melbourne 1983) and *SENSE; Studies to Encourage Non-Sexist Education* (CDC and Education Department of South Australia). See also Szirom (1988).

25. *Taught Not Caught*, op. cit., p. 21.

26. Cf. Tsolidis 1984, Kalantzis and Cope 1987, Weiler 1988.

REFERENCES

Acker, S., Megarry, J., Nisbet , S. and Hoyle, E. (eds.) *Women and Education* (World Yearbook of Education 1984). London, Kogan Page.

Amos, V., and Parmar, P. (1984) 'Challenging Imperial Feminism', *Feminist Review* 17 (July): 3–19.

Andrae-Thelin, A., and Elqvist-Saltzman, I. (1989) 'Sweden'. In G. Kelly (ed.), *International Handbook of Women's Education*. Westport, Greenwood Press.

Anyon, J. (1983) 'Intersections of Gender and Class: Accommodation and Resistance by Working-Class and Affluent Females to Contradictory Sex-Role Ideologies'. In S. Walker and L. Barton (eds.), *Gender, Class and Education*. London, Falmer Press.

Barrett, M. and McIntosh, M. (1985) 'Ethnocentrism and Socialist-Feminist Theory'. *Feminist Review* 20: 23–47.

Belenky, M.F., Clinchy, B. McV., Goldberger, N.R. and Tarule, J.M. (1986) *Women's Ways of Knowing*. New York, Basic Books.

Bennett, D. (1982) 'Ideology and Research: Some Examples for Discussion'. Paper presented to the *AARE Annual Conference*, Brisbane.

Bowles, G. and Duelli, Klein, R. (eds.) (1983) *Theories of Women's Studies*. London, Routledge.

Brown, S. and Fitzpatrick, J. (1981) 'Girls, Boys and Subject Choice'. Discussion Paper No. 11, Research Branch, Education Department of Western Australia, Perth.

Comber, L.C. and Keeves, J.P. (1973) *Science Education in 19 Countries*. Stockholm, Almqvist and Wiksell.

Cunningham, S. (1984) 'Women's Access to Higher Education in Scotland'. In S. Acker, J. Megarry, S. Nisbet and E. Hoyle (eds.), *Women and Education* (World Yearbook of Education 1984), London, Kogan Page.

Davies, B. (1989) 'Education for Sexism: A Theoretical Analysis of the Sex/Gender Bias in Education'. *Educational Philosophy and Theory* 21 (1): 1–19.

Dugdale, A. (1983). 'Feminist Curriculum vs. Non-sexist Curriculum'. *Bluestocking* 44: 1–2.

Elliott, C. (1983) 'Women's Education and Development in India'. In S. Acker, J. Megarry, S. Nisbet and E. Hoyle (eds.), *Women and Education* (World Yearbook of Education 1984), London, Kogan Page.

Evans, T. (1983) 'Being and Becoming: Teacher's Perceptions of Sex-Roles and Actions Toward Their Male and Female Pupils'. *British Journal of Sociology of Education* 3 (2): 127–144.

Foster, V. (1989) 'Is "Gender-Inclusive" Curriculum the Answer for Girls?'. In G. Leder and S. Sampson (eds.), *Educating Girls*. Sydney, Allen and Unwin.

Freire, P. (1972a) *Pedagogy of the Oppressed*. Harmondsworth, Middlesex, Penguin.

Freire, P. (1972b) *Cultural Action for Freedom*. Harmondsworth, Middlesex, Penguin.

Friedan, B. (1963) *The Feminine Mystique*. New York, Norton & Co..

Gilligan, C. (1977) 'In a Different Voice: Women's Conception of the Self and Morality'. *Harvard Education Review* 47 (4): 481–517.

Gilligan, C. (1982) *In a Different Voice: Psychological Theory and Women's Development*. Cambridge, Harvard University Press.

Girls, School and Society (1975) Report of a Study Group to the Australian Schools Commission, Canberra.

Greenberg, S. (1982) 'The Women's Movement: Putting Educational Theory Into Practice'. *Journal of Curriculum Theorizing*, 1 (1): 287–298.

Haley, E. (1973) 'A Catholic Girlhood'. In S. Higgins and M. Venner (eds.), *Women and Sexist Education*. Women's Studies Conference Papers, Adelaide.

Hamilton, D. (1980) 'Some Contrasting Assumptions About Case-Study Research and Survey Analysis'. In H. Simon (ed.), *Towards a Science of the Singular*. Norwich, University of East Anglia.

Hamilton, D., Jenkins, D., King, C., McDonald, B. and Parlett, M. (eds.) (1977) *Beyond the Numbers Game*. London, Macmillan.

Kalantzis, M. and Cope, B. (1987) 'Cultural Differences, Gender Differences: Social Literacy and Inclusive Curriculum'. *Curriculum Perspectives* 7 (1): 64–68.

Kelly, A. (1981a) *The Missing Half: Girls and Science Education*. Manchester, University of Manchester Press.

Kelly, A. (1981b) 'Sex Differences in Science Achievement: Some Results and Hypotheses'. In A. Kelly (ed.), *The Missing Half*. Manchester, University of Manchester Press.

Kelly, A. (1987) *Science for Girls?* Milton Keynes, Open University Press.

Kelly, G. (1989a) *International Handbook of Women's Education*, Westport, Conn., Greenwood Press.

Kelly, G. (1989b) 'Achieving Equality in Education—Prospects and Realities'. In G. Kelly (ed.), *International Handbook of Women's Education*. Westport, Conn., Greenwood Press.

Kuhn, T. (1970) *The Structure of Scientific Revolutions*. University of Chicago Press.

Martin, J.R. (1982) 'Excluding Women from the Educational Realm'. *Harvard Education Review* 52 (2): 133–148.

Martin, J.R. (1984) 'Bringing Women Into Educational Thought'. *Educational Theory* 34 (94): 341–353.

Martin, J.R. (1985) *Reclaiming a Conversation: The Ideal of the Educated Women*. Yale University Press.

McClintock Collective (1989) 'A Science Teachers' Collective'. In G. Leder and S. Sampson (eds.), *Educating Girls*. Sydney, Allen and Unwin.

Middleton, S. (1984) 'The Sociology of Women's Education as a Field of Academic Study'. *Discourse* 5 (1): 43–62.

Moss, J.D. (1982) 'Towards Equality: Progress By Girls in Mathematics in Australian Secondary Schools'. *ACER Occasional Paper* No. 16. Melbourne, ACER.

National Policy for the Education of Girls in Australian Schools (1987) Schools Commission, Canberra.

Popkewitz, T.S. (1984) *Paradigm and Ideology in Educational Research*. London, Falmer Press.

Pringle, R. (1988) *Secretaries Talk*. Sydney, Allen and Unwin.

Roberts, J. (1981) *Doing Feminist Research*. London, Routledge.

Scott, H. (1984) 'Women's Efforts to Achieve Sex Role Equality in Sweden'. In S. Acker, J. Megarry, S. Nisbet and E. Hoyle (eds.), *Women and Education* (World Yearbook of Education 1984). London, Kogan Page.

Spender, D. (1980) *Man Made Language*. London, Routledge.

Spender, D. (ed.) (1981) *Men's Studies Modified*. Oxford, Pergamon Press,

Spivak, G.S. (1987) *In Other Worlds: Essays in Cultural Politics*. New York, Methuen.

Stanley, L. and Wise, S. (1983) *Breaking Out: Feminist Consciousness and Feminist Research*. London, Routledge.

Stretton, H. (1969) *The Political Sciences*. London, Routledge.

Suggett, D. (1987) 'Inclusive Curriculum: A Gain or Loss for Girls?' *Curriculum Perspectives* 7 (1): 69–74.

Szirom, T. (1988) *Teaching Gender*. Sydney, Allen and Unwin.

Taylor, S. (1989) 'Empowering Girls and Young Women: The Challenge of the Gender-Inclusive Curriculum'. *Journal of Curriculum Studies* 21 (5): 441–456.

Tsolidis, G. (1984) 'Girls of Non-English speaking background: Implications for an Australian Feminism'. In R. Burns and B. Sheehan (eds.), *Women and Education, Proceedings of the 12th Annual Conference of the ANZCIES,* La Trobe University.

Tsolidis, G. (1986) *Educating Voula: A Report on Non-English Speaking Background Girls and Education*. Melbourne, MACMME.

Vale, C. and Roughead, C. (1987) 'Whose Culture Does Education Transmit? Exclusive Curriculum as a Source of Inequality'. *Curriculum Perspectives* 7 (10): 58–61.

Walkerdine, V. and Lucey, H. (1989) *Democracy in the Kitchen*. London, Virago Press.

Weiler, K. (1988) *Women Teaching for Change: Gender, Class and Power*. South Hadley, Mass., Bergin and Garvey.

Weiner, G. and Arnot, M. (1987) 'Teachers and Gender Politics'. In M. Arnot and G. Weiner (eds.), *Gender and the Politics of Schooling*. London, Hutchinson and Open University.

Westkott, M. (1983) 'Women's Studies as a Strategy for Change: Between Criticism and Vision'. In G. Bowles and R. Duelli Klein (eds.), *Theories of Women's Studies*. London, Routledge.

Williams, R. (1976) *Keywords*. London, Fontana.

Wilson, B.R. (ed.) (1974) *Rationality*. Oxford, Blackwell.

WOW Project (1987) *Including Girls*. Canberra, Curriculum Development Centre.

Yates, L. (1983) 'The Theory and Practice of Counter-Sexist Education in Schools'. *Discourse* 3 (2): 33–44.

Yates, L. (1985) '"Curriculum Becomes Our Way of Contradicting Biology and Culture"—An Outline of Some Dilemmas for Non-Sexist Education', *Australian Journal of Education* 29 (1): 3–16.

Yates, L. (1987a) 'Theorizing Inequality Today'. *British Journal of Sociology of Education* 7 (2): 119–134.

Yates, L. (1987b) 'Australian Research on Gender and Education 1975–1985'. In J. Keeves (ed.), *Australian Education: Review of Recent Research*. Sydney, Allen and Unwin.

Yates, L. (1988) 'Does "All Students" Include Girls? Some Reflections on Recent Educational Policy, Practice and Theory'. *Australian Educational Researcher* 15 (1): 41–57.

Yates, L. (1990) *Theory/Practice Dilemmas: Knowledge, Gender and Education*. Waurn Ponds, Deakin University Press.

Schooling and the Imperial Transformation of Gender: A Post-Structuralist Approach to the Study of Schooling in Bali, Indonesia

JAN BRANSON AND DON MILLER

La Trobe University

•

Monash University, Victoria

Throughout the world people strategically orient themselves towards their environment and their fellows to satisfy physical, social and emotional needs, guided in these orientations by their understanding of the world and their place in it—by their understanding of the *cosmos*. In framing a *cosmology*, an understanding of their cosmos, people do so, usually unconsciously, in a culturally and historically specific style. This mode of thought, of speech, possibly of writing, of reading, this way of seeing, this way of articulating the cosmos is their *epistemology*, an articulated bundle of dispositions towards themselves, others and the rest of the cosmos—animal, vegetable, mineral and spiritual. In this chapter we explore a range of epistemological problems as we examine the transformation of consciousness through the agency of Western-style schooling in Bali, Indonesia. They are epistemological problems for the researcher, the Balinese and the reader. As the people of Bali are experiencing challenges to their world view, so we are challenged to question our deepest assumptions about our world and the way we are disposed to approach it. For the exploration of epistemological transformations in Bali is at the same time a critical assessment of the epistemological foundations of those Western academic enterprises which seek to understand such transformations.

We the researchers are challenged on the one hand by the task of understanding the people we have lived with in Bali, and on the other by our on-going attempts to understand our own society, to understand the links between our deep-seated epistemologies and the systems of inequality and accompanying exploitation that characterise social relationships in Western capitalism. Both enterprises are intertwined as we explore the relationships between epistemological transformations and the transformation of inequalities based in gender, in the distinction between "male" and "female," in a Balinese market town. Our prime focus here is on the part formal schooling plays in these transformational processes.

As Indonesia has emerged through Dutch colonialism and Independence as a political unit oriented, through centralised bureaucratic control, towards coherent economic, social and cultural development, schooling is assumed both within and beyond Indonesia to be a vital ingredient in achieving these unitary aims. But what is in fact happening as students are provided with "literacy" and participate in a process assumed to hold out enormous promise? What are the links between the schooling process and the wider socio-cultural environment? To what degree do theories developed in the context of understanding schooling in capitalist societies provide the basis for understanding schooling in Bali? In order even to begin to answer these questions we must enter the realm of ethnography. We must come face to face with the problem of representing socio-cultural processes *in our terms.*

The schooling process is now virtually universal. Access to schooling is, throughout most of the world, an assumed right if not a compulsory experience. Denial of access to formal schooling is taken either as a sign of extreme underdevelopment or of political oppression. Formal schooling is assumed by the vast majority of humanity to be something they or their children must have. But when it comes to the comparative examination of formal schooling much is assumed, little is understood. Not only are cross-cultural comparisons assumed unproblematic, through rational analysis, but the comparative analysis of formal schooling is regarded as particularly so. Thus the literature on "education in the Third World" in the main documents the spread of

Western education, measured in terms of "schools" and the achievement of "literacy". This is not the literacy or schooling of monastery, gurukul, mosque or gurdwara. They are the "traditional" forms. "Schooling" is assumed of a kind, a cross-cultural, even acultural, activity which prepares students in such a way as to enable them to move between cultures in pursuit of cumulative transcultural educational qualifications, in pursuit of "reason," of the kind of knowledge assumed relevant to our modern, transnational, corporative world.

In the West, however, this complacent assumption that schooling is a singular, transcultural, international phenomenon has been disturbed by a new anxiety about "culture", about education in a "multicultural" society, for the Western colonists of old now find their countries full of former colonials and a host of other migrants, as well as assertive indigenous minorities. "Culture" and not just language must be confronted as a factor relevant to the transmission of knowledge. We are urged to respect "other cultures", other traditions, where once it was assumed that they must be assimilated into the host culture and its traditions. While "multi-cultural education" is toyed with as a new ideal, few question that the society's educational outcome should be the imparting of a scientific, rational education to all, even if the way it is taught may need to change. However, in response to the new consciousness of culture there has been, among a few academics, a serious questioning of assumptions about cross-cultural communication. Their questions seriously challenge comparative education in a number of ways.

Recent theorizing on the gathering of ethnographic material has stressed that the writing process, whether it be the writing of field notes or the analysis of the information collected, is an interpretive, inventive process. It is 'caught up in the invention, not the representation, of cultures' as it 'decodes and recodes' (Clifford 1986: 2). Writing can no longer be regarded as a transparent medium for the unproblematic recording of experience but as a 'fictional' process, a process of recoding bound by the stylistic conventions and epistemological assumptions of Western literacy, 'all constructed truths . . . made possible by power "lies" of exclusion and rhetoric' (ibid.: 7). So the ethnographer viewed others through a distinctly Western lens, recording/recoding what was thus seen via the far from neutral medium of a distinctly Western literacy.

This lack of neutrality remained hidden beneath the facade of reason, of scientific rationality. Firmly held by the hegemony of scientific rationality, Western academics unwittingly engaged in

> the epistemic violence that constituted/effaced a subject that was obliged to cathect (occupy in response to a desire) the space of the Imperialist 'self-consolidating other'. (Spivak 1987: 209)

They became complicit in the presentation to the world at large of views of the colonized as variations of the "other" against which the colonizers from the West measured their own progress and through which they rationalized their imperialism. Certainly "traditional", possibly "primitive" and "*pre*-literate", definitely not based in "rationality" or "science" but rather "superstitious', the colonized were mechanistically, phallogocentrically defined as singular subjects, members of monolithic, unitary, tangible "societies" and "cultures". The process has been phallogocentric in that it has not only involved the logocentric creation of changeless, static concepts, but the organization of these static concepts in a way which privileges the status of the male. The process is well summed up in Chris Weedon's comment on the French feminist Helene Cixous, revealer and opponent of such phallogocentrism. Weedon writes:

> Her work is influenced by the anti-essentialism of Derrida's deconstruction and she brings together his notion of logocentrism and phallocentrism. She argues that masculine sexuality and masculine language are phallocentric and logocentric, seeking to fix meaning through a set of binary oppositions, for example, father/mother, head/heart, intelligible/sensitive, logos/ pathos, which rely for their meaning on a primary binary opposition of male/female (or penis/lack of penis) which guarantees and reproduces the patriarchial order. This hierarchization of meaning serves to subordinate the feminine to the masculine order. (Weedon 1987: 66)

Such phallogocentric Cartesian dualism permeates the society as a whole, receiving its most powerful expression and creative force in the writings, the research, the analyses, the diagnoses of its ideologues, its academicians.

So Western intellectuals "created" "the Orient",[1] "the *traditional* Indian/Malaysian/Javanese/Balinese/ . . . village",[2] "tribal societies", "hunter and gatherers", even "Hinduism' among a host of "isms". This intellectual imperialism was thus a vital ingredient in the overall imperial domination of the non-Western world and, as discussed below, in the continuing domination of the Third World beyond the colonial era. But before we explore the contours and consequences of this epistemic violence further we should enter a word of caution. While the work of new-style cultural relativists such as Clifford justifiably warns against the perpetuation of intellectual imperialism through ethnography, we must ensure that we do not continue to frame problems and issues in an imperialist manner through a kind of inverted snobbery. The new version of cultural relativism warns against imposing our epistemologies, our cosmologies, our textualisations/fictions on "them". It is even asserted that we should use "their" epistemologies. Apparently hypersensitive to epistemological issues, the new cultural relativists continue to frame their critiques in a phallogocentric way. Their warnings may be an important antidote to the arrogant claims of scientific rationalism, but by phrasing their criticisms in relation to bounded uniform cultures within which coherent epistemologies and cosmologies are supposed to operate, they lead us straight back into the world of structural-functionalism where order and consensus reigned supreme in a world of socialised puppets, of unitary "others".

Here we explore the transformation of the construction of subjectivities in Bali as new epistemologies and cosmologies are encountered via formal schooling. The people of Bali are experiencing a form of epistemic violence which continues to mould the Third World to Western ways and Western interests and which, in the process, creates new modes of oppression. By following Spivak in her explorations of these epistemic modes of oppression we can move beyond Bourdieu's (1977) view of practice to reveal limits to strategic action which encompass those imposed by structurally-based variations in cultural capital, revealing the contours of symbolic violence and of forms of oppression which Bourdieu does not deal with—sexism and imperialism—and for Spivak it is imperialist oppression which characterises sexism.

Our approach to the problem of understanding the processes of schooling in Bali is post-structuralist, proceeding via theories which focus on the decoding, the deconstruction of "language", of cultural "texts". Languages take many forms beyond speech and writing as do their texts but here our concentration will be on the deconstruction of Western literacy, as it is transformed within the Balinese context, and its agent, schooling.[3] Our approach is stimulated by current feminist theorizing of essentialism—Western thought's fundamental dependence on a unitary subject, its humanism, its logocentrism. Weedon sums up the dynamism of feminist post-structuralisms as follows:

> The terms subject and subjectivity are central to poststructuralist theory and they mark a crucial break with humanist conceptions of the individual which are still central to Western philosophy and political and social organization . . . Humanist discourses presuppose an essence at the heart of the individual which is unique, fixed and coherent and which makes her what she is . . . Against this irreducible humanist essence of subjectivity, poststructuralism proposes a subjectivity which is precarious, contradictory and in process, constantly being reconstituted in discourse each time we think or speak. (Weedon 1987: 32–33)

We thus approach the problems of schooling in Bali aware of the problems of translation and of the distorting qualities of textualisation, open to other epistemologies and seeing therein clues to greater understanding, but aware that we must not engage in the epistemic violence of creating unitary others such as "the Balinese", so easily used to mean not the inhabitants of Bali but those sharing "Balinese culture", or "the Balinese woman", or "Balinese religion", or "the Balinese student'. People have always engaged in cross-cultural communication aware of language differences, different styles and values, to be stimulated positively or negatively by these differences. We have created "cultures" and "epistemologies" as things, as orders, inhabited bounded spaces, to contain creativity, control identity, and limit cultural manoeverability. Rather, we must escape the temptation of a unitary, logocentric consciousness through a constant deconstruction process. We must follow Spivak (1988) and "read against the grain" as we enter those "other worlds".

THE COSMOLOGICAL TYRANNY OF SCIENCE

When the Western colonists entered those "other worlds" and sought to build effective political and ideological bases for the pursuit of the all-important economic activities which were the lifeblood of empire, they did so as "rational" administrators whose imperial right was seen to lie in their having entered the "scientific" age. Their cosmos was a cosmos devoid of any mysteries other than the wonders of science. To understand the processes of intellectual imperialism and the place of schooling in this process we must understand the historical and cultural contours of the rise of "science" for only then can we transcend the ideology of acultural rationality and understand its current hegemony.

The triumph of what we today regard as "science" over other sciences occurs as part of the economic and political transformation of Britain and Europe from the fifteenth century. In an era of economic, political and religious upheaval, with the authority of church and state seriously questioned, the established, clerically-based intellectual traditions were seriously challenged. One sort of science, a mechanistic science, that of Newton, Galileo and Copernicus, triumphed as the basis for a new materialistic cosmology. Why and how did that particular science triumph? Essentially, as we show below, *because it served the economy and the polity well.*

From the beginning of the battle between mechanistic science and the non-mechanistic sciences it was the non-mechanistic sciences which were radical, which rebelled against the establishment. But a mechanistic science triumphed. Uberoi writes:

> The victory of official modernity in the scientific revolution of the mid-seventeenth century, which ran parallel to the restoration of the monarchy over the ruins of the Puritan revolution in England (1660), is to be dated with apparent finality from the battle of Kepler the continental against the science and the philosophy of Fludd, the last Paracelsian in England (1621, etc.) [sic] . . . [which] became recessive

> and went underground for the future. Elements of the latter remained secretly active in Europe, however, viewing the so-called Copernican revolution as essentially a counter-revolution according to their radical faith. If the world-view of Copernicus, Galileo and Newton came to be embodied in the recovered myth of Prometheus, the official hero of European modernity and the benefactor of mankind who defiantly stole fire from Olympus and suffered the vengeance of the gods, then the Paracelsian world-view also came to be embodied in the more popular myth of Faust, the anti-hero of the underground who sold his soul to the devil in exchange for knowledge and power in his own lifetime. (Uberoi 1984: 21)

The establishment of the science of Copernicus, Galileo and Newton as the *official* scientific method was overtly political, the result of overt patronage by the establishment, in particular the founding of the Royal Society of London after the restoration of the monarchy in 1660. "Truth" did not win out. Nor did the new supersede the old. To quote Redner:

> . . . this new scientific authority structure incorporated by Royal edict was closely related to as well as dependent on the political authority of the newly arisen absolutist monarchies . . . the authority of the cognitive norms of the new Mechanical Philosophy was itself protected by royal power from the challenges of politically more dangerous approaches to science then current: for example, those deriving from such Baconian reformists as Comenius, and from Paracelsian iatrochemists and hermeticists like Fludd . . . a 'harmless' and politically innocuous scientific approach was instituted at the expense of more dangerous radical rivals, which were thereby suppressed and repressed into irrational currents of popular science and the occult. (Redner 1987: 44–45)

"Science" thus meant "the mechanical model" and was oriented towards technological supremacy as a means to the effective *control* of nature *and of humanity* for economic and political gain. But science soon penetrated everyday life as the scientific experts became the "theologians" serving the interests of those in positions of economic and political power. Glorification of God was displaced by a glorification of the *scientific method*—rational, and ordered, the produce of human minds but beyond any individual mind—a logical procedure free of individual vagaries. Faith in God gives way to a faith in science, a faith in the reproduction of rational knowledge and advancement towards the rational society.

With orthodox science firmly set in its mechanistic mode the scene had been set for the intellectual euphoria of the so-called Enlightenment. "Progress" was now assured through science, 'an autonomous human creation, not the expression of the divine purpose working itself out on earth' (Kumar 1978: 22).

> The future beckoned urgently, and the promise it held out could only adequately be gauged by the chaos that might result if the forces of progress were not all combined in the task of bringing the new society into being. Of those forces the most important were science, the men of science, and all those who could see in the achievements of the scientific method the highest fulfilment of the Enlightenment, and the key to the future direction and organization of society. (Ibid: 26)

The new science banished its more radical opponents to the realms of poetry and the occult. So Blake wrote in *Jerusalem*:

> . . . O Divine Spirit! sustain me on thy wings,
> That I may awake Albion from his long and cold repose;
> For Bacon and Newton, sheath'd in dismal steel, their terrors hang
> Like iron scourges over Albion. Reasonings like vast Serpents
> Enfold around my limbs, bruising my minute articulations.
>
> I turn my eyes to the Schools and Universities of Europe
> And there behold the Loom of Locke, whose woof rages dire,
> Wash'd by the Water-wheels of Newton: black the cloth
> In heavy wreaths folds over every Nation: cruel Works
> of many Wheels I view, wheel without wheel, with cogs tyrannic,
> Moving by compulsion each other, not as those in Eden, which,
> Wheel within wheel, in freedom revolve, in harmony and peace.
>
> William Blake, *Jerusalem*
> (p. 388)

The Eden referred to is a cosmos understood in terms of alternative "sciences". It is the "nature" of Paracelsus, of Goethe, of Steiner which sees the individual not as a unitary subject but expressive of diverse qualities and rhythms in the natural world of sensitive chaos, of flux, not ordered and governed by laws but constantly forming and transforming, in chaos and in harmony. It is Cixous' "Realm of the Gift." It is a world in stark contrast to the logocentric, unitary, law-governed ordered image that comes down to us in the science of Copernicus, Galileo and Newton.

Their "progress" was/is a narrow progress firmly grounded in capitalist production, and the spread of education in the new science was itself influenced by the demands of the mode of production. This is not to say that the system of formal education was not at least relatively autonomous, developing an historical dynamic of its own, spurred on by a religious fervour for the spread of "reason," in pursuit of a progressive, rational world. The educational development promoted by the so-called "Enlightenment" of the eighteenth century, and pursued with fervour through the nineteenth century, followed, in form and content, the contours of a society egalitarian ideologically but unequal in practice, a practice shaped by unequal relations of production.[4] Its commitment to rationality and individual competition has served ideological ends and its practice has served economic ends as it has reproduced the cultural differences basic to the reproduction of unequal classes.

Schooling in the West is therefore an historically and culturally specific part of Western capitalist society, its "rationality" no more culture free than any other rationality. That education system has not only been a misrecognised mechanism for the transmission of privileges via the unequal distribution of cultural capital, it has also played a vital part in the transformation of consciousness as ideological commitments to individual achievement through competition and the secular basis of knowledge in formally, secularly-trained scientific specialists have been firmly entrenched. All knowledge is ideologically presented as tangible and accessible to all through schooling via its commodification, its packaging, in books, software and videos, as well as in the formal, temporally-programmed classroom. All knowledge, including family life, sexuality, and religion are so packaged. The knowledge itself derives not from the creative, aesthetic, intuitive qualities of awesome sages, that is "irrationality," but from the command of scientific techniques. This secular rationality is the ideological lynch pin in the reproduction of the individualistic, egalitarian, competitive consciousness basic to capitalist relations of production and of its political servant, democracy.

IMPERIALISM, SCIENCE AND EPISTEMIC VIOLENCE THROUGH SCHOOLING

But the capitalists and their ideologies have not stayed at home:

> The need of a constantly expanding market for its products chases the bourgeoisie over the whole surface of the globe. It must nestle everywhere, settle everywhere, establish connexions everywhere . . .
>
> Just as it has made the country dependent on the towns, so it has made barbarian and semi-barbarian countries dependent on the civilized ones, nations of peasants on nations of bourgeois, the East on the West. (Marx and Engels 1970: 38–9)

It has searched not only for markets but for new production sites where labour (variable capital) is cheap, manipulable and relatively free from unionization. Where once it sought stable markets and production sites through overt colonial control, it now seeks them through covert neo-colonial influence to ensure the maintenance of the necessary political conditions for capitalist activity, including the universality of "rational" bureaucratic administrations and their prerequisite, a pool of rationally schooled individuals to ensure the viability of international economic and political activity.

Cautiously the West initiated and then controlled the spread of Western-style education in and through "literacy" and "reason" to those deemed "backward" or "un/under developed" so that they too could step onto the path to "progress." In practice they laid the foundations for continued capitalist expansion. Also, in the process, they cast all other forms of knowledge, literate and non-literate, by the wayside. Devalued are the skills of oratory, the orally-transmitted myths and legends, the lore of clan and tribe and village. Cast aside as irrelevant to, even antagonistic to, progress are the works of great teachers, literate or not, Western and non-Western, which are not in the "scientific" mode. Kabir, Mohammed, the Buddha, Nanak, the authors of the Upanishads, Paracelsus, Goethe, Weil, Ibn Kaldhun, among so many, are dismissed as "religion" or "metaphysics" or "poetry."

So a highly selective form of knowledge, taught through a narrow bureaucratically-manageable form of schooling, has spread throughout the world, and although transformed in the process, a vital agent of Western imperialism and international capitalism. The political, economic and intellectual leaders of the West and the agents of Western "national" and international interests elsewhere thus play God, attempting to mould the world at large in their image, legitimizing their conduct through ideologies of "freedom," "equality," "individualism" and "development," all ultimately based in an ideology of "reason," in faith in a rationality that, it is believed, transcends culture. This too is the faith that has guided the study of other cultures, no more so than in the field of comparative education.

Through colonial pasts and into neo-colonial presents, the West has measured its progress against the "underdeveloped" "peasant" and have set out to assist "him," through colonialism and aid, creating a dependency on the West of the most fundamental kind, a dependency not only for material goods—spare tractor parts, fertilizer, hybrid seed, . . . —but for intellectual goods as well, to establish an epistemic, a cosmological dependency. We brought them "literacy"; we brought them "schools." Amid a host of contradictions imposed by imperialism, the people of the world found themselves defined by others and then, in pursuit of "independence," by themselves in national terms (see Anderson 1983). They were bundled together as "underdeveloped," "developing" "countries," as the "Third World," part of an international economy and polity with needs and aspirations which seemed increasingly inevitable and even desirable, not least the need for "literacy," for "education," as though they had never been educated before.

If the Western missionary zeal for spreading the gospel of "reason" has in part led to the international drive for "literacy" through "schooling," so too has the colonial need for literate bureaucrats; the need of a burgeoning and politically vital press for readers; businesses for literate clerks and agents; the factories for workers who can read instructions. The former colonies assume that they need schools because education is an assumed prerequisite for development, despite the fact that there is no evidence that schooling generates economic growth. Economic growth may in fact generate schooling (see Hutchins 1970: 45ff). Whatever the stimuli, the myth of the need of the former colonies for Western-style education reproduces their dependency on their former rulers as their future political, economic and intellectual leaders travel to the West for higher educational qualifications, often unwitting agents of the West's promotion of itself as the harbinger of progress through its ultimate monopoly of "knowledge." More than this, these systems of education initially imposed from without have become part of the social and cultural life of the former colonies, strategically manipulated, covertly and overtly, to suit the economic, political and ideological ends of those in positions of national power.

In the process the pre-colonial modes of thought and action and the bearers of "traditional" knowledge, of cosmologies not bound by Western concepts of nature and reason, are reevaluated. They are dominated, displaced, redefined not only by new political leaders, but an imperial, unitary, logocentric consciousness. As Spivak's essays collected under the title 'Entering the Third World' all reveal (Spivak 1987: 179ff), in India Western educated Indians replace the British as the imperial intellectual presence, wreaking epistemic violence on the unschooled, defining them in unitary, logocentric terms, "insidiously objectifying" those whom they would claim to understand. So too in Bali, through the new "literacy" and its accompanying containment and commodifation of knowledge, as well as through the transformation of dance, drama and other forms of socio-cultural expression, the consciousness of the Balinese people is being transformed. This is the process that we set out to document below.

SCHOOLING AND INTELLECTUAL IMPERIALISM IN BALI

Made is 14 years old. It is not yet 7 A.M. but she is off to school, resplendent in her crisp uniform. She has already swept her room, the courtyard, fed the pigs, washed and breakfasted, having cooked her own breakfast. She was up at 4 A.M.. She lives in the house of a local school teacher with 12 other girls and 15 boys from out of town. In the small room she shares with one other girl are her text books, exercise books and some much prized magazines such as *Femina*. She pays board and is expected to help with household chores. She is here in the market town of Pekengede, away from her home village, to be educated. Her family must do without her help in agricultural and household production, particularly in the preparation and presentation of religious offerings.

But the sacrifice and the expense are assumed necessary. Schooling is a necessary part of childhood and, if at all possible, of adolescence, integral to the maintenance of the family's, even the lineage's, status, their honour. It will be important in the settling of her marriage. Hopefully it will lead to prestigious, non-manual employment. For Western-style, school-based education has become a time-consuming, expensive part of the Balinese life cycle, a choice for them and their children which is hard to resist for the majority of Balinese as they strategically orient themselves towards the achievement of economic, social and spiritual sustenance. If as Wolf (1966) claimed, the peasant's allocation of resources is towards a "replacement fund," a "ceremonial fund," and a "fund of rent," it now also, throughout much of the world which continues to rely heavily on peasant-based production, involves an "educational fund," a fund to be strategically used to gain maximum returns for outlay, manoeuvering among the myriad school types—a high status to low status among private, religious and state schools—and through levels of schooling, deciding where that education should stop. Family pride, available economic resources, local expectations and adolescent aspirations all play a part in the strategic allocation of resources. School-based education is increasingly a rite of passage into adulthood, an event to be experienced and enjoyed, an experience to be proud of, the lack of it bringing shame.

Occupational aspirations and expectations for students and their families alike are conditioned by the implicit and explicit promises that schooling holds out—explicit promises by government associated with their high profile publicity for development and modernization, and the implicit but often unstated expectations that a new institution generates.

In Bali, the mysterious expectation of enlightenment and qualifications comes readily in a society imbued with a respect for knowledge through literacy. Situated in the most auspicious quarter of the town, the schools of Pekengede encompass the old seat of learning, the house of the Pedanda Pekengede, the high priest. For the Dutch did not bring either education or literacy to Bali.

Most Balinese lived in hierarchical social environments where there was a clear division between a small literate elite and a majority of non-literate commoners (see Miller and Branson 1989 and Miller 1982, 1983). Literature was varied, ranging through poetry, sacred texts and medicinal texts associated with healing. Above all, literacy was associated with access to power, to the sacred. While the sacred Hindu texts, the *wedas*, were the province of trained Brahmana priests alone, including women, literacy itself was not. The stress was on initiation into the mysteries of literacy through a teacher (*guru*) and was open to non-Brahmana and to women as well as men. To quote Rubenstein:

> The emphasis on being an initiate as opposed to a layman as a precondition for access to literacy and texts highlights a fundamental Balinese belief: letters have a divine origin and are imbued with divine and supernatural potency: writing and reading, therefore, are sacred activities that cross the threshold of the divine and the supernatural. (Rubenstein 1984: 2)

The power of the initiate highlighted the impotence of the laity. Dependent politically and ritually, their political-economic oppression, their ritual impotence and their illiteracy were integrally tied. As we have discussed in detail elsewhere (Miller and Branson 1984), the Balinese Hindu cosmos embodied the constant struggle between forces of creation, sustenance and destruction. Human beings trod warily in a world that can move from plenty to plague and pestilence in an instant. Their survival depended upon the control of the awesome powers that surrounded them through a maze of ritual in which they were utterly dependent on those with "spiritual power," with "*sakti*," the initiates. Those with *sakti* were always as potentially dangerous as they were protective and thus to be treated with respect. Through these ever-present and vital rituals the Balinese experienced the ideal sanctified images of good and evil, male and female, aristocrat and commoner, initiate and layman. The socio-cultural definitions of roles and norms as defined by the elite were thus legitimised through their location 'within the sacred and cosmic frame of reference' (Berger 1969: 33), a diverse cosmos in constant flux, not unitary or centred, ordered or bounded like the cosmos of Western science (see Hobart 1985). The reverence for literacy remains strong, a reverence which gave added legitimacy to the architects of Indonesian independence. But their "literacy" was a new literacy, a literacy of Western hue.

The access to Western education by a select few Indonesians did not lead on the whole to a rejection but rather to a reformulation, a transformation of their cultural heritage, to a desire to mould a new Indonesian nation based on the Western ideals of individual freedom and development. They saw, in classic Western ideological fashion, the education of the individual freeing them from the bonds of tradition and releasing creative energy which would build a new enlightened nation. The Dutch began to fear the rampant spread of education, especially through highly-idealistic private schools and attempted to control educational developments through the licencing of private schools, and by restricting access to secondary education. The confrontation only heightened hopes and strengthened determination:

> The Netherlands government was looking for peace, for order and for gratitude and sought through village education to extend welfare and prosperity and to abolish illiteracy. It hoped for a docile and relatively inexpensive labour force for the lower ranks of the civil service and business concerns, but . . . while the public prosecutor was endeavouring by police state methods to control the growth of national sentiment, the Director of Education, through the extension of schools, was opening the flood-gates which fed this stream. (Zainu'ddin 1970: 52)

But while they did indeed 'open the floodgates' to the flood of aspirations which, with the timely intervention of the Japanese occupation, would wash away the Dutch, the Dutch educational policies also accentuated and gave new content to existing class, racial and status divisions in Indonesian society, thus playing a vital role in the subtle processes of class formation:

> Dutch educational policies . . . emphasised class distinctions with the reservation of Dutch language education for a select group . . . and the provision of lower-standard vernacular schools for 'other natives'. They emphasised racial distinctions by the division of Dutch language schools along racial lines, and religious distinctions . . . In so far as Western education was accepted, it undermined the traditional society and created divisions between the older and younger generations . . . and it created a work force which it was beyond the capacity of the existing economic structure to absorb—and thus created discontent instead of docility. (Ibid.: 55)

The imminent Japanese occupation from 1942 to 1945 was to level these trends to some degree but a Western educated elite had emerged and their cultural competence was to favour them in an independent Indonesia in which an education, essentially Western in nature and linked to a range of educational opportunities in the West, was a vital factor in gaining access to positions of privilege in government, in the professions, and in national and international commerce.

While it is doubtful therefore whether formal Western-style educational systems held much meaning for the vast majority of Indonesians, especially since what elementary schooling existed was poor in quality and for the majority led nowhere, the Dutch education system was bringing together the future leaders of Independent Indonesia through their common participation in further education in Java and the Netherlands. They were sharing the frustrations of colonial status, frustrations highlighted by their exposure to Western ideals of individualism, equality, and progress.

Such leaders sought liberty for Indonesia and national unity through a common sharing of a unified education in a national language. Cultural barriers would be transcended through a universal language and curriculum. The pursuit of these aims was hastened by the Japanese occupation which broke the links with the Dutch as European schools were closed, Dutch books and the Dutch language banned and Dutch teachers were expelled. The Indonesian language was encouraged and educational uniformity sought. The final struggle against the Dutch as the former colonial power brutally attempted to re-establish control over Indonesia, and Java in particular, drove the Indonesian leaders into closer contact with villagers. As they fled the cities to organise resistance in the countryside they brought to the fore the role not only of the common people in the struggle for nationhood but also reinforced an ideological commitment to the creative role of the youth of the country in the unifying "revolution" against the Dutch, in the building of a unified independent nation. What had been a fairly disparate movement for independence prior to the war was now a united struggle against the invaders.

EDUCATION AND THE SEARCH FOR NATIONAL UNITY

Youth movements had been an integral part of the Independence movement since the early 1900s and symbolised the break with traditional society and culture associated with a Western education. Today, the revolutionary role of the youth of Indonesia (*pemuda*) in the fight for independence has taken on a mythical character. But whereas the heroes and heroines of the Hindu Epics who feature so prominently on the stages, puppet theatres and popular bookstalls of Indonesia symbolise the ideal wife, husband, ruler, son, daughter, servant and their battles with evil forces in a golden *past*, the *pemuda* ("youth") of the struggle for independence of this new epic, symbolise the young people of Indonesia at the front line of the ongoing revolutionary transformation of Indonesian society towards national unity and development. The school children of Indonesia are its potential heroes and heroines, the building blocks of a new national culture. But they must be guided firmly, bound together ideologically so the edifice of the nation does not crumble. Education is the mortar. In the words of a former Minister of Education and Culture, Daaoed Joesoef, 'education is an integral part of culture . . . a method used to transfer cultural values' (Joesoef 1978: 5) the means 'to process our culture into a civilisation' (ibid.: 6) for 'the smooth implementation of development' (ibid.: 7).

The motto of Indonesia, *Bhinneka Tunggal Ika*, 'They are many, they are one' or 'Unity in Diversity' is an aspiration of its leaders yet to be realised. The unity felt in common opposition to the Dutch remains a focus for national ritual but the government is consciously engaged in building a national culture: 'cultural development is needed to enrich the culture of the Indonesian—both materially and spiritually' (ibid.: 13), involving the development of 'an Indonesian personality' which will foster 'national resilience and unity' (ibid.: 18). Moral education towards such ends is an increasingly vital ingredient in curriculum development and the early stress of the architects of Indonesian Independence on the *right* of all Indonesians to receive education now means the right to receive the right education, to be taught the basics of Indonesian culture, to learn their national ideology, their *Pancasila* or 'the philosophy' which gives the spirit for the development of the national culture is Pancasila' (ibid.: 18). Courses based on *Pancasila*, the 'five principles' which are the basis of the Constitution—Belief in God; National Unity; Sovereignty of the People; Internationalism or Humanitarianism; Social Justice—are conducted throughout the school years and on into adulthood with teachers and public servants all attending increasingly advanced courses on the application of the principles to all aspects of private and public life. Sacred texts, historical facts, familial roles, political and economic goals, are all understood in the light of government's intepretation of *Pancasila*, to support the government's view of Indonesian society.

In fits and starts, modern Indonesian education has expanded at all levels, especially since the Second Five Year Plan (*Repelita* II 1974–79) until today primary schooling is available to the large majority of Indonesian children with secondary and tertiary education facilities increasing rapidly through the late seventies and on into the eighties through a combination of state schools and government-assisted private schools. Recent curriculum developments are oriented towards providing a general education through to junior secondary by the year 2000. When this is achieved, the vast majority, particularly outside urban Java, will be receiving a "general education" oriented towards general literacy, numeracy and personality and cultural development. How is this sudden transformation of childhood affecting the social relationships among Indonesia's many and varied communities? What do they expect of education? What does the future hold in store? For the girls? For the boys? In particular, what part is education playing in the formation and transformation (reproduction) of social inequalities based on sex, class and status? What transformations of consciousness are going on? In order to begin to answer these questions we turn to the development of education in Bali.

THE DEVELOPMENT OF SCHOOLING IN BALI

In contrast to many other parts of Indonesia, Dutch penetration of and control over Bali came slowly and piecemeal and not without violent struggle and heavy losses on both sides. It was the beginning of the twentieth century before the Dutch had control of all of Bali, having set up a capital in north Bali in 1882. A number of native language elementary schools oriented towards little more than literacy, and leading nowhere as far as secondary and further education were concerned, were set up in the first decades of the twentieth century. From 1914 a few "Dutch native" schools were established for the Balinese elite, with teaching in Dutch and opportunities for further education possible, though not in Bali. A Dutch Chinese school was also established and in 1916 a European school. From then on, the major developments during the colonial period were private initiatives by the Balinese, particularly by self-consciously Hindu groups, or other Indonesians, including the establishment of a women's school—*Sekolah Perempuan Shanti*. A Kartini School (see fn. 5) was established in Den Pasar in 1936. It was 1950 before Bali got its first senior secondary schools; prior to that time all students wanting to go on to further education had to go to Java. More recent expansions in education have been dramatic, especially since the 1970s, and private schools continue to be a vital ingredient in Balinese education.

The expansion of Western education in Bali was therefore slow and essentially supported the local hierarchical structure and the economic pre-eminence of the Chinese. The independence movement in Bali was relatively low-key and even the post 1945 period was dominated by relatively peaceful Balinese-Dutch cooperation with the reestablishment of Dutch rule from 1946 until 1948. During this period roads were repaired, irrigation systems repaired and upgraded and schools, clinics and hospitals restored and expanded (Hanna 1976: 109ff). Bali was declared an autonomous state in the Republic of East Indonesia and became a Dutch showpiece. But the autonomy and the good times were not to last. The Republic of East Indonesia was disbanded and the Balinese felt the heavy political and economic hand of Javanese "imperialism". The polity, the administration and the economy were dominated by Javanese, many of whom looked upon the Balinese as collaborators with the Dutch and as heathens. Not until the late 1960s did Bali again begin to experience any real sense of autonomy culturally, politically, or educationally. Today under a Balinese governor and an administration increasingly staffed by Balinese, and with more adequate tertiary education facilities minimising the need to travel to Java to gain qualifications, Balinese cultural consciousness is high.

Balinese increasingly assume that their children will go to school. It is now part of childhood. What they expect of the school is of course, a matter for research and cannot be assumed. We will come to that below. But there is no doubt that "schooling" is valued, that literacy is regarded as important and potentially "powerful'", and that there are pressures to extend schooling for as long as possible. Some of those pressures come from the government, others from the community, others from the parents and of course from the children themselves. The standards and content of that schooling are treated below.

The proliferation of schools in Bali over the last two decades in particular has been enormous. The expansion of schools and pupils has far exceeded the number of teachers, let alone those who are adequately trained, as well as the number of buildings. When a middle school was "opened" recently in a hill village outside Singaraja, it had no building and few teachers who were not already teaching in one or other of the village's primary schools. The middle school used the primary school building and most of its teachers in the afternoon. The primary school was held in the morning. Multiple use of buildings and teachers is common at all levels of education in Indonesia—primary, secondary and tertiary. Education must be seen to be done. The government regards it as fundamental to national achievement. Foreign aid earmarks it for attention. Balinese society is changing. Education is expanding.

SCHOOLING AND THE TRANSFORMATION OF GENDER

As schooling spreads it bombards its students with images of themselves and others in the context of their nation, Indonesia, and their "culture," Bali. Evaluations, implicit and explicit, of social relationships and modes of behaviour fill their lessons, their text books and the magazines and books to which their literacy gives them access, evaluations often at odds with those of parents and/or grandparents, and often contradicting the relations basic to the family's modes of production and consumption. Sacred texts and genealogical texts, once the province of an elite group of elders, are now available in the bookshops. Those now deemed "educated" are increasingly young and divorced from the cosmos of their antecedents. To assess, at least in part, the impact of schooling on the collective consciousness of current Balinese adolescents we turn to the question of gender, the cultural construction of "male" and "female," and in particular to the view of the "female." First we turn to Bali's pre-colonial heritage.

The pre-colonial position of women in Bali was complex (see Branson and Miller 1988 and Miller and Branson 1989). Economically they were relatively autonomous. Trading was, and still is to a large degree, the work of women. Medhurst, an English medical missionary who spent three months in Bali in 1829–30, commented on 'the male's predilection for cock-fighting, drinking, and gambling, while allowing the women to perform the manual labour' (Hanna 1976: 21), and the Danish trader Mads Lange who lived at Kuta in South Bali from 1839 until his death in 1856 found that not only was all inland trade controlled by the Balinese but that all transportation of goods through the hinterland and to the coast was in the hands of women (see Nordholt 1981). Indeed it was 'the leading lady of the royal descent group of Pamecutan (who as early as 1800), had built houses in Kuta for Chinese and Buginese traders to attract trade and wealth' (ibid.: 22). Lange's colleague reports how when a ship arrived to purchase animals:

> . . . it was only necessary to send (notice) a few days in advance to a dozen or so of the Balinese ladies, who acted as our agents in such matters, and on the appointed day, the beach near which the vessel lay

> would be crowded with many times the number of animals wanted . . . Here, for instance, is . . . Abaj Agybg . . . the wife of Gusti Made Dangin, a noble rank . . . (ibid.: 30–1)

Brahmana women had access to literacy in sacred texts, took a leading part in ritual and could themselves become high priests (*pedanda*) though only on the death of a *pedanda* husband. Satria, Wesia and commoner women, as well as Brahmana women, all engaged in commercial activity, the dominant presence in the market at all levels of trading, the decision-makers as far as capital outlay and the expenditure of profit was, and still is concerned. *Homo oeconomicus* was and still is to a large degree typically *femina oeconomica.*

This relative economic autonomy did not however signal, or result in social relationships in which women were equal with men. Ritually and politically women were clearly inferior and sub-ordinate to men. The images of women told in myth and experienced through ritual operated to counter-balance their autonomy in the economic realm and to maintain overall male control. Today, even that relative economic autonomy is being threatened.

Men are increasingly evident in trading activities at both administrative and commercial levels. The formerly widespread view of commercial activity as "female" is thereby redefined in line with the government's stress on the need for economic initiative and for men to take the lead in development. Both the nation state and the national economy are viewed by the government and western advisors like as "male". The familiar Western division of the world into the private female realm and the public male realm governs policy-making as Western educated administrators and advisors, as well as Western experts, convey a view of the family which stresses that the woman's prime place is in the home. This view of woman has been particularly prominent since the Second Five Year Plan (*Repelita* II 1974–79) as the UN declaration of a decade of women promoted an overt concern with the development of a coherent view of woman as the mothers, the homemakers, of society. The women's organisations focus on family planning, homewifely pursuits, and on an image of the family gleaned from the writings of Western-educated and Western anthropologists such as Koentjaraningrat and the Geertzs. An aspect of the early women's movement has thus encompassed it totally, and now it is men, not women who orchestrate the "women's movement". Women's organisations are on the whole organisations of wives, wives of public servants, wives of businessmen, wives of politicians—dressed for public participation in tight sarongs, high stiletto heels, their hair meticulously groomed and complemented by carefully pinned hair pieces, the anti-thesis of the economically-active woman. The division of labor in "modernised" Indonesia increasingly portrays women in jobs defined in the West as "female"—teachers, nurses, air hostesses. These are the images that fill the school text books. It is men who are portrayed as the architects of a new Indonesia. Despite statements about opportunities for women, the images that confront the public in school, in magazines and on television show women relegated to the background, as assistants and nurturers.

But not only do the media portray the new Indonesian woman as privatised, submissive and totally maternal in orientation, also portrayed, also constructed is an image of "traditional Balinese culture." The invention of "tradition," which is central to the colonial construction of the "other," in opposition to, acting as an ideological foil to Western modernity and its notions of progressiveness, individuality, creativity, has been incorporated into the very heart of Indonesian nationalist ideology. So the learning of Balinese language also affirms the national motto. It is an expression of the diversity, the cultural diversity, a diversity of unitary "cultures": of "Balinese culture," "Timorese culture," "West Irianese culture," and so on. The images projected in the language text books are the romantic, intensely colonial images of Dutch-inspired Balinese art, but with a twist, a twist ensuring that the image of the "traditional Balinese" does not contradict the images of the family and its division of labour and responsibility central to contemporary Indonesian society. Gone is *femina oeconomica* and her other half the indolent male. Instead we have the beautiful, decorous, curvaceous but submissive female alongside the equally beautiful but assertive, industrious and dominant "traditional Balinese male peasant." Even the current exploitation of the industrious Balinese women as cheap labour power is revised and romanticised in these drawings, the labourers curvaceous and demure showing no signs of exhaustion or wear.

With a stroke of the pen the education system would, like the structural-functionalist anthropologists of old, wipe away the diversity, the creativity, the strategy, the contradictions of Bali and its cultural processes to give prime of place to a unitary, unreal, "Balinese culture." So "Balinese culture" becomes the "other" against which modern Indonesian Balinese measure their modernity, their nationalism, and in terms of which they feel cultural pride. Schooling is the prime agent in this process.

But while schooling is promoted as the basis upon which the revolution was won, and through which the development will be achieved, and while it is overtly utilized as the prime medium through which to mould and unify the personalities and thereby the culture of Indonesians and Indonesia, it operates in a wide variety of socio-economic contexts—from heavy urbanisation and industrialisation on the one hand, to subsistence, horticulture and agriculture on the other. Balinese education takes place in the context of low-level urbanisation and industrialisation.

THE BALINESE ECONOMY

Those aspects of social change which the Indonesian government considers most important for 'the smooth implementation of development' are:

1. The intensification and expansion of literacy;
2. the development of occupational specialisation, referred to as professionalisation and involving the increase and upgrading of specialised training facilities;
3. an effective network of administration; and
4. the development of cities, or urbanisation. (see Joesoef, 1978)

The assumed inter-relationships between these elements is linked to an overtly Western view of progress. This involves increasing differentiation of the population through increased specialisation, associated with industrialisation and urbanisation, and requiring increased levels of literacy and increased bureaucratization. Such models, derived largely from the Parsonian theories of socio-economic development (see Parsons 1966), may bear some relationship to processes at work in parts of Indonesia, and particularly in urban Java, but they have little relevance for the current and future shape of the Balinese economy.

In Indonesia's overall plans for development, Bali features as an area for the promotion of tourism and small-scale cloth manufacture. Tourism is carefully confined territorially, draws its workforce from further afield than Bali alone, and is subject to widespread fluctuations influenced by intense international competition. While those directly engaged in hotel and travel work now often need tertiary qualifications to enter hotel training schemes—involving long periods learning mundane tasks such as how to fold paper napkins—the vast majority of people who live off tourism—the market and itinerate sellers, the drivers, the crafts-people, and so on—do not require any formal educational qualifications at all and none above basic literacy. Small-scale cloth manufacture is labour-intensive, using traditional technology and requiring little or no formal education. Urban development is very limited with both the current capital, Den Pasar, and the former Dutch capital, Singaraja, no more than administrative and market centres. Despite projections of expansion in the workforce involved in industry (cloth manufacture), in retail trading, hotels and restaurants, in administration, construction, transport and military and social services, in contrast to a projection of stasis in agriculture (Kantor Statistik Propinsi Bali 1983), the large majority of the population in fact operate now, and in the foreseeable future, within the agricultural sector. Thus while the 1980 census figures show 50.74 percent of the workforce engaged in farming (including livestock, forestry and fishing), of the 49.26 percent of the workforce in non-farming occupations (18.33 percent are in civil and military service, 2.21 percent in transport, 14.52 percent in retail trading, hotels and restaurants, and 4.82 percent in building), the vast majority are oriented towards the farming sector providing administrative, educational, transport, financial, retail trading, building and social services. Of these services, only those in the civil (including teaching), military and social services have anything like a link with schooling beyond basic literacy and numeracy and will not be able to absorb the products of the education explosion. The link between employment prospects and the implementation of educational policies involving the rapid increase of vocational training facilities at secondary and tertiary education level, is minimal. The orientation of educational planning is primarily towards national unity through cultural integration with increased vocational training rationalised as integral to "development", tangentially linked, at best, with whatever employment opportunities are available.

The prospects for girls, like Made mentioned earlier, within this general picture seem particularly problematic. It is true that they have access to the areas of trained employment which are ear-marked for expansion, namely teaching, nursing and general office work, but their access to the military and to positions of administrative authority and professional responsibility is limited by the current stress on women as wives and as occupants of distinctly female 'buffer zone' occupations. The government declares that sexual equality has been achieved:

> Hardly a century has passed after Kartini has made known her noble ideas and ideals about the emancipation of the Indonesian Woman, and lo . . . the Indonesian Woman today has become the Equal of the Indonesian Man in every respect, in every field. (quoted in Manderson 1980: 69)

Kartini[5] equals female emancipation equals education for girls. Equal access to education is assumed, as in the West, to equate with equal occupational opportunity. As Manderson has pointed out, the stress on responsibilities of girls as future wives and mothers is extremely strong and yet housework is not categorised by the government as "work". Housewives are not listed as part of the workforce in either towns or villages. Activities integral to household production and formerly valued as such are now devalued. Accompanying these changes is a changing view of childhood. Childhood in its integral association with school is increasingly removed from any responsibilities for tasks linked to production. Households are no longer necessarily perceived as integral to production involving a redefinition of the place of women in the productive process. A private female realm is being constructed in contrast to a public male realm, a situation far removed from the traditional one and an opposition which potentially restricts the degree to which girls see themselves as belonging in the world of work.

Before returning to the market town of Pekengede (a pseudonym), it should also be noted that, given the fact that expansion of civil, military and social services, and especially of Balinese involved, is very recent (numbers having more than doubled over the past decade—the civil and military services rose from 8.28 percent of the workforce in 1971 to 15.33 percent in 1980, almost a tripling of the population involved)—the proportion of parents who can provide current adolescents with a realistic understanding of work prospects through their own example and understanding will be small.

PEKENGEDE: A CASE STUDY OF BALINESE ADOLESCENTS

Pekengede, with a population of around 2,500, is 1½ hours' drive west from the capital of Den Pasar along the main highway linking the capital with Java, via the ferry at Gilimanuk on the western tip of the island. Pekengede straddles the highway and what was, little over fifteen years ago, a quiet main street echoing to the calls of market sellers, the hooves of horses in horse drawn carts, and the rumble of the occasional bus, broken only by the horns and roar of speeding trucks heading to and from Java, is now a speedway for the seemingly endless stream of express buses, increasingly large trucks, frenetic minibuses ("colts") seemingly intent on suicide, and covered utility trucks (*bemo*) which transport both goods and people to and from the market and between local villages. Pekengede serves as a market and educational centre for surrounding villages. There are pockets of cash crops other than rice (mainly coconuts and bananas), but for the majority of farmers, rice is the main crop. Yields per acre are lower than in the wetter areas of Bali and many farming families can no longer provide sufficient food for themselves but must look to alternative sources of income to provide for household needs, a trend present with varying intensity throughout Bali, and exacerbated by the complex technological and soil management problems associated with the cultivation of new varieties of rice (see for example Conner 1983: 56ff). Men look to casual labouring jobs, women intensify their market activities, and children are encouraged to look to education and future employment beyond agriculture for a way out.

Despite the rapid expansion of secondary education in Bali, many students do not have ready access to lower secondary education within the close vicinity of their own villages. They must, therefore, often at very real cost to their parents, either travel each day to nearby towns or board in a village or town with secondary education facilities. For many, attending post primary education means living away from home for much of their adolescence. Those with relatives in towns such as Den Pasar, Singaraja, Tabanan and Klungkung, where prestigious academic schools are available, will often travel far to stay with their relatives, seeking the best avenue to university entrance. This is particularly the case with higher secondary education since higher secondary schools are restricted in the main to regional capitals.

Of the final year students in lower secondary schools (SMP) in Pekengede, half came in from other villages in the area. There are four SMP in Pekengede, three of them government schools and the fourth a private "Saraswati" school. Government schools are generally regarded as more prestigious but cannot cater to the demand for secondary education. Of the students living away from home, a few lived with relatives, but the majority boarded in dormitory accommodation, often run by local teachers. For example, one teacher from the Saraswati school had fifty students living with him, fifteen girls and thirty-five boys, each paying a monthly rental of 500 rupiahs plus five kilogrammes of rice. They lived three or four to a room, sleeping on board beds with a mat on top. Each room had a table and oil lamp. They cooked for themselves on wood or spirit stoves and lived on a diet of rice and fried vegetables. Like most Balinese, the students were up at four in the morning, the girls sweeping their rooms and the courtyard and carrying water from the well and the river, the boys sweeping their own rooms but otherwise, in contrast to the girls, not expected to engage in everyday housework. School is attended six days a week, but when not at school the boys tend to play sport while the girls pound banana plants to feed the pigs, fetch and carry. Within the context of these varying role expectations, all students exhibited a high level of self-reliance and were oriented to individual achievement.

The actual group of adolescents to be dealt with below were all the students in the final year of lower secondary school in Pekengede, a total of 467 students drawn from eleven classes across four schools. In considering what the information gained from these students by questionnaire (administered in class in 1983), complemented by sample interviews and participant observation within the village, can tell us, it is vital to consider the very high drop-out and non-starter rate within Balinese education. Those adolescents who feature here are in fact a very select sample of Balinese youth. In 1979 when the current sample were in primary school (SD), and field work in Pekengede began, there was a total of 1,218 primary school students in Pekengede alone. At the same time, there were 556 high school students from the village. This halving of school numbers between primary and secondary schooling is exacerbated by the very large proportion of children who leave primary school before grade six. Class sizes in primary school often range from forty or more in grade one to twenty or less in grade six. Similarly, many students do not complete lower secondary school. In 1979, the records of the Pekengede Saraswati school showed that of those who finished lower secondary school, 60 percent of the girls and 75 percent of the boys went on to higher secondary education of some sort. In any year, approximately one quarter of the girls at lower secondary school and one half of the boys will go on to higher secondary education.

The barriers to proceeding on through the education system are many and varied—economic, cultural, geographic, social, structural, physiological—but they consistently operate to the greater detriment of girls. It would appear that while there is no initial impediment to girls starting school, either at home or elsewhere, there are processes at work all along the line which ensure that girls drop out or fail to continue to another stage of schooling at a far more alarming rate than for boys. Those girls who do continue on to higher secondary school are far more likely than boys to attend religious and vocational, as distinct from academic, schools. The government can claim therefore that equality of opportunity exists, that girls have equal *access* to education, but as in Australia, subtle processes are at work which give rise to decisions being made, by the girls themselves and by their parents, to withdraw from schooling or to channel educational choices in particular directions.

These processes are to a very large degree cultural, and we will return to them below, but what emerges in particular from the discussion above is that the students who are the informants in an exploration into adolescent attitudes are a select and potentially highly motivated group of students. Of the 467 students surveyed, 50 percent were boys and 45 percent girls. What was also clear was that these students were looked on by their non/ex-student peers as an elite, as achievers, as trend setters, as achieving enviable status honour.

What then of the ideals and practice of schooling when examined in relation to the reproduction/transformation of gender? There was no evidence that parents were more prepared to face education costs for sons than for daughters. The students coming in from outlying villages to live in Pekengede were equally divided between the two sexes. Given the costs involved in supporting students living away from home, including the loss of their labour at home, there is clearly a genuine belief in education for youth in general. Family size was also another variable which we felt might affect participation for economic reasons but students from large families of more than eight children were as much in evidence as those from smaller families of three children or less and birth order of student was of no significance.

But having facilitated equal access initially, did parents provide greater encouragement, help and facilities for the boys? Studies of academic achievement in the West have stressed the importance of discussion and conversation at home for success. In the case of the Balinese students studied, no sex differences emerged with regard to involvement with parents in conversation, nor with regard to help received with school work. Twenty-five percent had no one to help them with their school work, a few reported that their parents did help but half the students said that they received most or all assistance from brothers and sisters. *The strong bond between siblings and reliance on each other emerged constantly, stressing the degree to which modern education cut this generation off from their parents as they experienced a childhood markedly different from that of previous generations.* Where parents were brought into the education process, correcting their children's speech or discussing school, the boys were most likely to be involved with their fathers and the girls with their mothers.

When asked which out-of-school activities were most important, 80 percent said homework. Fifteen percent of the girls saw household tasks as most important and 16 percent of the boys saw assisting with the parental occupation as most important. Involvement in household tasks was virtually universal for the girls (98 percent) and involved three-quarters of the boys. Girls were only slightly more involved in ceremonial activities. There is therefore widespread involvement by both sexes in tasks of one kind or another but boys are more involved with the public "male" world of what is *now* formally regarded as "work" while girls are more involved with the private "female" world of the household production. When it came to other out-of-school activities, the vast majority of both sexes read, mainly newspapers, about one-third of both sexes watched television and almost half listened to the radio. Access to television was for the majority of students a mark of superior status. When it came to peer group activities, a marked sex difference did emerge with 70 percent of the boys playing sport but only 18 percent of the girls doing so. The majority of girls spent time talking and studying with friends when not involved in household tasks. Thus the contemporary image of the energetic, competitive male in contrast with the inactive demure female, a stark contrast to former gender-based imagery in Bali, was coming to the fore as students turned to their own devices—or rather what was available and valued—in their leisure time. They interpreted the present and the future through the "modern" media, through the new "sacred texts"—the newspapers, magazines and school textbooks, and through the "theatre" of radio and television. The world of their hopes and expectations was, on the whole, far removed from experience, as the examination of their aspirations and expectations showed.

STUDENTS' ASPIRATIONS AND EXPECTATIONS

Of the 467 students, only five said that they wanted to finish school at the end of that year. Half of the boys and two-thirds of the girls saw their education terminating at the end of higher secondary school, the rest wanting to go on to tertiary courses. When it came to expectations, as distinct from aspirations, while seventeen students expected to leave, as distinct from five who aspired to do so, the vast majority of students made no distinction between aspirations and expectations, despite the fact that drop-out rates between lower and secondary school are in fact high. Such unrealistic expectations seem to be linked to the government's promise of a new Indonesia led by the youth through education. *The views of the future relate only very marginally to experience.* But the expectations, realistic or not, did reveal important sex differences for not only did fewer girls aspire to tertiary education, but the majority of girls opted for religious, home economic and vocational higher secondary schools while only one third of the boys were so inclined. When it came to aspirations to university , that majority of the girls who were orienting themselves to tertiary training looked to vocational diplomas and first degrees, while the majority of the boys were setting their sights on professional degrees and higher degrees.

What were the subtle mechanisms which were leading girls to self-select themselves out of the upper echelons of tertiary education and the labour market? How were they interpreting gender in the context of this new post-colonial cosmos?

Of those students who did not aspire to tertiary education, or expect it, more than half of the boys said it was for financial reasons, while only 20 percent said they were not bright enough to continue. In contrast only a third of the girls said that they could not afford to go on but half attributed their decision to not being intelligent enough to attempt higher education. Very few adolescents expressed a disliking for school. What did emerge was the feeling of family involvement in eventual decision-making about their educational and vocational future. The girls' lack of confidence, and the boys' confidence, were obviously tied to expectations about parental response to further education. Here the father emerged as the most important figure for almost two-thirds of the students, slightly more so for boys than girls who also saw siblings as playing an important role, indicating the degree to which men rather than women are now being identified with decisions beyond the home. In considering their families' aspirations for them vocationally, the main occupations chosen by the girls were teaching (35 percent), office work (41 percent) and medical doctor (12 percent), while the main occupations given by the boys were medical doctor (20 percent), engineer (10 percent), police (10 percent) and teaching (23 percent). The patterns are remarkably similar to the Australian results and reflect a clear perception of the labour market as involving a division of labour along sex lines, of certain occupations as relevant for girls and others as relevant for boys, perceptions which the students identify with their parents' aspirations for them. What then of their own occupational aspirations and expectations?

On the whole, the students looked upon education as the way out of traditional occupations. Despite the realities of the very restricted Balinese labour market, students were aspiring to occupations identified with the government's image of a developed Indonesia. Few wished to be farmers or to pursue traditional craft occupations. Instead their hopes were set on office work, university lecturing, engineering, medicine, teaching, nursing and the police force. Not surprisingly, the sex differences which characterised students' views of their parents' aspirations were evident in the students' own aspirations and expectations. University lecturing, the judiciary, engineering, medicine and senior office work featured most prominently among the boys, while the girls were mainly oriented towards teaching, medicine (nurse and doctor), and office work. Some of the newer occupations which do not have a direct link to education such as driver and mechanic were not seen as desirable. When they were asked what the least preferred occupation was, one third of the boys and 23 percent of the girls said stone mason. Indeed, if all the traditional craft occupations are combined they account for 57 percent of the students' least desired occupations. These were followed by *bemo* driver, and the traditional religious positions of *pedanda* (high priest), *pemanku* (temple priest) and *balian* (healer)—the traditional literati—as well as labourer. In fact, *almost every student listed the traditional crafts as one of the least desired occupations and one third listed the religious specialists.*

CONCLUDING REMARKS

These initial findings from Pekengede indicate that a range of subtle cultural pressures are at work which channel girls' aspirations both for education as such and towards particular kinds of education and specific sections of the labour market. Their decisions are governed by views of the self, generated and nurtured in family, school and community. They have lower opinions of their ability than the boys and downgrade their aspirations, processes all too familiar in the Australian situation.

The main contrast between the Australian and Balinese situations with regard to education is that for the majority of Balinese students, even those from relatively wealthy homes, there is little or no understanding of the relationship between modern education and the labour market transmitted through socialisation. Modern education is not "known" or "understood", it is not integral to the cultural competence they bring to the school. What is clear is that the emerging sexual division of labour in contemporary Bali is being produced through the agency of Western-style schooling. Schooling is integrally involved in the transformation of relationships between the generations, of relationships between the sexes and of attitudes towards those in positions of traditional secular and religious authority. Traditional occupations which are still the backbone of the Balinese economy are being devalued.

In a passage quoted bove, Zainu'ddin points out that in the colonial period,

> In so far as Western education was accepted, it undermined the traditional society and created divisions between the older and younger generations . . . and it created a work force which it was beyond the capacity of the existing economic structure to absorb—and thus created discontent . . . (Zainu'ddin 1970: 55)

That process is no longer limited to a mainly Javanese elite but is now encompassing much of Balinese (and indeed Indonesian) society. These processes are at work because the education system is a symbol of, and an agent in the production of, individuality, which contrasts with the household focus of traditional activity. The students look to achievements as individuals in jobs as far removed as possible from the traditional division of labour. They are isolating themselves from their homes as a labour pool develops which no longer focusses on community needs and is not based on face to face relations but rather on abstract qualifications. Through their individuation they are becoming alienated labour power. Such qualifications, and therefore access to this now desirable way of life, are apparently available to all through equal access to constantly increasing education facilities. Education thus becomes the primary agent in the processes of individuation and alienation, providing apparent equal opportunities to all its individual students. It is also the agency through which subtle processes of selection operate channelling some back into agricultural production, and others to the many and varied corners of labour market, which varies enormously in the rewards it offers.

In contemporary Bali "the transmission of power and privileges" is no longer legitimised through an overt ideology of hierarchical and hereditary rights. The government espouses an egalitarian and individualistic view of society and yet inequalities are as evident as ever. But these inequalities are now rationalised as the consequence of individual achievement. Inequalities based on sex and status have apparently disappeared.

Schooling is above all seen as the path to a modern world, standing in stark contrast to that unitary, encompassed "other"—the "traditional," agriculturally-based, pre-colonial, pre-Independence "other." The diverse, rich worlds of their parents and/or grandparents are thoroughly devalued, "insidiously objectified" through constant epistemic violence, both creating and created by a new unitary consciousness. But given the large agricultural base and low levels of industrialization and urbanization in Bali, the creation of discontent as students are forced to turn to occupations and household tasks which they overtly devalue as irrelevant to their generation, this time by a government intent on unity and development, seems inevitable.

And yet both the Indonesian government and the West are as intent as ever on schooling. The recent Jackson Report (*Committee to Review the Australian Overseas Aid Program*) stresses that 'education is critical to the development of human resources' and recommends that 'assistance for education within developing countries should be emphasised in bilateral country aid programming' (1984: 8). Educational aid is presented as unproblematic, the only problems being to ensure that the aid is actually spent on education. The content of that education is not discussed, let alone its consequences, which are assumed to be "development".

So the Report recommends that 'more support should be given to curriculum development and teacher training for primary, secondary, and vocational schools' (ibid.). Problems such as the transformation of childhood in areas predominantly concerned with primary produce through household production are not considered, let alone the way in which education becomes critical for the creation and sustenance of new forms of social inequality. What this paper demonstrates is that educational aid emerges as just as potentially damaging and insidious as any of the many and varied forms of international aid which the Report sees as fraught with problems.

The irony is that while educational policies, bolstered by Western aid, are alienating a generation from their economic and cultural background, and in the process producing Western-style patterns of sexual discrimination and social inequality, tourism, through its promotion of dance and drama rituals as entertainment is, as we have explained elsewhere (Miller and Branson 1989), reinforcing those traditional images of women which stress their subordinate position in society. Their *traditional* commercial autonomy and their vital and valued role in household-based production is being destroyed. At the same time the provision of educational opportunities, the skilful transformation of the women's movement into "legend" (cf. Levi-Strauss 1977: 266–7) which legitimises their wifely role, and the secularisation of dance and drama for tourist consumption operate to ensure the effective sub-ordination of women in all realms of social activity.

The contradictions generated and promoted by Western imperialism are mirrored in and at least in part reproduced through the schooling system. As a symbol of a new era, the school stands in opposition to the knowledge of old, relegating that knowledge and literacy to a newly segregated "religious" realm. "Religion" is taught as a subject, to instil national pride, to manifest the cultural diversity of Indonesia. The myths become no more than legend. Their potency is reduced. *Sakti* is downgraded. The magic of literacy fades as a new increasingly demystified literacy takes over and spreads. Schooling beyond literacy holds out a promise that is rarely, increasingly rarely, fulfilled. Privileges remain, the privileged the first to be schooled, the most "educated," but the power assumed to lie in knowledge is increasingly hollow. The new education, associated as it is with the modern, the urban, the overtly "non-traditional," devalues the very rurally-based lifestyle that the vast majority of the newly educated must lead.

In the past, and still for some, literacy was a reward in itself. Literacy was power. Now literacy is an assumed means to an end but the destination is frequently unknown. Schooling is displayed; occupations available to few aspired to by many. Newspapers must be read. The town must be confronted. The "new," the "modern," the "fashionable," creates its opposite—the "traditional," the "antiquated," the "unfashionable." What were valued as diverse and live-in mysteries become unitary, singular "religion." Those uninitiated into the modern through schooling become a monolithic "other."

The imperialist epistemic violence that was imposed from without becomes internal and endemic.

We have moved far beyond an unproblematic, rational concern with the spread of literacy through schooling into a world of intellectual turbulence. As we recognise the cultural and historical specificity of our own intellectual traditions and the epistemic violence they have generated we are brought face to face with the potential tyranny of our own intellectual pronouncements, of our own disciplined academic activity. We have shown that to make the grand gesture and declare that other cultures must not be distorted by our epistemologies but must be understood in their own terms is to adopt a new cultural relativism which is as tyrannical as the rationalism it seeks to destroy. The people that we study in the so-called Third World do not live in insulated unitary cultures.

We have concentrated on the transformation of consciousness, on the transformation of cosmologies, of the way the world is perceived and thus understood. The tyranny of capitalism and the tyranny of scientific rationality, of Western phallogocentrism have been shown to go hand in hand, hand in hand also with the tyranny of nationalism.

NOTES

1. See E. Said, *Orientalism*, Routledge and Kegan Paul, London 1978 and Penguin Books, London, 1985.

2. On the invention of "tradition" see Hobsbawm & Ranger 1983.

3. "Literacy" is a complex concept, a concept usually understood entirely in Western, logocentric terms. The impact of literacy has been discussed in an anthropological context by Goody (1979) and Street (1984), but for a discussion of "literacy" in terms particularly relevant to this discussion see Derrida (1976) and especially Spivak's "Introduction."

4. See Jan Branson & Don Miller, *Class, Sex and Education in Capitalist Society*, Melbourne, Longman Sorrett, 1979.

5. Raden Adjeng Kartini, a Javanese aristocrat who died in 1904 at the age of 25, has become the symbol of women's emancipation in Indonesia. Kartini saw Western education as the path to a better life for women. Her own limited access to Dutch education had opened the way to liberal ideas, particularly those of the Dutch feminist movement of the turn of the century, which reinforced her questioning of traditional Javanese practices. Her conviction that education for girls was the path to freedom was embodied in the establishment of a school for girls of the nobility in her own home, a venture which had barely begun when she died soon after the birth of her first child. She had inspired Europeans and Indonesians alike and her example was followed throughout Indonesia. The Indonesian women's movement had begun and formal education for girls was integral to it. The demands were social: for the abolition of child marriage and polygyny; for the right to participate as creative activists in the modernisation and eventual emancipation not only of women but of Indonesia (see Zainu'ddin 1980).

REFERENCES

Anderson, B. (1983) *Imagined Communities: Reflections on the Origin and Spread of Nationalism*. London, Verso Pres.

Anderson, P. (1974) *Passages from Antiquity to Feudalism*. London, New Left Books.

Berger, P. (1969) *The Sacred Canopy: Elements of a Sociological Theory of Religion*. New York.

Bourdieu, P. (1977) 'Cultural Reproduction and Social Reproduction' in J. Karabel and A.H. Halsey (eds), *Power and Ideology in Education*. New York, Oxford University Press.

Branson, J., and Miller, D.B. (1977) 'Feminism and Class Struggle', *Arena*, 47–48.

Branson, J., and Miller, D.B. (1979) *Class, Sex and Education in Capitalist Society: Culture, Ideology and the Reproduction of Inequality in Australia*, Melbourne, Sorrell.

Branson, J., and Miller, D.B. (1988) 'The Changing Economic Fortunes of Women in Bali'. In G. Chandler, N. Sullivan and J. Branson (eds.), *Development and Displacement: Women in Southeast Asia*. Centre of S.E. Asian Studies, Monash University.

Clifford, J. (1986) 'Introduction'. In J. Clifford and G. Marcus (eds.), *Writing Culture: The Poetics and Politics of Ethnography*. Berkeley and Los Angeles, University of California Press.

Clifford, J., and Marcus, G. (eds.) *Writing Culture: The Poetics and Politics of Ethnography*. Berkeley and Los Angeles, University of California Press.

Committee to Review the Australian Overseas Aid Program (The Jackson Committee) (1984) *The Australian Overseas Aid Program*. Canberra, AGPS.

Connor, L.H. (1983) 'Healing as Women's Work in Bali'. In L. Manderson (ed.), *Women's Work and Women's Roles: Economics and Everyday Life in Indonesia, Malaysia and Singapore*. Canberra, ANU.

Derrida, J. (trans. G.C. Spivak) (1976) *Of Grammatology*. Baltimore, Johns Hopkins University Press.

Easlea, B. (1981) *Science and Sexual Oppression*. London, Weidenfeld and Nicolson.

Goody, J. (1979) *The Domestication of the Savage Mind*. Cambridge University Press.

Hanna, W.H. (1976) *Bali Profile: People, Events, Circumstances 1000—1976*. New Hampshire, Whitman Press.

Hobart, M. (1985) 'Anthropos Through the Looking Glass: or How to Teach the Balinese to Bark'. In J. Overing (ed.), *Reason and Morality*. London, Tavistock.

Hobsbawm, E., and Ranger, T. (eds.) (1983) *The Invention of Tradition*. Cambridge University Press.

Hutchins, R.M. (1970) *The Learning Society*. Harmondsworth, Penguin Books.

Joesoef, Daaoed (1978) 'The Era of Cultural Development and its Relation to Education'. *Indonesian Quarterly* VI (3) July.

Kantor Statistik Propinsi Bali (1983) *Keadaan Angkatan Kerja Di Bali Pada Pelita III Dan Proyeksinya Pada Pelita IV*. Denpasar.

Kumar, K. (1978) *Prophesy and Progress: The Sociology of Industrial and Post-Industrial Society*. Harmondworth, Penguin Books.

Levi-Strauss, C. (1977) *Structural Anthropology*, Vol. II. London, Penguin.

Manderson, L. (1980) 'Rights and Responsibilities, Power and Privilege: Women's Roles in Contemporary Indonesia'. In *Kartini Centenary: Indonesian Women Then and Now*. Melbourne, Centre of South East Studies, Monash University: 69–92.

Marks, J., and de Courtivron, I. (eds.) (1981) *New French Feminisms*. Brighton, The Harvester Press.

Marx, K., and Engels, F. (1970) *The Communist Manifesto*, in *Selected Works*. Progress Publishers, Moscow.

Miller, D. (1982) 'The Brahmin/Kshatriya Relationship in India and Bali', *South Asia* V (1), June.

Miller, D. 'Hinduism in Perspective: India and Bali Compared'. *R.I.M.A.*, December.

Miller, D., and Branson, J. (1989) 'Pollution in Paradise: Hinduism and the Subordination of Women in Bali'. In P. Alexander (ed.), *Creating Indonesian Cultures*, Oceania Publication: Sydney University Press.

Nordholt, H.S. (1981) 'The Mads Lange Connection. A Danish Trader on Bali in the Middle of the Nineteenth Century: Broker and Buffer'. *Indonesia*, Cornell: 16–47.

Pachter, H.M. (1951) *Magic into Science: the Story of Paracelsus*. New York, H. Schuman.

Parsons, T. (1966) *Social Evolution*. Englewood Cliffs, NJ: Prentice-Hall.

Redner, H. (1987) 'The Institutionalisation of Science: A Critical Synthesis'. *Social Epistemology* 1 (1): 37–59.

Rubinstein, R. (1984) 'The Magic of Literacy'. Paper presented at the Fifth National Conference of the Asian Studies Association of Australia.

Spivak, G.C. *In Other Worlds: Essays in Cultural Politics*. New York, Methuen.

Treet, B.V. (1984) *Literacy in Theory and Practice*. Cambridge, Cambridge University Press.

Uberoi, J.S. (1978) *Science and Culture*. New Delhi, Oxford University Press.

Uberoi. J.S. (1984) *The Other Mind of Europe*. New Delhi, Oxford University Press.

Vreeve-De Stuers, C. (1960) *The Indonesian Woman, Struggles and Achievements*. The Hague.

Weedon, C. (1987) *Feminist Practice and Poststructuralist Theory*. Oxford, Basil Blackwell.

Zainu'ddin, A. (1970) 'Education in the Nederlands East Indies and the Republic of Indonesia'. In R.J.W. Selleck (ed.), *Melbourne Studies in Education*, 17–83.

Zainu'ddin, A. (1980) 'Kartini—Her Life, Work and Influence'. In *Kartini Centenary: Indonesian Women Then and Now*. Melbourne, Centre of South East Asian Studies, Monash University: 1–29.

Empowering Women Through Knowledge: International Support for Nonformal Education

NELLY P. STROMQUIST

School of Education
University of Southern California, USA

The last decade has witnessed a tremendous growth in the number of nonformal education offerings. Although not always identified by that name, nonformal education (NFE) is increasingly seen by both government and non-governmental organizations as a critical resource that will allow marginal and destitute populations to acquire skills and knowledge to become more effective members of their societies. In the case of women, nonformal education is being advocated not only as a resource that will enable them to become "integrated" in the development process but also as a resource much more attainable than capital and land.

The social science research findings produced in the last 15 years have questioned the claim that women are not "integrated" in their societies. Women participate constantly and on a daily basis in the reproduction and maintenance of their respective societies. It has been demonstrated—rather convincingly—that the problem of women is not lack of integration but rather integration under conditions of subordination, which does not allow women to attain the full range of social and financial benefits produced by the collectivity, and which oppresses them through an unfair social division of labor that assigns them in-home child-care responsibilities and restricts the range of occupations they may fulfill outside the home.[1]

Advocates and skeptics of "integration" for women agree that NFE has a critical role to play among poor and destitute women. Numerous activities and projects having knowledge and skills components addressed to out-of-school, adult populations have already been implemented. It might therefore be appropriate at this time to examine what the main contributions of NFE toward the condition of women have been. In this context, we can ask ourselves several questions: What kinds of NFE activities for women have been put into place through international agency support? What knowledge have women gained through the various efforts? In what ways has the condition of women been improved through this knowledge? Under what conditions can women attain useful knowledge? These are some of the questions that I would like to explore in this paper.

The study is based on information from 11 multilateral and 7 bilateral development agencies.[2] The information was first obtained some years ago when I interviewed personnel involved in basic education projects in these agencies (Stromquist 1986). Since then I have updated the study primarily through the analysis of reports and policy documents produced by these agencies.[3]

It is difficult to obtain a clear picture of the activities covering nonformal education that are funded by the international development agencies. Problems emerge because relatively few nonformal educational projects are funded under that name. A multitude of projects involving knowledge transmission or the acquisition of skills take place in areas such as agriculture, health, population, and water and sanitation. On the other hand, these activities tend to be planned with little consideration for their educational dimensions. Rare is the program—judging from project description documents—that considers carefully the content of the training or extension program, the outreach and delivery strategies, the training of NFE instructors, or the selection of and incentives for the participants. Those projects that do receive recognition as NFE tend to be but a small fraction of the agencies' educational budget. SIDA, one of the agencies most committed to NFE, assigns to it only 11% of its educational resources (SIDA 1987), a situation that SIDA attributes to the recipient governments' preference for formal, particularly higher, education. The World Bank, one of the largest sources of educational financing, pays practically no attention to NFE. One of its more recent policy documents ('Education in Sub-

Saharan Africa', 1988), clearly defines World Bank strategies as focused exclusively on the formal educational system.

And yet women tend to represent a large proportion of the enrolment in NFE projects. A 1985 study of 15 educational projects funded by the World Bank in Africa found that 70 percent of the enrolment was female. The same study also observed that the NFE components received the smallest share of overall project funding, frequently less than 1 percent of all assignable project funds (Fryer 1985: 3).

THE QUESTION OF USEFUL KNOWLEDGE FOR WOMEN

The assessment of the usefulness of the NFE programs for women has to be preceded by an understanding of women's current conditions and a vision of the new social order we should create. Since at present women play heavy reproductive roles (i.e. bear children, raise them, and manage the home), it is clear that NFE programs for women should seek to provide them with the skills and knowledge that would make the execution of these current reproductive tasks less demanding and more efficient. At the same time, since a considerable portion of women's subordination has been traced to their lack of financial autonomy, NFE programs should seek to provide women with marketable skills that would enable them to develop their own source of income. And yet, nothing of this would be sufficient if women were not given the opportunity to realize that they live under conditions of subordination and were not given skills to change the current social order. In other words, NFE would have to provide women with skills and knowledge that would allow their emancipation from unequal labor and social relations. To reach an effective combination of these three types of skills, for reproduction, for production, and for emancipation, is by no means an easy task. But, obviously, any one-sided approach would not be addressing the nature of women's condition.

The provision of these three types of skills for women in turn makes a number of logistical demands on project design and implementation. It would be overwhelming for women to receive and acquire reproductive, productive, and emancipatory skills simultaneously or in a short time; therefore, the design of NFE projects for women would have to use medium- and long-time frames, so that it is possible to work consistently with women and carry their skills/awareness through different stages of development. Since one of the consequences of women's subordination is that many of them have become passive social actors, NFE programs would have to consider as a key objective the involvement of women in project activities in ways that go beyond their role as mere beneficiaries. In other words, the NFE projects would have to pay a great deal of attention to the process itself, so that women would have a say in the various aspects and stages of the NFE activity.

Finally, since women at present carry heavy responsibilities associated with child and home care, NFE activities would have to consider the provision of "supportive services" to enable poor and overworked women to participate in educational activities. These supportive activities refer to the provision of incentives such as child care services, transportation, bonuses and so on, that would allow women to meet immediate reproductive responsibilities and thus free them for new tasks.

EXISTING PATTERNS OF NFE FOR WOMEN

As one tries to identify the range of NFE activities offered to women, it becomes clear that these activities vary substantially depending on the identity of the institution executing the project. There are three main actors in the area of NFE: the national government and its various ministries and agencies (which will be named the State in this paper), the international NGO and its network of national branches, and the national NGO and its network of local branches.

A characteristic of most NFE projects conducted by the State, particularly in capitalist developing countries, is that these activities tend to be compartmentalized into established fields of social action, e.g. health, agriculture, education (literacy and production skills), home economics, and income-generating activities.

Governments provide a substantial amount of training for women in the area of health. This is a major concern of multilateral organizations such as WHO, UNICEF, and UNFPA, and many bilateral organizations and their grants and loans to governments reflect this concern. Attention to issues such as malnutrition, maternal–child health, immunization, nutrition, and family planning is also high among most bilateral agencies, and NFE programs are designed so that ministry personnel at the local level, working from medical posts of community health centers, convey this "critical" knowledge to women. Indeed, the role of women as key actors in the transmission and implementation of new health approaches and technologies is solidly entrenched in many development agencies.

Another sector in which women receive considerable attention by the government is home economics. Again, this is an area in which development agencies are in agreement. Within home economics, information regarding cooking, sewing, child care, and handicrafts is conveyed, usually by home economics or community workers affiliated with ministries such as agriculture, rural development, or social welfare. Some agencies, particularly FAO, have grown more sophisticated in their understanding of home economics and have expanded the field to cover information regarding food crops, animal raising, and uses of fuel energy. Nonetheless, a large amount of funds in these projects still goes to traditional home economic activities. A review of CIDA projects by staff in the country missions noted that during 1979–81 as much as 64 percent of the funds spent on women-oriented projects went to pilot and training projects in skills such as sewing, embroidery, crafts, weaving, and home economics.

Technical skills in agriculture constitute an important part of NFE activities, but these continue to be given mostly to men, a situation caused in part by the fact that most extension agents are men, which facilitates their access to men but limits access to women. This predominant attention to men was detected more than 15 years ago; unfortunately, it continues to be the pattern. A 1985 evaluation coordinated by UNDP of the women-related activities performed by 13 UN agencies in four countries (prepared for the closing of the UN Decade for Women) found that women still face difficulties in obtaining extension advice on "equal footing with men." The same evaluation remarked that many of the projects still assumed that husband and wife operated as "farm families," a concept that emphasizes harmony within the household and ignores the unequal division of labor among family members. A consequence of this was that the 'content of some extension and training [was] more appropriate to men's needs than to women's' (UNDP 1985: 17).

Literacy occupies much of the core of NFE activities. And yet, surprisingly few of these projects have been designed to address women's needs exclusively. Most of these projects seek to serve men and women indistinctly, even though in practice the majority (often between 70 and 80 percent) of the participants in these projects are women. In the few cases where literacy projects are designed for women, the content concentrates on 'child rearing, home management, nutrition, and similar 'feminine' subjects' (UNESCO 1985; Stromquist and Kuhanga 1990).

In recent years a new type of activity, the income-generating project, has emerged in development projects and, particularly, among women-oriented projects. This type of activity holds great potential for women given its practical emphasis on enabling women to attain financial resources—certainly an appealing feature to women living in conditions of abysmal poverty and usually facing serious economic and social responsibilities as heads of households. It can only be said that this area has potential because it has not been fully exploited either in terms of understanding its unique advantages for women or in terms of allowing a reasonable implementation of the concept. In other words, there are many income-generating projects today but they are typically underfunded, understaffed, and exceedingly short term.

The general picture of the NFE projects for women run by the State is that they are segmented, in that they deal usually with one sectoral activity under the aegis of one single ministry. Exceptions to this are the few cases of rural integrated development projects, but even here—when one reads the fine implementation detail—it can be seen that the activities, although conveying information on agriculture, health, nutrition, water, and so on, consist of a series of discrete courses with little integration among them. Seldom, if ever, are these State-run projects accompanied by gender-awareness discussion or mobilization/organizational skills that would enable women to question the gender-based division of labor in society and to adopt new identities.

An important characteristic of State-run projects is that they address mainly the reproductive roles of women; they seek to make women more informed mothers, more efficient family caretakers, more effective home managers. Although some NFE programs seek to provide marketable skills for women, the benefits are often seen within the context of women as important family members. Thus, the transmission of marketable skills to women is usually justified along the lines that, when provided with these skills, the women will be able to feed and clothe their children better, to improve their housing, to raise the sanitary condition of their homes, etc.

Another characteristic of State-run NFE projects for women is that they rarely contain the provision of supportive services; only in a few cases is some provision of child care services contemplated. Most of the time, women are supposed to take care of these difficulties by themselves. From the UNDP evaluation focusing on projects concerning women in four countries, we learn that the NFE schemes there 'were not geared to women's lack of mobility, time constraints, and child care responsibilities' (1985: 3). From a country study conducted by UNFPA we can surmise that minimal child care is still being provided in its projects because the document recommends that 'serious attention should be given to establish part-time work and child-care facilities on site for UNFPA-supported projects that involve women either as workers or trainees' (UNFPA 1984,: 82).

Projects run by NGOs, on the other hand, offer some interesting and positive characteristics. NGOs are not an homogeneous group and some of them hold traditional attitudes toward women. However, the activities by NGOs offer much more diversity, more creativity, and often provide women with more comprehensive educational approaches. While it is also true that very few NGOs offer supportive services, this condition is mostly the result of having to operate with the smallest of budgets. Yet, in several instances, NGOs have provided alternative child-care services, usually through non-institutional approaches.

My study found that it was the NGOs almost exclusively that offered NFE in the area of civil rights—meaning awareness of gender, family and labor legislation, and social and economic conditions. Initiatives by international NGOs such as the International Planned Parenthood Federation (IPPF), the Women's International Tribune Center, the Overseas Education Fund (OEF), and the Women's Information and Communication Service, International (ISIS), have been essential in providing women with the skills and awareness necessary for their advancement. Within numerous countries, it has been through the work of national NGOs that women have received critical knowledge about their conditions of subordination at home, in the workplace, in their sexuality. Women-run NGOs in Colombia, Brazil, the Philippines, Peru, the Caribbean, and Nigeria have initiated and implemented NFE activities dealing with diverse but nonetheless important issues such as labor rights for women in the domestic service (a major source of women's work in the informal sector), "legal literacy campaigns," and information about women's sexuality. Often with a minimum of economic resources and limited staff, these NGOs have been able to gain access to destitute women, conduct critical tasks, and attain goals not easily matched by State efforts.

The most successful cases of income-generating projects are being implemented by NGOs. These successful projects are characterized not only by the attainment of profits by women but also by their involvement in decisions regarding the functioning of the project instead of being mere beneficiaries. These projects have also enabled women to enter economic roles traditionally reserved for men such as the construction of wells, mechanical repairs, and the creation of agricultural cooperatives. The initiatives conducted by Women in Development (WAND) in the Caribbean, the Bangladesh Reconstruction Advancement Committee (BRAC) in Bangladesh, the Staff-Employed Women's Association (SEWA) in India, the women's associations in countries such as Kenya and Peru, the projects conducted by various religious organizations, and the multiple projects coordinated by the IPPF, the consortium of Private Agencies

Collaborating Together (PACT) and OEF, not only provide women with marketable skills but at the same time raise the awareness about their conditions and possible ways to modify these conditions.

In other words, it is often the case that women NGOs run programs that combine skills with gender awareness. They also tend to provide simultaneously organizational and mobilization skills by making women active participants in the activities. The success of these NGOs—success measured in terms of the satisfaction of the participants and the continued existence of the NGO—indicates that the positive results attained by these groups derive perhaps less from resources and formal management than from patience, commitment to serve women, and considerable sensitivity to local needs. It is not that managerial and financial resources are not important; rather, they do not seem sufficient to ensure project success.

THE POTENTIAL FOR THE STATE AND NGOS TO PROVIDE EFFECTIVE NFE PROGRAMS FOR WOMEN

To what extent do the executing agencies have abilities that either set limits or offer possibilities for certain types of action designed to help women? The basic differences between the State and NGOs are in their legitimacy, size, amount of resource, personnel, objectives, and proximity to the target population. When comparing these two groups in terms of their ability to help women, one additional dimension must be added: the question of willingness.

The State

The State is supposed to be a neutral vehicle for the articulation of citizens' interests and the distribution of resources. Because of its large size and relative stability compared to other social institutions, the State is expected to be able to carry out comprehensive actions: since its ministries and local offices touch many parts of the national territory, the State, in principle, is capable of carrying out massive projects, with almost nationwide coverage. Its national budget should allow for the implementation of large-scale projects or at least of projects that will be in effect over several years. Its personnel, on the average much better educated than the rest of the population, are supposed to represent competent human resources capable of transmitting to other social groups the skills and support necessary to undertake development efforts. Another feature of the State is that since it proceeds according to national development plans, then the various activities it undertakes, including NFE, can be coordinated with a maximum of impact and a minimum of waste. As to proximity to target populations—i.e., the poor sectors of the population, peasants, women—the assumption is made that the State represents their interests and that these subjects indeed see the State as a supportive actor.

Actual performance by the State, however, challenges each of the preceding expectations. In many developing countries, there is an increasing realization that the State has adopted a model of development that favors industrialists and large entrepreneurs over peasants; that the State often allocates more resources to urban than to rural areas. One often finds among destitute segments of the population a mistrust of the State. It is constantly noted that in rural areas, government action is seen as a prelude to some sort of demand such as taxes, military service, or labor. Ministry personnel at the local level, although in fact better educated than the villagers, tend to adopt city-like and paternalistic attitudes in dealing with them. In addition, ministry personnel do not always deal with the neediest of the people; often their contact is limited to the notables or influentials of the community, whom they see as the most likely to behave as "change agents." The State's presence in many parts of the national territory is rendered ineffectual by the limited contact between government officials and the society they serve and because most projects represent ideas from the central government and target groups rarely participate in the definition of their problems or the identification of possible solutions.

Regarding the case of women, the majority of the states—except in the case of some socialist governments—manifest a lack of desire to develop projects sensitive to women's problems and needs. According to personnel of some bilateral agencies, the recipient states were often identified as a major obstacle to the development of women's projects because of failure to consider women's issues seriously or to identify women's projects for funding. Women's issues reportedly "come up from time to time" in the annual meetings of the multilateral agencies and in the negotiations of country programs between recipient governments and the bilateral agencies, but these issues are lost by the time of actual programming. And in cases where the State does seek to benefit women, it often has problems reaching them because of a lack of awareness on the part of planners about common conditions of women. A SIDA review of its support to Vocational Training Institutes in Bangladesh, for instance, found that women rarely participated because admission required eight years of prior schooling which most women did not have. Women were able to participate only after the introduction of a six-month modular NFE training course. But since only technical skills were provided, with no organizational or marketing skills, the graduates experienced difficulties finding employment or setting themselves up in self-employment (Lofstedt 1986).

A significant factor for the non-inclusion of women's issues in the design of country programs seems to be related to the absence of women in negotiating teams. Reflecting on her experience, which involved mostly negotiation among men, an agency administrator remarked, 'You have a game that goes back and forth. Neither the government nor the donor agency considers women's programs important and therefore both of them suggest other things.' And why is it that so few women are found in government negotiating teams and so few also in teams that design and implement projects? A basic reason is that the State is perhaps one of the most male-dominated institutions of society. The low levels of electoral participation by women, a result in large part of a domesticating socialization, lead not only to male over-representation in the legislature but also to the emergence of a bureaucracy that is predominantly male. Although certain men indeed understand the situation of subordination of women, most are inclined to preserve the *status quo*. This attitude is particularly intense in societies where cultural and religious norms have institutionalized and legitimized the subordination of women.

The NGOs

The characteristics of NGOs are not easy to summarize because diversity among them predominates. They vary a great deal in size, objectives, and population served. A survey of nine active NGOs in Bangladesh, for instance, identified groups as small as 667 members and as large as 45,000 (Lofstedt 1986). Most of the NGOs are young, perhaps no more than ten years old. Nonetheless, in their brief existence they have earned a reputation as organizations that operate with flexibility, encourage self-reliance, and are able to get closer than most government agencies to grassroots groups and to social strata not usually touched through large-scale projects.[4] Some of the flexibility of NGOs has been demonstrated not only in their speed to introduce project changes to suit local conditions but also in their ability to involve the community in design and implementation decisions.

It has been observed that the fairly simple administrative structures of NGOs require their personnel to be responsible for multiple tasks in the organizations, a feature that results in greater speed of operation and less bureaucratization. It has also been noted that the products of NGOs are much more end-user oriented than those of the State (IDRC 1984).

In several instances, also, NGOs have been successful mediators between the poor and the State, when they have 'assist[ed] the poor in articulating their needs and insisting on their rights, and serving as intermediaries between the poor and local authorities' (Lofstedt 1986: 27). A recent development in India seems to be the emerging linkages between NGOs and the creation of mass movements. These mass movements are able to aggregate substantial numbers of individuals and to articulate coherent philosophies of social change. Also in India, there are signs that a strong reciprocal relationship is being forged between NFE activities and the strengthening of mass movements.

While NGOs tend to be more sensitive to gender issues than the State, many NGOs have not succeeded in incorporating this concern in their fundamental objectives (see Yudelman 1987). But women-run NGOs have both abilities and concerns that translate into beneficial efforts to help women. Findings from the Yudelman in-depth study of five women-run NGOs in Latin America and the Caribbean showed that one of them, WAND, had played an instrumental role in prompting governments in seven of the Caribbean islands to establish women's bureaus. A second group, the Honduras Federation of Peasant Women (FEHMUC), had participated actively in pressing the government to pass agrarian reform legislation. A third group, the Center for Working Women in Mexico (COMO), had played an important role in forcing factories to set up health rooms and nurses on site for their predominantly female personnel (Yudelman 1985: 19–20).

There is also evidence that NFE methodologies and content originally developed by NGOs are later utilized by the State or other NGOs. The Yudelman study reported that WAND's training on participatory methodologies is now being used by ministries of agriculture and community development on several islands. The same study found that the courses in human development and training of trainers developed by the Federation of Voluntary Agencies (FOV) of Costa Rica were being used by government officials and personnel from other NGOs.

In the case of NFE, NGOs have been able to introduce innovative educational practices with great appeal among adult learners, such as music, popular theater, role playing and puppetry. Another positive trait of NGOs, also linked to NFE, is that they are much more comfortable than government agencies in dealing with projects that involve multiple sectors—a frequent feature of effective projects for women. It is indeed projects run by female-run NGOs that tend to present a package approach, combining elements of community health, agriculture, income generation, and literacy. Finally, as noted above, NGOs have shown significant willingness to deal with non-traditional roles for women and to engage in conscientization and mobilization efforts—objectives that must be considered essential in projects that seek to advance the status of women.

SOME EVALUATIONS OF NGO WORK

As noted by Buvinic (1984) there are several NGOs run by persons with good intentions but limited skills and competence. But, by and large, NGOs present a strongly competitive edge over the performance of the State and its multiple agencies.

A survey of executing agencies for projects supported by German funds indicated that 90 percent of the projects implemented by religious German NGOs and 50 percent of the projects implemented by other NGOs yielded positive impacts for women compared to 17 percent of the projects implemented by GTZ (which operates mainly through governments) (OECD 1985: 8). Further suggesting that NGOs, and particularly female-run NGOs, are efficient and effective implementors of women's projects is the shift in the allocation of funds reported by UNIFEM (previously known as UNDFW). When this agency started supporting women's projects in 1978–79, it gave 6 percent of its funds to NGOs; by 1982–83, NGOs were receiving 45 percent of its funds (UNDFW 1985: 11)[5]. An evaluation of its seven years of work led this agency to assert that:

> Entrusting project execution to local groups strengthens them and permits the idea of incorporating women into economically-oriented development projects to take root with the community. National expertise is allowed to surface and is reinforced, lessening dependence on imported talent. With nationals in charge, activities have a better chance of prevailing in the long run. (Ibid., p. 11.)

A few evaluations have been conducted of women-run NGOs in terms of their ability to implement successful income-generating projects. An assessment of female NGOs in various developing countries found that their income-generating projects tended to degenerate into welfare activities (i.e. away from profit making and more toward the execution of traditional roles for women, such as sewing, knitting, cooking, etc.) (Buvinic 1984). The same study, however, recognized that these groups received hardly any help to allow them to improve their management and administration. A study by Blumberg of 45 AID-supported income generating projects in Latin America and the Caribbean found that the women's NGOs selected for the projects had paid little attention to marketing and long-term viability. Blumberg concluded that these income-generating projects 'were given too few resources to make a substantial difference in the participants' lives' (1985, p. 51).

An in-depth and more recent evaluation of five projects run by female NGOs in Latin America and the Caribbean (Yudelman 1985), found that these NGOs are a training ground that offers opportunities for professional and personal growth that women would not be able to find in male-run organizations. It is also noted that these projects build confidence and provide important skills for women. Further, when provided with sufficient access to technical assistance and credit, women-run projects have been found capable of implementing projects successfully, and lenders find women to be more reliable borrowers than men (p. 28).

The findings by Buvinic and Blumberg, on the one hand, and those by Yudelman, on the other, are not contradictory. Together, they tell us that women have performed poorly when they have not been provided the minimum training and financial resources and that they have done quite well when these inputs were in place.

In the last decade, NGOs have made improvements despite the relatively small funding they have received from development aid agencies. Some NGOs have been able to attain considerable size and impact such as in the cases of the Grameen Bank, the Women's World Banking, the Women in Development Unit (WAND), the Bangladesh Rural Advancement Committee (BRAC), and the Self-Employed Women's Association (SEWA) of India. The Grameen Bank covers about 14,000 villages in Bangladesh. The Women's World Banking has affiliates in 22 countries and is developing new branches in 11 other countries. WAND operates in 10 Caribbean islands and provides technical assistance in consciousness raising, leadership, and organizational skills, and in setting income-generating projects. BRAC operates in over 1,000 villages in Bangladesh and serves approximately 10,000 women, 9,000 of whom are in non-craft production.

Several national NGOs have countrywide national networks; this is the case in countries such as India, the Philippines, Kenya, and Brazil. Several international NGOs, such as the IPPF, the YWCA, the International Council of Women, the International Cooperative Alliance, the World Council of Indigenous People, the International Association of Business and Professional Women have reached a level of development that includes the creation of branches in many Third World countries as well as the provision of technical assistance to these branches.

DONOR AGENCY SUPPORT OF NGOS

Aware of the positive role NGOs can play in the identification and implementation of projects to benefit women, development agencies are increasing their funding of NGOs. CIDA's support of NGOs increased from CAD$5 million in 1968 to CAD$243 million in 1987–88 (CIDA 1987), but even so NGO support represents only 9 percent of CIDA's funds (a figure that also includes funds given to firms in the private sector). Many agencies have attempted to involve NGOs in greater numbers. These include UNICEF, UNDP, WHO, IFAD, ILO.

Although the information is sketchy, it appears that a considerable proportion of the funds given to NGOs is spent in NFE, and that much of these efforts consider women as target groups. In the case of CIDA, it is estimated that about one-third of the NGOs conduct educational work, although this proportion might overestimate management training and underestimate training in health and agriculture. In the case of SIDA, 35.8 percent of NGO funds were spent in education, 29.5 percent in health, and 10.9 percent in rural development in 1983–84 (SIDA 1985).

Despite the substantial—if not institutionalized—work conducted by NGOs on behalf of women, the proportion of funds that NGOs receive is quite small. SIDA, an agency which has traditionally supported NFE, allocated 23 percent of its NFE funds to NGOs in 1986–87, but this amount represented a miniscule proportion of the overall development assistance funds. However, in 1986 SIDA set up a special fund of about US$1 million for direct support of female NGOs in developing countries. Even in the case of CIDA (the agency reporting the largest increase of funds going to NGOs) the total proportion of development funds assigned to NGOs has never surpassed 11 percent.

While it is not certain that all the international and national NGOs could absorb sudden and large budget increments—in fact some NGOs express fears that too rapid a growth might diminish their ability to produce a personalized and flexible service—it is clear that some groups would benefit significantly from increased funds. UNIFEM, the major UN agency addressing women's concerns, indicated at one point that because of budget constraints it was forced to reject one half of the requests it receives, many of them from NGOs (UNDFW 1985: 27). YWCA administrators consider that "at most" they can fund two-thirds of worthy projects. MATCH, a Canadian NGO that provides critical funding support to small women's groups in Third World countries, is able to satisfy only 25 of the approximately 150 annual requests for help from grass-roots groups.

Notwithstanding the potential of NGOs for addressing women's concerns, it must be noted that additional funding of NGOs will necessitate the establishment of mechanisms to ensure accountability. From the donor agency's perspectives, one of the advantages of dealing with the State is that of dealing with stable institutions with well-identified chains of command and responsibility. These fcatures are lacking in NGOs and will pose problems as more funds are disbursed to them. The possibility of fraud, although not very high, is there. Anecdotal information indicates that in certain countries, Sri Lanka for instance, several unscrupulous persons are "jumping the NGO bandwagon" and setting up local groups with scant community support; these people reportedly do very little work but trick donors into believing that they are quite active in the community. The proper identification of NGOs should become therefore very important and steps must be taken to monitor their work and weed out the incompetent or false groups. On the other hand, the need for accountability should not result in oppressive reporting procedures that consume substantial NGO energies.

BEYOND NONFORMAL EDUCATION AND TOWARD THE PROVISION OF CAPITAL

Although certain types of knowledge and skills are beneficial to women, one should not lose sight of the fact that poor women, before anything, need financial resources. In this respect, credit schemes are very important to women, and there is evidence suggesting that when credit is provided, even if training is not, women realize financial benefits for themselves and their families. Evidence from credit projects comes at this point from the experience and achievement of NGOs such as the Grameen Bank, the Women's World Banking, various NGOs in Latin America supported by the Inter-American Foundation, and several projects throughout the developing world coordinated by PACT. In many cases, loans given to poor women have allowed them to organize both farm and nonfarm activities that have raised their incomes and enabled them to repay the loans. Evaluations from the Grameen Bank indicate that the credits have resulted in increases as high as 31 percent in the per capita income of the household, that the participants have improved their housing, and that their children tend to remain at school longer (Hossain 1984: 128); the average repayment rate in the Grameen Bank is reportedly 98 percent (Yanus 1990). Evaluations of the activities of the Women's World Banking found that the loans resulted in profit increase for clients of about 40 percent per year and in the creation of one new employee for every US$200 to $1,000 loaned (Trade and Development International Corp. 1985: 10). Preliminary reports from PACT indicate that women who get credit tend to repay their loans at very satisfactory rates.

The lessons to be drawn from the performance of credit schemes for women so far, is that poor women possess high levels of ingenuity and resourcefulness that might be better utilized if they are given the opportunity to render concrete their ideas. This also suggests that if credit schemes were able to combine financial inputs with new knowledge/skills, the benefits for women would be even greater.

SOME ISSUES RELATED TO THE ROLE OF NGOS IN DEVELOPMENT

Three issues emerge as we try to conceptualize the role of NGOs in development efforts. These touch the issues of whether one should follow micro vs. macro strategies of social and economic change, whether women could be helped through women-only projects as opposed to "integrated" approaches, and the extent to which the State should be the key actor in the development process.

1. Micro vs. Macro Strategies of Socio-Economic Change

One of the frequent reasons expressed by agencies not willing to support NGOs was that they can conduct only small projects, and that small projects are inefficient because they are not "transferable," "replicable," or "generalizable." In contrast, large-scale projects tend to be seen as much more desirable.

Several observations are in order here. Large-scale projects should not be equated with success or efficiency. "Large-scale" is a notion that reflects more an administrative than a delivery reality: even in the case of the largest of projects, the delivery of services and treatments occurs at the community level. Large-scale projects, because they tend to be centrally designed and managed, arrive at the community level as top-down decisions and with personnel relatively alien to the community. While these characteristics are negative in projects where most participants are men, they are more serious for projects that seek to benefit women. These large-scale projects will reach few women and those reached will not be encouraged to develop new identities because they will be mere beneficiaries rather than active participants in development efforts.

Agencies with extensive experience in dealing with community groups maintain that the question is not of "scaling up" the projects but rather of finding ways to scale them down. In the case of women, intense and patient work is needed to reach the very poor, marginal, often demobilized women. This calls for projects with a great amount of interaction with participants, with many decisions and activities emerging from meetings and through trial and error.

It may be appropriate to consider here the theoretical contributions of Antonio Gramsci regarding the role of "civil society" in social change efforts (Guibal 1981). Gramsci often contrasted the civil society (the conglomeration of private institutions and groups) to the political society (the public or governmental machinery) to indicate that it is the former which provides the consent necessary for the State to operate beyond coercion. He argued that in order to challenge the hegemonic power of the State changes were needed in the civil society and that these changes would have to be introduced by the people themselves. He argued that the individuals who comprise the civil society can attain social changes by being critical and developing a coherent view of their world. Such alternative world view can break the existing hegemony of dominant groups. But to make this possible, it is necessary to enable dominated groups to discover their knowledge and to find modes of expression (Martinic 1984.). Under those conditions, if one seeks to transform society, the most effective way might be by developing gradually the critical understanding of the members of that society, i.e. the fibers of the civil society. This understanding will emerge only through the constant recombination of action and reflection.

This approach implies working with individuals from the very beginning. And individuals are best approached through small groups. In this case, acting at the micro level is necessary, and it is by passing through this scale that macro results will be attained. This implies a theory of social change that moves through expanding concentric circles, creating multiple groups first at the community level, then regional levels, and ultimately the nation.

This idea of giving more importance to individuals is also present in the comments by Rajni Kothari, the well-known scholar and activist. He says that when we talk about power we should not merely consider the capture of State power but, instead, envisage a process of redefining the whole concept and structure of politics with a view to empowering the masses. As he sees it, it is not a question of inheriting or seizing power but recreating it (Kothari 1984).

There is evidence suggesting that the micro-macro link can be established. The experiences reported by organizations supporting NGOs in substantial numbers (such as the Ford Foundation, the Inter-American Foundation, and the Carnegie Corporation) and NGOs themselves such as IPPF and WAND indicate that community-level projects can grow in sophistication and over time create similar models in other sites within the country.

2. *Women-only vs. Integrated Projects*

Another reservation observed among international agency staff is that they fear setting up many "small, isolated women's groups that will not benefit from the mainstream development efforts." The prevailing belief is that to benefit women planners should consider them within the large, nationwide projects. "Integration," although a desirable goal, does not always produce the desired objectives. Integration in terms of considering female and male recipients alike or assuming that the activities will naturally benefit both sexes has been found to result both in projects that are difficult to evaluate and in projects where the greater proportion of funds go to men.

In some instances, women-only projects can certainly be nothing but isolated and forgotten dead-end initiatives. But research from the social sciences regarding small group behavior informs us that, because of diffuse but internalized social expectation, individuals having low-prestige status in society tend to participate much less in group discussions and decisions than those having high-prestige status (Berger, Cohen, and Zelditch 1972). We also know that high-prestige individuals (i.e. men in this case) tend to behave more assertively in mixed-gender groups than they would in all-male groups.[6] It follows then that to develop certain skills in women, such as organization, public speaking, and leadership skills—basic skills that many men have already mastered by adulthood—women-only groups may be the most effective first step.

Preliminary findings from NGOs' experiences suggest that if well-conceived, women-only projects can produce extremely positive results. Women-only projects have been found to produce benefits for women to become active participants, to find support in persons with similar experiences, and to develop basic skills usually already mastered by men, such as expressing opinions in public and addressing a group. Interviews with women participating in women-only groups have identified the following advantages to joining this type of group:

> First, they want to run their own organizations.
>
> In male-dominated groups, such as cooperatives and agricultural associations, women are not even given the opportunity to participate, let alone manage. Second, they want to earn and control their own income. Since men control the finances in most families, it is only through their own projects that poor women can hope to earn income. Third, they do not want to assume the debts of men. They are well aware that the cooperatives and agricultural associations in their communities are often in debt. Finally, they realize that their financial

> contributions lead to changes in attitude on the part of their husbands. In the Dominican Republic, for example, several members of one MUDE group noted that, as a result of the group's successful cultivation and marketing of rice, their husbands now consult them about household expenses. In Honduras, FEHMUC women who have increased family incomes are treated with new respect by their husbands. (Yudelman 1985: 10)

Women-only projects tend to be small in size and require small amounts of funds compared to large infrastructural projects, but they do not necessarily result in inconsequential outcomes. Women who develop skills in participation and mobilization are able to transfer those skills to other facets of their daily lives. Data from several Latin American countries indicate that some women's groups have been able to make this transition. Yudelman (1985) reports that the Honduras Federation of Peasant Women, the only peasant women's federation in Latin America and which claims over 5,000 members, representing 13 of the 15 departments of Honduras, started initially as a homemakers' club (p. 3). Also, women-only projects can be quite "integrated," if by integration we mean the combination of income-generating skills with knowledge in certain areas such as health, leadership, literacy, management, etc.

The experience of development aid agencies active in women's issues has taught them that it should not really be a question of integrated projects vs. women-only projects. Rather, these approaches must be seen as complementary in many cases. Given the complex situation of poor women and the diversity of the political and cultural contexts in which they live, a combination of both approaches is advocated to ensure that, on the one hand, some critical skills are developed and, on the other hand, that women's needs and problems are not "ghettoized." The challenges ahead are to determine when to promote which type of project and how to make sure that "integrated" projects do not mean absorption to the point of invisibility for women. There are no easy prescriptions here; each situation will have to be examined in its own specificity and context.

3. The Role of the State in National Development

Among donor agencies there is a marked tendency to consider the State in developing countries as their main, if not exclusive, interlocutor. And yet, the State plays a major role in the subordination of women. It does so through the public institutions it maintains and through the family dynamics it protects both through coercion and socialization. Therefore, it should not be surprising to realize that many of the governments of developing countries play a conservative rather than an innovative role regarding the identification and implementation of projects for women. The performance of most states regarding the condition of women leaves much to be desired: Governments have shown a tendency to accept almost gender-free approaches to the expansion and improvement of formal educational systems and to prefer reproductive over productive and certainly over emancipatory objectives in the design of NFE projects for women.

International development agencies, particularly the bilaterals, also represent the State. But several of them represent states where women have been able to demand and obtain greater social and economic concessions. Some bilaterals, in consequence, reflect national policies strongly committed to the advancement of women that translate into progressive development assistance for this group.

In the early years of international development, there was a belief that the State, given the deficiencies of private economic agents and those of the free market, was the most suitable "protagonist" of development. The Economic Commission for Latin America, for instance, consistently attributed a rational and planning role to the State, whose intervention was seen as necessary to promote economic growth, to distribute fairly the fruits of that growth, and to decide what and how to produce (Gurrieri, p. 8). This romanticized version of the State was tempered subsequently as the question of power and its internal and external manifestations on government decisions was taken into account. Today, there is a greater awareness in that organization and others regarding the limits of the State in conducting democratic planning. However, although there are increasing references in development agency circles to strengthen the democractic forces in society, the consequences of this objective for increased attention to and support of NGOs, particularly women-run NGOs, have not been fully grasped.

Kothari considers that the State, previously viewed as an instrument of transformation, is now in decline, 'in part simply due to proven incapacity for government to perform, but in good part by deliberate design' (1984: 24). He argues that the State is neither distributive nor mass oriented. It is 'an agent of technological modernization,' more interested in serving the elites than in coping with the 'pressing, often desperate, needs and demands of the poor' (ibid.). What Kothari and others, including myself, have in mind is not the emergence of private enterprise as the solution to underdevelopment. Rather, we consider that grass-roots groups and other types of organized citizen initiatives should be encouraged to become alternative institutions for social change. Kothari makes a distinction between NGOs, which he considers apolitical and somewhat coopted bodies, and what he calls "non-party political formations." I do not make the distinction. I argue simply that non-governmental institutions, even if they do not have a comprehensive political agenda, can play important roles, particularly for women.

It should be remarked that we are not proposing the end of the State. The empowerment of grass-roots groups and the NGOs that aggregate their interests should in fact work toward the emergence of a more representative and sensitive State. In this matter, the State will be made not only the subject but the object of development, as observed by Gurrieri (1984).

The State has assumed varying positions toward development and governance. There are countries where the State has practically withdrawn from an active role in development and where privatization policies prevail; Chile under Pinochet was a case in point. In such cases, the NGOs play an essential function either in narrowing the social services gap or in preserving democratic and social interests. In other countries, we find that the State is active in development but that the model of development pursued emphasizes economic growth and fails to deal with certain issues and certain populations. In India, for instance, the State tends to neglect the problems of pavement dwellers, women, and displaced peoples. In this context, NGOs play a dissident role and put pressure on the government to address the needs of marginal populations. They also play a role in the creation and implementation of development alternatives. In yet other countries, we find that the State has embarked on a development model that enjoys social consensus. In those cases, NGOs can cooperate with the government and undertake activities that fall within their comparative advantage. It is clear, therefore, that the approaches to development taken by the State influence significantly the roles NGOs can and do take, but it should be equally clear that female NGOs are likely to be the best vehicles to serve women's needs in all cases.

CONCLUSIONS

International cooperation has supported important and numerous activities in NFE but the privileged recipient has been the State. The main consequence of having the State as the key intermediary between donor agencies and low-income women has been that NFE programs have been segmented, have not paid attention to the educational component in them, and have been designed with little sensitivity for women's concerns.

What knowledge have women gained through NFE? By and large they have received conventional skills and knowledge, mostly linked to their maternal and domestic roles; thus, the emphasis on health, nutrition, water, and sanitation, appropriate technologies, and home economics. Women, thus, have tended to be seen as tools for social purposes rather than as the objects and subjects of a new social order.

Only in a few cases have women received knowledge in organizational and leadership skills that would allow them to take more active roles in decision making. In even fewer cases have these women increased their awareness of their subordination because topics such as gender consciousness-raising have been covered only in selected instances, mostly when projects have been run by NGOs, and particularly when these have been run by female NGOs.

Although knowledge can have a social and political empowering function, the type of knowledge most low-income women receive through international cooperation cannot be said to be conducive to their empowerment and emancipation.

Under these circumstances, the condition of women has not changed dramatically. It could be maintained that with the conventional skills perhaps women are becoming better home managers, better transmitters and implementers of basic health technologies, and less inefficient domestic/subsistence producers. But, from a feminist perspective—meaning a posture that seeks gender equality—it could be asserted that these new skills and information are perhaps contributing to solidify the reproductive role of women and to render more elusive than before the emancipatory goals for women.

The evidence so far indicates that it is doubtful that the State can be counted on as a willing partner in women's quest for emancipation. The few instances of NFE and related initiatives helpful to women have come from alternative agencies, the NGOs, and it is with them that the potential for social change along gender lines lies.

In an insightful article, Maxine Molyneux makes the distinction between "practical gender interests" and "strategic gender interests," defining the former as short term and linked to immediate needs arising from women's current responsibilities vis-a-vis the livelihood of their families and children, while the latter address larger issues such as the sexual division of labor within the home, the removal of institutionalized forms of gender discrimination, the establishment of political equality, freedom of choice over childbearing, and the adoption of adequate measures against male violence and control over women (n.d.: 5–6). Molyneux observes that even in the case of a socialist state such as Sandinista Nicaragua, the question of women's emancipation (i.e., the strategic gender interests), tends to be subordinated to a wider strategy of economic development, which tends to address mainly women's practical interests.

If such is the behavior of the State even in systems that admittedly seek a better social order, then it becomes evident that women must protect their interests through independent bodies. In that case, NGOs, and especially women-run NGOs, offer substantial evidence of and potential for addressing successfully women's concerns. This, however, does not preclude the possibility that under certain circumstances, it may be possible for the State and NGOs to work together toward some common goals.

For those agencies interested in strengthening women-run NGOs, the advice is challenging: fund them so that they can design activities that have both immediate and longer-time frameworks; give them support to improve both its personnel and its basic infrastructure; and allow them to provide some form of credit to the participants in their programs so that knowledge and skills result in actual applications.

NOTES

1. For an excellent synthesis of such literature, see Gita Sen and Caren Grown (1985) *Development, Crisis, and Alternative Vision: Third World Women's Perspectives*. New Delhi, DAWN.

2. The agencies considered in this study were: Canadian International Development Agency (CIDA), Commonwealth Secretariat, Food and Agriculture Organization of the United Nations (FAO), Ministry of Foreign Relations, Cooperation, and Development (France), German Agency for Technical Cooperation (GTZ), International Fund for Agricultural Development (IFAD), International Labor Office (ILO), Department for International Cooperation (Italy), Overseas Development Administration (ODA), Swedish Agency Development Authority (SIDA), United Nations Children's Fund (UNICEF), United Nations Educational, Scientific, and Cultural Organization (UNESCO), United Nations Development Program (UNDP), United Nations Development Fund for Women (UNIFEM), United Nations Fund for Population Activities (UNFPA), United States Agency for International Development (USAID), World Bank, World Food Program (WFP), and World Health Organization (WHO).

3. It should be noted that since the end of the UN Decade for Women there has been much less attention given to gender issues in development, which is reflected in the paucity of current reports and evaluations dealing with them.

4. For careful examinations of the performance and potential of NGOs in development efforts, see Drabek 1987, and Broadhead et al. 1988.

5. The figures for UNIFEM's direct support of NGOs for 1990 are 7 percent, or US $400,000 out of a total budget of US $6 million. It appears, however, that this apparent decrease may be a function of the new accounting procedure that differentiates between direct support and subcontracting.

6. For additional references see Lockheed, 1976.

REFERENCES

Berger, J., Cohen, B. and Zelditch, M. (1972) 'Status Characteristics and Social Interaction'. *American Sociological Review* 37: 241–255.

Blumberg, Rae (1985) 'To What Extent Have Women Been Taken Into Account in US Foreign Aid in Latin America and the Caribbean. Clues from the Paper Trail of Agency for International Development Projects'. Report prepared for AID, mimeo.

Brodhead, Tim, Hebert-Copley, Brent, and Lambert, Anne-Marie (1988) *Bridges of Hope? Canadian Voluntary Agencies and the Third World.* Ottawa, The North-South Institute.

Buvinic, Mayra (1984) *Projects for Women in the Third World: Explaining their Misbehavior*. Washington, D.C., International Center for Research on Women, April.

CIDA (1987) *Sharing Our Future. Canadian International Development Assistance.* Ottawa, CIDA.

Drabek, Anne (ed.) (1987) 'Development Alternatives: The Challenge for NGOs'. *World Development*, supplement, Vol. XV, Autumn.

Filion, Louise, Laforce, Jocelyne, and Pesant, Louise (1985) *Contribution de l'ACDI à l'alphabetisation et à l'education de base des femmes dans les pays en development. Rapport Final. Volume II.* Ottawa, Cooperative d'Animation et de Consultation.

Fryer, Michelle (1985) 'Education Lending in Sub-Saharan Africa. Expenditures on Females, 1983–1985'. Washington, D.C., Educational Policy Division, The World Bank, November (mimeo).

Guibal, Francis (1981) *Gramsci. Filosofia, Politica, Cultura.* Lima, Tarea, Centro de Publicaciones Educativas.

Gurrieri, Adolfo (1984) *Vigencia del Estado Planificador en la Crisis Actual.* Santiago, CEPAL.

Hossain, Mahabub (1984) *Credit for the Rural Poor. The Grameen Bank in Bangladesh.* Dhaka, Bangladesh, Institute of Development Studies, Research Monograph No. 4.

IDRC (1984) 'Seminar Report. Southeast Asia Non-Government Organizations: Research Practices and Potential. May 28–31, 1984'. Singapore, IDRC Regional Office (mimeo).

Kothari, Rajni (1984) 'Grass Root Movements. The Search for Alternatives'. *The Illustrated Weekly of India*, April 29: 24–31.

Lockeed, Marlaine (1976) *The Modification of Female Leadership Behavior in the Presence of Males*. Princeton, Educational Testing Service.

Lofstedt, Jan-Ingvar (1986) *Female Participation in Production in Bangladesh. An Area for Development Assistance?* Stockholm, Institute of International Education, University of Stockholm.

Martinic, Sergio (1984) *Saber Popular e Identidad*. Paper presented at the Third Latin American Seminar on Participatory Research. Sao Paulo, 14–17 October.

Molyneux, Maxine (n.d.) 'Mobilization Without Emancipation? Women's Interests, State and Revolution' (mimeo).

OECD (1985) *Summary Record on the Meeting held on 29–31 January*. Paris, Development Assistance Committee, Expert Group on Women in Development.

SIDA (1985) *Study of the Development Assistance Capacity of Swedish Non-Governmental Organizations*. Stockholm, SIDA,.

SIDA (1987) *Swedish Support to Non-Formal Adult Education Programmes*. Stockholm: SIDA, February.

Stromquist, Nelly (1986) *Empowering Women through Knowledge: Policies and Practices in International Cooperation in Basic Education*. Report prepared for UNICEF (mimeo).

Stromquist, Nelly and Nicholas Kuhanga (1990) *Feasibility Study for the Creation of a World Literacy Center: A Global Response to a Global Problem*. Report prepared for the International Council of Adult Education, March.

Trade and Development International Corp. (1985) *Evaluation of Women's World Banking. Final Report*. Prepared to US Agency for International Development. Needham, Maryland, Trade and Development Corp.

UNDFW (1985) *Farmers, Merchants and Entrepreneurs. A Report of the United Nations Development Fund for Women*. New York, UNDFW.

UNDP (1985) *Inter-Organizational Assessment of Women's Participation in Development. FAO, IFAD, ILO, UNCDF, UN/DTDC, UNDP, UNESCO, UNFPA, UNICEF, UNIDO, VFDW, World Bank, WFP, WHO*. Evaluation Study No. 13. New York, UNDP.

UNESCO (1985) *The Development of Adult Education. Aspects and Trends*. Paris, UNESCO.

UNFPA (1984) *Report on the Evaluation of UNFPA-Sponsored Country Programmes in Democratic Yemen, 1979–84 and the Role of Women in It*. New York, UNFPA.

World Bank (1988) *Education in Sub-Saharan Africa.* Washington, D.C., The World Bank.

Yanus, Muhammed (1990) 'For Dispossessed Women, A Godsend', *Los Angeles Times*. April 4.

Yudelman, Sally (1985) 'Women's Development Organizations: Successes, Constraints and Problems'. Paper presented at the meeting on Anthropological Perspectives on Women's Collective Actions. An Assessment of the Decade, 1975–1985, held at Mijas, Spain, November (mimeo).

Education and Cultural Reproduction in India: A Content Analysis of Selected Textbooks

TIMOTHY J. SCRASE

Charles Sturt University, New South Wales

This chapter intends to address the broad area of cultural reproduction theory and its relationship to comparative education research, particularly through a case study of Indian textbook content. There are two prime objectives in this chapter. The first is to provide a brief review of social and cultural reproduction theory and discuss its applicability to education in India. In addition, I examine the concept of hegemony and explain its relationship to the politics of schooling. The second objective is to provide an analysis of Indian school textbook content and relate the findings of this analysis to questions of cultural reproduction which occur in India. Additionally, my analysis shall also broach broader questions of the function of dominance and ideology which arise at the school level.

REPRODUCTION THEORY AND INDIAN EDUCATION[1]

Writing in 1982, Michael Apple posed four fundamental questions that summarized the issues raised in radical education scholarship of the past decade. These questions were:

> (1) Do schools primarily reproduce the social division of labor or are they avenues for lessening the existing inequality of power and knowledge in our society? (2) Are schools 'strongly determined' by ideological, economic, and cultural forces outside of them or do they have a significant degree of autonomy? (3) Do theories of economic

> reproduction adequately respond to the cultural and ideological roles played by education? (4) What actually happens within the school (the curriculum, the social relations, the language and culture considered legitimate) that may provide answers to these questions? (Apple 1982b: 1)

In order to situate the discussion on reproduction theory, it is necessary to return briefly to the middle 1970s and broach the writings of two American scholars—Samuel Bowles and Herbert Gintis.

In *Schooling in Capitalist America* (1976), Bowles and Gintis provided a comprehensive study on the role of schools in reproducing the social division of labour in the United States. Their study raised a number of important, and no less, controversial issues about the relationship of schools to capitalism. One of their main arguments was basically that '... the education system serves—through the correspondence of its social relations with those of economic life—to reproduce economic inequality and to distort personal development' (1976: 48). The notion of correspondence implies a direct relationship between two or more entities. For Bowles and Gintis, this relationship is between schools, on the one hand, and capitalism's need to sustain its economic and political dominance, on the other hand. In order to explain the correspondence principle they argued that:

> The structure of social relations in education not only inures the student to the discipline of the work place, but develops the types of personal demeanour, modes of self-presentation, self-image, and social class identifications which are the crucial ingredients of job adequacy. Specifically, the social relationships of education—the relationships between administrators and teachers, teachers and students, students and students, and students and their work—replicate the hierarchical division of labor. (1976: 131)

Arguing for reproduction in education through a correspondence principle evoked much response and criticism. On a positive note, it has been argued that the correspondence principle has contributed much to our knowledge of issues such as: the mechanisms of the hidden curriculum; the relationship between class and gender specific modes of schooling with social processes in the workplace; and has illuminated the non-cognitive dimensions of schooling (Giroux 1983: 85).

Influenced by social reproduction theory, at least to some degree, has been the research of, for example, Kelly and Nihlen (1982) and Anyon (1981; 1980).

Social reproduction theory in many ways spoke for a neo-Marxist view of education under modern capitalism. Yet, there remain some fundamental weaknesses in this approach. One writer argued that Bowles and Gintis end up with a theory of social reproduction that is much too simplified and over-determined: 'Not only does their argument point to a spurious 'constant fit' between schools and the workplace, it does so by ignoring important issues regarding the role of consciousness, ideology, and resistance in the schooling process' (Giroux 1983: 84). Carnoy (1982: 110) claimed that little understanding is presented which can provide an explanation of the contradictions and nature of class struggle in the educational setting. A further criticism levelled at Bowles and Gintis was their neglect of the micro-level school processes; namely, the curriculum and classroom interaction (Sarup 1983). Thus, it was argued that a strongly functionalist theme in radical educational theory emerged (Shapiro 1988: 419).

Schools, it is argued, epitomize the society; they are a microcosm of social life in the sense that wider political, ideological and cultural struggles are fought out at the level of the classroom, the school, the community, and the State. In this chapter I take the point that Bowles and Gintis make regarding social reproduction, yet I am cautious to generalize, especially in the context of comparative educational systems (and hence comparative social and cultural experience). For instance, social reproduction in education does occur in India. In a study of Bombay schools by Michaelson (1983) she argued that: 'The educational choices of Bombay parents serves to reproduce a diversity of labour skills needed in the continuity of the productive process' (1983: 345). Yet, there remains the need to theorize further; that is to say, we must contextualize the problems of education in the framework of a political economy of schooling in which important questions of not only agency and structure are considered, but the significant issues of the State and politics, and of ideology and culture, are addressed.

In the case of India, this contextualization, as it were, is historically contingent upon the relationship between the development of schooling under colonialism and the development of capitalist relations of production (see, for instance, Carnoy 1974). In contemporary India there currently remains a serious inconsistency with education policy. On the one hand, mass schooling has benefited India in terms of modernising its economy. On the other hand, the benefits of this modernization have gone primarily to a minority of Indians that control India's social and economic life—the middle classes and indigenous capitalists. The catch, of course, is that although schooling is free and available, only those who are already financially secure can hope to complete their schooling and so compete with others in the middle class job market. As stated above, schooling is also about other issues: ideology, culture, and politics. School knowledge, in the form of curriculum and textbooks, encapsulates these issues.

While social reproduction theorists have rightly recognised the link between the needs of the capitalist economic system and schooling, they have failed in terms of providing a comprehensive analysis of human agency and social structure. Importantly, the use of the concept "culture" is missing in their analysis. In contrast, theories of cultural reproduction attempt to focus the argument around curriculum issues, social class and culture. In other words, the aim is to show how capitalist societies reproduce themselves within the cultural sphere of the school. Importantly, cultural reproduction theory examines the mediating role of culture, rather than economic imperatives, in the reproduction of class societies. In this instance, the writings of Pierre Bourdieu (1977a; 1977b) and with Jean-Claude Passeron (1977) are of particular importance.

After having undertaken an extensive sociological study of the link between people's occupations and cultural habits and practices in France, Bourdieu is able to argue that the French school curriculum serves the cultural, and therefore class, interests of the middle and upper classes. He states:

> The educational system reproduces all the more perfectly the structure of the distribution of cultural capital among classes (and sections of a class) in that the culture which it transmits is closer to the dominant culture and that the mode of inculcation to which it has

> recourse is less removed from the mode of inculcation practised by the family. (Bourdieu 1977a: 493)

Thus, those students that already have the highly valued culture, who possess high "cultural capital", passed on from their parents (through a complex socialization process Bourdieu terms the "habitus") are directly benefitted by the school system in terms of the school structure, curriculum content and teaching practice. From this position, two important points have to be recognized:

> First, the dominant classes exert their power by defining what counts as meaning, and in doing so they disguise this 'cultural arbitrariness' in the name of neutrality that masks its ideological grounding . . . Second, class and power connect with dominant cultural production not only in the structure and evaluation of the school curriculum, but also in the dispositions of the oppressed themselves, who actively participate in their own subjugation. (Giroux 1983: 89)

Power, in the sense that Bourdieu and Passeron write, has an inherently symbolic effect (1977: 10). That is, social power is exercised and enforced in society in ways that appear indirect, but the eventual outcomes (the domination of the subordinate groups) is achieved. In schools, for example, the dominant classes exercise their power symbolically in the sense that the cultural capital of the dominant classes is reproduced in language, curriculum and pedagogy.

For Bourdieu, then, the school is in many ways a reflection of bourgeois family life, cultural patterns and authority structures. Interestingly, many of Bourdieu's observations on language and its relationship to the distribution of power and culture in schools (articulated in the notion of "symbolic violence"), show a similarity to the findings of Basil Bernstein (1971) in his outline of the speech code patterns and the reproduction of inequality in British schools.

To pursue this point in the context of Indian schooling and culture raises an important issue. In India, English is the language that is most often appropriated by the dominant classes. English, therefore, in Bourdieu's terms, is a component of the dominant classes' cultural capital. From the middle class home to the school, the Indian middle class children have the decided advantage as proficiency in English language (along with a solid post-secondary education) enhances employment success, status and prestige. In addition, English also acts as a (another) barrier for the subordinate classes to overcome. The dominant classes can effectively marginalize the majority of the subordinate classes and guard against incursion across their cultural barrier by exercising their knowledge of English. Thus, while this cultural power is symbolic, its effects remain real.

Bourdieu's contribution to reproduction theory and culture remains incisive and challenging. His writings have come in for much criticism from leftist scholars, especially for his incorporation of seemingly functionalist interpretations, in particular those based on the legacy left by Durkheim (as in the view that cultures are arbitrary). Essentially, one could say that he has developed a theory of functionalist Marxism. In a recent critique, however, Miller and Branson (1987) have argued that this is a basic misreading and misinterpretation of Bourdieu's theories. Other critics have not been as kind. Both Giroux (1983: 90–95) and Willis (1981: 54–56) criticize Bourdieu for his failure to link schools with the notion of cultural production, his unwillingness to link the notion of domination with the materiality of economic forces, and for offering no theoretical insights into notions of youth resistance. Nevertheless, the theoretical implications of the term "cultural capital" provide particularly useful ideas for exploring the cultural context of educational inequality in India. I shall turn to this point shortly.

This discussion of cultural reproduction theory cannot be completed without mentioning the research of one other important scholar. Paul Willis's (1977) writings are interesting in that he arrives at a theory, through ethnography, which basically explains how working class students are marginalized in the school setting. The outcomes of failure at school for the students he studied were bleak—unemployment, factory work and poverty. Yet, what is important is that these students did not accept their position lying down. Instead they struggled against the hegemonic domination of the school rules and authority, albeit within the structural and ideological constraints imposed by the capitalist social system. Nevertheless, they were able to develop their own specific culture based upon their class-located, parent cultures.

The students that Willis studied were essentially part of a sub-culture. That is, they comprised a small group bound together by a particular adherence to a common life-style or pattern. The common, and dominant feature of this sub-culture was resistance. The accounts presented by Willis detail the situations when the "lads" constantly disobey and confront their teachers and the school authorities. These "lads" had no need to obey, no need to conform, as the logic of their cultural vis-à-vis class position resigned them to the scrapheap of society. As Willis explains,

> The working class does not *have* to believe the dominant ideology. It does not need the mask of democracy to cover its face of oppression. The very existence and consciousness of the middle class is deeply integrated into that structure which gives its dominance . . . The working class is the only group in capitalism that does not have to believe in capitalist legitimation as a condition of its own survival. (1977: 123; original emphasis)

The essential point that Willis makes, and what distinguishes his position from that of Bourdieu's, is that despite the reproduction that occurs in schools, the working class are able to generate their own oppositional culture and ideology; that is, they produce a counter-culture and ideology that is oppositional to the middle class, dominant culture. Nevertheless, the degree to which this oppositional culture can effectively challenge the dominant culture is severely limited. Sub-cultural formation represents a form of resistance to the established order in capitalist society, but it inevitably ends up being concerned with fashion, taste or aesthetic design. Rarely does it involve an effective, well-organized campaign for political change that would be of benefit for all marginalized groups and alienated workers (including women and blacks). As critics of Willis have argued, the "lads" he studied were overtly sexist, racist, and politically reactionary (Macdonald 1980; McRobbie 1980), and rather than seeing this as a positive thing (i.e. because they rebelled against authority), the emphasis should be on understanding how theories of resistance can account for the way in which class and culture combine to offer outlines for a theory of cultural politics (Giroux 1983: 101).

While the views of Bourdieu and Willis are somewhat divergent, they provide some interesting possibilities for theorizing and analyzing the ideological construction of knowledge in Indian school textbooks. Let us consider each point separately:

(i) The basic premise behind Bourdieu's notion of "cultural capital" is that the culture of the dominant classes is reproduced in the schools, especially in terms of the curricula, school rules, teaching style (in other words, the school culture). Yet, undeniably, culture is also produced in the schools. Schools cannot be separated from the wider social context. In India, the attempt to re-structure and modernize the economy on capitalist lines continues. Educational policy speaks of the pivotal role education can play in training an educated, technically-skilled workforce. It logically follows that, at the psycho-social level, the middle classes must be imbued with the same "modern" and technically oriented image. Therefore, one can expect to see a degree of re-orientation in the school curricula and textbooks which emphasize the changing character of the Indian economy at the wider social level. The point remains, however, that this re-orientation of school knowledge basically occurs in the interests of the dominant culture—the Indian middle classes.

(ii) Following Williams (1976)[2] I would contend that when theorizing cultural change in India one must consider the impact of "residual" cultural forms. For example, the influence of caste is especially important in terms of comprehending inequality based on gender and class divisions. Therefore, while school knowledge may show a tendency toward reflecting the "modern" (the emergent culture), the veneer of pre-existing (or traditional) residual cultural patterns are expected to remain for some time.

(iii) Resistance in Indian schools does occur. Resistance, in this context, is more often than not expressed in a form, or forms, of disobedience. School students in India may tend to be naughty and rude to a teacher, but this is deflected onto the teacher, not onto the school as an institution. Education in India is still highly valued, even though it remains out of the reach of a great number of children. It follows, therefore, that the creation of an effective counter ideology is restricted, or more accurately, negated as, on the one hand, the majority of students have a limited social, cultural, and political experience and, on the other hand, aspirations for education remain high.

(iv) Finally, the Indian middle class (like most classes) wants to advance economically. Their advance, however, is at the social and ideological expense of the subaltern classes. This raises the issue of cultural politics in Indian education; that is, the cultural politics of the Indian middle classes is expressed in the ideology of school knowledge. Yet, what complicates this picture is the influence of the residual cultural forms on the entire construction of a middle class culture. Expressed in another way, the dominant culture, as Bourdieu argues, has to do two things: effectively marginalize subaltern culture; and, in so doing, justify its own social dominance and significance. Thus, the imperative for the Indian middle class in education (one of the major cultural institutions under its control) is to legitimate its own dominance.

HEGEMONY AND EDUCATION

In order to clarify the process of cultural reproduction in Indian education, it is appropriate to now discuss hegemony. The concept of hegemony forms the central component in the work of the Italian Marxist Antonio Gramsci, particularly in his influential studies contained in *Prison Notebooks* (1971). In his earlier works, Gramsci applied the term in the sense of building class alliances. In his later work, however, hegemony comes to signify a complete fusion of economic, political, intellectual and moral leadership which will be brought about by one fundamental group, and groups allied to it, through ideology (Sarup 1983: 141). Further, hegemony does not imply mere reciprocity or one-sided domination. Its operation is far more subtle as classes struggle to contest for self interest and control. As Sarup explains,

> A hegemonic class is a class that has the ability to articulate the interests of other social groups to its own by means of ideological

> struggle. In order to exercise leadership the class must genuinely concern itself with the interests of those social groups over which it wishes to exercise hegemony. In other words, hegemony is constructed, not by the domination of one class or group, but with the consent of different groups—it is the terrain on which ideological struggle takes place. (1983: 41; original emphasis)

The notion of tacit "consent" among the (antagonistic) classes is perhaps an acknowledgement of the deeply rooted processes of socialization, of power and of indoctrination that characterize modern capitalist society. This aspect of hegemony as deeply saturating the consciousness of a society seems to be fundamental (Apple 1979: 5). As Williams states,

> (Hegemony) is a whole set of practices and expectations; our assignments of energy, our ordinary understanding of the nature of man and of his world. It is a set of meanings and values which as they are experienced as practices appear as reciprocally conforming. It thus constitutes a sense of reality for most people in the society, a sense of absolute . . . (1976: 205)

Thus, effective class struggle necessitates both an *ideological* as well as an *economic* purpose. In this way, we can thereby see that the process of hegemony incorporates a threefold dimension: ideological; cultural; and economic.

Concerning education, this conceptualisation is especially relevant in terms of cultural reproduction which occurs in schools. As Williams puts it: 'The educational institutions are usually the main agencies of the transmission of an effective dominant culture, and this is now a major economic as well as cultural activity . . .' (Williams 1976: 205). Schools perform many functions. They teach students. They socialize students and inculcate knowledge and values. They act also as agents of both cultural and ideological hegemony through the process of selective tradition (Apple 1979: 6). The dominant culture in the school is passed off as the "tradition" or "the significant past" and thus legitimized as the culture that is common to all. The selection process ensures that certain meanings and practices are chosen for emphasis while others are excluded. 'Even more crucially, some of these meanings and practices are reinterpreted, diluted, or put into forms which support or at least do not contradict other elements within the effective dominant culture' (Williams 1976: 205). In this sense, the cultural practices of the dominated classes can be appropriated and reformed so as to aid class oppression, even to the extent of historical omission or misrepresentation. It is this point that is essential in any consideration and analysis of the ideology inherent in textbook content.

HEGEMONIC PROCESSES IN INDIAN EDUCATION

At this juncture, there are three fundamental areas that I wish to address: (i) the role of the State in Indian education; (ii) textbooks and ideology; and (iii) cultural domination and control in schooling.

Following Carnoy (1982), and others, I would agree that schools serve to maintain hegemony. Take the following examples:

> At the process (instrumental) level schools reinforce and consolidate hegemony largely through their own internal logic and procedures. They emphasize things like rule following, punctuality and hierarchy . . . Schools typically reflect their own reward system—both in what kind of thing is rewarded and how it is rewarded—the reward system of capitalism—individual 'payment' for individual work. Through these processes schools reinforce the values of possessive individualism and achievement motivation. And it is important to note that such values are of critical importance not just to 'attitudinally attune' students to the demands of the workplace (which is where Bowles and Gintis place much the greatest emphasis), but also to socialize good consumers and good citizens. [Furthermore] . . . what the country is about is reflected and reinforced in what is taught (and much more in what is *not* taught) in schools, and in their rituals. (Carnoy 1982: 150–151; original emphasis)

Focusing on the structure and processes in Indian education we can appreciate some of the points and issues that Carnoy raises. In the first instance, the State assumes control over the vast majority of schools in India. The State's hegemonic control is therefore exercised in two important areas: (i) in that textbooks and curricula adopted for use in schools are invariably sanctioned by the State (by state appointed committees that ensure the textbooks and curricula contain the essential knowledge for passing state controlled exams); and (ii) because the large majority of schools are sanctioned by the State through their affiliation to particular Boards of Education.

The next important consideration relates to school knowledge. As the majority of textbooks used in Indian schools are state sanctioned then it follows that the information contained in them, as well as their structuring of lessons and stories, are equally state approved. Guidelines for textbook preparation, at the national and regional level, recommend that these textbooks closely follow the ideals laid down in the Indian Constitution and the National Policy on Education (the latest being released in 1986). Essentially these textbooks contain an explicit ideology (in, for example, the fostering of national goals) but also an implicit ideology, or set of ideologies, that either complement these national goals and ideals or, more often than not, are in contradiction to the ideals of fostering equality in education.

Finally, there arises the third issue of cultural domination and control in Indian schooling. My aim in analyzing English language textbooks, below, is to reveal the nature of the ideology that the large majority of the Indian middle class are exposed to. I argue that this identifiable textbook ideology largely serves middle class interests to the detriment of the class and cultural interests of subaltern groups. In other words, the hegemonic function of this ideology is to reproduce the dominance of the middle classes in Indian society.

In summary, the attempt to analyze textbook content is based upon the idea that schools are not merely social, but cultural institutions as well. They are sites where the culture of the dominant classes is established and legitimated and, moreover, this legitimation serves an ideological function of suppressing and marginalizing subaltern culture in the established arrangements of social order and structure of Indian society.

CONTENT ANALYSIS OF SCHOOL TEXTBOOK AND CURRICULUM STUDIES

Recent research in the United States and Europe has revealed many inherent problems in textbook knowledge and curricula content. In the

US, for example, some writers have sought to clarify the relationship between school textbooks and the curriculum to the ideological function of schools in maintaining social class division and social inequality (see Anyon 1981, 1980, 1979a, 1979b, 1978; Lukes, Jenkins and Abernathy 1974; Taxel 1984, 1980, 1978/79; and Popkewitz 1977). Issues of racism, gender and class bias have been addressed in Britain by Dixon (1977a, 1977b) and in the US by Sadker and Sadker (1977). Gilbert's (1984) study of ideology in the social science curriculum in England is noted for its depth of analysis and discussion of the political nature of an ideologically biased curriculum. Luke (1988) has investigated in detail the issues of language, textbooks and ideology while a similarly incisive discussion of the politics of language and literacy has been published by Freire and Macedo (1987). Finally, as an indication of the degree to which interest in textbook and curriculum studies in the West has grown, the recent publication edited by deCastell, Luke and Luke (1989) contains numerous scholarly articles on several aspects of textbook form, knowledge, and production and issues of language, authority and criticism in textbooks.

While many important studies such as those mentioned above have contributed significantly to the sociology of school knowledge in the West, it is disappointing to note the failure of Indian scholars to consider the important contribution of cultural reproduction theory and theories of ideology and dominance in relation to educational inequality. This has been, and continues to be, a significant deficiency in Indian sociology of education research. Just how deficient can be gleaned from the studies conducted by Thirtha and Mukhopadhyay (1974) and Chitnis (1974). While both reviews are of research conducted predominantly during the 1960s and early 1970s, the literature they reviewed shows a strong theoretical bias toward the dominant, structural-functionalist paradigm.

Throughout the 1970s, the Indian research effort was largely confined to liberal perspectives that linked schooling with social inequality.[3] Solutions to the problem were more often than not couched in terms of equality, quality and quantity. However, in recent years there have been a few exceptions, most notably in the area of textbook and curriculum studies.[4] Kalia (1979) shows in what ways Indian textbooks stereotype males and females and thus propagate gender inequality through sexist ideology. He discusses themes in stories like: the images assigned to male and female characters; the sex-ratio of authors; language and anti-feminism; authority relationships; and the occupational role models.

Kumar (1986) stresses the importance of textbooks in India as the basis of thc exam-oriented, educational culture. Elsewhere, he inquires into the role that Indian textbooks perform in the process of child socialization (1981) and again in 1989 (especially ch. 3). He has published important material on issues of power and dominance in the school that function to marginalize lower class students from the learning process. In West Bengal, it has been argued that modern language textbooks reflect the values and experiences of the elite cultural groups, the *bhadralok*,[5] resulting in the working class and peasants becoming culturally alienated from the mainstream education system (Acharya 1986, 1981). Most often in India, however, the research interest in textbooks has been generated by a political controversy in which the new state power had planned to amend the school curriculum and texts to suit their particular political ideology (see, Rudolph and Rudolph 1983; Acharya 1982).[6]

TEXTBOOKS AND CULTURAL REPRODUCTION IN WEST BENGAL, INDIA: A SAMPLE STUDY

Data was collected during fieldwork in Calcutta, West Bengal, India.[7] A number of English language textbooks—primers and readers—were chosen for analysis.[8] English language textbooks were selected for two reasons. First, because mastery of English has now assumed major importance for the middle and upper classes in India, particularly with respect to professional employment, and so maintains class and status differences. Second, language textbooks, as opposed to social studies, history or civics textbooks, were selected because of the importance and stress placed upon reaching a level of literacy, both reading and writing, that is fundamental to all learning. Freire eloquently puts it this way:

> Reading does not consist merely of decoding the written word or language; rather it is preceded by and intertwined with knowledge of the world. Language and reality are dynamically interconnected. (Freire and Macedo 1987: 29)

As mentioned above, English has now become the language of the elite and so perceptions and images of the oppressed classes in these textbooks raise important questions as to the processes which maintain the elite's ideological and cultural, hence hegemonic, dominance particularly as it is this group which will advance into important jobs in government, industry, commerce, the media and education. Thus, understanding the processes of transference of the hegemonic dominance of this class through education is of crucial importance.

The textbook materials gathered for this study are currently in use in both primary and secondary schools in West Bengal. For the purposes of this paper, a qualitative, rather than quantitative, analysis of the textbook content will be undertaken. Importantly, consideration is also given to the textbook silences and omissions. What the textbooks don't say about the life of the subalterns is just as significant as the distortions, stereotypes and ideological bias. Textbooks used in schools affiliated to three Boards of Education (CBSE; WBBSE; ISSC) will be analysed.[9] In all, 195 stories and lessons were analysed.

Textbook Analysis

In order to discern levels of class and cultural bias in the textbook content a number of categories of analysis were chosen. As the results of this analysis form part of a much larger study (Scrase 1989) then I shall restrict my discussion to the following categories: spatial scene; families; recreational activities; and, finally, the subordination of females.

Spatial Scene

The data indicates that, firstly, there is little difference between urban location for scene (18.5 percent) and a combined rural/village category (21.6 percent). This is a significant result. As West Bengal is predominantly a rural or village-based economy and society, and is one in which most of the superior social classes in Bengal reside in district towns and in Calcutta, then the textbook setting would seem to over-emphasize the urban or built environment, the social milieu of the middle and upper classes. In other words, we find an over-representation of urban scene in proportion to the numbers of Bengalis that live in urban areas.

The relatively high proportion of stories in which spatial scene was not detected (22.6 percent) is possibly because textbooks and readers are often deliberately portrayed in vague terms so as not to be unsuitable in any milieu (Kumar 1981: 125, following Weinreich 1978). Other points to make are: (i) of the 11 cases where schools were the location of the story, none were in a village, poor or urban slum school; (ii) regarding the relationship of spatial setting to time, while urban settings are portrayed as contemporary, rural or village scenes are more often set in the past or given an indeterminate status.

What is revealing from the analysis is that many of the middle class stories are enacted across settings. Qualitative analysis of many selections shows that the middle class children, in an urban setting, are often acting outside the confines of their home—in a restaurant, travelling for holidays, in a park, on an excursion. The subalterns, in contrast, are generally shown to be tied to a specific place (their land, village or home) and in a work situation. They are therefore depicted as not exploring outside the confines of their immediate social milieu. If these textbooks did contain more detailed stories of urban working class children then perhaps the situation would be different. Working class children in the course of their everyday activities do encounter varied social contexts. While the middle class children do have frequent access to broader social spaces, such as those engaged during travel, the working class child is likely to be responsible for marketing, running errands, and engaged in some form of wage-labour (for example, as domestic servants). Thus, these children in the urban environment also often experience a wider social context beyond the confines of their family or neighbourhood.

These stories portray the cultural limitations of subalternity contrasted against the limitless experience accorded to the superior social classes. They reflect an ideology of confined subaltern culture by restricting them to an established, one-dimensional setting (further emphasized by historical or indeterminate status) rather than showing them in places like schools or going on pilgrimages and to festivals (this point is elaborated upon in the section on "recreation" below). The reality for rural Bengalis is that they do drop out of school, do not travel, and are tied to the land. Youth that I met in a rural town (Krishnanagar) often expressed the desire to travel. A day in Calcutta was considered a luxury, yet it was only one hundred kilometres away. In one sense, at least, it was their economic situation that restricted their movements.

The culture of the rural Bengalis is constructed around their immediate lifestyle, just as it is for the middle and upper classes. The difference is that for reasons of higher income and residential location, the immediate lifestyle for the dominant classes is more broadly based and culturally more exposing (because, for example, they reside in an urbanized, multi-faceted environment). Here we can comprehend the idea of the socio-spatial dialectic (see Soja 1989: ch. 3). For the peasant, it is the dialectic between the natural environment and the mode of production which confines and restricts them to the landscape in which their labour is undertaken. This spatial confinement results in closely tied social groupings (of caste, kin and ethnicity) and hence a more limited (though not necessarily demeaning) cultural and world view.

Families

The family in India was, until recently, based on the joint or extended family model in which two, or perhaps three, generations lived under the one roof. Family authority was vested in the senior male household heads. The family was patriarchal, with property being inherited through the male line. Other manifestations of patriarchal forms included male members assuming preference over females in activities like eating meals first, gaining an education, or paid employment. Today, however, the joint family has been substantially eroded, especially in urban centres and rural towns. Male authority and patriarchy are still strong but the exercise of that power is varied as women of the professional classes move to join nuclear families, and also because of changes in the authority structure within the joint family (see Liddle and Joshi 1986: ch. 19). The main point to consider, therefore, is the changing nature of the family, and questions of family authority and power. The textbooks and readers, to a limited extent, implicitly and explicitly discuss the nature of Indian families.

The total number of stories in which family relationships were discussed or present was only fifty-eight (29.7 percent). Well over half of these reflected the nuclear family situation. Considering the importance placed upon the family for childhood socialization in India then it could be expected that families would appear in a greater proportion of selections. Looking at family authority and power, the selections tend to reflect the established patterns. Children are portrayed as subservient to their parents with respect to obedience, helping out when told, and taking advice. Girls are portrayed as relatively docile, participating in house-work, doing homework, and playing non-physical games. Adult women are stereotyped as care-givers, and undertaking domestic labour, which is in contrast to adult men who are more often than not giving advice, disciplining, or assisting with study.

The stories focusing on middle class families tend to show them in a variety of activities such as taking holidays, going on a picnic, or having parties. Parents are depicted taking an interest in their children's study. Middle class children generally appear as happy and content with their home and among their family. This view fits well with the established middle class lifestyle. In contrast, the subaltern classes are rarely portrayed in situations outside the context of their labour. Some exceptions do appear ("The Harvest Festival") but even in this example, the festival is intrinsically connected to their labour (i.e. harvesting the crop).

Single parent families, or families in a crisis, are rarely portrayed. The textbooks tend to deny that the problems facing families do exist. The stereotyping of the ideal, happy family is not only common to Indian textbooks. Sadker and Sadker (1977: 21) see this neglect as a major problem in US children's textbooks and literature. The problem is that the textbook writers tend to offer the ideal norm, rather than the realism of daily life. Thus, stories can be negatively interpreted, in an emotional sense, especially for the more senior Indian school children, as the ideals that they see portrayed do not reflect the reality of family conflict and problems in their home life. The children in the stories are rarely shown resolving conflict; rather their life and decisions are determined by their parents or others in authority. When they do act on their own, it usually results in a mistake and they are then made to feel foolish and to seek forgiveness. This type of portrayal thus creates a sense of dependency by defining the identity of the child through elders.

Recreational Activities

The analysis of recreational and leisure pursuits also added to an overall cultural framing of the textbooks. Activities like playing sport with equipment (e.g. cricket), travelling, undertaking hobbies and reading were most commonly represented. Other, less common forms of activity shown in the textbooks include: walking in a park or garden; playing a flute; singing with a guitar; story-telling; watching television; writing to pen friends; telling jokes; exploring a beach; swimming in a pool; painting and drawing; knitting; playing cards. Forms of recreational activities associated with religious festivals and pujas were seldom presented. This point will be addressed shortly.

Overall there appears a class and sexist bias reflected in the leisure activities and these mirror some of the wider societal divisions. Equipment, in the form of bats, balls, and toys is often shown (17 percent). Moreover, equipment is most often utilised by boys. My visits during fieldwork to two contrasting schools (elite and poor neighbourhood school) also serves to highlight these biasses. At the elite school in Calcutta, physical education was part of the curricula. This form of organized exercise involved both general exercise, and sport utilizing equipment (e.g. cricket; tennis). Recreation in this case was not only for reasons of improving health, but instilled discipline and a sense of working together (e.g. in team sports). The poor, local school in the town of Krishnanagar did not conduct physical education. During recess the children would play games in the small dirt yard.

Gender segregation was obvious. The boys played "tag" or marbles and the girls skipped or chatted. The games did not incorporate any equipment, mainly because it was too expensive.

In the textbooks, play without equipment usually centres around a family gathering, is set in someone's house or garden, and sometimes involves taking part in Western-style party games. Stamp-collecting and reading, two popular middle class activities that require expense (for the stamps and books) and time (to actually read) are mentioned on a number of occasions. Travel is represented in nine cases but does not involve members from the rural classes (for instance, there is not one story about pilgrimage). On the whole, girls are under-represented in recreational activities (35 percent) and, when they are present, they are displayed in passive activities like knitting and painting. Few indigenous forms of activity and recreation are presented.

Drama, dance, art, festivals, plays and music have a pivotal role in the process of cultural unification and celebration in India (see Lannoy 1971: 190–98). These forms of cultural expression are usually divided between the Little Tradition (folk culture) and the Great Tradition (classical culture). Lannoy argues that:

> Brahmins generally acted as patrons, supervisors, teachers, choreographers, 'script writers', but were also performers, particularly in the Sanskrit media belonging to the Great Tradition. On the other hand, vernacular cultural bearers and cultural performers of the Little Tradition were generally representatives of a caste such as potters, weavers, basket-makers. (1971: 190–191)

In relation to Bengali society, Ostor (1984) discusses the significance of *purana, jatra, puja* (myth, theatre, and ritual) and its relevance to the process of indigenous cultural formation.

The essential point here is that the textbook omissions reflect the continual disintegration of indigenous forms of recreation, leisure and celebration. The marginalization of folk culture, music and handicrafts (except of course when its ascetic value appeals to the consumer public) is occurring at the same time as other forms of artistic expression like classical dance and music are losing their allure.

Women, Girls and Subordination

Much international research has been undertaken in the past decade on the issue of women in school textbooks (see also the related chapter by Branson and Miller in this volume). The findings from these studies range from blatant and derogatory levels of sexism in textbooks (Kalia 1986), to more subtle, but equally offensive, material which present the female in a marginal role not merely by limited characterizations, but

> . . . when those few female characters are analyzed by type of role and activity, themes of passivity, weakness are consistently associated with women involved in frivolous social or home nurturing activities. (Biraimah 1982: 163)

Extensive research views the transmission of gender inequality in schools as an all-encompassing process in which school authorities, curriculum, and teachers all play a direct, and indirect, part in promoting sexism and patriarchal attitudes (see Arnot and Weiner 1987).

In my textbook sample, women and girls are generally confined to the home. In addition, the discrimination of women is occasionally overt, but more often than not it is subtly inferred. For instance, one story, "Looking For Mother", outwardly portrays the theme of kindness to animals:

> . . . A bird flew into the room. It flew around the room. And it flew out of the room. It flew to a tree.
>
> "That's the mother bird", said Mona's mother. "She's looking for her baby".
>
> Mona ran out of the house to the tree. She saw a nest on the tree. She ran back to her mother.
>
> "Mother! Mother!" said Mona. "There's a nest on that tree".
>
> "Let's put the baby in the nest", said Mona's mother.
>
> Mona and her mother took the baby bird to the tree. Mona's mother put the baby bird in the nest.
>
> "Tweet, tweet", said the mother bird. "Tweet, tweet", said the two baby birds.
>
> "They are saying 'Thank you'," said Mona's mother.

Thus, the mother bird is back where she belongs—in the care of her baby birds in the nest. The hidden ideology in the story is somewhat more revealing especially as it subtly reinforces the traditional domestic relationship. The (Indian) mother should be at home looking after her children. Children must be cared for and looked after by their mothers. Danger lies ahead for the children if the mother is not at home with them.

A more realistic representation of women's oppression is found in the story "Mr. Hossain's Family". Mr. Hossain is a school teacher and he is pictured reading a newspaper while his wife and daughter are together in the kitchen preparing a meal:

> . . . Mr. Hossain's wife, Satera, does everything in the house. She cleans the rooms, washes the clothes, and cooks the food. She gets up before sunrise and works throughout the day. She keeps their house very neat and clean.
>
> Zareen, their daughter, gets up quite early, too. She helps her mother in the kitchen. She makes tea and helps her mother to prepare breakfast . . .

Unlike some stories that have a sexist innuendo, this story comes straight out and describes the hard work of the mother. The realism in the story is perhaps meant to draw the students' attention to the difficulty of a mother's life. I would think that the opposite would occur. It was especially disappointing, but perhaps expected, that the questions following this story were not at all to do with the plight of the mother nor designed to generate sympathy for the fact that the mother laboured from early morning to late at night. Moreover, unless the students had a conscious teacher this story, like so many others, would reinforce the taken-for-granted attitude that is so often accorded to women.

The need to focus on sexism as a separate issue in the textbooks stems from a desire to uncover the contradictory aspects in educational policy, bias in textbook writing and wider gender inequality in Indian society and culture. The woman in Bengali society is both admired and abused. In one sense, the adoration of "womanliness", femininity, stems from the ideal of the mother as the unifying force in the family (see Lannoy 1971). However, the subjugation of women to daily forms of exploitation within and outside the home negates this position. This ideological dualism, materialising from the social arrangements of power and authority, saturates Indian society at large. Furthermore, I would contend that exploitation in society is expressed both openly, such as in labour discrimination or sexual abuse, and ideologically, in forms of textual meaning and representation. The textbook image of the happy and dutiful housewife contests the notion that her position in that role results more from her exploitation as a woman than from any inner desire to be a good wife and mother—unemployed and confined to the home. The subordinate role of the woman in Indian society emerges from the combination of complex religious values, societal attitudes and a patriarchal ideology that has formed, and is re-formed, constantly over many decades. The school contributes to the process of reproducing and maintaining such ideologies by essentially promoting male-centred, authoritarian culture.

In analyzing the textbooks the data indicate that women are still by and large accorded a marginalized and passive role in Indian society. Their discrimination is realized through stereotypes ranging from caring and compassionate (which should also be attributed to male characters more often) to those in low-value employment and labour. Overall, women are pictured as subservient and external to the majority of plots, scenes and overall narrative in the textbooks.

SUMMARY OF FINDINGS

A number of issues and arguments have been raised in the discussions above. Settings are constructed in such a way as to reproduce the fact that middle class Indians have a wide social experience and that this experience contributes to their overall cultural formation. This is in contrast to the subaltern classes, whose cultural reproduction is determined by their labour and their immediate social environment. The portrayal of families in the textbooks is relatively infrequent and the nuclear-conjugal family is the type most commonly presented. Recreational activities are extremely gender specific and notable is the absence of indigenous forms of art and leisure. Finally, it was noted that the portrayal of women is highly stereotypical and patriarchal, with the textbooks reproducing the subservient role of women and girls in areas like employment and recreation, as well as in the home.

To a degree, these images reflect the present social hierarchy of prestige and power in India. In the first instance, they represent a hegemonic determination in that the culture of the subaltern classes is narrowly represented. In the second instance, they reproduce established forms of power and authority. The cultural codes embedded in the texts signify the dominance of males over females, middle class over subaltern classes. The middle class imagery espoused is now the dominant form of cultural expression in India. However, the basis of its determination lies in the elements of residual cultural formation defined by, for instance, the traditional view of male dominance over females, of mental over manual labour, of high culture over folk culture.

CONCLUDING REMARKS

The culture of the elite and middle class are constantly reproduced in the textbooks. This presentation is hegemonically defined in the sense that opposing cultural images are not accorded equal status and, as such, are not legitimated in the eyes of the dominant classes. This hegemonic process that in turn legitimates the dominant culture operates at two levels; overtly, in the sense of bias, stereotype and distortion of proletarian culture; and covertly through omission and silences of proletarian culture in the textbook content.

As I mentioned earlier, hegemony incorporates a threefold dimension incorporating ideological, cultural and economic factors. In order to understand fully the relationship between the hegemonic process and educational inequality (through social and cultural reproduction), in India, then one would need to examine and discuss at length the nature of present Indian social structure. As space precludes such an in-depth analysis, then I would like instead to offer a few thoughts on how an examination of textbook content can contribute to an understanding of what is known as cultural hegemony.

Firstly, in the sense of ideology, textbook content is ideological in that it forwards a particular world view that is more often than not held by the dominant Indian social classes. In the case of Bengali society, this world view is held commonly by the *bhadralok*[5] and the middle classes. English language proficiency is an important factor as, in the case of the former group, it maintains social status and, for the latter, it is a means to obtain respectable, relatively well paid, white-collar employment. Consequently, this also increases the status of this group through their ability to acquire material (mainly Western) possessions. Indeed, as capitalism continues to transform Indian society then the older, traditional factors that delineate class and status are being replaced by modern, capitalist-derived ones. For instance, the institution of caste, particularly in urban centres, now plays a less important role as a status maintainer. However, the ideological component of caste distinction indirectly continues through social and cultural institutions like education. Mass schooling has resulted in increasing enrolments of lower class students at the primary level, although completion rates above Grade VI are still dismal. As we have seen, however, textbook content discriminates widely against the social and cultural interests of this group. In many cases this is an extension of pre-modern, ideological caste distinction. The idea that peasant and manual labour is demeaned has its roots in the caste ideology that places the Brahmin on top of the occupational, hence social ladder (see, for example, Dumont 1972; Srinivas 1962). For Brahmins, their social distinction was, and is, maintained through their aversion to manual labour. As capitalism penetrates Indian society, caste barriers are removed. Social class, in turn, then becomes a more prominent factor of social division. The ideological component of caste, therefore, has merely adjusted to new forms in order to maintain the power of the dominant social classes. This process continues ultimately into the economic and cultural sphere.

The Indian economy has continued to industrialise and mechanise rapidly since World War II. New technologies developed in India and elsewhere have contributed to this growth, and in the 1980s computer technology has become a central component in planning and development. Estimates of the number of Indians engaged in middle class occupations are now put at one hundred million. Development and growth in modern India now more than ever rests upon excellence in manufacturing and commercial enterprise rather than upon the skills of the village artisan or peasant cultivator. In terms of textbook content, there seems to be a direct relationship between the positive contribution of modern Indian lifestyle and the negatively portrayed, traditional social and economic modes of living. Their generally positive portrayal of a middle class, comfortable lifestyle set against the negative imagery accorded to peasants and manual workers serves to re-affirm their economic, hence dominant class position in Indian society. Covertly, it promotes the value of modern capitalist forms of labour and production in contributing to the growth of India while alternatively implying that traditional forms are either impractical or not socially significant. This is borne out, for instance, in stories which portray peasants as irresponsible and foolish. One does not expect such people to be the captains of industry, or in the "important" jobs as administrators, clerks, teachers, or computer programmers and hence, directly involved in the building of the modern Indian economy.

Finally, the textbook content elucidated both ideological and economic components which combine to continue the process of cultural hegemony. It is hegemonic in the sense that oppositional forms of ideology or economic rationalism are not presented. Furthermore, it is culturally hegemonic as the textbook content evokes a moral picture of the positive elements of the culture of the dominant social classes at work and in their leisure pursuits. The structure of the Indian education system, with its rigid curriculum and examination system, its factory-like training of teachers, and its reliance upon textbooks such as those that I have analysed, ultimately means that counter-hegemonic practices are severely limited. Of course, many teachers do attempt to circumvent the restrictive structures imposed upon them. Yet many more take the easy way out and continue to allow the textbook to teach for them.

There are obviously no easy solutions as the education system is but one of the numerous social institutions that maintain the social and cultural dominance of the elite and the middle class. Therefore, this chapter has attempted to introduce and address an educational problem rather than present any fixed ideas on its solution. The task for comparative educators must be one that is imbued with a sense of critical awareness of the ideological constructs in Third World societies. Not to recognise these constructs when attempting to resolve educational problems may indeed only lead to the creation of new and more complex dilemmas.

NOTES

1. Discussion of reproduction theory, and of issues relating to the sociology of school knowledge, may be found in: Apple (1982a); Apple and Weis (1985); Carnoy (1982); Green (1986); Olson (1981); Walker (1986).

2. As Williams has elaborated, residual culture means:

> . . . that some experiences, meanings and values which cannot be verified or cannot be expressed in terms of the dominant culture, are nevertheless lived and practised on the basis of the residue—cultural as well as social—of some previous social formation. (1976: 206)

On the other hand, emergent culture as he puts it means:

> . . . that new meanings and values, new practices, new significances and experiences, are continually being created . . . We have to see, first as it were, a temporal relation between a dominant culture and on the one hand a residual and on the other hand an emergent culture. But we can only understand this if we can make distinctions, that usually require very precise analysis, between residual-incorporated and residual not incorporated, and between emergent incorporated and emergent not incorporated. (1976: 206)

3. For a useful summary of this conceptual approach see: Naik (1975).

4. See also: Ehsanul-Haq (1976); Kakar (1971).

5. The *bhadralok*, literally "respectable people", are considered to be the cultural elite in Bengali society. They are mainly the Westernized, Hindu middle class who dominate Bengal's cultural and political life. With respect to their special relationship to education, Broomfield argues that as they were the bearers of learning, the custodians of art, the interpreters of philosophy doctrine then as a natural consequence they set great store by education (Broomfield 1968: 232). In modern Bengali society it is the *bhadralok* who are now experiencing a decline in their status as a more materialist, middle class consumer culture emerges.

6. Altbach (1987, 1983) provides further insights into problems of textbooks in the Third World. See also Kumar (1986) for a discussion on

textbooks in Indian education. A special edition of *Social Education* (1986) contains a variety of interesting articles on global education and textbooks.

7. Fieldwork was carried out between December 1986 and April 1987 in Calcutta. Part of the fieldwork expenses were funded by a research grant from the La Trobe University, School of Education.

8. The texts are: New Radiant Readers Books 1–4, Allied Publishers, 1986; Adventures in Reading Books 2b-5, Oxford University Press, 1984; English Reader-Special Series Books 1–3, NCERT, New Delhi, 1986; Books IV-V, NCERT, New Delhi, 1985; Let's Learn English-Special Series Books 103, NCERT, New Delhi, 1986. Using Good English Books 1–4, Allied Publishers, 1986; Learning English Step 1–4, West Bengal Board of Secondary Education, Calcutta, 1983; Read for Pleasure Books I-V, NCERT, New Delhi, 1986.

9. The abbreviations are: CBSE—Central Board of Secondary Education; WBBSE—West Bengal Board of Secondary Education; ISCC—Indian School Certificate Course.

REFERENCES

Acharya, P. (1986) 'Development of Modern Language Text-Books and the Social Context of 19th Century Bengal'. *Economic and Political Weekly* XXI (17).

Acharya, P. (1982) 'Abolition of English at Primary Level in West Bengal'. *Economic and Political Weekly* XVII (4).

Acharya, P. (1981) 'Politics of Primary Education in West Bengal—The Case of Sahaj Path'. *Economic and Political Weekly* XVI (24).

Altbach, P.G. (1987) 'The Oldest Technology: textbooks in comparative perspective'. *Compare* 17 (2).

Altbach, P.G. (1983) 'Key issues of textbook provision in the Third World'. *Prospects* XIII (3).

Altbach, P.G., Arnove, R., and Kelly, G.P. (eds.) (1983) *Comparative Education*. New York and London, Macmillan.

Anyon, J. (1981) 'Social Class and School Knowledge'. *Curriculum Inquiry* 11 (1).

Anyon, J. (1980) 'Social Class and the Hidden Curriculum of Work'. *Journal of Education* 162 (Winter).

Anyon, J. (1979a) 'Ideology and United States History Textbooks'. *Harvard Education Review* 49 (3).

Anyon, J. (1979b) 'Education, Social Structure and the Power of Individuals'. *Theory and Research in Social Education* 7 (1).

Anyon, J. (1978) 'Elementary Social Studies Textbooks and Legitimating Knowledge'. *Theory and Research in Social Education* 6 (3).

Apple, M. (ed.) (1982) *Cultural and Economic Reproduction in Education*, London, Routledge and Kegan Paul.

Apple, M. (1982) 'Reproduction and Contradiction in Education: an Introduction'. In Apple (1982, ibid).

Apple, M. (1979) *Ideology and Curriculum*. London, Routledge.

Apple, M. and Weis, L. (1985) 'Ideology and Schooling'. *Education and Society* 3 (1).

Arnot, M. and Weiner, G (eds.) (1987) *Gender and the Politics of Schooling*. London, Hutchinson, in collaboration with the Open University Press.

Bernstein, B. (1971) *Class, Codes and Control—Vol.3: Towards a Theory of Educational Transmissions* (2nd ed.). London, Routledge and Kegan Paul.

Biraimah, K. (1982) 'Different Knowledge for Different Folks: Knowledge Distribution in a Togolese Secondary School'. In Altbach, Arnove and Kelly (eds.), ibid.

Bourdieu, P. (1977a) 'Cultural Reproduction and Social Reproduction'. In J. Karabel and A.H. Halsey (eds.), *Power and Ideology in Education*. New York, Oxford Review Press.

Bourdieu, P. (1977b) *Outline of a Theory of Practice*. London, Cambridge University Press.

Bourdieu, P. and Passeron, J.C. (1977) *Reproduction in Education, Society and Culture*. London, Sage.

Bowles, S. and Gintis, H. (1976) *Schooling in Capitalist America*. London, Routledge and Kegan Paul.

Broomfield, J. (1968) "The Non-Cooperation Decision of 1920'. In D. Low (ed.), *Soundings in Modern South Asian History*. Berkeley, University of California Press.

Carnoy, M. (1982) 'Education, Economy and the State'. In M. Apple (ed.), *Cultural and Economic Reproduction in Education*. London, Routledge.

Carnoy, M. (1974) *Education as Cultural Imperialism*. New York, David McKay Inc.

Chitnis, S. (1974) 'Sociology of Education: A Trend Report'. In *A Survey of Research in Sociology and Social Anthropology Vol. 2*. New Delhi, Indian Council for Social Science Research.

de Castell, S., Luke, A. and Luke, C. (eds.) (1989) *Language, Authority and Criticism: Readings on the School Textbook*. London, The Falmer Press.

Dixon, Bob (1977a) *Catching Them Young 1: Sex, Race and Class in Children's Fiction*. London, Pluto Press.

Dixon, Bob (1977b) *Catching Them Young 2: Political Ideas in Children's Fiction*. London, Pluto Press.

Dumont, L. (1972) *Homo Hierarchicus*. London, Paladin.

Ehsanul-Haq (1976) 'Sociology of Curriculum: the Role of School Textbooks in Nation Building'. *Indian Educational Review* 11 (1).

Freire, P., and Macedo, D. (1987) *Literacy: Reading the Word and the World*. Massachusetts, Bergin and Garvey

Gilbert, Rob (1984) *The Impotent Image: Reflections on Ideology in the Secondary School Curriculum*. London, The Falmer Press.

Giroux, H. (1983) *Theory and Resistance in Education*. London, Heinemann.

Government of India, Ministry for Human Resources Development (1986) *National Policy on Educatio*. New Delhi.

Gramsci, A. (1971) *Selections from Prison Notebooks* (ed. and trans. Quinten Hoare and Geoffrey Smith). New York, International Publishers.

Green, B. (1986) 'Reading Reproduction Theory: On the Ideology-and-Education Debate'. *Discourse* 6 (2).

Kalia, Narendra Nath (1986) 'Women and Sexism: Language of Indian School Textbooks'. *Economic and Political Weekly* XXI (17).

Kalia, Narendra Nath (1979) *Sexism in India Education-The Lies We Tell Our Children*. New Delhi, Vikas Publishers.

Kakar, S. (1971) 'The Theme of Authority in Social Relations in India'. *The Journal of Social Psychology* 184.

Kelly, Gail P. and Nihlen, Ann S. (1982) 'Schooling and the Reproduction of Patriarchy: Unequal Workloads, Unequal Rewards'. In M. Apple (ed.) ibid.

Kumar, Krishna (1989) *Social Character of Learning*. New Delhi, Sage.

Kumar, Krishna (1986) 'Textbooks and Educational Culture'. *Economic and Political Weekly* XXI (30).

Kumar, Krishna (1981) 'Literature in the School Curriculum: A Comparative Study of the Library Materials Approved for Use in Grades Four, Five and Six in Madhya Pradesh, India, and Toronto, Canada'. Unpublished PhD Thesis, University of Toronto.

Lannoy, Richard (1971) *The Speaking Tree: A Study of Indian Society and Culture*. New York, Oxford.

Liddle, Joanna and Joshi, Rama (1986) *Daughters of Independence: Gender, Caste and Class in India*. London, Zed Books.

Luke, Alan (1988) *Literacy, Textbooks and Ideology*. Lewes, Sussex, The Falmer Press.

Lukes, W., Jenkins, F., and Abernathy, L. (1974) 'Elementary School Basal Readers and the Work Mode Bias'. *Journal of Economic Education* 5 (2).

MacDonald, M. (1980) 'Socio-Cultural Reproduction and Women's Education'. In Rosemary Deem (ed.), *Schooling for Women's Work*. London, Routledge.

McRobbie, Angela (1980) 'Settling Accounts With Subcultures'. *Screen Education* 34.

Michaelson, Karen L. (1983) 'Education and the Reproduction of Social Hierarchy: Bombay'. In Gira Raj Gupta (ed.), *Main Currents in Indian Sociology, Vol. 4—Urban India*, New Delhi, Vikas.

Miller, D. and Branson, J. (1987) 'Pierre Bourdieu: Culture and Praxis'. In D. Austin-Broos (ed.), *Creating Culture*. Sydney, Allen and Unwin.

Naik, J.P. (1975) *Equality, Quality and Quantity: The Elusive Triangle in Indian Education*. Bombay, Allied Publishers.

Olson, P. (1981) 'Laboring to Learn: How Working Theory Gets Down to Classroom and Kids'. *Interchange* 12 (2).

Ostor, Akos (1984) *Culture and Power: Legend, Ritual, Bazaar and Rebellion in a Bengali Society*. New Delhi, Sage.

Popkewitz, T.S. (1977) 'The Latent Values of the Discipline Centred Curriculum'. *Theory and Research in Social Education* 5 (1).

Rudolph, L., and Rudolph, S. (1983) 'Rethinking Secularism: Genesis and Implications of the Textbook Controversy, 1977–1979'. *Pacific Affairs* 56 (1).

Sadker, M.P., and Sadker, D.M. (1977) *Now Upon a Time: A Contemporary iew of Children's Literature*. New York, Harper and Row.

Sarup, M. (1983) *Marxism, Structuralism and Education: Theoretical Developments in the Sociology of Education*. London, Falmer Press.

Scrase, Timothy J. (1989) 'Image, Ideology and Inequality: An Examination of Social and Cultural Reproduction in School Textbooks From West Bengal, India'. Unpublished PhD Thesis, Centre for Comparative and International Studies in Education, La Trobe University, Melbourne, Australia.

Shapiro, Svi (1988) 'Beyond the Sociology of Education: Culture, Politics and the Promise of Educational Change'. *Educational Theory* 38 (4).

Social Education (1986) Special Number: 'Global Education and Textbooks' 50 (5).

Soja, Edward W. (1989) *Postmodern Geographies: The Reassertion of Space in Critical Social Theory*. London, Verso.

Srinivas, M.N. (1962) *Caste in Modern India and Other Essays*. Bombay, Popular Prakashan.

Taxel, J. (1984) 'The American Revolution in Childrens Fiction: An Analysis of Historical Meaning and Narrative Structure'. *Curriculum Inquiry* 14 (1).

Taxel, J. (1980) 'The Depiction of the American Revolution in Children's Fiction: A Study in the Sociology of School Knowledge'. Unpublished PhD Thesis, University of Wisconsin, Madison.

Taxel, J. (1978–79) 'Justice and Cultural Conflict: Racism, Sexism and Instructional Materials'. *Interchange* 9 (1).

Thirtha, N. and Mukhopadhyay, M. (1974) 'Sociology of Education: A Trend Report'. In M. Buch (ed.) *A Survey of Research in Education*. Baroda, Centre of Advanced Study in Education.

Walker, J.C. (1986) 'Romanticising Resistance, Romanticising Culture: Problems in Willis's Theory of Cultural Production'. *British Journal of Sociology of Education* 7 (1).

Williams, R. (1976) 'Base and Superstructure in Marxist Cultural Theory'. In R. Dale et al. (eds.), *Schooling and Capitalism: A Sociological Reader*. London, Routledge and Kegan Paul.

Willis, P. (1981) 'Cultural Production is Different from Cultural Reproduction Is Different from Social Reproduction Is Different from Reproduction'. *Interchange* 12 (2–3).

Willis, P. (1977) *Learning to Labour*. Aldershot, Gower.

Ethnic Diversity and Multicultural Education

KEITH SIMKIN AND EMMANUEL GAUCI

La Trobe University

•

Department of Labour, Victoria

INTRODUCTION

The responses by educational institutions in Australia to ethnic and cultural diversity, the result of 200 years of immigration to a continent peopled by Aborigines, have collectively been given the label of multicultural education. What the label actually means for educational practice and what kind of society this type of education is supposed to produce are issues of keen debate.

It is useful to try to characterise educational responses by looking at what the various State educational authorities in Australia recommend for schools in terms of purpose, structures and programs: their multicultural education policy statements. Because of the variation between these policy statements, however, it is necessary to turn to comparative education to try to identify appropriate criteria with which to locate Australian responses in terms that are comparable to responses in other parts of the world. In the final section of the chapter, the relationships of multicultural education policy responses, academic comparative educational research and actual school practice are examined to show the gaps that exist between each.

INSTITUTIONAL RESPONSES TO ETHNIC DIVERSITY

Australia has a federal political system, with most of the responsibility for the provision of education falling to the various States and Territories. Consequently, we have to look to the States' policy statements on multicultural education to assess the range of educational responses to ethnic diversity and to establish any commonality. In 1987 the National Advisory and Co-ordinating Committee's report, *Education in and for a Multicultural Society* (NACCME 1987) set out a response to diversity at the Federal level: but like the States' multicultural policy statements, this document is hortatory rather than binding in terms of both policy and practice. Similarly, its definition of ethnic diversity excludes for the most part reference to Australia's Aboriginal people. This separation is a common feature of policies and programs at Commonwealth and State levels. In this paper the focus is on multicultural rather than Aboriginal policies.

State educational authorities throughout Australia have tackled the issue of multiculturalism in a variety of ways: through policy statements, the provision of specialist or new services at school and at system level, or through the incorporation of multicultural concerns within the daily practice of relevant support staff.

The analysis of these policy statements is based on three questions. How do educational authorities conceptualise the problem? Whose problem is it? How is it proposed to resolve the problem? The emphasis here is on the translation of multiculturalism into educational rhetoric and practice. This analysis recognises that, as a relatively new concept in the Australian educational sphere, multiculturalism is considered problematic and attempts to define its implications for educational practice have therefore been seen as resolutions of a "problem".

(i) Definition of the problem

Multicultural education is generally understood to be about the preservation of social cohesion: despite cultural diversity, Australia has to remain a stable, united, cohesive society. Cultural diversity is the sticking point. Having recognised that it exists, what do authorities do with it? Australian educational authorities do not consider the unbridled promotion of cultural pluralism desirable. Limits must be placed around its development to protect society: for example, 'the New South Wales Government is committed to fostering and promoting multiculturalism in the context of a cohesive democratic society' (1983: 1).

Within this framework, authorities differ in the way in which they perceive cultural diversity. For some, the task is the resolution of potential or existing tensions:

> All Queensland State schools must help all children cope with the realities of living in such a society; secure in their own personal and cultural identities and tolerant of those of others; but aware of the strains and tensions implicit in multiculturalism and conscious of their responsibility to contribute to the national identity in the changing and growing 'common culture'. (Queensland 1979)

> Multicultural education must thus address this paradox: the need to maintain and sustain the striving for identity without sacrificing equity and justice, or jeopardising the integration of all groups in the common political and moral order of society. (NACCME 1987: 21)

For others, diversity is seen as a constant feature of Australian society, one that 'can be utilised and developed for the national good' (Tasmania 1988: 1). For example:

> Education in, and for, a multicultural society is built on two basic principles: it accepts that past and present diversity is a significant influence on Australia's development and it demonstrates a commitment to fostering linguistic and cultural diversity within a cohesive society. (Victoria 1987: 6)

> The principles of multiculturalism described here emerge from a broad view of multiculturalism as a social philosophy. The major elements of this philosophy are linked to the value which is placed upon the fact of linguistic and cultural diversity in our society and the need to maintain it; the wish for a cohesive but resilient society through common and shared understandings; and the acceptance of all citizens to participate in decisions and to have equitable access to social outcomes and services. (South Australia 1987)

Implicit in these policy statements is a view about culture and social change. Very few statements explicitly define the term "culture". A generous interpretation would be that authorities recognise that "culture" is a dynamic rather than static phenomenon. The best explicit definition of the term is in the Victorian policy:

> The concept of culture embedded in multiculturalism as described in this paper is broad and dynamic. Culture is not static and unchanging. It is not composed solely of rituals or objects nor is it a discrete entity that some people have and others do not. Culture is created and expressed throughout the complex range of social experiences of all groups and individuals. Differing life experiences and perceptions result in individuals and groups developing a variety of cultural understandings and behaviours. (Victoria 1987: 5)

On the other hand, authorities have very clear expectations about the nature and direction of social change within a multicultural Australia. The development of a "common culture" or a "cohesive society" involves a progressive change in values and behaviours. While all statements pay lip service to the importance of building tolerance and understanding of cultural differences (new values for Australian society?), there is nonetheless a clear expectation that Australia's "common culture", its democratic framework, its moral and political order, will remain largely unaltered. The Tasmanian draft statement, for example, encourages in students 'the development of cultural understanding and linguistic competence which will equip them for full participation in Australian society' (1988: 2). This involves, among other things, 'meeting the individual needs of all students, . . . recognising the importance of cultural heritage and identity for the development in all students of a source of personal worth and self-esteem' (1988: 3). Similarly, the Northern Territory policy lists as one of its aims 'encouraging children to understand the culture of their own background and its relevance to Australian society' (Bull and Tons 1985: 69).

The Western Australian Multicultural Education Committee's statement perhaps best expresses this view:

> Social cohesion is assisted by the acknowledgement of a set of core or common values which make individuals uniquely Australian. These include acceptance of the following:
>
> * English as the working language of the nation
> * western style parliamentary democracy as the most desirable system of government
> * freedom of each individual to pursue social objectives and economic opportunities to the maximum extent possible
> * the right of others to express opinions, practise beliefs which are acceptable to society as a whole and promote their views
> * the English system of common law. (WAMEC 1986: 7)

It is not surprising therefore that there is little explicit discussion of racism, it being subsumed by debate on cultural diversity, tolerance and understanding. While a number of authorities, e.g. ACT, South Australia and Victoria, make direct reference to racism, prejudice and to the Aboriginal component of Australian society, there is no sustained discussion in these documents of the nature of racism in Australian society nor of the way in which multicultural education can move beyond acceptance of cultural diversity towards a more active anti-racist education. The exception to this trend has been the 1987 NACCME report which discusses curricular strategies to combat racism, but this perspective is not developed nearly as far as in ILEA policy statements (Cole 1986).

Finally, few policy statements recognise the structural concomitants of minority status, what NACCME describes as the "equity element". In its most blunt form, minority status is synonymous with educational and economic disadvantage, with limited access to and problematic participation in education and subsequently in the workforce. In most cases, where disadvantage is recognised in the documents it is seen to be due to a limited knowledge of the English language. The South Australian, West Australian and Tasmanian policy statements identify the importance of promoting equity for the individual to achieve educational access and outcomes. The Victorian and NACCME statements present a stronger argument, linking equity with cultural diversity and identity:

> Education in, and for, a multicultural society aims to improve the life-chances and options of all students. If educational opportunities are to be equitable, *all* students must be provided with appropriate experiences at school. Curriculum planning that does not acknowledge the past and present diversity of Australian society disadvantages students. It does not equip them with the knowledge and ability to participate in a multicultural society. In addition, many students suffer because their out-of-school experiences are ignored and devalued or dismissed. (Victoria 1986: 6)

Summarising, multiculturalism is perceived to be about containing and directing cultural diversity to preserve Australian society. The problem for education authorities is to ensure that while individual cultural heritages are respected and tolerance encouraged, there is nonetheless a recognition and promotion of Australia's core values. The potential for multicultural education to contribute to the development of a more equitable and less racist society has been largely ignored.

(ii) Ownership

> Because of its broadly educative goals, multicultural education, in contrast to migrant education, is considered to be a concern for all schools and all students: Multicultural education is not a separate subject in schools and colleges; rather, it should form an integral part of all aspects of the curriculum. Nor is it a programme only for immigrants; it has relevance for all Australians, irrespective of age and heritage. (Western Australia 1981: 1)

This is a commonly held position about what *should* be the major curricular response to ethnic diversity.

In practice, some authorities emphasise the difference between migrant and multicultural education, while others combine the two. The Western Australian Education Department, for example, has two separate statements, one on the Child Migrant Education Programme and another on education for a multicultural society. In contrast, the New South Wales Education Department's policy differentiates between processes for all schools—multicultural perspectives in the curriculum and intercultural education—and programs for students according to need and interest, specified as English as a second language (ESL), transitional bilingual education, community/language education and ethnic studies.

This development is not surprising, given the history of educational endeavour in this field. The existence for some time of two separate Commonwealth funding programs for English as a second language and multicultural education with substantially different resource levels, histories and purposes lent itself to the creation of dual administrative structures in educational authorities, especially at school level. The fact that this separation did not reach its logical conclusion in all authorities is as much due to the views of relevant officers as to the limited resource base allocated by authorities to this field. The continuation of separate Commonwealth funding and philosophical bases for English as a second language on the one hand and languages on the other will preserve this dualism in educational responses. While some commentators have argued strongly for the integration of migrant and multicultural education (Bull and Tons 1985: 59), others argue that this separation is not harmful. Campbell, in his review of the national ESL program argued that 'multiculturalism should be freed from its special relationship with ESL to exert a more pervasive influence upon the curriculum and that ESL should be strengthened by its inclusion within a coherent language programme, comprising as well, English as a mother tongue, language-across-the-curriculum, bilingual studies and "foreign" languages' (Campbell and others 1984: 100).

While all policies embrace a broad view of the responsibility of every school to deal with and incorporate multiculturalism in their pedagogy, curriculum, organisation and assessment procedures, this breadth of vision is not always applied to the definition of participants in multicultural education. Education is usually presented as a school matter, to be dealt with by teachers and schools in the normal course of their work, with the support of resources and officers from the school authority. What is not always so clear is the contribution which owners of different cultural capital can make to the development of school policies, the preparation of curricular materials, or to the teaching and assessment of students.

The importance of this issue varies with authorities. For some it is a few lines of appropriate rhetoric; for others it is a theme that runs through their statement. For example, the Northern Territory identifies as one of its aims 'increasing opportunity for both English speaking Australians and Australians of non-English speaking backgrounds to share experiences that will lead to the understanding of cultural groups other than their own' (Bull and Tons 1985: 69).

In contrast, the South Australian Education Department lists as a principle of multiculturalism maximising 'the involvement of staff and families from different linguistic and cultural backgrounds in structures which lead to decision making about schools and education' (1987).

Parents and community members are viewed in one of three lights: as contributors of ethno-specific knowledge to a classroom activity or school program; as equal partners in the school's decision making processes with an opportunity to influence the organisation, curriculum and operation of the school; or as participating in order to be taught about Australian schools. To quote NACCME: 'participation in schooling offers ethnic minority parents the opportunity to replace with a positive direction, their more commonplace dissatisfaction with Australian schooling' (1987: 35).

(iii) Solutions to the problem

It is perhaps not surprising that this conceptual soup has led to an array of proposed solutions. Five programmatic arrangements can be identified:

A. The core-plus model exemplified in the New South Wales statements. All schools do multicultural perspectives and intercultural studies; some schools take on ESL, bilingual education, community languages and ethnic studies;

B. The common model suggested by NACCME and South Australia, that is, 'a common inclusive curriculum which provides a set of common skills and knowledge . . . fortified by the values of cultural pluralism' (NACCME 1987: 38);

C. The process and content model. The elements of this model are illustrated in the Victorian statement which proposes multicultural perspectives in content, teaching styles and school curriculum, relevant and appropriate to all students, participatory decision making and pedagogical styles, and inclusive critical curriculum;

D. The add-on model, as illustrated in the Queensland policy, which can include specialist programs such as ESL, with changes made to the content of traditional areas of learning;

E. The linguistic model, adopted in the ACT, which emphasises ESL and the learning of LOTE (Languages other than English).

What is noticeable in this array of strategies is the low profile given to serious social education. For policies designed to promote social cohesion, very little is said about how that will occur. The assumption seems to be that if schools teach minority children English and learn a bit about their culture they'll feel more at home and schools will become more understanding and tolerant as a result! How this is to effect social cohesion is unexamined.

(iv) Overview

Australian education authorities have taken a conservative approach to multiculturalism. Their goal is to preserve Australia against the threat of cultural diversity which may lead to a divisive society, a breakdown of common moral, social and political order. The term "multicultural education" has become an umbrella term to describe a range of diverse programs for immigrant and Australian children.

While there is general recognition of the importance of tolerance and understanding, and a recognition of the presence of cultural diversity, the bulk of the teaching strategies recommended do little to promote serious social education around these issues. Discussion about racism is generally avoided, with pedagogical options subsumed under the rubric of intercultural education. All authorities make reference to community participation in multicultural education, but few appear to recognise or admit the critical role which the community ought to have in defining and teaching a common, inclusive curriculum or a curriculum with a multicultural perspective.

COMPARATIVE APPROACHES TO MULTICULTURAL EDUCATION

Given the variety in the State multicultural policy statements, it is necessary to caution against overgeneralising about 'Australian' responses to ethnic diversity. But some generalisation is required if we are to make comparisons between Australian and other responses.

Australian academic comparative education research has made some contributions to our understanding of educational responses to ethnic diversity. This research and its contribution can be divided into several distinct approaches to the nature of comparisons. These are:

i. model-building and classification,
ii. cross-national comparisons,
iii. implicit comparisons,
iv. selective cultural borrowing,
v. internal comparisons.

In covering such a range of material, it should be emphasised that this is not a review of research. Rather, it is an attempt to evaluate the extent to which several strands in Australian comparative education have contributed to our understanding of 'the content of education within groups, as well as the interrelationship between groups . . . (to) . . . assist those who conduct schooling' (White 1981: 317).

(i) Model-building and classification

A useful way to get an overview of how Australian responses to ethnic diversity can be related to those in other countries is to examine cross national taxonomies and classifications of multicultural education options and policies. International comparisons of the way in which education systems respond to diversity are often made at two levels: an ideological level (definition of the problem) and a programmatic level (range and targets of programs). Several Australian comparativists have attempted this exercise, but before we look at their work it would be useful to locate the Australian response in comparison with other countries.

To do this we will use Churchill's (1987: 64–99) synthesis of educational policy trends in multicultural OECD countries. The model represents what appear to be sequential historical stages of policy development, what Churchill describes as 'how education has become multicultural or the process by which educational systems adapt to accommodate diverse language and cultures reflected in the make-up of each country's population' (1987: 64). The model was built using data from nineteen national surveys or studies which contributed to the CERI project on the financing, organisation and governance of education of special populations. It excludes countries with relatively old established minority situations whose major customs were defined at least fifty or more years ago (Belgium, Finland and Switzerland).

The model contains six stages, although it presumes a seventh which is ignoring the existence of special educational needs of minorities. Stage 1, the learning deficit model, recognises that certain groups of students perform less well than their peers. For example, they have poor grades, discipline problems, drop out of school in greater numbers and at an earlier age than the norm. It is assumed that for minority students this deficiency is a result of an inadequate knowledge of the majority language caused by use of the mother tongue. In Stage 2, socially linked learning deficit, the broader social problems associated with lower school performance are recognised, for example, parents' unfavourable socio-economic situation. Churchill argues that these two stages appear to be universal in OECD countries with the exception of Finland and Switzerland. Our analysis of Australian policy statements finds examples of these positions, especially the emphasis on educational disadvantage or life chances and the importance given to the teaching of English.

Churchill describes the third stage as multicultural education. 'It assumed', she contends, 'that minorities suffer from learning deficits at least in part because of the failure of the majority society—particularly its education system—to recognise, accept and view positively the culture of the minority' (p.97). She suggests that the essence of this stage is the recognition of the right to be different and be respected for it, but not necessarily to use a different language. She believes this concept is gaining ground in Western Europe. Many Australian policies fit neatly into this stage, for example, the focus on multicultural perspectives and ethnic studies.

Stage 4, mother tongue deprivation, identifies the major cause of learning deficits among linguistic minorities as the failure to develop children's mother tongue. The policy implications of this stage include support for home language learning and transition bilingual programs. Australian equivalents can be found in State language policies rather than in their multicultural policies although there are some exceptions, for example, the NACCME statement (1987).

The final two stages have developed in countries with established minorities. Stage 5, language maintenance for private use, recognises the subordinate and weaker position of minorities and their right to maintain and develop their language for private purposes. Programmatic applications of this principle include the use of minority languages for instruction in the initial years of schooling. Where this stage differs from the preceding stage is the assumption about the long term role of the minority group in the country involved. This view may in part sustain the Australian Commonwealth Government's ethnic school funding program where funds are provided to ethnic community organisations to operate language programs (although this may be a generous interpretation).

The final stage grants full official status to the minority language for use in public institutions and in the broader economic life of the country. It is Churchill's view that this stage has been reached in very old bilingual or multilingual states such as Belgium, Finland and Switzerland.

While recognising that the differences between the various stages are not always clear cut, Churchill argues that the fundamental difference lies in the way in which language and culture are viewed. In Stages 1 to 4 they are treated as a handicap, while in Stages 5 and 6 they are considered to be a positive asset for the individual and for society.

These differences become more apparent when one examines how authorities have defined the role of culture within this context. Churchill postulates that there are three positions:

A. Minority has difficulty in adapting to a majority culture. Children are not accustomed to "modern" situations and so need assistance to overcome the handicap of their culture and to learn the new culture and its demands.

B. Minority suffers from discrimantion and from negative attitude of majority and majority culture. Therefore offer the home culture as a subject of interest to all children to promote better human relations and attitudinal change. In some cases the need for culture-related instruction for minority group members is recognised.

C. Minority suffers from non-equal status and lack of positive valuation of its culture. The minority culture is considered an enduring concern for the majority, expressed for example in obligatory instruction in the minority language on the majority.

Viewed in this light, the conservative nature of Australian responses as well as the scope of the debate find ready counterpoints in other systems. Australian statements contain the rhetoric of all of Churchill's six stages, with more recent documents espousing a more sophisticated line of argument. However, the programs offered or recommended in the State's policy documents clearly locate Australian programs within the first two definitions of the role of culture and primarily within the third stage of Churchill's model.

In European and American comparative education there is a tradition of developing ideal-typical theoretical models aiming to impose some conceptual order on disparate phenomena and to identify empirical similarities and differences in education system responses. The processes of classification and taxonomy building are accepted as essential preconditions for systematic comparisons at the macro level and devices for fruitful reflection on the implication of related case studies. As Hoy (1983: 251) has commented:

> Overall it is not a question of whether models or unique case studies provide the most useful comparative analyses, but rather that each complements the other at different stages of the researcher's work.

In Australian comparative educational research on responses to diversity, it seems that this mutual reinforcement through complementary strategies has yet to be achieved. Rather, taxonomies and classificatory model building seem to have been utilised mainly for the purpose of reducing some of the conceptual confusions that bedevil discussions of multicultural education and to make explicit the program implications of various policy choices.

Smolicz and Secombe (1979) developed a model of possible forms of interaction between two cultures, in terms of methods of adaption to these cultures by individuals and the resulting consequences for belief systems at the individual and group level. Building on this humanistic sociological theorising, and on the work of Nicoll (1977) on the categorisation of migrant education programs, Holenbergh Young (1979) outlined a typology combining the following elements: methods of adaption to cultures A and B by individuals, definition of education, cultural elements, targets for change, social effects and curriculum consequences for each type of education desired. She identified six definitions of multicultural education, ranging from the assimilationist end of the continuum (definitions 1–3, targetting migrants for change), through integration (definitions 4 and 5, targetting migrants and Australians) to pluralism (definitions 5 and 6 targetting all groups) in its extreme form turning into structural pluralism involving separate development for minority students.

In some ways this is a more coherent model than Churchill's. Its logic is more apparent, it is based on continua that are widely recognised, it is not drawn from any historical progression and would appear to be universally applicable. Holenbergh Young refers to Australian and international programs that exemplify some aspects of the model, but she doesn't use it for cross-national comparisons. She employs it as an heuristic device, to suggest where, and how, comparative research could be systematised. It is surprising that a model with such potential for theory development appears to have been neglected.

In contrast to Holenbergh Young, Jayasuriya (1987) has drawn on North American taxonomies of multicultural education (Gibson 1977; Young 1979; Magsino 1985) to classify Australian educational system reactions to ethnic diversity. His taxonomy of conceptions of multicultural education distinguishes six policy options:

A. Education for an emergent society, emphasising unity through basically assimilationist programs.

B. Education for the culturally different, aimed at overcoming minority deficits through remedial, often assimilationalist programs.

C. Education for cultural understanding, aimed at all students, emphasising cohesion rather than minority identity.

D. Education for cultural accommodation, aimed at preserving cultural diversity within group equality.

E. Education for cultural preservation, aimed at minority students through language programs and separate "ethnic" schools.

F. Education for multicultural adaption, for all students, aiming at unity within diversity, allowing for mixed cultural identities.

Jayasuriya employs this taxonomy primarily to compare Australian responses to diversity at different points in time. His analysis suggests that Type 1 responses were characteristic of the 1960s, Type 2 responses were reflected in the reformist policies of the Whitlam Labor administration, and that Types 3, 4 and 5 have co-existed throughout the 1970s and 1980s. There are allusions in his discussion to "Head-Start" programs, bilingual programs in North America and Sweden, the Canadian "socio-cultural" emphases and British "race relations" emphases in multicultural education programs. The taxonomy is not used explicitly for cross-national comparisons, and given the variety within various State systems in Australia it is probably better to commence with intra-Australian comparisons. However, the potential is there for the taxonomy to be used in comparative educational research.

The three examples of model-building and classification that have been discussed indicate the difficulties of comparison at this level of generality. Devising appropriate categories is not easy, for there are so many criteria to be considered. These include pedagogic assumptions, policy purposes, target groups, economic and social status of minority students, status of mother tongue, status of the language(s) of education, notions of culture, the role of the State vs private educational agencies and the degree of diversity/assimilation or structural/cultural pluralism that is thought to be desirable.

Each of the models categorises combinations of these elements in different ways, providing alternative criteria for comparisons over time or space. Historical data are employed to suggest some sort of sequencing, but care has been taken not to infer any sense of regularity or progression in institutional responses. These classifications are not causal models. They are general constructs based upon historical data and ideal types and inferences drawn from policies to inentions. This is not to deny their validity. Without them we remain tied to selective cultural borrowing and uncritical repetition of contradictory meanings of multiculturalism. We need these general guidelines for reflective, more systematic and more productive comparisons of responses to diversity. The problem is, however, that there is hardly any fruitful interaction occurring between model and case study of the type alluded to by Hoy (1983).

Our comments, and those of Jayasuriya, have pointed to the difficulty of generalising about responses at the national level. The National Advisory and Co-ordinating Committee on Multicultural Education policy document is not enforceable. Neither are the States' policy recommendations. Most are ignored or are too general to be translated into practice. The response of each State, region, school is different. It is not difficult, therefore, to find responses to diversity that fit into all of the categories of all the taxonomies. At this stage in the Australian situation, the major task is to look for variations in emphasis over time and space, to go beyond the policy statements towards comparisons of practice, structures and programs. This means that for

Australian comparativists there will for a long time continue to be an important role for case studies (Crossley and Burns 1983).

(ii) Cross-National Comparisons.

Perhaps because of the difficulties outlined in the previous section, and perhaps because of the decline of centralised national bureaucracies as the most important influence on educational responses, there have been few cross-national studies of multicultural educational responses by Australian comparativists. The phenomenological perspectives of the 1970s shied away from the nation state as the unit of comparison, and "national character" is singularly inappropriate as a conceptual tool for analysing multicultural education. National level aggregated "variables", manipulated by multivariate analysis, have been more popular instruments in studies of educational participation and attainment than of multicultural education. The comparativists who have tried to generate theoretical perspectives for comparing responses to ethnic diversity have tended rather to emphasise issues relating to how we conceptualise culture, how we understand its significance, and which cultures survive in altered forms in ethnically diverse societies.

A group of papers delivered at the 1983 Conference of the Australian and New Zealand Comparative and International Education Society illustrates this (Sheehan 1983). Crossley and Burns argued for the use of case studies to compare a set of educational ideas on curriculum content and process in developed and developing countries. Benoit and Cumming argued for the concept of "cultural accommodation" as a basis for comparing internal cultural colonisation in Australia with the colonialisation of the Third World by First World cultures. White used the Yipirinya Aboriginal school in Alice Springs as an example of how comparativists could usefully concentrate on the central questions of all education: 'the problem of the determination of a direction to schooling by groups, and the relationship of those groups to one another' (1983: 107).

There have been several comparisons of a particular aspect of multicultural education in Australia and another country, and anthologies in which multicultural education in several countries has been compared, implicitly rather than systematically (e.g. Smolicz 1984; Corner 1983; Hoy 1983; Modgil 1986; Bell 1987). The outstanding cross-national research effort in this area, however, is Bullivant's *The Pluralist Dilemma in Education* (1981). Bullivant compares the responses to the problem of balancing cohesion and diversity in Britain, Canada, Fiji, the USA, Hawaii and Australia. He concludes that naive multiculturalism is disadvantageous to minority individuals and to the survival of the societies in question.

> The task for educationalists is to achieve a form of pluralist education which recognises the challenge of the survival imperative. (p. 244)

His plea for the term "polyethnic" rather than "multicultural" to describe Australian society has not been heeded, but his work on the analysis of multicultural education has been influential on Australian discussions of the most appropriate responses to ethnic diversity.

(iii) Implicit Comparisons

It would probably be true to say that a good deal of the academic analysis of responses to diversity by Australian educational institutions has been based on theoretical perspectives derived from outside Australia. A lot is also based on viewpoints about the most appropriate responses to diversity in other countries that now are part of the world's stock of cultural understanding via the normal processes of knowledge diffusion, mostly from the Northern to the Southern hemisphere. Judgments about actual and desirable Australian responses are based, therefore, on comparisons, but these comparisons are often implicit, embedded and almost taken for granted as natural reference points.

The most influential of these perspectives in the analysis of Australian responses to ethnic diversity are described here as (a) structuralist, (b) redistributionalist, (c) celebration of diversity, and (d) race relations perspectives. There are some similarities in these to the categories outlined in the taxonomies discussed earlier. This is quite natural, as the perspectives are analysing similar features of institutional responses: Education for whom? In which language(s)? For whose benefit? How do we balance cohesion and diversity? Some readers will demur at the aptness and the inclusiveness of the characterisations. They are set out here as suggestive rather than as definitive devices.

A. Structuralist Perspectives. These perspectives have as a general focus the problem of how to maintain basic social structures, cohesion and core values. Diversity is seen to be a major problem: cultural but not structural pluralism is permissible, but only to acceptable limits. In some instances the perspectives seem to have roots in American structural-functionalism, and, in others, European liberalism. The educational responses advocated emphasise English as a second language and a classic conception of cross-cultural and intercultural studies as the pathway to awareness, understanding, empathy and tolerance of diversity (Schools Commission 1979; Committee on Multicultural Education 1979; Australian Institute of Multicultural Affairs 1980).

A major problem with this perspective is that Aborigines are seen to be a special problem and have to be argued as a special case.

> Australia has rejected any notion of a class or caste structure that places one person or one group in a position of automatic superiority over another . . . Our approach to where people live and with whom they work is not constrained by any form of apartheid or separate development policy . . . However, Australia's Aboriginal people have certain special claims because of their dispossession during the process of colonisation. These might ultimately be met through the assignment to them of areas for their exclusive use. This would not imply separate development, as Aboriginals would remain free to choose at any time their identity and lifestyle. (Australian Council on Population and Ethnic Affairs 1982: 27–8)

Bullivant's perspective is distinctive for the explicitness of his comparisons, but in important ways it has strengthened the emphasis in Australian comparative research on questions of structure. Bullivant's viewpoint on the dominance of Anglo elements in Australian society has led him to point to the dangers to minority children if their mother tongue and culture are developed to the point that they are prevented from acquiring English language and cultural skills that will lead to social mobility. In a neat irony, Birrell and Seitz have argued more recently (1986) that we have evidence that many minority children are now succeeding in school. Consequently, there is no longer a strong justification for teaching their mother tongue and culture (cf. Bullivant 1986).

B. Redistributionist Perspectives. These perspectives are critical of the emphasis in official policy statements on social cohesion and the superficial aspects of culture at the expense of recognition of structural inequalities that relegate minorities to the lowest economic, political, social and cultural status (e.g. Bottomley and de Lepervanche 1984; Kalantzis and Cope 1988). Official multicultural policy is seen as an instrument of State control, dividing oppressed groups to draw attention away from class conflict (e.g. Jakubowicz 1984; Foster and Stockley 1984). There has been a growing emphasis in these perspectives on the incorporation of multicultural education into a broader social justice policy context, targetting ethnicity, social class and gender as inter-related components of disadvantage (e.g. Bottomley and de Lepervanche 1984).

Appropriate educational responses have been spelled out in greater detail than has been the case with some of the other perspectives. Some of these responses are reflected in the more recent of the policy statements, for example, the NACCME and Victorian emphases on equitable multiculturalism. There are programs in several States that go beyond the "culturalist" approach and provide students with resources and experiences to examine critically the structural constraints on equality (e.g. Kalantzis and Cope 1981; Keen 1988).

C. Celebration of Diversity Perspectives. In a country of several hundred languages and cultures, it is not surprising that a large amount of analysis has been devoted to issues of ethnicity and identity, language and culture teaching, intercultural and ethnic studies, and ethno-specific compared with mainstream provision of services.

In 1978, Martin's *The Migrant Presence* described how, in the preceding two decades, educational responses moved from assimilation to a recognition of the needs and rights of immigrant children and their parents. In the decade since, the legitimation of diversity has proceeded apace.

One strand has emphasised the importance of maintaining cultural identity and the psychological costs of persisting with monolingual, monocultural, assimilationist educational practices (e.g. Isaacs 1981; Rado 1984). Working in a European humanistic sociological tradition, Smolicz (1979) has emphasized the virtues of education for additive biculturalism. Rationales and programs for bilingual education from the Council of Europe and North America have been particularly influential in the development of transition and maintenance bilingual programs in Australia. Conspicuously lacking, however, are systematic evaluations of the relevance of programs transplanted from abroad (Rado 1984; Clyne 1987). This might be rectified if proposals put forward in the *National Policy on Languages* (Lo Bianco 1987), itself a reflection of European and American influences, are put into practice.

There has been a small but smouldering debate in Australia about the provision of ethno-specific educational services, especially since the 1978 *Review of Migrant Services and Programs* institutionalised Commonwealth Government assistance to ethnic community schools and welfare agencies (Galbally 1978). The least controversial response in this area has been the growth of "insertion" classes, in which languages other than English are taught by members of minority communities in State (and some private) schools (Harris 1984). More problematic has been public and official acceptance of funding for separate ethnic community schools. These are mainly part time (evening and weekends) but increasingly full time private fee paying schools that are manifest indications of a growing structural pluralism (Kringas and Lewins 1981; Norst 1983). Aboriginal groups are developing their own models (White 1983; Sokoloff 1987).

In the areas of intercultural education and ethnic studies, borrowing from overseas has been common, but largely unacknowledged. It is common because much of the curriculum and many of the techniques and technologies were developed first in the UK, US and Canada, and quickly transplanted. It is largely unacknowledged since the language of such programs is increasingly becoming universal: an emphasis on tolerance, understanding and sympathy for all, and the maintenance of identity, self esteem and cultural pride for each minority group.

Fortunately, this accommodation of concepts has not led to a homogenising of perspectives. There has been a growing body of criticism of intercultural studies programs as failing to go beyond superficial concepts of culture, for avoiding discussions of racism in anything other than attitudinal perspectives, and for failing to explore pedagogies emphasising similarities rather than differences (e.g. Nemetz Robinson 1985; Kalantzis 1988).

There has also been a change in the context of intercultural studies that could have implications for this type of response to diversity. From 1979, the Federal Government funded intercultural studies through its Multicultural Education Program. In 1984 a review of the program pointed to deficiencies in its impact (Cahill 1984), and the 1987 *National Policy on Languages* report suggested that intercultural studies could fruitfully be incorporated into language courses. Subsequently, the MEP was discontinued and the Multicultural and Cross-Cultural Supplementation Program commenced. The effect of this will arguably be to deprive intercultural studies of an independent bureaucratic and financial base, and to accelerate the trend towards ESL and LOTES as the main components of the response to diversity. This perpetuates the too widely-held belief that multicultural matters are properly the concerns of non-Anglo minorities and their teachers.

D. Race Relations Perspectives. A concern about social cohesion has been an enduring focus of multicultural education in Australia. It has become much more pronounced since the 1970s when it became apparent that the Asian component of Australia's immigration/refugee intake was increasing. Anxiety about the so-called 'Asian invasion' erupted into political, public and academic controversy in 1984 and 1988 (Blainey 1984; Markus and Ricklefs 1985; Markus and Rasmussen 1985; Castles and others 1988; Collins 1988).

Anti-racism strategies discussed in Australia have been similar to those employed in various parts of the world: anti-discrimination legislation, anti-racial incitement legislation, community education, anti-prejudice and intercultural curricula in schools, and longer term policies for the improvement of the economic, social and political status of minority groups (e.g. Minister for Ethnic Affairs, Victoria 1984; Pettman 1987).

There are distinct approaches to the issues. The human rights approach, internationalist in derivation, includes racism along with other sources of discrimination and denial of rights and freedoms (e.g.

Pettman and Henry 1986; Debney Park High School 1986). A deconstructionist approach emphasises the importance of understanding the structural underpinnings of racism in modern industrial societies. In most educational responses, these issues are usually omitted from the curriculum.

> Issues pertaining to structural racism, such as underachievement at school, the need for alternative credentialling for indigenous people and those of non-English speaking background, inadequacies of access in the transition from school to work, the traumas of settlement and serious cultural conflict, are all sidestepped. The fact that some people consider Australian Aborigines in their daily interactions today as inferior does not itself create their inequality. Their current position can only really be understood in terms of the structural effects of racism in Australian history. (Kalantzis 1988: 94)

Another approach could loosely be labelled as 'pragmatic' in that its aim is to provide teachers with workable anti-racist strategies at the classroom and school level. Its intellectual basis is eclectic, derived from various strands of humanistic psychology and sociology, administrative theory and community studies (e.g. Lippman 1973; Skelton 1985).

To say that the perspectives described in this section are based on implicit rather than explicit comparisons is not to be critical, but to note that the borrowing of parts of the world's cultural capital is taken for granted, assumed to be as applicable to Australian diversity as to anwhere else.

(iv) Selective Cultural Borrowing

Borrowing of a different sort has long been described in the comparative literature, often looked down upon as bad comparison and worse policy. Such judgments are probably too harsh, and anyway irrelevant. Selective borrowing is rampant in Australian education's response to ethnic diversity: ESL methodology, LOTE methodology, bilingual programs, on-arrival and settlement programs and anti-prejudice programs. In many cases it would be foolish to maintain that the inadequacies of these programs are due to their overseas genesis. More to the point is that they are seldom properly evaluated at all.

There has, indeed, been some felicitous borrowing. One example relates to the way in which Australian scholars have adopted the ideas in Barker's *The New Racism* (1981), which describes the post-war emergence of racism in Britain based upon the 'common sense' notion that all people "naturally" prefer to live among others similar to them in colour, language, religion and culture. This and related studies of the "racialisation" of British politics in the 1960s (e.g. Miles and Phizacklea 1984) has, by contrast and analogy, facilitated Australian studies of racist controversy and its implications for language, the media, politics and education (Markus and Ricklefs 1985; Markus and Rasmussen 1987; de Lepervanche and Bottomley 1988).

Another example is the type of cultural borrowing advocated by Hannan (1982). In his analysis of some curriculum material—from Italy, but it could equally well be taken from any of the students' cultures—he illustrates how students could study a topic from multiple cultural perspectives, not just from the host culture's interpretation. The underlying point of the comparison is very important.

> Relevance comes from comparison and contrast. Some subjects are probably too close to home and too sensitive to approach directly. Youth culture comes to mind. So does the family. And sex-roles. Their very centrality makes them hard to approach directly in a critical way. The same may well be true of some ethnic themes. The hot ones, and there are plenty of them, have to be handled from a cool distance. The aim, after all, is not to resolve old conflicts with simplistic analyses, but to equip people first of all to look at culture and society critically. (p. 91)

In other words, critical cultural borrowing can be of great importance in achieving a more enlightened response to ethnic diversity at the practical level of the classroom.

(v) Internal Comparisons

In Australia, as in other host countries, internal comparisons of the educational and subsequent occupational profiles of immigrant compared with native born children have been used by academics, minority groups, politicians and education authorities as a barometer of the responses of educational institutions to ethnic diversity. In Australia, as in other countries where indigenous peoples have been displaced and disinherited, there is a double difficulty in interpreting the barometer. Consequently, ideological and political considerations are never far below the surface of these internal comparisons.

The documentation of these comparisons is voluminous. In the field of ethnic and cultural diversity related to education, we can now evaluate Australian educational responses in several distinct areas. These include:

A. the performance of minority group children on intelligence/ achievement tests (e.g. de Lemos 1975; Marjoribanks 1980),

B. the retention and participation rates of minority group children in different levels and sectors of education (e.g. Meade 1983; Birrell and Seitz 1986),

C. the adaptiveness of schools to minority group characteristics (e.g. Gauci 1983; Poole and others 1985; Hartley and Maas 1987),

D. the effectiveness of minority groups in translating school performance into workforce participation (e.g. Young and others 1980; Sturman, 1985; DEET 1987),

E. the receptiveness of schools to the special needs of minority group girls. (e.g. Tsolidis 1986; Porter 1986; *In Our Own Words* 1988)

It is difficult to generalise about such a broad range of internal comparisons of the experiences of minority children. The comments that follow are, therefore, speculative.

A. Australian educational institutions appear to have had some impact on the mobility of *some* minority groups, but other groups, particularly Aborigines and those with cultures very dissimilar to the Anglo majority, are severely disadvantaged;

B. there are insufficient data to make clear judgments about the relative contributions of school programs, home background factors and 'ethnic' influences on the educational and occupational attainments of minority group students;

C. the absence of sufficient data to indicate in detail the patterns of educational participation and occupational attainment of minority group youth, after forty years of significant post war immigration, suggests an inadequate and uncaring response by Australian institutions to the immigrant contribution;

D. the inadequacy of the data on educational/occupational performance has allowed opponents to argue for a reduction in multicultural programs on the grounds that the success of many immigrant groups has obviated the need for special assistance;

E. many of the comparisons have looked only at the educational and occupational "success" of minority students in comparison with the Anglo majority. What is conspicuously absent has been a serious attempt to analyse what is lost to minority individuals and to the nation as a whole when "success" is defined only in terms of the dominant culture's criteria, and when one set of cultural characteristics has to be abandoned for 'success' to be possible. Many of the comparisons assume a zero sum conception of culture rather than explore an additive notion implying change for both minorities and the majority.

MULTICULTURAL EDUCATION: POLICY AND PRACTICE, AND COMPARATIVE EDUCATION.

In 1983 Simkin argued that the gap between academic comparative education and school policies and practice in multicultural education might be reduced if comparativists looked at some of the following issues:

(i) What is the range of acceptable mulicultural policies in Australia, and how could they best be translated into viable programmes at the school level?

(ii) What happens in local multicultural programmes and how can they be compared with those interstate and overseas?

(iii) How do pressure groups affect the life and death of different sorts of responses to ethnic diversity?

In the intervening period there has been, as we have seen, some research in each of those areas.

The argument put forward in this chapter, however, has been that comparative theory building in the area has been negligible in Australia and there have been few systematic comparisons leading to knowledge relevant to either policy or practice. Most of the Australian research has been based on implicit comparisons, the adoption of overseas perspectives or selective cultural borrowing. Thus there has been (with a few exceptions) little direct relationship between academic comparative education and policies or practice in Australian multicultural education.

The policy statements of the State educational authorities show great variability, stretching across a number of continua, reflecting the wide range of response options available in multicultural education:

(i) *in* a multicultural society (present reality) or *for* a multicultural society (future ideal)?

(ii) for intergroup tolerance or for increased access and equity?

(iii) for social cohesion or the increased rights of minority groups?

(iv) for minority or for all children?

(v) specific programs (ESL, LOTES, intercultural studies) or a perspective infused into the total curriculum?

(vi) mainstream or ethno-specific programs?

(vii) determined mainly by the authorities or based on community input?

In addition to this variability, there are significant differences between responses to diversity at the policy level, and responses at the level of academic research and of actual practice in schools. Some generalisations for consideration are:

(i) In the policy statements, the term 'race' is rarely used. The term 'racism' is employed, often equated with prejudice, and usually seen to be a matter of attitudes that can be therapeutically treated. In the academic literature this notion has been criticised by drawing attention to the structural components of racism that have been ignored in policy. In practice, a high degree of racism exists in many schools, prejudice is shown by teachers as well as students, institutional structures disadvantage minority students, and bilingual/bicultural skills are discounted (Debney Park High School 1986; Fields 1986; Tsolidis 1986; Orfanos 1987; cf. Bullivant 1986).

(ii) The concepts "multiculturalism" and "multicultural education" are defined differently in various policy documents. There is no agreement about these concepts in the academic literature either, and the press coverage of controversies relating to immigration and multiculturalism would indicate confusion at the public level as well. Recent policy (e.g. NACCME 1987) and academic comment suggests a tendency towards a "social justice" conception that views ethnic diversity with other factors such as gender and class as targets for social engineering. The implications of this for educational responses are not yet clear.

In practice, multicultural education is a low priority in most schools. It is seen as appropriate for minorities, to help them solve their "problem", and as irrelevant for "real Australians" by large numbers of school principals, teachers, parents and students. Multicultural perspectives are rarely infused into the whole curriculum. Teachers lack either commitment or expertise and do not see how they can include racism (or sexism or peace studies) into their already overcrowded curricula (e.g. Pratt and Lenton 1984).

(iii) The concept of "culture" is largely unexamined in the policy statements and its meaning and characterisation have been problematic (NACCME 1987). Recent academic analysis has tended to criticise the highly "culturalist" orientations of responses to ethnic diversity with their emphasis on language learning and maintenance, music, dance, food and festivals. In practice, linguistic responses continue to dominate. Most effort is put into ESL programs for non-English speaking students, and next into LOTE programs, especially for minority group mother tongue speakers (Lo Bianco 1987). The first emphasis, if unaccompanied by other responses (as is usual) is assimilationist. The second, because of inadequate staff, resources and lack of continuity, is too often tokenistic. The performance of most Anglo majority students in learning another language continues to be less than inspiring.

(iv) Most of the policy statements assume a common Australian culture with "core values", towards which minority cultures will contribute but will be eventually assimilated into, retaining only exotica and perhaps vestiges of the mother tongue. Much of the academic analysis sees the limits to responses to diversity in cultural pluralism, not structural pluralism (except for some Aboriginal groups). The practical situation in schools probably is one of the unremitting assimilation of minority children. There is a major exception in the form of the growth of ethnic community schools, increasingly full time, fee paying, ethno-specific. Parents supporting these schools argue that they have been driven to this solution because State responses to their linguistic and cultural needs have been inadequate. This growing structural pluralism is a political time bomb.

(v) Some of the policy statements and the academic literature make the point that schools must draw on the resources available to them in the community. There must be a dual

> interaction, in which schools adapt their programs and structures to suit the wishes of the clientele. In practice, little of this occurs. The curricula, structures and language of education do not reflect community diversity. This only reflects the continuity of our response: as Martin (1978) and Foster and Stockley (1984) have illustrated, minority groups have never had equal access to the definition and control of appropriate solutions to the 'problem' of diversity.

Academic researchers might like to think that they influence multicultural education policy, which in turn directs everyday school practice. With a few exceptions this is fantasy. Theory and research, policy and practice seem rather to be three separate reactions to diversity, sometimes parallel, mostly distinct, occasionally connecting.

It is difficult to predict future responses in Australian education to ethnic, cultural and linguistic diversity. No doubt, small groups of dedicated academics, policy makers, principals, teachers, parents and students will continue to strive for improved responses to diversity. They will continue to re-invent the wheel, be unaware of each others' successes and failures, see good programmes wither and many opportunities go to waste (Martin 1978; Cahill 1984, cf. NACCME 1987).

Educational responses will probably continue to reflect the responses of the nation as a whole. It might be, as Liffman suggests in "Immigration and Racism in the Land of the Long Weekend" (1985), that xenophobia rather than racism characterises our response to cultural difference, and that indifference rather than active opposition will determine the future of educational responses. It might be, however, that Australian politics has become irretrievably "racialised" and that controversies over Aboriginal land rights, racial discrimination legislation, Asian immigration and foreign ownership of property, resources and finance will inevitably polarize political parties' attitudes to multicultural education. About the only certainty is that, in a country committed to continuing immigration and dependent on it for a significant component of population and economic growth, the issue of diversity will always be with our educational institutions.

REFERENCES

Bell, R. (1987) *Multicultural Societies: A Comparative Reader*. Sydney, Sable.

Barker, M. (1981) *The New Racism*. London, Junction Books.

Birrell, R. and Seitz, A. (1986) 'The Ethnic Problem in Education: the Emergence and Definition of an Issue'. Paper delivered at the AIMA Conference on Ethnicity and Multiculturalism, University of Melbourne, May.

Blainey, G. (1984) *All for Australia*. Sydney, Methuen Haynes.

Bottomley, G. and de Lepervanche, M. (eds.) (1984) *Ethnicity, Class and Gender in Australia*. Sydney, George Allen and Unwin.

Bull K. and Tons, J. (1985) *Multicultural Education: From Practice to Policy*. Adelaide, Education Department of South Australia.

Bullivant, B. (1981) *The Pluralist Dilemma in Education: Six Case Studies*. Sydney, George Allen and Unwin.

Bullivant, B. (1986) *Getting a Fair Go. Studies of Occupational Socialization and Perceptions of Discrimmination*. Human Rights Commission, Occasional Paper No. 13, Canberra, AGPS.

Cahill, D. (1984) *Review of The Commonwealth Multicultural Education Program*. Report to the Commonwealth Schools Commission, Vol. 1, Canberra, Commonwealth Schools Commission.

Campbell, W.J., Barnett, J., Joy, B., and McMeniman, N., (1984) *A Review of the Commonwealth English as a Second Language (ESL) Program*. Canberra, Commonwealth Schools Commission.

Castles, S., Kalantzis, M., Cope, B., and Morrissey, M. (1988) *Mistaken Identity. Multiculturalism and the Demise of Nationalism in Australia*. Sydney, Pluto Press.

Churchill, S., (1987) 'Policy Development for Education in Multicultural Societies. Trends and Processes in the OECD Countries'. In Centre for Educational Research and Innovation (CERI), *Multicultural Education*, Paris, OECD: 64–99.

Clyne, M. (ed.) (1987) *An Early Start: Second Language Learning at Primary School*. Melbourne, River Seine.

Cole, M. (1986) 'Teaching and Learning about Racism: A Critique of Multicultural Education in Britain'. In S. Modgil, G.K. Verma, K. Mallick, and C. Modgil (eds.), *Multicultural Education: The Interminable Debate*. London, The Falmer Press: 123–147.

Collins, J. (1988) *Migrant Hands in a Distant Land*. Sydney, Pluto Press.

Committee on Multicultural Education (1979) *Education for a Multicultural Society*. Report to the Schools Commission.

Corner, T. (1983) *Education in Multicultural Societies*. British Comparative and International Education Society, Kent, Croom Helm.

Crossley, M. and Burns, R. (1983) 'Case Study in Comparative Education: An Approach to Bridging the Theory-Practice Gap'. In Sheehan (1983): 1–18.

Debney Park High School (1986) *Human Rights*. PEP Schools Resource Program, Cultural Support.

de Lacey, P. and Poole, M. (eds.) (1979) *Mosaic or Melting Pot. Cultural Evolution in Australia*. Sydney, Harcourt, Brace Jovanovich.

de Lemos, M. (1975) *Study of the Educational Achievement of Migrant Children*. Melbourne, Australian Council of Educational Research.

Department of Employment, Education and Training (1987) *Ethnicity, Education and Equity*. Canberra.

Fields, E. (1986) 'Italo-Australian Girls' Perceptions of Home and School'. Unpublished M.Ed Thesis, La Trobe University.

Foster, L. and Stockley, D. (1984) *Multiculturalism: The Changing Australian Paradigm*. Clevedon, Multicultural Matters.

Galbally, F. (1978) *Migrant Services and Programs*. Report Vol. 1, Vol. 2, Appendices. Canberra, AGPS.

Gauci, E. (1983) 'Applying Empirical Methods in Comparative Research: An Example'. In Sheehan (1983): 57–77.

Gibson, M. (1977) 'Approaches to Multicultural Education in the United States: Some Concepts and Assumptions'. *Anthropdogy and Educational Quarterly* 7(4): 7–18.

Hannan, B. (1982) 'The Multicultural School—or Schools in Search of Their own Culture'. In G. Dow (ed.), *Teacher Learning*. London, Routledge and Kegan Paul: 79–110.

Harris, J. (1984) *Study of Insertion Classes under the Commonwealth Ethnic Schools Program*. Canberra, Commonwealth Schools Commission.

Hartley, R. and Maas, F. (1987) *Getting a Lot Further*. MACMME, Australian Institute of Family Studies.

Holenbergh Young, R. (1979) 'Ethnic Identity and Education'. In de Lacy and Poole (1979): 343–365.

Hoy, C. (1983) 'Comparative Methodology and Its Application to Multicultural Societies'. In Corner (1983): 247–67.

Isaacs, E. (1981) 'The Relation Between Home and Educational Progress as it Affects Greek Children Attending State Schools in Sydney'. PhD thesis, School of Sociology, University of NSW.

Jakubowicz, A. (1984) 'State and Ethnicity: Multiculturalism or Ideology'. In J. Jupp (ed.), *Ethnic Politics in Australia*. Sydney, George Allen and Unwin.

Jayasuruja, L. (1987) *Australian Multicultural Education in a Comparative Perspective*. Paper for the Conference, Canada 2000—Race Relations. Carleton University, Ottawa, Canada.

Kalantzis, M. and Cope, B. (1981) *Just Spaghetti and Polka? An Introduction to Australian Multicultural Education*. Sydney, Social Literacy.

Kalantzis, M. and Cope, B. (1986) *Pluralism and Equitability: Multicultural Curriculum Strategies for Schools*. NACCME Commissioned Research Paper No. 3, Canberra, NACCME.

Kalantzis M. and Cope. B. (1988) 'Why We Need Multicultural Education: a Review of the "Ethnic Disadvantage" Debate'. *Journal of Intercultural Studies* 9(1): 39–57.

Keen, I. (1988) *Being Black: Aboriginal Cultures in 'Settled' Australia*. Canberra, Aboriginal Studies Press.

Kringas, P. and Lewins, F. (1981) *Why Ethnic Schools*? Canberra, ANU Press.

Liffman, M. (1985) 'Immigration and Racism in the Land of the Long Weekend'. In Markus and Ricklefs (1985): 112–118.

Lippman, L. (1973) *The Aim is Understanding*. Sydney, ANZ Book Company.

Magsino, R. (1985) 'The Right to Multicultural Education: A Descriptive and Normative Analysis'. Unpublished paper, quoted in Jayaswriya (1987).

Markus, A. and Rasmussen, R. (eds.) *Prejudice in the Public Arena: Racism*. Monash University.

Marjoribanks, K. (1980) *Ethnic Families and Children's Achievements*. Sydney, George Allen and Unwin.

Markus, A. and Rucklefs, M. (eds.) (1985) *Surrender Australia*? Sydney, George Allen and Unwin.

Martin, J. (1978) *The Migrant Presence*. Sydney, George Allen and Unwin.

Meade, P. (1983) *The Educational Experience of Sydney High School Students*. Report No. 3, Canberra, AGPS.

Miles, R. and Phizacklea, A. (1984) *White Man's Country: Racism in British Politics*. London, Pluto Press.

Minister for Ethnic Affairs, Victoria (1984) *Racism in the 1980s. A Response*, Office of the Minister for Ethnic Affairs, Victoria.

Modgil, S., Mallick, Verma K., and Modgil, C. (eds.) (1986) *Multicultural Education: The Interminable Debate*. London, The Falmer Press.

NACCME (1987) *Education in and for a Multicultural Society: Issues and Strategies for Policy Making*. National Advisory and Co-ordinating Committee on Multicultural Education, Canberra.

Nemetz Robinson, G. (1985) *Crosscultural Understanding*. Pergamon Press.

New South Wales, Department of Education (1983) *Multicultural Education Policy Statement*. Sydney, Department of Education.

New South Wales, Department of Education (1987) *Curriculum Implementation: Multicultural Education, Aboriginal Education*. Sydney, Department of Education.

Norst, M. (1983) 'Ethnic School or Community Language School?' In B. Falk and J. Harris (eds.), *Unity in Diversity. Multicultural Education in Australia*. Carlton, Victoria, The Australian College of Education, pp. 108–115.

Orfanos, S. (compiler) (1987) *My Language, My Life*. PEP.

Pettman, R. and Henry, C. (1986) *Teaching for Human Rights: Grades 5–10*. Canberra, Human Rights Commission, AGPS.

Pettman, J. (1987) 'Combatting Racism in the Community'. In Markus and Rasmussen (1987).

Poole, M., de Lacy, R., and Randhawa, B. (eds.) (1985) *Australia in Transition. Culture and Life Possibilities*. Sydney, Harcourt Brace Jovanovich.

Porter, P. (1986) *Gender and Education*. Deakin University Press.

Pratt, C., and Lenton, S. (1984) *Teacher Attitudes to Multicultural Education*. Perth, Western Australian Multicultural Education Advisory Committee.

Queensland Department of Education (1979) 'Policy Statement on Multiculturalism'. Education Office Gazette (81, 5).

Queensland, Department of Education (1982) *Education for a Multicultural Society: Curriculum Guidelines for Primary Schools*. Brisbame, Department of Education.

Rado, M. (1984) Teaching in the Multilingual Classroom. Canberra, CDC.

Simkin, K. (1983) 'Educational Comparisons and the Educator'. In Sheehan (1983): 108–124.

Sheehan, B. (ed.) (1983) *Comparative and International Studies and the Theory and Practice of Education*. Australian Comparative and International Education Society.

Skelton, K. (1985) *Combating Prejudice in Schools. Identifying Issues and Implementing Strategies*. Richmond, Victoria, RCEC.

Smolicz, G. and Secombe, M. (1979) 'Cultural Interaction in a Plural Society'. In de Lacey and Poole (1979): 6–22.

Smolicz, J. (1984) 'Is the Monolingual State Out-of-date? A Comparative Study of Language Policies in Australia and the Philippines'. *Comparative Education* 20(3): 265–285.

Sokoloff, B. (1987) 'Culture, History and Change: Aboriginal Education in Australia'. *ANZAAS Congress Papers* 56, Paper 340: 1–9.

South Australia, Education Department (1987) 'The Philosophy and Practice of Multiculturalism in the Education Department'. Education Gazette Notice (15, 29).

South Australia, Education Department (1988) *Developing Culturally Inclusive Practices in the Curriculum: A Framework*. Adelaide, SAGP.

Sturman, A. (1985) *Immigrant Australians. Education and the Transition to Work*. NACCME Discussion Paper No. 3, 1985.

Tasmania, Department of Education (1988) Position Paper on Multicultural Education (draft, mimeo).

Tsolidis, G. (1986) *Educating Voula*. MACMME.

Victoria, Ministry of Education (Schools Division) (1986) *Education in, and for, a Multicultural Victoria*. Melbourne, Ministry of Education.

Western Australia, Education Department (1977) 'Child Migrant Education Programme'. Policy from the Director-General's Office, No. 11.

Western Australia, Education Department (1981) 'Education for a Multicultural Society'. Policy from the Director-General's Office, No. 33.

Western Australian Multicultural Education Advisory Committee (1986) 'Multiculturalism in Education: Implications for Systems, Teachers and Students.' Policy document (mimeo).

White, D. (1983) 'The Methodology of Comparative Education and its Clarification as a Basis for its Contribution to the Theory and Practice of Education'. In Sheehan (1983): 101–107.

Young, J. (1979) 'Education in a Multicultural Society: What Sort of Education?'. In J. Mallea, R. John, and J. Young (eds.), *Cultural Diversity and Canadian Education*. Ottawa, Carleton University Press.

Young, C., Petty, M., and Faulkner, A. (1980) *Education and Employment of Turkish and Lebanese Youth*. Canberra, Commonwealth Department of Education.

School and Work in the Philippines: Is the Cost Too High?

COLIN B. COLLINS AND ROSELYN R. GILLESPIE

University of Queensland

Before examining the various aspects of the education/employment connection in the Philippines, two very broad areas need to be briefly addressed. The first is concerned with the question; what is unique about the Philippines? The second is concerned with one of the main problems which bedevils much of educational argument, namely the relationship between efficiency and equity and how educational aims centralized around these two realities also confound so many educational planners and administrators.

To the Westerner first visiting the Philippines, there does seem to be a large number of factors that are familiar to anyone who knows even the bare minimum about developing countries. Comprised of over 7000 islands the country is relatively small in area (115,600 square miles) but has a population of some 58,000,000 people which makes it much more heavily populated than, say, most countries in Latin America or Africa but is not exceptional in Asia. About two-thirds of the labour force are classified as agricultural workers. The Philippines has a very small manufacturing base; its service sector is also very modest, even that part employed by the government bureaucracies.

Although the official figures for unemployment are relatively low (about 5 percent), those for underemployment are much higher and some estimates indicate that two-thirds of the Filipino people either live at survival level or under it. As in Latin America, a small number of families (80 in this case) control much of the land and income is skewed with the top 20 percent of income earners accounting for 52.6

percent of earnings and the bottom 60 percent accounting for only 27.2 percent of earnings.[1]

Two dominant features are very much in evidence in the Philippines. The first is the domination of one metropolis. Some—perhaps exaggerated—estimates are that 10 million people live in Metro Manila, a fifth of the country's people. The next largest city is Cebu with a population of only 2 to 3 million. This concentration of political, social, economic and educational power in one city has an enormous influence on the education-employment relationship. All roads may not lead to Rome but most students with higher education set their sights on the air-conditioned comfort of a Manila office.

The other dominant feature is that of cronyism. Although the word may have been coined in the Philippines and although cronyism, under Marcos, may have been brought to an art form seldom witnessed elsewhere, the patronage system is endemic in developing countries (and elsewhere as well, though less obviously). It certainly has not disappeared with the removal of Marcos.

Hence the Philippines; rich in human potential, poor in technological resources. With a per capita income of $600US it is by no means in the poorest country category. But with a foreign debt of almost $30 billion, it is one of the great debtor nations of the world. (Budgetary allocation for 1987 was Pesos 160 billion; the debt service for the same year was Pesos 75.2 billion.)

A very familiar picture, but, what about the differences? Although there are many pre-Malay inhabitants and many different dialects, the majority of the inhabitants are of Malay origin. What makes a highly observable difference is their dual colonization by the Spanish for 333 years ending in 1898 and by the United States beginning in 1898, officially ending in 1946 but unofficially still very much in evidence. Of the first observation, much could be said—the Spanish names, Spanish blood, the formality of the Filipino people. But, for our purposes, the most important aspect of the Spanish heritage is the dominance of the Catholic Church. Eighty-five percent of the population profess Catholicism and the public display and practice of religion is very much in evidence—far more so than in Europe or even Mother-Spain, and even more so than in the Spanish colonized Latin

American countries. For the purposes of this paper, however, we are primarily concerned with the predominance of the Catholic Church in the education sphere. Although the position has changed drastically over the last 20 years, as a single force the Catholic Church still dominates the tertiary education system and the high school system. This dominance of private/denominational schools and colleges is probably more widespread here than in any other country; it has significant implications for education-employment connections.

The second colonization has been by the US. Other than making the Philippines an English speaking country with a dual medium education system (Tagalog and English), the music, sport, many of the films, the folk-art of the "jeepneys" are so American—perhaps a little dated but stamped, "U.S.A." As shall also be noted this has influenced the educational system, especially in its broad aims, its nomenclature and, above all, in the status of these new illustrados who hold degrees from US universities.

The second introductory point can be made succinctly; it is concerned with the convoluted relationship between the utopian aim of equity (in the Philippine context, the word democratisation is used more frequently) and the more pragmatic aim of efficiency. First regarding efficiency, which is really the concern of this essay. In every government document on education, sooner or later the phrase "to improve the productive capacity of the nation" appears. Whatever proportion education is of a government's budget, significant amounts are always spent on the educational systems of nations. Other than the political payoff, the main belief underlying most 3–5–10 year plans in education is that an increase in educational budget ultimately leads to an increase in private and public productivity. Use of this "Human Capital" approach is based on so-called orthodox economic theory. A sub-set of this theory is dual market theory which divides modern and traditional economic systems in developing countries. This suggests that there is a modern, industrialised sector which is being constrained by and has to support a lagging traditional agricultural sector. There is however another set of theories of production and labour market segmentation which enables the observer to make connections between world capitalism and the dependence of so-called peripheral economies on the more powerful ones. To describe these two theories in detail would be too digress too far from our main purpose. (For details see Carnoy 1977.)

What should be maintained at this stage, however, is that the belief in the Human Capital approach persists, no matter what kind of mitigating or even contradictory evidence is brought forward. Twenty to thirty years ago, academics worked in very broad categories when writing of development, progress, industrialisation. They noted that if a country had an under 30 percent literacy rate it would not be industrialised or developed. If over 70 percent of the population were literate, it would have a significant industrial or modern section and therefore could be considered as developed.

These days, connections are more sophisticated, though no less significant. What is of primary importance is that during the last ten years, a great amount of evidence has indicated that industrialised nations, especially the US, are overschooled and that particularly at tertiary level, more schooling can make persons less productive (Berg 1971; Squires 1977; Collins 1979). One of the conclusions was that industry was simply using higher and higher educational credentials purely as screening devices.

This same message was shown to be the case by Dore (1976) in the less developed countries he investigated, where he found educational systems to have expanded enormously in the development decade of the sixties. As this happened, employers have demanded higher and higher qualifications and made these demands, not because they thought the graduates were better, but because they were better screened. These works certainly indicate that many countries are overschooled. And this has led to one of the great problems of the less developed world—the educated unemployed and underemployed.

It would seem, therefore, in the interests of efficiency that there should be less rather than more schooling; perhaps at high school, but certainly at college and university level.

Contradicting this pragmatic aim of creating an *efficient* education system, or one that conforms to the manpower needs of a nation, is that of *equity* or *democratisation.* To suggest that education should be cut down would be political suicide. Throughout the world, and more especially the developing world, parents view schooling as the way out of poverty for their daughters and much more so for their sons. Even in the days of Marcos, the educational share of government expenditures dropped from approximately 25 percent to 10 percent. But the numbers of students in the system increased. Under President Aquino, the great cry has been reemphasized that every child has a right to school, not merely to elementary school but to high school as well. This cry does not make economic sense. And although the aims of education are certainly far more than just economic ones, the mismatch between the labour market and schooling has become one of the most serious problems of the Third World. Its dimensions will now be examined. Before doing so, it should be emphasized that accurate statistics, especially regarding the economic system, the labour force and most particularly concerning employment and unemployment are notoriously difficult to obtain. Or rather, they vary widely according to sources. Statistics concerning employment and unemployment in a country that is two-thirds agricultural are not only difficult to obtain, but signify different tradition than do comparable measurements in developed countries.

THE FILIPINO LABOUR FORCE

The per capita income of the Philippines is about $600 US.[2] This places the Philippines slightly above the "poorest" nations of the world category. After negative growth rates towards the end of the Marcos era, the growth rate had picked up to 5.6 percent p.a. for 1986. But, as already mentioned, the Philippine economy has been propped up by enormous borrowings from overseas, namely $28.6 billion. Over 40 percent of the government budget is taken up with servicing this debt. All of which makes it very difficult for the big money spenders: defence, because of the insurgency problem, health services and education, not to mention improvement that should be occurring in the all important agricultural sectors. A concise summary of the historical aspects of the economic face of the Philippines is given by Tan (1985: 109).

A brief economic boom immediately after 1945 was not sustained, and food deficits became a major problem. The country's earnings from primary products such as minerals, timber, sugar, coconut and fibres were used to import food, and what was left from the food bill was siphoned off as capital for manufacturing industries in the cities. Manufacturing was inward looking, i.e. largely import-substituting, and its products were intended mainly for domestic consumption rather than for export. High tariff walls propped up inefficient industries, while an over-valued currency and artificially low interest rates on capital for the so-called infant industries made those industries heavily capital-intensive. All these circumstances reduced the capacity of the country to absorb labour in gainful employment.

Manufacturing grew by taking advantage of short-term gains up to the limits of artificially cheap capital and of what could be supported by domestic markets. As the limits of the latter were nearly reached, growth rates could not be sustained. The frontier was soon reached because the rural sector was virtually neglected, rural institutions and land tenure were obsolete, not to say feudal, and agriculture was technologically stagnant. Food prices were kept low in favour of the politically articulate city dwellers but to the disadvantage of farmers and producers. Consequently, except in a few areas, the productivity of farms was generally low and the purchasing power of farmers and the rural population was at a standstill, even declining. This resulted in a massive move to Manila where the population increased from just over 2 million in 1960 to its current 10 million. Although efforts were made to increase industrial development and to improve agricultural production, all these efforts fell into disarray with the OPEC shock of 1974. Coupled to this, a state of emergency had been declared by Marcos in 1972.

During the decade 1975–1985, the economy became increasingly beleaguered. It was propped up by huge overseas loans, a considerable amount of which were creamed off by cronies. Manufacturing, in many cases, was dependent on multi-national corporations' capital. Agriculture was being impeded by feudal land ownership and increasing insurgency. The country sank lower and lower into economic depression.

More to the point of this chapter is the question of the different sectors of the economy, growth or decline in each sector and employment rates over against the unemployed. Research studies have shown the sectoral employment of workers in the Philippines over the last nine years (Philippine Yearbook 1985, NEDA 1986, Manila p.467). EDA 1986. Over the last ten years, employment grew from 15 to 20 million. Manufacturing grew only slightly whereas community, racial and personal services employees almost doubled.

What is much more significant to this study is the way in which individuals are declared to be employed or unemployed:

> . . . labour force is the part of population 15 years old and over that is either employed or unemployed during the reference period. Prior to November 1976 survey, labour force was defined as the part of the population 10 years old and over that is either employed or unemployed during a reference quarter period. In any case, employed persons include all those who were reported at work, those with a job but not at work while unemployed include all those who were reported as wanting and looking for work anytime during the reference quarter whether on a fulltime or part time basis. Also included are persons reported as wanting but not looking for work because of the belief that no work is available or because of temporary illness, bad weather or any other reasons. Persons not in the labour force are those who are not at work and without jobs and not wanting work, or wanting work but not looking for work for the reasons that a person is disabled, retired, schooling or housekeeping. Also included are those seasonal workers who are not working and not looking for work during the survey period. (Yearbook 1985: 466)

It should be noted that people are counted as employed if they work for one hour in the reference quarter. Thus the official figures for unemployment are much lower than the actual numbers. For example, unemployment was said to be 8.5 percent in 1961 and 7.8 percent in 1968 and 3.9 percent in 1974. However, as Tan states (1985; 172).

> These rosy figures were no more than estimates from head counts of persons who had worked during the 'reference week'. The estimation never considered how much time was spent at work or how much income was earned from that work, and hence, the figures never accounted for underemployment and its full arithmetic equivalent in

> unemployment. However, indirect estimates by the ILO Mission showed that far from the 4 to 8 percent range, unemployment could be placed at 25 to 35 percent of the labour force in 1971.

Other estimates indicate that up to 50 percent of the working population are either unemployed or underemployed.

It should also be mentioned that it is so difficult to obtain work that the number of workers now exported from the Philippines has grown phenomenally in the last 10 years as indicated in the following tables (Yearbook 1985: 471, 485). Between 1975 and 1985, the number of contract workers in overseas countries grew from 5000 to almost half a million. The unofficial figures are thought to be well over a million.

To complete the picture of the employment situation, the figures for labour force participation rates for the Philippines over the last decade should be considered: (Yearbook 1985: 470). The picture that emerges from these statistics is that although over 21 million Filipinos were "in the labour force" in 1985, the participation rate was only 63.4 percent. It should also be remembered that in that year the population of the country was 55 million, half of whom were under the age of 21. As will be seen when absorption rates of the educated are cited, many of those who work, especially many in the agricultural sectors and the marginals in Manila and other cities and towns, do not have regular full-time salaried jobs. For most of those workers who are "in the labour force," work means seasonal or part-time work or buying or selling on street corners. As already mentioned, about two-thirds of the population live at survival level or less. The fortunate minority are those who have full-time work in industry, commerce, service (government or otherwise) or who own enough land to be economically self-sufficient.

THE EDUCATIONAL PICTURE

Once more only those aspects relevant to school/employment connections need to be given to indicate the gross statistical picture of education over the last two decades. (See Philippine Education Indicators 1965–1985: 3, 4.)

Several comments can be made from these data:

1. While the proportion of the budget given to education has dropped from 28.47 percent in 1965 to 13.70 percent in 1985, actual figures have increased from over half a billion pesos in 1965 to over 8 billion pesos in 1985. During these 20 years, enrolment in all sectors increased from 7 1/2 million to 12 1/2 million students. The Aquino government has promised a greater share of budgetary allocation to education (15 billion pesos were allocated for 1988). So far this has not been done to any considerable extent, except to increase teachers' salaries in the public sector. It should also be noted that, in the main, the private schools and colleges are self-supporting and that many *barangay* and provincial schools have to find a considerable proportion of their own finance. Hence, the public and private total amount spent on financing schools is considerably higher than the official DECS figures.

2. Over the last 20 years, state involvement in elementary schools has increased somewhere on the order of 50 percent. Secondary education increased by 183 percent (Education Indicators, p. 11). This latter increase was mostly due to the increase of government high schools (as also at the tertiary level).

3. The predominance of the private sector at both secondary (57 percent vs. 43 percent of enrolments) and at the tertiary level (77.7 percent vs. 22.3 percent) should also be noted (Education Indicators; p. 12, 13).

4. In 1985, 25.53 percent of the Filipino population was at school. In itself, this figure is as high as many industrial countries. As will be further discussed, the ratio between levels is much more significant; 16.48 percent of the population are in elementary schools; 6.23 percent in high schools and 2.82 percent at the tertiary level.

Flowing from these general observations, certain points more specific to the education/employment situation should be made. The first point is concerned with retention rates. Of an elementary school total of almost 9 million in 1984/5, only a little over a million graduated from Grade VI. As in all less developed countries, the great cluster of elementary school students are in the first four years and scarcely become literate before dropping out. Out of a total of 3.3 million students in secondary school, 618,000 graduate are in their final year. As can be expected, this is a much higher proportion than in elementary schools (19 percent opposed to 11 percent).

The factors that will influence the school/employment connection are as follows:

(a) The location of the educational institute. Students from a National High School in Manila are far more likely to succeed than those from a local *barangay* school. At the tertiary level, the University of the Philippines graduates have much higher status than small provincial or country ones (UP has half the library books of the entire state university system of 78 institutions).

(b) Pupil-teacher ratios are also significant. In the Philippines, numbers per class run at about 40 students per teacher in both elementary and secondary schools. This figure is high compared to industrialized countries.

(c) The length of time students spend at school. The average time is five years for the total Filipino population.

(d) The private/public school dichotomy. Students who attend private schools usually come from richer and more well-educated parents.

(e) The vast majority of schools are of an academic nature. Very few technical schools exist and still fewer are effective. Like virtually all developing countries, the preference is for schools that prepare students for professional and white collar jobs rather than manual occupations. In the tertiary sector, for example, less than 3 percent of students enrol in agriculture.

From a schooling point of view, the Philippines compares well to many other developing countries, especially in the tertiary sector with its more than 1000 institutions and 1.5 million students (1987). The questions which remain to be asked are: What are the connections between school and employment? Does education increase a person's work chances or make him or her more productive? Does education add to the productivity of a nation, or should it merely be considered as a service to the nation's people? What kind of education are Filipino children receiving and is it suitable for a country that is two-thirds agricultural? An attempt will be made to outline some of the given answers to these questions and to analyze the kinds of solutions which have been suggested.

THE CONNECTION BETWEEN SCHOOLING AND EMPLOYMENT

An educational system is not merely an instrument of manpower planning. In all policy statements, many other lofty aims are espoused, such as the development of a child's intellectual, emotional, spiritual and physical well-being, the democratisation of the nation, the production of well-adjusted citizens and, in many cases, God-fearing and loving persons. Our concern is, however, much narrower.

Firstly, one question that is perhaps the most frequently asked is whether an individual's work chances are improved by education. Answers to this usually take the form of mobility studies or analyses of the educational qualifications of workers in various categories and their income attainment.

Regarding social mobility, the pattern is almost always the same. The work cycle commences with the father's occupation. If it is high status and well-paid, the child is likely to end up in a private elite school and, eventually a well-paid job. Many variables enter into this circle. A few such variables are in the family life: socio-economic status, parents' occupation, their educational achievements, gender, location of family (rural or urban) and home attitudes to school and work. All these predetermine which school the child enters and what happens in the school. At school, various forces will come into play such as the administration of the school, quality of teachers, the attitude and quality of the students, the kind of curriculum undertaken (academic or vocational) and which subjects are taken, as well as the achievement of the particular student. Finally, entry into the workforce depends on what work is available, contacts and so on.

This circle can be a very felicitous one for those from the upper classes but is horrendous for a large proportion of Filipino students who come from less favoured backgrounds. In short, as many authors demonstrate, (for example Bowles and Gintis 1976) schools re-enforce class distinctions. In answer to the question of whether schools improve a person's life chances, these authors reply positively but state that class factors already predetermine schooling and eventually work.

Jaime B. Valera (1982 and 1983) has examined the circle for certain groups of Filipino students. Some of his conclusions are somewhat at variance with the above. In his paper, "Does Education Pay?," he states:

> Is education a passport to social mobility? Compared to social background in the given model it appears that educational attainment is the most important determinant of occupational and earnings attainment for urban residents. For rural residents, education comes second only to vocational background, where the respondent spent his youth. Yet in contrast to what is suggested in stratification or mobility studies we find no strong evidence that paternal social status to be more important than educational attainment. (Valera 1982: 10)

He does suggest, however, that

> to attain these dreams of better occupation and hence better incomes, it is important to be a parent to have a relatively high education. (Valera 1983)

Clearly, schooling usually does benefit the individual in terms of status and earnings, but it only does so among a cluster of many other variables.

Another way to make connections is to look at the educational qualifications and earnings of workers in various graded occupations. We have not been able to locate any statistics presented in these forms for the Philippines, except for rather general studies (such as Richards and Leonor 1981) or highly specific studies, such as Valera (1986), who deals with tertiary agricultural graduates.

Another way is by following up the employment and unemployment data of students particularly from the tertiary sector. This has been done for the Philippines by Editha A. Tan and Mauricio Leonor in a work edited by M.D. Leonor, *Unemployment, Schooling and Training in Developing Countries* (1985) and in Arcelo and Sanyal, *Employment and Career Opportunities After Graduation: The Philippine Experience* (1987). One rather startling conclusion comes from an ILO Mission report of 1974 (tertiary education has been considerably expanded since then). Their conclusions were that:

The utilisation rates of human resources were rather low, especially among school drop-outs, the lowest being among those who dropped out of college. The base figures of "college to 3 years" in 1965, including their projections for 1969 and 1974, never reached 39 percent, suggesting that the non-utilization rate was 61 percent, or that about 6 out of every 10 educated persons in this category were not working. Of course, many of these (prospective) workers were attending school rather than work, but even for those who had completed college, i.e. four or more years after high school, the figures seem to suggest an increasing number who were not working, that is, from 1 out of 4 in 1965 to 6 out of 10 mentioned above.

They note that with the rapid expansion of the tertiary systems of education and the economic depression since 1974, the situation has certainly deteriorated. This ILO study also examines the various areas from which students graduate in the tertiary sector and notes that 56 percent are from business, teaching and agriculture.

There have not been detailed studies of employment, underemployment and unemployment of elementary and high school students in the Philippines. However, judging by the relatively small proportion employed in white collar work in this country, the underemployment and unemployment rate of high school students must be extremely high.

And it is, in the final analysis, that an answer to the question of whether schooling increases a nation's productivity is at least partially answered by the underemployment rates and unemployment rates of its better educated citizens. Some estimate these joint rates to approximate 60 percent which fact means either that the educational system is overexpanded particularly at its top end, or that it is the wrong kind of education which attracts students to white collar urban jobs rather than to agricultural activities.

No one is really able to say how efficient a schooling system is in terms of a country's productivity. Even in a highly urbanised and an industrialized country such as Australia, at least half of school-leavers learn their work on the job. Efficiency can only be partially judged when considering the upper echelons of occupations such as doctors, lawyers and high technology workers. But one all-important conclusion that can be reached and has been much written about in the developing world since Philip Coomb's, *The World Educational Crisis* (1966), is that in the Philippines there are too many educated for too few jobs, and that there is too much education of a largely academic rather than a vocational kind. It is rather ironic that the Philippines has already exported almost half a million of its educated unemployed to other countries!

The Philippines does not stand alone in this respect. Overeducation and underemployment/unemployment is endemic to most Third World countries. The fantasy (for the many) is that high education will get them jobs or better jobs. This happens for a minority of school and university products (see Blaug 1974, Coombs 1966, Leonor 1985). But where the beliefs and expectations of the masses remain the same, are there any solutions?

POSSIBLE SOLUTIONS

A first set of solutions is of the liberal reformist kind and is usually exclusively concerned with educational matters (see Blaug 1974, and many others). The second are concerned with a nation's economy and are somewhat more radical in tone though sometimes emanating from conservative sources. We shall turn first to the educational solutions.

A first cluster of solutions is what to do about the size of the educational system. The present Aquino government has, in response to popular demand, said that it will expand the system so that eventually all Filipino children will acquire high school certificates. Although this is not really a response to the problems discussed above, the effect of expansion can keep the unemployment figures down. This is certainly true in a provisional sense. The higher the retention rate in schools, the fewer young unemployed—the group most affected by the problem. This is certainly a major reason for educational expansion in industrialised countries.

A second solution is to reduce the educational system, or at least reduce the number of rapidly escalating small colleges at tertiary level. Although there have been three recent studies on tertiary education, little suggestion has been made of reduction in numbers. In one of these reports, *Report on State Universities and Colleges in the Philippines* (MECS, Feb. 1987), suggestions are made for the consolidation of smaller colleges and for the elimination of many oversubscribed courses in, for example, commerce. In fact, a report, *Images from the Future: The Philippines in the Year 2000* (1978), makes some amazing connections between schooling and productivity. Its conclusion is:

> For our economy to grow at the target 8 percent yearly we will be needing among other things a tremendous amount of high-quality laborers. This requirement, in turn, will help to increase the pressure on our educational system. It is now up to us to make sure that the educational system passes the test with high marks! (p. 47)

The solution of contracting the system by having fewer high schools and colleges has been attempted in some socialist countries as, for example, Tanzania (Leonor 1985). It would probably be political suicide for any government in the Philippines to do so.

A third suggestion has been that of a *laissez-faire* policy, a kind of supply and demand free market setup. To a certain extent this has been the policy of past Filipino governments—hence the proliferation of private institutions. Especially in the last 20 years the government has built up a very impressive elementary system. During the 1980s, however, the rhetoric continued to be towards expansion.

A much more obvious form of supervision is to prevent wastage by having quality control between the various phases of education and more especially from high school into colleges and universities. This has been done in the Philippines when in 1976, the National College Entrance Examination (NCEE) was introduced. As stated in the

Philippine Yearbook 1985 (p. 204): "This test is held every year to identify the top 55 percent who can be accommodated in college and consequently absorbed into the job market." A further solution addresses the need to make the schools more relevant to the requirements of a nation, and more especially its economic needs. This has been called the "vocationalizing of education". Its main tenet with reference to developing countries has been that because a nation such as the Philippines is almost two-thirds agricultural, its educational system should be more directly concerned with agricultural pursuits. (The whole "vocational education fallacy" has been hotly debated since Foster's (1966) article. For a summary of the debate see Lillis and Hogan 1983).

Although the Philippines obviously has technical schools and colleges and a well-developed agricultural educational sector, these efforts have hardly dented the academic character of the high school or the fact that only 2.6 percent of tertiary students are enrolled in agriculture courses. (Ministry of Education, Culture and Sports Annual Report 1985: 41.) And although it is obvious that education only becomes vocational at tertiary level, more than a third of Filipino tertiary students go into Commerce and Business Administration while another 20 percent go into Engineering and High Technology. When the low manufacturing and service base of the Filipino labour force is considered, unemployment or at least underemployment of those graduates is quite understandable.

There have been a number of educational experiments in the Philippines during the last two decades. These involve the agricultural orientated high schools called Barrio schools. The results of such experiments have been somewhat dubious, except in the case of the Bayanihan School Programme (Palao 1987). Such combinations of school and work have rarely met with success in capitalist countries (for a discussion of such experiments, see Gillespie and Collins 1987).

Other suggestions for vocationalizing education would be to have a common curriculum core for, say, six years, and then a break into academic and vocational schools. Liberal democrats would argue about the justice of such a scheme whereas radicals would point to the class re-enforcement of such a move. Our own position is that such a move can only be justified if (1) special provision is made for students from rural backgrounds getting into the academic stream and (2) special provision is made to ensure that adults can return to the schooling system after being employed (or unemployed) for a while.

Another set of educational solutions to modify the mismatch between education and employment is to build up the informal and non-formal sectors of education. This has been done in the Philippines but to a degree that is marginal when compared to the formal educational system. Perhaps an exception to such marginality is the encouragement that is now being given to private enterprise to train their own workers on-the-job.

Many other suggestions for remedying the mismatch between education and employment have been made such as improving the information process concerning jobs or encouraging graduates to accept lower jobs for a limited period of time. But these kind of suggestions are usually of a band-aid nature, though they may help individuals and should, therefore, be encouraged. As in most developing countries, individual solutions usually occur through "whom one knows."

These are just some of the main educational suggestions which have been propounded to help rectify the education/employment mismatch. As is obvious from the above, the Philippines is not set on a course to rectify this problem. There are many writers, however, who would say that changes in the educational system would not appreciably alter the mismatch. Instead they maintain that the employment or economic and political realities of a country need to be changed before its educational institutions can be altered.

Regarding economic matters, writers such as Carnoy (1977), and others are quite categorical:

> —the solution to unemployment and to educated unemployment, as well as to the rapid, uncontrollable migration from rural areas to the urban sprawl of shanty towns lies not in the restructuring of the production system. We can no longer rely on the emergence of new entrepreneurs to organize financing, marketing and production for new employment; although there are many talented entrepreneurs in LIC's, the production of foods and services does not maximize employment—it maximizes profit. (Carnoy 1977: 80)

Although many other writers would not go as far as this, it is interesting to see how other economists and planners have come to the same kinds of suggestions when looking at economic factors (see, for example, "Education and Employment: From World Capitalism to the Rural Thais," 1985).

Put simply, the problem is not primarily an educational one. Unemployment or underemployment, especially of the educated, can be solved by the creation of more or better jobs. Both Carnoy and the Thai report discuss plans for the urban and rural sectors.

For urban areas, Carnoy (1977) for example suggests that direct central government employment on public works projects such as roads, dams, rivers, irrigation and school buildings should be tempered by the "public financing of producer cooperatives" and "—with the financing of co-operatives and the direct employment of the unemployed could be tied to training programs—not training for private sector jobs but programs which would provide the skills needed in local producer co-ops, worker-run plants financed with government credits" (Carnoy 1977: 79).

The Thai report suggests moreover that, as in the Philippines,

> Industries in Thailand are that heavily dominated by import substitution types. In theory, once these industries have been established there should be a general reduction of imports. (1985: 41)

As this hasn't happened, the report goes on to state criteria for desirable industries (most of which would not be of the multi-national variety). They should have low import content, have good export potential, should generate a sufficient amount of income and employment, have technological linkages, but with domestic control and so on (actual industries are suggested such as processed foods, garments, etc.) Carnoy (1977: 73) also suggests that job creation can be improved by direct subsidies to firms, the taxation of high income earners, and the increase of government services. These and other reports also make a pre-eminently important point. If employment is to be increased in the rural areas and if people are to be kept in the country, life in the country has to be made more acceptable. Various suggestions are made, some of which include:

1. Re-distribution of the land to farmers. (Under the CARP scheme, this has scarcely been commenced in the Philippines where much of the best land is held by the few.)
2. The building up of rural co-ops and the training of people in their management.
3. Support for individuals and organisations who play an active part in field work (instead of viewing them as agitators).
4. Direct action by provincial and central authorities in the area of constructing infra-structures.
5. Efforts to increase rural productivity and the possible raising of agricultural prices in order to increase the purchasing power of the rural sector.

These suggestions and many more are summarized by (Carnoy 1977, 82):

> —If, however, rural education is accompanied by the extension of credit to small farmers, high prices for products which they can produce, land reform and advice on cooperative arrangements and the leasing of machinery then there is a real possibility of such education leading to greater productivity and more employment in rural areas.

What chances are there for any of these changes to be implemented in the Philippines? At the moment very little is being done to direct the country towards greater employment strategies along the lines indicated. The fundamental contradiction is that more jobs are not being created because industry is dominated by the multi-nationals, and land by the few. To add to this, an educational system is increasing the numbers of educated unemployed. Where so many people live at survival levels, it is small wonder that schools become leaky life-rafts and that others have turned to revolution. Small wonder the Philippines is going through such turbulent times.

To end on a more positive note: a chapter of a NEDA document on "Education, Manpower and Labor" is part of the "Updated Philippine Development Plan 1984–87". Although it has a conservative tone in that it endeavours to align education and the economy more closely, it also contains many educationally reformist ideas discussed in the latter part of this paper. Naturally enough it does not promote the twin ideas of local (and popular) ownership of industry or redistribution of land ownership, the cornerstone of the more radical economic suggestions. It does, however, suggest a general slowing down of the system by a temporary moratorium in the conversion of barangay high schools into national high schools and of public secondary schools into state colleges and universities (p. 179). It also suggests "full support for the balanced Agro-Industrial Development Strategy," for new skills training and vocational/technical education and even that

> the focus of the investment program will shift from large-scale and foreign exchange oriented activities to those which are small and medium-scale and less foreign-exchange dependent. (p. 188)

All of which is to say that there are positive ideas available, if only there were the political ability to implement them. The ultimate irony, however, is that this same document recommends the increased exportation of overschooled and unemployed Filipinos to the rich world—at the moment, the country's greatest source of foreign earnings! This represents yet more commodification of education, at the expense of more responsible forms of development which would aid the wider populace.

NOTES

1. *Trends Focus* (14), August 17–23, 1987.
2. IBON, *Facts and Figures* X (3/16), February 1957, p. 8.

REFERENCES

Government Sources

Images from the Future: The Philippines in the Year 2000. Population Center Foundation, Manila 1978.

The Philippine Yearbook 1985. Manila, 1986.

Philippine Educational Indicators, 1965–85. Moving Upward in Education: 1985. Ministry of Education, Culture and Sports.

Report on State Universities and Colleges in the Philippines, 1987. MECS, Feb.

Updated Philippine Development Plan 1984–87. September 1984. National Economic and Development Authority.

Other

Arcelo, A.A. and Sanyal, B.C. (1987) *Employment and Career Opportunities after Graduation: The Philippine Experience*. Manila, UNESCO.

Berg, Ivar (1970) *The Great Training Robbery*. Harmondsworth, Penguin.

Blaug, M. (1970) *An Introduction to the Economics of Education*. London, Penguin.

Blaug, M. *Education and Employment Problems in Developing Countries*. Geneva, ILO.

Bowles, S. and Gintis, H. (1974) *Schooling in Capitalist America*. New York, BASIL Books.

Carnoy, M. (1977) *Education and Employment: A Critical Appraisal*. Paris, UNESCO: International Institute for Educational Planning.

Collins, Randall (1979) *The Credential Society*. Academic Press.

Coombs, Philip (1968) *The World Educational Crisis: A Systems Analysis*. London, Oxford University Press.

Dore, J. (1976) *The Diploma Disease*. London, Allen and Unwin.

Education and Employment: From World Capitalism to the Rural Thais 1985. Bangkok, The National Education Commission, Office of the Prime Minister. Institute of Human Resources, Thammasat University.

Foster, P. (1965) 'The Vocational School Fallacy in Development Planning'. In C.A.B. Anderson and M. Bowman, *Education and Economic Development*. Chicago, ALDINE.

Gillespie, R.R. and Collins, C.B. (1987) 'Productive Labor in Schools. An International Evaluation'. *Prospects* XVII (1): 11–26.

Leonor, M.D. (ed.) (1985) *Employment, Schooling and Training in Developing Countries*. London, Croom Helm.

Lillis, K. and Hogan, H. (1983) 'Dilemmas of Diversification; Problems Associated with Vocational Education in Developing Countries'. *Comparative Education* 19 (1): 89–107.

Palao, M.P. (1987) *The Bayanihan School Programme: Equitable and Quality Education for Rural Countries.* 1987 Congress, Baguio City, May 20–22, 1987.

Richards, P. and Leonor, M. (1981) *Education and Income Distribution in Asia.* London, Croom Holm.

Tan, E.A. and Leonor, M. (1985) 'The Philippines'. In M. Leonor (ed.), *Unemployment, Schooling and Training in Developing Countries.* London, Croom Helm.

Valera, J.B. (1982) 'Government Schools and the Process of Occupational Attainment'. Professorial Chair Lecture June 25, UP at Los Banos.

Valera, J.B. (1983) *Does Education Pay: The Influence of Schooling an Occupational and Earnings Attainment in Rural and Urban Philippines.*

Valera, J.B. (1985) 'Employment and Schooling: The Case of Higher Education in Agriculture'. In *Proceedings, Regional Service versus Higher Education in Agriculture and Rural Development*, May 13–15. Los Banos, Philippines, SEARCH.

Learning and Employment: A Perspective of Lifelong Change*

EDMUND KING

Professor Emeritus, University of London, Great Britain

INTRODUCTION

Mankind has always had a tendency to regard the present state of affairs as permanent—not only permanent but evidently self-justified, and indeed "natural". Even revolutionaries about to establish a new system have relied on a sense of permanence—in heaven, in the rational process, or in "natural laws" of some kind that could be invoked to regulate and perhaps "predict".

Thus the Founding Fathers of the United States of America could pronounce: 'We believe these truths to be self-evident: that all men were created equal, and that all are equally endowed with certain unalienable (sic) rights. . . .' And so on. "Rationality" grafted on to British customary administrative and legal organisation in the newly independent American colonies gave rise in due course to the "American way of life" which, as everyone knows, it is still near-sacrilege to challenge. In the "University of the State of New York" (i.e. that state's educational system) an attempt was made to establish a logical pyramid of educational provision for all the state's foreseeable needs.

The French revolutionaries, for their part, used almost the same words as the new Americans to justify their new political order (not surprisingly, because both parties relied on a formulation by the Englishman Thomas Paine); but the French drew on the concepts and centralism of the Catholic Church, as well as the administrative heritage of the Roman Empire, to build the pyramidal system of educational provision and controls we have learned to call "Napoleonic". The essential assumption was that everything is capable of logical formulation, and controllable by rules beyond the present vagaries of mankind.

Marxist theory has relied on the supposed existence of permanent and controlling 'scientific laws' which could enable party leaders objectively and accurately to establish not merely general political principles but the details of decision and planning in particular cases. For decades the USSR and Eastern Europe were ruled by such formulae, even in economic management. Despite the last five years of *perestroika*, the 1989 collapse of communist regimes in Eastern Europe, and the 1990 relinquishing of political monopoly in the USSR itself, compliance with the interpretations of official ideology still survives at the very heart of "communist morality", which (according to Lenin and his latter-day followers) is still the end-purpose of all education in the USSR.

Until "reconstructed" by Gorbachev and his supporters, the Soviet Union programmed its political, economic and educational development systematically through interlocking five-year and other plans—for example, by forecasting manpower needs in a whole hierarchy of categories and by moulding formal and informal educational provision to match them. Though not so tightly or continuously, the French have somewhat similarly forecast their future development and shaped or reformed official education to suit it—by instruments of state. In the US, despite apparently diffused responsibility for education, long-term manpower planning by industry and commerce since the 1950s has (through its financial incentives) been profoundly influential in shaping what is expected of school- and college-leavers.

Important though the differences are between these three examples when studied individually, they are perhaps more significant for my present purpose when considered together as embodying the assumption that the future is foreseeable, plannable, and contrivable by means of formal education systems managed by the State—if not owned by the State. Indeed, states have behaved as though they also owned the young people being educated, and their careers, as though they were a commodity called "manpower". Despite truly humanitarian considerations motivating many educational developments, scholastic provision has usually been construed as something decided upon in the long term, and managed consistently from the top downwards.

It is this central assumption which is now fundamentally challenged, for technological, political and educational reasons. The central challenge for today is that we must work towards *Education for Uncertainty* (King 1979a)—and most of all in everything that pertains to young adults (a newly recognised "problem" constituency in three senses: socially, economically and politically) (King, Moor and Mundy 1974, 1975). Young adults are now very important politically, since in many countries they have the vote at 18 and in others are liable to conscription. They are a source of economic anxiety—as potential workers or as unemployed—and demographic fluctuations referred to below accentuate that anxiety. Socially, they have largely overthrown the norms of older generations in sexuality and life-style preferences. However, the emphasis in this chapter is on their profound—indeed central—challenge to all previous educational assumptions and provision for the threshold between juvenility and engagement in acknowledgedly adult life.

On whose behalf are upper-secondary education and training at that level provided? In industrially developed countries, today's young adults (i.e. those over the age of about 14, but including some younger) are expected to be "in school'"—in marked contrast to all previous generations, and unlike their peers working responsibly or raising families in the agrarian societies where most of mankind still lives. Yet school and training systems developed in the past 150–200 years have never been intended to recognise and serve "young adults" as such. In so far as they have prepared "youth" for "transition" to someone else's prescription for adult life, that initiation process has been based upon "perennial" assumptions for a future that is now technologically obsolete, unpredictable and indeed dependent upon development by young adults themselves through a network of contacts, communications and learning resources without precedent.

The whole of education's relationship with society and work in industrialised (increasingly "post-industrial") communities is on a moving frontier. Young adults are a frontier population par excellence. That is why an analysis of their situation is pivotal to any decisions about education. Education of any kind is essentially forward-looking, and today's young adults will have to make and re-adjust that relationship continuously.

That is the essential point of principle we must accept. It is pivotal to all thinking about education. Who educates whom? For what? How, when and where? And what are today's and tomorrow's instruments and occasions of education? What kinds of participation, partnership and feedback will be conducive to educational development and reform? These are the key questions—quite different in emphasis from those which have exercised older educators. The answers are to be found—provisionally, and with continuous correction—by successive generations of young adults along a frontier of rapid and universal change.

Comparative studies of education are especially challenged by this transformation of the educational context. Quite apart from the fact that such studies used to be almost exclusively intended for teachers in initial training, or postgraduate specialists—thereby omitting from involvement most of the people active or passive in the business of education—there has been a change in the prime area of concern. In the past, Comparative Education has been mainly preoccupied with documentation, classification, "currents", "trends", so-called "cause-and-effect" relationships, and (sad to say) presumed "predictions" or even "laws" of development. Studies of real-life policy formation, decision-making, implementation and partnership with the real world of headlong technological/occupational readjustment are much rarer and more recent; and they have seldom been supported by empirical research.

In any case, the key challenge lies in the whole notion of educating an entire population for a life of continuous, self-managed change in a network of re-learning such has never existed. That concept has never been provided for, never contemplated (King 1979b). Above all, our educators have never appreciated that they too must be learners together with the young adults who are making or shaping tomorrow's world. That is a notion which stands most conventional Comparative Education on its head.

A DEFINITION OF 'NEW ADULTS': A CHALLENGE FOR EDUCATORS

When, in the early postwar years, fresh educational and social concern was expressed about the consequences of having so many more young people staying on at school or in training beyond the age of compulsory attendance, nobody spoke about "young adults". The talk (and therefore any research or planning that went on) was all about "youth" or—at best—"young people".

Such expressions implied that anyone between the age of about 14 and the end of schooling—or even up to the age of about 25—was of conditional status. Their lives and needs were thought of in terms of older people's judgements, and always assessed on the assumption that they would have to fit into patterns of life and work with which older people were familiar. Existing courses of instruction or training, and therefore systems of examination and occupational entry, were all imagined to be semipermanent or even everlasting.

However, some of us became aware that changes brought about by the increased numbers "staying on" in schools and training institutions, and the ever-extending length of their enrolment, required much more investigation. My own Comparative Research Unit at King's College in the University of London originally set out in 1970 to investigate 'newness' in full-time post-compulsory education in five Western European countries: newness in the composition of those enrolled between the ages of about 16 and 20 (for example by including more girls, or students from different social backgrounds); newness in the kinds of school or study they had come from; newness in the institutions now provided to accommodate them, and still more in their courses or teaching methods for the "new" population; newness in the further courses or careers available after extended schooling; and—above all—newness in the "inside view" of the students themselves and their teachers.

Over our three-year period of research it became abundantly clear that all the students were "new" in this age range. The very fact of having a larger population enrolled, with a different "mix" and a wider range of studies or expectations, was sufficient to ensure radical change in educational provision and style. To accommodate this larger student body, many European countries began to establish or adapt 'post-compulsory' institutions of a more comprehensive nature than previously.

Everyone noticed a "more adult atmosphere" as a distinct educational advantage, even in establishments that were only adapted upper-secondary schools. Some newer types of organisation, however, combined immediately post-compulsory provision with "community college" services for the older general public, and thus false distinctions between the age groups participating in education quickly faded. That has been especially true of the vast amount of part-time education in evening institutes.

Of course, it should have been obvious that the over-16s (and some younger people) enrolled in schools during the daytime were really adults in many respects outside school hours if not during them. Throughout the 1950s there had been a crescendo of appeals to young people's maturing ambitions in "pop" songs, in fashions, in the contraceptive pill, in magazines, in the media.

Moreover, those enrolled were not all simply 'staying on' beyond compulsory schooling. In Sweden, for example, more than a quarter had been out at work and had returned to fulfil study or training, though still usually at an early age; some students elsewhere were taking advantage of workers' supplementary education schemes (like that in France or the '150 hours' in Italy). Yet others had returned to that level of learning at a much later age, perhaps because of job changes (frequent among the young), because of the need to learn new subjects or skills, or for a whole range of reasons.

Perhaps in consequence of this wider demographic and social "mix", many students from comfortable homes who previously would almost certainly have opted for "academic" courses gradually began to broaden their study choices with "practical" or pre-vocational programmes—partly because of their intrinsic appeal, partly because they seemed to "make more sense" than previously familiar bookish courses, and partly because of their potential utility for a future job market. In any case, the adult world had by the late 1960s and early 1970s begun to show that prosperous and satisfying careers might more easily be enjoyed in the less academic occupations than in the precarious pursuit of professions prepared for in university courses and the like.

This kind of choice has been increasingly made by the over-16s in Norway and Sweden. In a not dissimilar way it has been noticeable that boys in Eastern Europe are often enrolled in employment-oriented courses during the later secondary school years, while the more theoretically 'academic' courses are apparently the province of girls. That is less surprising in countries which already have great strength in work-oriented higher education, of both an "academic" and a distinctly practical character; but one must also bear in mind the large proportion of students there who undertake higher education on a part-time basis while in paid employment. Since the mid-1960s nearly all the main industrialised countries have greatly expanded their higher education provision in the "applied" sciences; and a great deal of that has taken the form of "sandwich" courses (that is, alternations of theoretical and practical stages). The fact that even graduate unemployment had already become a familiar phenomenon, especially in many of the less industrialised countries, presented a warning to many young adult students still at school.

After 1973 the most insistent influence on study preference and career expectation during post-compulsory education was, of course, juvenile unemployment on a vast scale; it shattered all previously assured prospects from school at this age- or attainment-level. Nevertheless, it would be a great mistake to suppose that only disruption of occupational prospects or a demand for new groups of competences prompted re-thinking about education and training at the young adult level. In fact, demographic changes in most industrial countries have already introduced a fall in the total 16–20 age-group and are likely to bring about at least 10 percent–30 percent fall in the potential young adult workforce. That brings numerical implications for employment prospects, of course; but at the same time occupational shifts and technological innovation call for different kinds of "employability"—and personal choices.

Hence the re-thinking which started in the late 1960s and was made specially urgent by young adult unemployment and job impermanence has during recent years required more of a generic reorientation than simply a concern to mitigate the political perils of "youth unemployment". Because of the new awareness and the broader perspectives encouraged by new combinations of study—often in new-style institutions—the urgent need arose from the late 1960s onwards to recognise "post-compulsory education" as a characteristically new entity for an unprecedented group of educational requirements.

Yet the specific term 'post-compulsory education', with precise reference to the whole complex of interlocking needs with which we are now familiar, was not widely used until my research team adopted it; and even then we frequently had to explain its full significance. More strikingly, nobody spoke about "young adults" in that specific connection until in 1973/4 we publicised their educational significance as a constituency in their own right across the whole gamut of needs and aspirations in that age-range, as the Council of Europe recognised in Post-Compulsory Education in Western Europe—a new concept (King 1979).

Nowadays, of course, the term "young adult" is commonplace in many languages. It is perhaps most frequently used with reference to non-scholastic needs—no bad thing, because the adult dimension of young adults' life experience is of far greater significance than whatever formal "educators" devise in "schooly" terms. As we emphasised, post-compulsory education is the first stage of adult education, and all previous schooling must be a preparation for that: indeed, that stage itself is also pivotal to a future of lifelong self-education. Without recognising the importance of the 'young adult' frontier—not simply as "transition" or "initiation" but as a criterion for all that precedes and follows it—we miss its centrality for all educational evaluation and research.

The main reason for acknowledging the central importance of "young adult" education as a criterion by which to judge previous schooling as well as post-compulsory education is that at this age- or attainment-level the old differentiations between professional and personal preparation, between the "liberal" and the "vocational", between the "conditional" child and the adult making mature choices, are blurred. Scholastic "either/or" dichotomies are shown up as fictional; it is much more a case of "both and"—both learning and working, both "humane" and practical training, both ad hoc and long-term preparation.

In other words, young adults and we ourselves face a new synthesis made possible and indeed necessary by new configurations of work prospects, by newly interactive constellations of study or training, and by the certainty that working and learning together for the future will require life-long and largely autonomous reappraisal. The scholastic "forecasting" of the past is becoming increasingly questionable—if not meaningless; therefore many of the old demarcations and hierarchies of esteem derived from the past are as unjustifiable as they are unreliable.

In any case, the "explosion of knowledge" which educators talked so much about in the early postwar years entails a necessary consequence: the incompleteness and indeed the obsolescence of previously acquired education and training. We still have not faced up to this problem. Scientists have long talked about the "half-life" of professions (the time taken before the graduation package is half useless or only half-complete)—five years in engineering, in medicine, in the communications sciences, possibly eight years in physics, and so on. The figures do not matter so much as the obsolescence, with the need for recurrent education in some form.

Quite apart from obsolescence, people often need to acquire some additional knowledge or professional insight at a later stage in their careers—such as another language and a "topping up" in science or mathematics. External considerations such as expanded contacts with other countries or indeed with other parts of industry or academia also call for updating and re-assessment of previous education. In many countries that has been partly provided by 'distance learning' schemes, with "open universities", "open colleges" and new forms of educative partnership with many kinds of enterprise. This whole area is rapidly developing to provide supplementary education and training.

The cumulative effect of all these transformations of the educational scene—at a time when many or all young adults' job prospects and career expectations are in question—is to make all young people aware that whatever school or initial preparation can offer them is of merely conditional relevance. Everything in future will depend on their own and their contemporaries' later modification of the system—by means which are at present probably outside the scope of the system.

As said before, the real conceptual point to recognise is that today's education must be responsible and ultimately self-directed education for uncertainty, and that the young adult frontier is its proving ground. By also acknowledging the situation of young adults in post-compulsory education as pioneering a new world for which there is no precedent in the tasks to be done, the skills to use, or the content and methods of learning, we can better direct our research endeavours in every aspect of learning and training.

CHANGES IN THE CONTEXT OF INVESTIGATION

Thus we have moved on from new concepts about "young adult" education to consider: (a) the wider context of occupational/technological changes; (b) the changing institutional framework within which and for which young adults must adapt themselves; and (c) the modes of learning and re-learning available.

New concepts raise fresh questions about intentions and interpretations. In our various countries we have all grown up with ideas inherited from the past, embodied in institutions and practices likewise inherited from situations very unlike today's. For example, everyone over the age of about 30 (and therefore nearly all teachers) grew up in a pre-computer age. By contrast, my youngest grandchildren have used computers all their lives—at home and in school. My oldest grandchildren already review computer programmes for specialist magazines. Most of today's patterns of employment, and certainly all previous methods of communicating and learning, are called into question by the offspring of transistors, of laser technology, of fibre optics, etc.

All our systems of formal education have been established by national laws, local customs, local or regional patterns of industry. They have been made rigid by those laws, by financial allocations, by the constraints of higher education and of occupational entry. But is our occupational framework predictable any longer? The staple industries of Europe and North America moved during two centuries from an agricultural to a heavy industry basis, and from that have been moving to a "service" or increasingly "post-industrial" economy. Meanwhile, those countries' heavy industrial production has been largely taken over by South Korea, the Philippines, Mexico and China, while around the Pacific rim the 'dawn technologies' of the newly industrialising countries (or NICs) are quickly outstripping our ancient economies. Correspondingly they are making our school and higher education systems irrelevant.

Obviously, one huge consequence was severe unemployment—most marked among the under-25s, who still constitute roughly half of the unemployed in OECD countries. People between the ages of 16 and 20 are three times more likely to be unemployed than the 20–25 group; and if they do succeed in finding a job the duration of employment is on average six months, alternating with five months unemployment, which in turn is usually followed by a different occupation. Discontinuity of career (and therefore of learning) is becoming the rule rather than the exception.

Alongside all these changes there has been steady urbanisation, followed by "suburbanisation" as possession of cars and mopeds has become more nearly universal. On the other hand, telecommunications bring the world's information resources instantly into every home; so expectations of higher living standards tantalise young people while differences in actual life-styles are accentuated. (That is to say nothing about the influences of migration.)

These and many other corollaries are the consequences of headlong technological and occupational change in industrialised and industrialising countries, and in urban centres throughout the world. In greater or lesser degree apparently similar problems are discussed at all international conferences, in increasingly comparable terms. Of course, the great majority of mankind still live in less developed countries (the average human being is either Chinese or an inhabitant of the Indian sub-continent, and most of mankind is under the age of 25); but "modernisation" usually entails urbanisation, and that adds "Western-style" problems to those of an indigenous nature.

Although these contextual changes and their consequential problems for society and education are to be found repeatedly throughout the world, it is obvious that local and national 'idioms' of perception, of remedies successfully tried, of indications for the future, can contribute a wide range of complementary insights, with valuable suggestions for on-the-ground as well as analytical research.

COMPARATIVE RESEARCH ON THE EDUCATION AND TRAINING OF YOUNG ADULTS

For as far ahead as we can see, realistic studies of education must be country- or culture-specific. Manifestly there are deep differences of ideological background, differences in the degree of socio-economic development, differences in resources and in the availability of suitable personnel, and so forth. Consequently, "reality" is seen through different lenses. That is of course obvious when we think of official planners and providers; but nowadays we must also take account of the massive input of all those other individual people and groups participating in the educational process. These participate in shaping their own education and that of their contemporaries; and in doing so, of course, they give a provisional shape to the immediate future. To an increasing extent they set the terms of reference for the next stage of the educational debate.

To capitalise on mankind's varieties of perception, experience and research, the World Council of Comparative Education Societies (WCCES) decided in 1984 to establish an international programme of cooperative, comparative research in which member societies (and some individual researchers or teams) were invited to take part. Since then, some 30 Comparative Education Societies and many teams and individuals have indicated eagerness to participate in a common research project.

The WCCES gave absolute priority to research on 'The education and training of young adults aged 16 to 25 in the perspective of technological and occupational change'. For a variety of reasons (some financial, some caused by the death or professional involvement of the prime movers), no really active impetus has so far been put into the research programme on a world basis; but academic contacts continue to this end, and some member societies are conducting promising researches.

PARTNERSHIP IN RESEARCH

At this point it seems appropriate to emphasise that the WCCES did not imagine that only societies or university departments and research units labelled with the title "Comparative Education" would be welcomed as research partners. On the contrary, many of the most serious comparative studies of education and its changing contexts and perspectives are undertaken by investigators in very differently designated enterprises. In universities, manifestly, some of these occur in departments of "politics", "government", "economics", and the like. Nowadays many industrial and commercial enterprises also scrutinise the international educational scene in the hope of improving performance and/or relationships; and so on.

The strict terms of membership enforced by some Comparative Education Societies in the past excluded from partnership many high-level scholars, research teams, and powerful financial supporters. They have sometimes indirectly caused the activity called "Comparative Education" to be considered a limited and perhaps irrelevant pedagogical exercise. Now, however, our partners in the comparative study of education are multiple, varied and practical. It is the hope of the WCCES that Comparative Education Societies will enlarge the range of their partners, thus (no doubt) increasing their influence and their membership. In particular, it is expected that the practicality and urgency of the chosen research theme will attract the attention and support of policy-makers and programmers.

That is particularly important not only for reasons of international scholarship and cooperation but because henceforth the continuation and fulfilment of education increasingly depend upon multiple networks of information, persuasion and training, by a multiplicity of means. These usually range far beyond the control—and often the awareness—of governments and formal educators. Education is more obviously made, and participated in, outside the school and college systems with which governments and researchers have hitherto been concerned. Feedback from experience, and self-correcting or "cybernetic" inputs, are becoming more and more influential in educational development; and in that sense 'participant' research which gives "the inside view" will become an ever-stronger element is scholarship as in market research.

That is why university and other specialist researchers, for "scientific" as well as humane reasons, must necessarily form new comparative partnerships—less "schooly", interdisciplinary, and by an adaptive variety of methods and contacts. Documentation will obviously be cumulative and of provisional relevance. Books in the field of Comparative Education will necessarily be less biblical, and teachers less prophetic. There is already more participation by Comparative Education's scholars in studies intended to clarify the formation of policy (which ultimately is the province of governments and those who pay). Problems of practicality and implementation—in schools or colleges and in the outer world where education and training are put to the test of experience—are likewise a rich field for case studies and operational investigation.

It goes without saying that real-life 'problem' studies and other forms of thematic treatment will be called for (always in a cooperative and comparative perspective, since omnicompetence or single-nation sufficiency is a delusion happily obsolete).

Of course, not everything can be done at once, and there must always be priorities of preference and topical urgency. That is why, in the present case, the many problems circling round the education and training of young adults in the perspective of headlong technological and occupational change were decisively selected by the World Council of Comparative Education Societies in 1984 as pivotal for comparative researchers across the world. They remain pivotal today.

NOTES

* Observations made in the middle section of this paper were presented in an earlier and shorter draft at the 1988 Budapest Conference of the Comparative Education Society in Europe, but have been edited and re-written for this volume.

REFERENCES

King, E.J., ed.(1979a) *Education for Uncertainty*. London and Beverly Hills, Sage Publications.

King, E.J. (1979b) *Post-Compulsory Education in Western Europe—A New Concept*. Council of Europe, DECS EGT (78) 30-E.

King, E.J., Moor, C.H., and Munday, J.A. (1974) *Post-Compulsory Education in Western Europe I—A New Analysis*. London, Sage.

King, E.J., Moor, C.H., and Munday, J.A. (1975) *Post-Compulsory Education in Western Europe II—The Way Ahead*. London, Sage.

Epilogue

ROBIN BURNS AND ANTHONY WELCH

OVERVIEW

This collection is distinguished by an interweaving of themes, within a range of innovative approaches to the study of comparative education. Studies of privatisation and legitimation, by the co-authors, represent important newer currents of comparative scholarship. The studies of small island states (Hindson), the training of technocrats from the Third World (Toh and Farrelly), and studies of the relationship between education and the economy in the Philippines (Collins and Gillespie) represent a contemporary move from traditional geographical foci of scholarship. There is also a break with the traditional assumptions in much of comparative research with respect to methodology and geographic-cultural aspects. Analyses have been presented which deal with commodification (specifically in Burns, implicitly in Scrase, and Toh and Farrelly), legitimation (Welch), ethnography (Crossley) and post-structuralism (Branson and Miller), and of comparative education as a subject (Price). Equally, the authors move away from a traditional concentration on Western nation-states, in two senses. The nation-states which are considered are almost entirely drawn from the developing world and include some case studies of particular contemporary interest (the Philippines and Papua New Guinea). More than this, however, some of the studies break altogether with the major nation-state unit of analysis, focusing supranationally (Hindson: small Pacific island states) or sub-nationally (Bali: Branson and Miller). Chapters also draw together other studies, especially on Third World education (Bacchus) and gender (Yates).

One of the threads which runs through all those chapters dealing with the Third World, and implicit in articles such as King, and Simkin and Gauci, concerns the conceptual tools for examining the role of education in a particular society and the possibilities for comparing what is happening in different societies, especially the possibilities for practical applications of such findings. While the latter has always been a key question in comparative education, since it is an item of faith used to legitimate the activity of comparison, it is rare to find such a reiteration in chapter after chapter of the necessity to examine the underlying concepts and to challenge the nature of the education-society link. Why is this felt so strongly by the contributors? A part of the answer, to be discussed in further detail below, may be the educational and socio-economic dependency which those working in Australia themselves experience. Australia's own educational dependency, which is nowhere more apparent than in the past history of comparative education itself in the country, and the ways in which comparative educators here have tended to work, largely outside the system of educational advice and expertise abroad, may have enabled a more critical perspective to be developed and sustained.

Toh and Farrelly, Crossley, and King address a further aspect of the role of comparative and international education, namely the role of the field of scholarship in actual framing of ideas and practice. Toh and Farrelly, and Crossley, point to ethical issues involved in the teaching of Third World students and in research in and on Third World countries. Crossley raises some centrally importrant aspects of this, through his use of local Pacific scholars' critiques, for example of the role of consultancies to outside agencies as a source of 'research' opportunities (see also Burns). King reports upon his substantial research project, which also raised new issues for comparativists and planners to confront, particularly the role of a group who were no longer in formal education, yet clearly needed to develop further skills, and who were in a sense the guinea pigs in attempts to forge more successful relations between education and employment.

Crossley, and Hindson, both remind us of the need to take 'insider' perspectives into account, stressing the problems with models, theories and even rationales for research which take a generalising or so-called objective perspective. Some of the problems of expertise which appears to be irrelevant stem from ignoring local issues, conflicts and possibilities. The nature of the models used, as well as the type of research undertaken, is challenged by these and other contributors, pointing to growing points in comparative and international education especially through the translation of analytic schemes such as Holmes into practice in research.

Focussing on methods is one way in which comparative links to and extends other fields of educational research. As in the growing relationships between anthropology and sociology, so the use of ethnographic methods in particular, while considered by Crossley to be particularly suited to the Third World, draws together a particular research intent in developed and developing countries. This is perhaps best exemplified when Bacchus writes about the emancipatory interest which guided the Progressive Education Movement of the 1920s and 1930s and is emerging again in some comparative work in the Third World. It may well provide a way of bringing together the concern of comparativists represented in this volume with making research more useful especially to kids and their parents and through them, their societies, in the Third World and in a sense providing an alternative source of theory and information to that of the international and governmental consultants. It links to the new sociology of education with its more localised concerns of researchers working within their own societies. How the comparative perspectives can be brought to bear on a particular society is the ongoing task of comparative methodology; how to convince others that it is useful to do so is at one level a test of the generality of the insights gained and of the possibilities for comparativists and others to interact.

Crossley introduces another important point when he considers the relevance of collaborative research both to theory and practice. It can be argued that researchers from the South Pacific, including Australians and New Zealanders, are in a strong position to put this perspective before our comparative and international education colleagues, since we are in an interstitial position in many ways between the intellectual, as well as the general politico-economic influences of the UK and US, and other countries in the region with whom we have been involved in a colonial or neo-colonial relationship. While not wishing to advocate the limitation of research to local people, nevertheless we can emphasise the importance of their equal partnership in it, and stress this on epistemological as well as ideological and ethical grounds. This is not a viewpoint often encountered in writings about the practice of comparative education elsewhere.

The importance of a "people's perspective", especially people who are largely regarded as objects and not active participants, is raised in a different way by Stromquist. Using both the contrast between the nature and activities of NGOs, and women, she indicates the nature of projects in the field of nonformal education and the effects of different approaches to this. These questions of nonformal education, and of the role of NGOs especially in the Third World, show the complexity of finding appropriate frameworks for educational action and the usefulness of cross-national work in the development of theoretical tools and of models of practice. Listening to the students, and understanding their context of action as well as their perspectives, is obviously crucial in work with women; looking at women in different Third World settings enriches not only comparative and international education but also feminism, since it challenges frameworks, assumptions and approaches which are often taken from middle class, white (and in the case of comparative education, male) perceptions and practice in an unreflected fashion. Her study which includes a critique of the role of the State, bears out Toh and Farrelly's points about the ways in which outsiders and national officials alike find it convenient to overlook the neediest members of society, as well as emphasising Bacchus' and others' concern with education as a tool for emancipation. Previous studies under the auspices of the Australian and New Zealand Comparative and International Education Society (ANZCIES) have shown the relevance of both such a perspective for the Pacific (e.g. Melville 1984). While most of the papers talk about a theory of development, Stromquist raises the issue of the nature of the State, and theories of change, which brings new perspectives especially relevant to educators, comparative and otherwise, since on the whole they are dealing with education as a State institution.

Scrase too takes the perspective of disadvantaged groups in his analysis, rather than simply accepting the idealized and caricatured images which fill the Indian texts which he studied. There is clearly room for this kind of perspective to be used more widely, not only to point out some of the substantial distortions which occur, but to reveal the underlying ideology of the process which results in such distortions.

Branson and Miller, too, are critical of the way in which the lives of many Third World individuals are dominated by newly imposed notions of what is appropriate, and just as important, what is no longer acceptable. Their analysis of the situation of Balinese women provides a cogent example of how new, "modern" images imported from the West can disempower traditionally important female activities, thereby de-legitimating the previously central role of women in that society.

Price's contribution raises the prospect of widening the debate considerably. This is not so much because of his powerful rejection of the positivist legacy of comparative research, since that is becoming a more widely held view among contemporary scholars. A more radical departure exists in his conception of education which is much more comprehensive than most, and which if accepted would fundamentally alter some of the conceptual categories and units of analysis that comparativists have traditionally taken for granted.

Yates, too, presents some substantial challenges to comparative research, in that implicitly, at least, she extends the concepts of culture with which comparativists are familiar to embrace the distinctive experiences of girls, whose needs are still often not met adequately within schools. She too rejects the culture of positivism, and its distortions to research.

Concepts of culture are at the centre of Simkin and Gauci's work too, and the extremely thorough taxonomy which is developed of the different formulations of multiculturalism in the different Australian states is one that could well prove suggestive for scholars in other federal states. What is equally striking in this chapter is the effective blend of argument and classification.

The dilemma which is presented by Collins and Gillespie is one increasingly common in several parts of the world. International political and economic crises are tending to leave in their wake a new shift away from equity and towards economic concerns such as efficiency and economy. Human capital theory, once again, underlies too many of contemporary policies and practices in education for many practitioners and scholars, who still believe in the ideals of individual and social advancement through education, as also that education is ultimately more an ethical than economic concern.

Lastly, the strains of research opened up by Welch and Burns each present substantial prospects for further work in comparative education. In an era of crises in many parts of the world, the concepts of the relationship between the legitimation of knowledge and the legitimacy of the modern state, and the analysis and exploration of commodification as a conceptual tool with which to make sense of changes in education in recent years, both possess considerable scope as research tools.

COMPARATIVE AND INTERNATIONAL EDUCATION 'DOWN UNDER'

The title of this volume, *Contemporary Perspectives in Comparative Education*, focuses attention on the linked themes of continuity and change. Comparative education has a history, and in both teaching and research there are continuities. Thus, for example, one of the editors was recently approached for assistance with establishing a course in comparative education in an African country. The inquirer had undertaken postgraduate studies in the US, including a course in 'traditional' comparative education which was based on the works of the founding fathers, and he wanted to do the same for his compatriot students. The fact that such an approach would be unlikely in the teaching of comparative education in Australia immediately raised questions about the role of institutions and the training of individuals in the transmission of the culture of comparative education. The subsequent employment of those persons is one of the sources of change, although in the case of the African, the change was more in terms of introducing history and philosophy rather than perhaps the more usual "national case studies" or "contemporary issues" which represents a change of a more cyclical nature.

In addition to continuity, the perspective from Australia and New Zealand, like that of places in the region more likely to be considered newly independent, includes the reality of dependency. The dependency of our institutions is nowhere more apparent than in the past history of comparative education itself in the country. Dependency of a different sort, on funds and opportunities, affects the ways in which comparative educators here have tended to work, largely outside the system of educational advice and expertise abroad, which may have enabled a more critical perspective to be developed and sustained.

How is comparative education conceived currently, especially in Australia, and what are the factors conditioning those concepts and the practices related to them?

STUDYING COMPARATIVE: THE TEACHERS AND THE LEARNERS

Since comparative education is compulsory in very few educational courses, and since there are only two sections of Faculties or Schools of education that have the words 'comparative education' anywhere in their designation, it is to the professional society that one can look to get a sense of what is happening in the field. That society, the Australian and New Zealand Comparative and International Education Society (ANZCIES), has maintained a steady membership of around 90–110 persons over the past decade, a slow growth since its beginning in 1972. Nearly all the members have had appointments in Universities or Colleges of Advanced Education, and of those all but two or three have been members of Faculties or Schools of Education. Retired academics and school teachers, mostly part-time higher degree students in education, have formed the rest of the membership.

In a survey of members in the second half of the 1980s, (Burns 1987) it was found that two-thirds of respondents had formally studied comparative and international education at some time, mostly at the graduate level and mostly as an elective, and that nearly half of those studies in comparative and international education had been undertaken overseas (Australian nationals and citizens of other countries currently employed here were not distinguished in the survey). Further, more than half had either a PhD or a Masters qualification from overseas. The Society thus represents educators, a number of whom have formal qualifications in comparative and international education, about half of those being from overseas (predominantly the UK or the US). The effects of this on the possibility for a distinctive perspective on the field are difficult to assess. One avenue for this might be to consider the relationship between qualifications, teaching and research interests.

The survey indicated that one-third of the respondents were not currently teaching any courses in comparative and international education. Only 19 claimed to be teaching one or more courses in comparative and international education. That this represents most such courses in Australia is cause for some concern. The concern is strengthened by the fact that, even taking small overall numbers of compulsory courses into account, only four teach compulsory courses in it (one of which was in Papua New Guinea) in comparison with six having themselves undertaken a compulsory course in their professional development. Most of the courses being taught are thus elective, and most (25 out of 32) are at the undergraduate, diploma or related level, rather than post-graduate. Most (26 out of 31) courses had 25 students or fewer (mean = 15). Sixteen individuals were supervising post-graduate students, though not all of these were directly working on comparative and international topics, and included post-graduates doing PhD or MEd/MA theses by research only as well as other qualifications. The picture of students working with the 30 comparativists is shown in Table 1.

TABLE 1: POSTGRADUATE STUDENTS, 1987

	Completed		Current (1986)	
	Male	Female	Male	Female
PhD	20	11	12	5
Research Masters	44	25	16	16
Coursework Masters Project	9	7	7	7
Graduate Diploma	6	0	0	0
Other	0	0	0	0
Total	79	43	39	25

In some cases, completed supervisions included other respondents, but even allowing for this, it can be estimated that some "reproduction" of comparativists is taking place. While information concerning the age of those supervised was not sought, the age distribution of respondents is seen in Table 2.

TABLE 2: AGE OF RESPONDENTS

Years	25–30	31–35	36–40	41–45	46–50	51–55	56–60	61–65
Number	1	1	3	8	4	5	7	1

Over half are into the second half of their careers. Thus there is a need for a steady stream of post-graduates, at least on the assumption that there is a continuing need for comparativists and that these will be recruited from within Australia.

GEOGRAPHICAL FACTORS

Australia is a "North" country in the southern hemisphere. Her nearest neighbours are Indonesia, Papua New Guinea and New Zealand. While all four are former colonies, Australia and New Zealand have more in common with each other through their former British colonial status, but Australia is the physical and economic "giant." In size alone, this is obvious. When taken together with its N-S and E-W extent, and with the fact that most of its relatively small (17 million) population clings to the coast, over 80 percent in the large connurbations surrounding the capital cities of the states (and almost half in greater Sydney and Melbourne), two features of relevance to the flow of educational ideas and people are evident. There is a communication problem, all capital cities except Perth being closer to an overseas city than to the other side of Australia, and contact with the "North" is always via the tropics with the exception of Latin America which is poorly served by direct air links, and to some extent Africa. It was in fact half-seriously suggested at an ANZCIES conference recently that not only inter-state comparisons, but study-tours would be an appropriate activity!

Both the fact of size and relative isolation, and of historical differences between the educational systems does place some mark on comparative educational activity. Further, colonial ties with some of our neighbours, and participation in a range of regional associations in which Australia and New Zealand are the sole 'western or 'North' partners, provides some reasons for particular educational links, for research, teaching experience and consultancy or development assistance. This is reflected in the work of the respondents to the survey.

Twenty-two had some overseas teaching experience (including school teaching, the majority of these in Papua New Guinea or the UK—a common way of financing post-graduate study abroad). Two had up to four different overseas teaching engagements, most (15) having one or two. Although this was not specified, in a number of cases such overseas assignments have led the person to undertake comparative or international studies, including post-graduate dissertations, on return, or to offer courses arising out of the experience.

Few of the respondents were actually undertaking research overseas, and the numbers have declined since the survey was undertaken. Of those who were, the most common research was on the history of a particular education system, and evaluation of a project or program (five each), curriculum, and educational planning (three each), or educational administration in developing countries (one). These are the most clearly "international" research projects out of a total of 44 projects listed. Only six said they had received funding other than through regular (and small, mostly covering only an airfare) internal institutional sources. There was a close relationship between current research listed and project undertaken on last sabbatical leave. However, since it is easier for university staff to obtain such leave for individual research, CAE staff using it more for professional development (e.g. undertaking further qualifications, looking at teaching or other aspects of the work of institutions rather than individual research for which resources are much scarcer even within CAEs), there was some divergence between ongoing research and leave projects. More than half of all respondents spent most of their last leave in Europe or North America, the others spending it in the SW Pacific (four), Asia (six) or Africa (two). Only two were able to obtain special funding for their leave projects.

Consultancies, usually arranged through regional or UN agencies, the World Bank or government-to-government bases, are another source of experience for comparative and international educators. Educational assistance overseas has not been a major feature of Australian bilateral aid programs (the situation in New Zealand, especially in relationship to Fiji and other Pacific Island states, has been different). Some Australians have worked as UNESCO consultants, and there has been considerable involvement in establishing and extending education at all levels in Papua New Guinea. It is only in the last few years, with national and international changes in approaches to educational assistance, especially through large educational projects funded by agencies such as the World Bank, that Australian involvement in such activities at an official level has developed to any extent.

Including four consultancies within Australia, these had been undertaken by 20 respondents. Four of the women had been involved, three on overseas assignments. Overseas assignments were concentrated in the Pacific (ten) and Asia (ten), with Papua New Guinea and Indonesia the most frequent (five each). Only six respondents had undertaken more than one consultancy, and none had been involved in one with other respondents (and the likelihood of other ANZCIES members being included was almost nil). The main agency to which the consultants were appointed included an individual school (two), a whole school system (thirteen), a government, not including those specifically working with a national education department (ten), a university (one), the International Development Program of the Australian Universities and Colleges (one), a UN agency (six), a US Foundation (two) and the World Bank (three). The main concerns of such consultancies were: some aspects of curriculum (seven), evaluation of projects or programs (four) and educational planning (three). The following areas had been the subject of one consultancy each: re-organisation of a national ministry of education, teacher education, resource development, university development, early childhood education, English language services and student exchanges.

HISTORICAL CONSIDERATIONS

The teaching, research and consultancy work of comparativists is thus to a significant degree related to the geographical region surrounding Australia, most strongly for consultancy work. This is not simply due to our location; however, as the next sections indicate, though given the extent to which the respondents had undertaken formal studies in the UK and the US, location has some effect on opportunities for comparative and international work.

The UK has been the dominant educational influence on Australia and New Zealand. Australia, as the administering power in Papua New Guinea, established the formal school system there, and while Fiji was also a British colony, New Zealand had a formative influence and formal educational role there. With the independence of both Papua New Guinea (1976) and Fiji (1970), the role of expatriate staff from Australia and New Zealand respectively, at all levels of the educational systems, has declined although World Bank-funded educational consultancies with Australian staff in particular are increasing in the region.

Of particular pertinence to considering the development and growth of comparative education in the area is the fact that, even today, the higher educational institutions preparing the teachers for and researchers into the national education systems are often non-nationals: if those with overseas higher degrees are included, the proportions of staff of those institutions with some or all of their education abroad are higher even in Australia, and to a lesser extent New Zealand, than in comparable European and North American institutions. On the surface of it, this paves the way for a "natural" place, in educational planning, in the education of teachers and in educational research, for comparative education. On the other hand, however, this gives rise to a cultural state which has been labelled "partial colonialism" (Thomas and Postlethwaite 1984) and it has three major implications for the explicit study and use of comparative education:

(i) The influence may simply consist of the unacknowledged and unexamined transfer of assumptions and concepts from one situation to the other, for the purpose of influencing the local situation, deliberately or through oversight and unreflected practice;

(ii) This leads in turn to a "backlash", at certain stages or in particular areas, so that there is a deliberate and conscious attempt either to "borrow" or to eradicate foreign influences;

(iii) At the micro level in particular, there is some indication that "system level" studies have become the focus for "foreigners", leaving the "locals" to undertake detailed "ethnographies". This in itself is an over-generalisation, but can be partially borne out in the contributions in this volume and in the analysis of the research and teaching commitments of foreign and local staff.

The emergent nature of all the societies in the region, and the transplanted nature of their formal educational systems, could also be expected to be a source of study for comparativists. The issues of educational transfer are studied by comparativists in the area. This volume shows productive ways in which local studies, espeially of gender and ethnicity, are also being undertaken. The survey respondents may have been those with a concern to keep alive a more traditional higher comparative and/or international profile. Their general comments showed some alarm at the decline of this type of study.

The experience of colonialism, and reciprocal ties despite historically and culturally diverse experiences, make the South Pacific a microcosm of those processes which form the substance of comparative and international studies. This provides some focus for the practice of the subject, though it is weaker than perhaps might be expected, and some reasons for this are explored in the next section.

PROSPECTS AND PROBLEMS

At least with the survey respondents, a process of continuous recruitment was taking place, although without examination of the actual higher degree topics, the directions which potential comparativists are taking are not known. Further, no account was taken of overseas higher degree students and hence the potential 'brain drain' from the region.

Five major sources for the development of comparative and international education are discernible:

1. Specific individuals, trained overseas, who were able to apply that training to the development of comparative education courses and research on appointment back in the region.

2. Specific individuals whose expertise in a particular aspect of education led them to international advisory or problem-solving roles in inter-governmental, regional or international agencies, for other governments or in their own government's aid to education projects. A sub-group of these are teachers with overseas, especially developing country, experience, who subsequently moved into the tertiary sector and maintained their interest in the education systems of other countries.

3. Individuals or groups who, through collegial contacts overseas, became involved in cross-national research, rarely specifically related to comparative education methodologically or feeding into comparative education publications or courses.

4. Individuals simply attracted to the study of education systems other than their own, or transplanted from one system to another, who began to research or teach comparatively.

5. On the "international" edge of a "comparative and international education formula", individuals with a vision more commensurate with that line traceable back to Comenius and more currently espoused by UNESCO, of the need for education to be seen in an international perspective, and to contribute towards 'international understanding'.

Until 1981, like-country studies and comparisons, and studies of developing countries, formed the major foci of activity. The comparativists in the region, perhaps like our colleagues elsewhere, are more in debt theoretically to structural-functional theory than to comparative. There has been some polarisation between modernisation and dependency approaches and both are still evident in teaching of and research in comparative. But as this volume shows, new theoretical directions are being actively and fruitfully explored.

This is coming about in part through engagement with other educational practitioners, the school systems and society at large and is stimulating a new phase in the theory and practice of the subject, here and elsewhere.

A little over a decade ago, Cleverley and Jones considered that there were three principal areas in which the international aspects of Australian education have come to the fore: the impact of immigration; the broadening of the cultural base of the curriculum; and education as a focus of foreign aid (1976). The three continue, albeit in somewhat changed form, and have given rise to activities, projects, exchanges and the like, but their significance outside limited, and often academic circles, is declining. This is not unique to the region, but one local effect has been to stimulate comparativists to seek actively to pursue, and to renew, their tasks in dialogue not only with other comparativists but with educators from other fields. This volume is intended as a contribution to that process of dialogue and development, one to which we hope the next generation of comparative scholars will be just as committed. It is them for whom this book is largely written.

REFERENCES

Burns, R. (1987) 'Comparative and International Education: Focus on Australia'. Paper presented to the *World Council of Comparative Education Societies Sixth World Congress*, Brazil.

Cleverley, J., and Jones, P. (1976) 'Australian and International Education: Some Critical Issues'. Melbourne, *Australian Education Review* No. 7.

Melville, L. (1984) 'Women and Their Education in the South Pacific'. In R. Burns and B. Sheehan (eds.), *Women and Education.* Melbourne, ANZCIES: 295–310.

Thomas, R.M., and Postlethwaite, T.N. (eds.) (1984) *Schooling in the Pacific Islands.* Oxford, Pergamon.

Index